IS THIS THE END
8 00 · 79 2 1355

Body Builders

Daily exhortations to stretch,
strengthen and build up your faith

Barry Stagner

Body Builders
Daily exhortations to stretch, strengthen and build up your faith
by Barry Stagner

Printed in the United States of America

ISBN 9781612154589

www.xulonpress.com

Dedicated to my loving wife Teri

I am a child of God destined to make a difference
I will not doubt or fear in the face of adversity
I am committed to Gods will for my life
no matter what opposition may come
I will praise God for every blessing and
through every trial for He will never fail me
I will put God first every day of my life
That I may hear Him say: Well done

Calvary Chapel Tustin Manifesto

January 1

Behold, I will do a new thing, now it shall spring forth; shall you not know it? I will even make a road in the wilderness and rivers in the desert.

—Isaiah 43:19

Idolatry and disobedience had led the children of Israel into captivity, yet here in Isaiah, the Lord declared His faithfulness as the one who had created them (Isa. 43:1), and the promise was made for "a road in the wilderness and rivers in the desert." What this means is that God was going to make a way home for His rebellious children and even provide for them along the way.

As a new year begins, many make resolutions of change. But the sad truth is, the common denominator for most resolutions is that they are broken. However, it is not so with the Lord. What He commits to do for us, He will do, including bringing new life and direction to barren and waste places.

Dear friend, if last year was not what it ought to have been or even could have been in your walk with the Lord, be encouraged by the fact that He has provided a way for you to walk on the path of His promises this year. It might seem a corny truth, but it is nonetheless true that the best way to keep from changing is to stay the same. We cannot do everything the same way we did last year yet expect a different outcome this year. We must seek, serve, and pray more if next year's resolutions are not to become a commitment to fulfill this year's.

God says this year can be richer and fuller than any other by simply putting Him first and above all else. No year will end in disappointment or fall short of your expectations when seeking first His kingdom is your reality. This may mean being more faithful at church or serving in ministry, but it may also mean giving your private and personal time with Him priority. It is *you* He wants to be intimate with, it is *you* He wants to commune with, it is *you* He wants to walk the path with, and it is *you* for whom He made the rivers in the desert.

So if this year is not going to be a repeat of last year, resolve to know and serve Him as never before. Then, when next year comes, He will have another new thing for you!

January 2

Let a man so consider us, as servants of Christ and stewards of the mysteries of God. Moreover it is required in stewards that one be found faithful.

—1 Corinthians 4:1–2

A steward in Bible times was one who had the responsibility to oversee and distribute the possessions of his master, using them to care for the well-being of the master's family. Paul says that we are such stewards in God's kingdom, entrusted with the Master's possessions for the care of His children, other believers. These possessions are both spiritual and material. We have been given His Spirit as a guarantee of our inheritance (Eph. 1:14), and we are recipients of countless material blessings as well. As stewards, we are required to be faithful with these gifts of the Spirit and the good gifts of material blessing.

We often hear of Christians longing for things to be as they were in the first-century church, because the book of Acts records such a powerful testimony of God's Spirit moving in His people. Acts 2:43–45 says, "Then fear came upon every soul, and many wonders and signs were done through the apostles. Now all who believed were together, and had all things in common, and sold their possessions and goods, and divided them among all, as anyone had need." The wonders and signs they performed show us they were faithful stewards of the Spirit, and regarding all they owned as common demonstrates faithful stewardship in their possessions.

Why was the church so powerful at its birth? Because men and women of God believed that all they had in spirit and flesh came from God and was not their own. This too is how we can live as faithful stewards, knowing that every good personal possession and even the perfect gift, the presence of His Spirit, is the Lord's. He has merely made us stewards over His possessions.

It is admirable to wish things were as they were in the early church, and the solution for achieving this is actually quite simple. If we will just do what they did *then*, we'll see what they saw *now*.

A loose grip on the things of this world and a tight grip on the things of God is a good way to describe the attitude and actions of the early church. It's also a good way to describe any church and certainly any Christian. Let's adopt an attitude of stewardship like theirs and make the early church and all that it experienced not just a wish but a reality!

January 3

Then I turned to see the voice that spoke with me. And having turned I saw seven golden lampstands, and in the midst of the seven lampstands One like the Son of Man, clothed with a garment down to the feet and girded about the chest with a golden band. His head and hair were white like wool, as white as snow, and His eyes like a flame of fire; His feet were like fine brass, as if refined in a furnace, and His voice as the sound of many waters; He had in His right hand seven stars, out of His mouth went a sharp two-edged sword, and His countenance was like the sun shining in its strength. And when I saw Him, I fell at His feet as dead.

— Revelation 1:12–17

I love how John — whether you read his gospel, his epistles, or the book of Revelation — is always talking about Jesus. The pinnacle of all His descriptions, I believe, is here in Revelation, because John describes Jesus in His heavenly physical glory, not in His humanity.

It is disheartening at times to realize the misconception many hold of both the Father and the Son. An angry, wrathful God of the Old Testament and an easygoing surf-cat Jesus of the New Testament seem to be the perception of many today. But Jesus told Philip and His other disciples that He and His Father were one and that if you have seen Him, you've seen the Father (John 14:9). It is also interesting that the Jews, who knew the Messiah was coming, missed in Scripture that He was coming twice. All they expected was the coming of a lion to free them from the hand of Rome, not the coming of a lamb to take away the sins of the world.

Many today seem to have fallen into the same trap, only in reverse. They perceive Jesus as a meek and mild lamb and forget that He's returning as a mighty lion from the tribe of Judah to judge the world. In other words, they see Him only as the forgiver of sin, not as the transformer of lives.

It is clear in our day that reverence for God has diminished greatly, and many simply want a god who is everything they want him to be. But God did not come into the world to be what we want; He came into the world to be what we need — the Savior who redeems and transforms all who believe in Him.

May we understand that Jesus is King of Kings and Lord of Lords, as are the Father and Spirit, and may we stand in awe of His majesty as we bask in His grace each day.

Yes, He is our wonderful counselor, but He is also almighty God. He is the Prince of Peace, but He will also rule the nations with a rod of iron (Rev. 2:27). So let's not diminish His greatness and majesty by only seeing Him for what we want Him to be. Let's see Him for who He is and worship Him as our mighty king!

January 4

Before I was afflicted I went astray, but now I keep Your word.

—Psalm 119:67

Though life itself has its twists and turns, it is also true that some of what we encounter are trials and afflictions allowed by God to strengthen our walks and increase our faith in His Word. When we are going through a time of trial or affliction, the important thing to remember is that there is more to be learned in a trial than just God's faithfulness to deliver us from it. And the lesson is usually somewhere in the middle.

I have often reminded saints encountering a time of trial to remember that the middle is not the end. In other words, don't stall out in the middle of a trial. There is a lesson there, and the faster we learn it, the quicker the recovery time (I am not talking about grief or trauma here).

There is nothing we encounter that God will not be faithful to see us through. But too often our trials and afflictions create a limited prayer life concentrated on what we think is the only good part of any trial or affliction: the end.

It is good and right to cry out to God for deliverance, but let's expand our cries to encompass the lesson in the middle. Yes, God will be faithful; yes, He will see you through; but what is it in the midst of the trial that He wants you to learn? You can be sure that there is one, for God does not allow anything in our lives that is not for His glory and our good.

Is there an aspect of His Word that He wants to increase your understanding of or that He wants you to begin to keep? Maybe He wants to teach you things like trust, steadfastness, or even how to walk in His will when you don't feel anything. These are the things that trials and afflictions often teach.

So make no mistake about it, friend. God is in control. His eye is on you, and His hand is under, over, and around you. That is true whether you're in a trial or not. But if trying times are upon you, seek Him for the lesson while you cry out for deliverance!

January 5

Therefore, since all these things will be dissolved, what manner of persons ought you to be in holy conduct and godliness.

—2 Peter 3:11

As God's people, we are to wait expectantly for the Lord. I have a card that sits in a stand on my desk that has two words on it: "Perhaps today." It is a continual reminder to me of two things. First, there are opportunities this day that may never present themselves again, and I am to treat this day as if it were my last opportunity to reach anyone for Christ. This makes every encounter more meaningful.

Second, the "conduct and godliness" aspect of expectancy is to be ever on my mind. Are there things God has been speaking that He wants me to change? Are there attitudes that need to be better aligned with His? Or even for some, are sinful patterns or habits that need addressing continually put on tomorrow's to-do list?

Perhaps today is the day the Lord comes for His people. Perhaps today is the last day before things begin to spiral toward the end that Scripture warns is coming. Every God-honoring Christian has things he or she hopes to do for the Lord "someday" when life settles down, when the job isn't so demanding, or when some other legitimate concern that demands attention is resolved. But Peter tells us we must always be mindful that time is a limited commodity. Whether globally or personally, time is running out.

Each day is the best day to live with urgent expectancy, as though the last witnessing opportunity with someone you know is before you. The day that you are now living is the best day to deal with some spots and wrinkles in your own life (Eph. 5:27). One day, someday, it will be *that* day.

Perhaps today!

January 6

Fear not, for I am with you; be not dismayed, for I am your God. I will strengthen you, yes, I will help you, I will uphold you with My righteous right hand.

—Isaiah 41:10

How often we face situations and circumstances as though this promise is not ours to redeem! When difficulty or challenges come our way, we need not fear or be dismayed. His strength is there for us, His help will enable us, and His upholding will carry us with His righteous right hand.

If we remember where Jesus is seated, at the right hand of the Father (Heb. 1:3), we will be reminded that these are things that are true for those who trust in Him. It is our relationship with Him that carries us through places others face without hope or strength.

Friends, if times are hard or life is tough, you are not alone. He is there to strengthen, help, and uphold you because you are His child, and nothing and no one can snatch you from His right hand (John 10:28).

Notice Isaiah does not say, "Try not to fear," or "See if you can avoid being dismayed." The Lord speaks His words of exhortation as a command, and remember, God never asks anything of us where provision has not already been made. This is yours and mine to embrace at all times.

So if you are in a season of difficulty, start looking for signs of His presence, for He is there with you. If dismay is setting in, remember, not only is He your God, but also dismay is not your portion. You are His child, and like any good parent, He seeks to encourage His children. Strength is there, help is there, and all you need to do is access it by remembering that you are His.

Whatever you are facing in your life, don't forget that if He allowed it, you'll be better for it. There are no exceptions to that truth—ever! He said do not fear and do not be dismayed, and He spoke it as a command. Then He said why: "I will strengthen you, yes, I will help you, I will uphold you with My righteous right hand."

Now that's a promise to change the outlook of any day!

January 7

You are the light of the world. A city that is set on a hill cannot be hidden.

— Matthew 5:14

Today is a great day to let your light shine. Remember the Sunday school song that said, "This little light of mine, I'm gonna let it shine"? Each day is filled with opportunities to let your light shine.

Sometimes we let our lights shine by doing the opposite of what everyone else is doing. Sometimes we let our lights shine by befriending those rejected by all others. Sometimes we let our lights shine by withdrawing from certain conversations or refusing to be dragged into dirty jokes and vulgar stories.

The opportunities to shine our lights are endless. Yet it seems as though many times we diminish those opportunities as invalid thinking. We need to remember, however, that being a witness, a light, is more visible then verbal. As it has been said, "You may be the only Bible some people ever read." So let your light shine today.

A T-shirt that I love says on the front, "Be the moon," and on the back it says, "Reflect the Son." This is our daily bread; it is each day's opportunity to reflect the Son and, if the door opens, to even use words to do so.

But the key, first and foremost, is to go public with our faith. This does not necessarily mean announcing at the sales meeting, "I am a Christian," or standing up in the locker room at school and shouting, "I am born again" (unless the Lord leads you to do so). But more likely it will mean being someone whom others recognize as distinct from the world, someone not like everyone else, someone who is a light in dark places. What God wants from you today is constant and continual behavior that shows others what Christ has done in your life.

Your workout today is quite simple: be the moon, reflect the Son!

January 8

Be sober, be vigilant; because your adversary the devil walks about like a roaring lion, seeking whom he may devour.

—1 Peter 5:8

I have taken many trips to Africa and have had multiple opportunities to go on a game drive. I can assure you firsthand that nothing is more chilling than the roar of a wild lion, especially if you cannot see it! Your mind begins to wonder about your unseen adversary. Is it a large older male accomplished in battle, or is it a young male, seeking to establish his own pride and willing to fight to obtain it?

But one thing we all know, whether learned from actually being in Africa or by watching the National Geographic or Discovery channels, is that lions do not usually roar when they hunt. We have all seen pictures of lions creeping stealthily along the ground, slowly and silently approaching their unsuspecting prey. To roar would be disastrous for the hunt.

There are two occasions, however, when lions will roar while on the hunt. When they are wounded or when they are sick and dying, they will roar out of rage and frustration. At that time, they pose the greatest danger and are most likely to attack prey not part of their usual diet.

This, dear brothers and sisters, is the case with our spiritual adversary, the devil. He was wounded severely by the Lamb of God and is now dying a slow death until the day of judgment when he will be finally put down. But in the meantime, he still seeks those whom he may devour: the wounded and the weak, those sick with sin. But resist him, and he will flee from you!

Even when the enemy's roar is loudest, remember, he has been defeated by the Lamb. If he is roaring at you, friend, stay in the herd (fellowship), because the ones he devours are those not watching, those unaware they are his prey. In watching lions hunt, we know the ones in the middle of the herd never get devoured, but the wanderers or the young on the perimeter of the herd are the ones the lion snatches.

Is the devil roaring in your life right now? Then get in church, read your Bible, pray, stay in the herd, and change your proximity to worldly things and desires. The things on the perimeter of God's will can never afford the safety and protection of the center. Take steps to flee and you won't be devoured.

The enemy is seeking those whom he *may* devour. This seems to imply both vulnerability and cooperation, vulnerability through being too close to his hunting ground and cooperation by not being watchful. Eliminate both of those things and the enemy will have to seek other hunting grounds!

January 9

But as for you, you meant evil against me; but God meant it for good, in order to bring it about as it is this day, to save many people alive.

—Genesis 50:20

Remember all that Joseph endured in his life? He was sold as a slave by jealous brothers, falsely accused by a promiscuous boss's wife, forgotten in prison by one he had helped, then finally remembered when Pharaoh had a dream.

Evil was meant for him, but God took the evil intentions and used them for good. Maybe that is where you are today. Maybe someone at work has it out for you, maybe a teacher at school is after you, or maybe it seems as though evil intentions are continually encroaching into your life.

Dear friend, you are God's child, and you are under His sovereignty and complete control and care. The lesson you can learn through this is not just that God will turn evil intentions for good, but that it is possible to stay faithful even when evil intentions abound.

Joseph runs with some pretty elite spiritual company. Although the Bible discloses many of the failures of some of its greatest champions (Abraham's lies, David's murder and adultery, for example), it also records the stories of those in whom was found no failure. Joseph is one of these, as is true for Daniel, Nehemiah, and the Hebrew boys Shadrach, Meshach, and Abed-Nego. Men with evil intentions surrounded these heroes, yet not even a momentary lapse of their faith is recorded. This can be our testimony too if we don't let the moment rule our attitudes.

Evil cannot overcome the goodness of God. So when we rub shoulders with it or the evils of this world impact us, let us consider them but momentary afflictions. Though they may be meant for evil, God will turn them into good. It was true for Joseph, it was true for Nehemiah, it was true for Daniel, and it is true for you and me too!

January 10

But I want you to know, brethren, that the things which happened to me have actually turned out for the furtherance of the gospel, so that it has become evident to the whole palace guard, and to all the rest, that my chains are in Christ; and most of the brethren in the Lord, having become confident by my chains, are much more bold to speak the word without fear.

—Philippians 1:12–14

One of the great joys of the faith is to be used by God to reach others and by that to bring Him glory. It is a special thing that makes us feel really good when we have spoken up or stepped out in faith. The interesting thing about that, though, is we often forget this great truth when facing hardship or heartache, when trials or troubles come our way.

Paul was shackled to a Roman guard by an eighteen-inch chain, twenty-four hours a day, seven days a week, yet he observed that this shackling actually turned out for the furtherance of the gospel.

Christian friend, a given circumstance can easily begin to dominate our thoughts and impede us in serving our great King. But any hardship is actually one of great opportunity. Paul said that his being chained to a Roman guard had furthered the gospel, and this in turn led to others' boldness.

Imagine if Paul had been bitter and complained because of his current situation. What would the whole palace guard have learned then? Would they have concluded that knowing God really doesn't change how a person faces difficulty? Would they have thought that joy can be experienced only when things are good, but bitterness and frustration take over when things get tough?

My friend, you are neither forgotten nor forsaken, and your current circumstances are some of your greatest opportunities. After all, fruit grows in the valley, not on the mountain peak. God, in His majesty and grace, for reasons that may never be known in this life, has allowed whatever difficulties you have encountered. But one thing you can know for sure: God wants to use you in them to further His gospel, and that, my friend, can even make hard times feel so much better!

January 11

My brethren, count it all joy when you fall into various trials, knowing that the testing of your faith produces patience. But let patience have its perfect work, that you may be perfect and complete, lacking nothing.

—James 1:2-4

What a monumental command! How do we couple trials and joy? I don't like trials; I like smooth sailing. But trials are inevitable for all of us, so we may as well seek to face them God's way — with joy.

Does that seems impossible in light of your present circumstances? Did God have James write this only to those "happy all the time" people (that's code for weird)? The thing you must remember is that God never asks of us what He will not do in us. I have found that one of the keys to having joy in trials is a simple, even silly, reminder: the middle is not the end.

You might be in the middle of a time of trial right now, but remember, this is not your permanent address. As a matter of fact, I believe that some trials become more difficult and are more prolonged than necessary because of our own attitudes or actions. God allows trials to perfect faith, and faith is not perfected through continual cries for the trials to end, but rather through worship and trust while in the middle of them.

There are seasons in life when it is hard to find a "this life" reason to worship, but worship is not about how things are going. Worship is about the worthiness of God and submitting ourselves to His will.

So if you feel stuck in the middle of a never-ending trial, remember, the middle is not the end, and praise at all times might be what God is trying to perfect in you!

January 12

Love suffers long and is kind; love does not envy; love does not parade itself, is not puffed up; does not behave rudely, does not seek its own, is not provoked, thinks no evil; does not rejoice in iniquity, but rejoices in the truth; bears all things, believes all things, hopes all things, endures all things. Love never fails.

—1 Corinthians 13:4–8

Interestingly, in John 13, Jesus commanded us to love one another. He even said this is how the world will know we are His disciples. He couldn't possibly expect us to love some of the people we know... could He? After all, some of them are not so loveable!

Paul's definition of love consists of fifteen Greek verbs describing the actions, attitudes, and abilities of love. If we understand love from this perspective, we can remove any misconception about how to love enemies and even difficult family members or friends.

Love is not a person, place, or thing. Love is a verb; it is something we do. We love because Jesus commanded us to love, and Paul defines for us what that love looks like. It is patient and kind, not haughty or self-promoting. It promotes the truth and even endures all things that threaten our forbearance of others.

If we make love a feeling-based action, we will find it impossible to practice real love. But if we understand love as Paul described it, the fifteen actions we can take when dealing with others—even the difficult "others"—we will find ourselves doing what Jesus said to do, and that always feels better than ignoring His commands. Then, the next thing we know, our actions will have redefined our attitudes, even toward difficult people.

Don't ask God to make you love someone. Just love them as defined here, and let the feelings and emotions take care of themselves. Find someone to practice this on today. In fact, I'll bet you've already thought of at least one hard-to-love person!

January 13

Do not love the world or the things in the world. If anyone loves the world, the love of the Father is not in him. For all that is in the world — the lust of the flesh, the lust of the eyes, and the pride of life — is not of the Father but is of the world.

— 1 John 2:14–15

Have you ever thought about the value and effort we place on things that mean nothing in heaven? The Bible does tell us to care for our homes and families and even tells us it is good to leave an inheritance to our grandchildren (Prov. 13:22), but isn't a godly heritage of more value than a material inheritance? It is so easy to lose sight of what is truly valuable in this fast-paced world, and it is even easier to feel slighted when our neighbors get a little bit ahead of us in their home improvements or the cars they park in their driveways.

So how do we stay balanced, and how do we leave behind a heritage and not just an inheritance? Colossians says to set our minds on things above, not on things below. I recommend that people frequently visit Hebrews 11 to see what a life of not loving the world looks like and those who excelled at it.

As they grow older, children adopt many of the values of their parents. If church and serving God play a secondary role in our lives, our children will grow up with the same approach. However, if we put God first and our lives revolve around serving Him as a delight rather than a duty, then that is exactly what our children will grow up believing and practicing.

Money is just an inheritance, but teaching others to live for Jesus — that's a heritage!

January 14

For the life of the flesh is in the blood, and I have given it to you upon the altar to make atonement for your souls; for it is the blood that makes atonement for the soul.

— Leviticus 17:11

We have all had those days, weeks, or even months when it seems like we are living under Murphy's Law. All that could go wrong does. In times like this, the enemy seeks to sow seeds of doubt and discouragement, and questions like *Where are you, God?* bombard our minds.

The battle against the doubts of dry seasons is best fought by remembering truth, and no truth is greater than the blood of Jesus Christ shed for our sins. Often we seem to gauge God's love through circumstances, but God's love is displayed for us on the cross in such a way that all doubt is driven out by remembering His shed blood.

Circumstances come and go, but the blood shed for you and me will never lose its power or meaning. It was you and I who deserved that cross. That death should have been ours, for it was we who sinned, not Jesus. Blood had to be shed to make atonement for our souls, and it was His blood, not ours, that did it.

So when the enemy seeks to wreak havoc in your thoughts about the love and commitment of God, don't look to your circumstances to see if He loves you and is committed to you. Look to the cross!

The blood shed on the cross tells us all we need to know about the love of God for you and me. The enemy has no defense against the blood of Jesus, and his tactics of doubt and despair are rendered ineffective by one thing above all others — the shed blood of Jesus for the atonement of our lost souls. Blessed be the name of the Lord!

January 15

I am the way, the truth, and the life. No one comes to the Father except through Me.

—John 14:6

Jesus had just told His disciples to not let their hearts be troubled because He was going to prepare a place for them (and us!). He basically told them, " If I go, I will come again and receive you. Where I am, you will be too; and where I go, you know; and the way you know too."

Thomas, hearing this, responded, "Lord, we have no idea what You are talking about. We don't know where You are going, so how can we know the way?"

Then Jesus spoke the words that ring through the realm of eternity to this very day: "I am *the* way, I am *the* truth, I am *the* life."

Jesus claimed an exclusive on how to enter the kingdom of heaven. It is this exclusivity that separates the Christian faith from all others, and it is this message we need to bring to others in this age of religious and political correctness.

Do not be ashamed of the exclusive claims of Jesus Christ as the only way to heaven. After all, He is the only religious leader who came from there in the first place.

Be bold and confident in the Word of the Lord today. Don't allow the world's reactions to dictate your actions. Jesus is the way, He is the truth, and He is the life. If we fail to tell the world this, how then can they find the hope of heaven?

We have all heard the saying "All roads lead to God," and that is true in one sense. But the question is, where do you go after you meet Him? Only through Jesus can you enter into eternal life.

Speak the truth in love today. Someone you know needs to hear it—even if they don't want to!

January 16

What shall we say then? Shall we continue in sin that grace may abound? Certainly not! How shall we who died to sin live any longer in it?

— Romans 6:1–2

I have always found it interesting to hear people say things like "We're not under the law" anytime a call to live holy or the doctrine of sanctification is mentioned. I like to call this group the "hey bros," for any mention to them of repentance or turning from sin is met with "Hey, bro, don't judge me, man. We're not under the law."

What Paul is saying to us in Romans is both simple and majestic. He is saying, since God so graciously sent His own Son to die for our sins while we were yet sinners, then why wouldn't we respond with disgust and hatred for the things that sent Jesus to the cross; namely, our own sins?

Holiness is not legalism, and repentance from sin is not law. Those things are ours by God's grace. Heaven's radical response to humanity's sin ought to create a radical response to sin in us. God has wiped away our sins with the blood of His Son, so how can we ignore His grace by continuing in the things He died for?

We are not under the law, to be sure, but that doesn't mean God doesn't desire that we live differently from the way we lived before we knew Him. As 1 Peter 4:3 says, "For we have spent enough of our past lifetime in doing the will of the Gentiles—when we walked in lewdness, lusts, drunkenness, revelries, drinking parties, and abominable idolatries."

Dear friend, you can't earn your salvation though works, but living a sanctified and holy life is not works, but rather proof that the past lifetime is just that—past.

It has been often said that Christians are the only Bible some people will ever read. What are they reading in you? Hopefully, it is a life that reflects in every act and deed what God has done for us!

January 17

Deliver those who are drawn toward death, and hold back those stumbling to the slaughter. If you say, "Surely we did not know this," does not He who weighs the hearts consider it? He who keeps your soul, does He not know it? And will He not render to each man according to his deeds?

— Proverbs 24:11–12

It has been reported by many who gather church statistics that 95 percent of all Christians have never led anyone to the Lord. I hope that bothers all of us, and I hope it challenges any of us who find this to be a personal truth.

These verses in Proverbs have been my life verses for many years. They are words that grip my soul and challenge my heart and mind. We all know people who are drawn toward the things that bring death, people stumbling along into things that will slaughter their lives and rob them of their souls. But God has said to deliver them and hold them back, and we cannot claim ignorance to the fact that we know people who are doing those things.

One of the greatest misconceptions at the root of the statistic mentioned previously is "looking for the door of opportunity." But Jesus said we have to go into the world to deliver and hold them back with the power of the gospel. Delivering those drawn to death and slaughter, however, will require getting out of our comfort zones and going into the world of the stumbling.

Your open door for the gospel is found in the nonbelievers within your daily circle of relationships: neighbors, coworkers, classmates, and, for some, even family. Tell them about Jesus and their need for Him and His love for them. Act as though their lives depend on their encounter with you, because you just might be the one that God uses to bring their deliverance!

January 18

Therefore know that the Lord *your God, He is God, the faithful God who keeps covenant and mercy for a thousand generations with those who love Him and keep His commandments.*

— Deuteronomy 7:9

Could you imagine life if we had to wonder if God was going to be faithful? Even when we wonder why God allowed this or what good can come from that, deep in our spirits we know that God keeps His covenant and that His mercy is for a thousand generations (a Hebraism for *forever*).

We know God is faithful, so we are free to live as though He is faithful. This belief in His faithfulness is the enemy of doubt and all its companions, such as discouragement, despair, and discontentment.

Life brings us many things that are unfair, but none of them will we face without God's faithfulness. He hasn't failed us when difficulty comes our way, but He will be faithful in the face of our difficulty. Even when we doubt, there is mercy to meet our lapses in faith.

Life would be unbearable if we really thought that God, even for a moment, was not faithful to His covenant promises. Satan wants to convince us that pain or sorrow is a lapse in God's faithfulness, but nothing could be further from the truth.

God is always there; He is always near. He cannot deny Himself; faithful is what He is — not what He does. It is impossible for Him not to be faithful. It is who He is; it is part of His character, a divine attribute. As Malachi 3:6 says, "For I am the Lord, I do not change; therefore you are not consumed, O sons of Jacob."

It is impossible for God to let us down. His faithfulness is eternal, as is His mercy when our faithfulness lapses. So why do we feel abandoned when trouble or tragedy strikes? Because we are human beings who dwell in bodies of flesh. But the day of trouble is exactly the time when we need to turn to an eternal God who is not limited to granting peace and hope only when things are good.

God has not changed — even when our circumstances do!

January 19

I have been crucified with Christ; it is no longer I who live, but Christ lives in me; and the life which I now live in the flesh I live by faith in the Son of God, who loved me and gave Himself for me.

—Galatians 2:20

One of the most amazing things to me in Scripture is how men and women of God expressed their relationship with the Lord in such intimate terms. John the apostle saw himself as beloved, even calling himself the "disciple whom Jesus loved" (John 21:7). Though we know Christ died for the sins of the whole world (1 John 2:2), Paul says here in Galatians that Christ lives in *me,* loves *me,* and gave Himself for *me.*

This is an essential practice to keeping your faith from becoming merely a religious ritual. You know God so loved the world that He gave His Son, but put your name in there today: God so loved *me* that He gave Himself for me and now lives in me, and by faith I can live for Him and He through me.

God cares about all that we do. We matter to Him, and each day is meant to be a glorious wonder-filled journey of Him living through us. Yes, that includes both you and me! This is especially important to remember when encountering the bumps and bruises of life, the traumas and tragedies that come to us all.

Consider that Paul wrote Colossians, Philemon, Ephesians, and Philippians from a prison cell; yet each of those letters is a monument of hope and even joy—from a prison cell! Paul understood the intimate love that God had for him. And God has this same love for you and me too.

God loves you, God gave Himself for you, and God lives in and through you—yes, you! Take that with you today and see how it changes your perspective. Remember the adage "One up-look can change your whole outlook."

He who is seated at the right hand of majesty on high loves you!

January 20

For this reason I left you in Crete, that you should set in order the things that are lacking, and appoint elders in every city as I commanded you.

—Titus 1:5

Paul had given a young pastor a monumental task. He sent him to a city that, by its own admission, had a horrible reputation. Paul said of the city of Crete in verses 12–13 of this same chapter that "one of them, a prophet of their own, said, 'Cretans are always liars, evil beasts, lazy gluttons.' This testimony is true."

Imagine Crete as your assignment as a young pastor—a daunting, intimidating challenge, to be sure. I could not help but think that, truth be told, we each have a similar ministry. As the lone Christian in many circumstances, we often find ourselves called to set things in order in the midst of a wicked and perverse generation.

To Titus, this meant implementing structure within the church leadership and cleaning up some doctrinal and theological errors. What does your assignment look like? What are the needs around you? What has God assigned for you alone to do for His name and glory?

This reminds me of a great truth: God has each of us where He wants us, and there are things for us to do right where we are! All around us, something is lacking in someone's life. For some, it is simply the lack of knowing Jesus. For others, it may be a lack of hope, a lack of joy, or a lack of peace. But there is a reason we are where we are, and the reason is the people around us.

Someone needs encouragement today, and someone needs to know the hope of forgiveness through Christ the Lord. Things are lacking all around you, and God has put you there to set things in order.

Right in the middle of a carnal, selfish, godless society, you are the one God wants to use today!

January 21

Now therefore, fear the Lord, serve Him in sincerity and in truth, and put away the gods which your fathers served on the other side of the River and in Egypt. Serve the Lord! And if it seems evil to you to serve the Lord, choose for yourselves this day whom you will serve, whether the gods which your fathers served that were on the other side of the River, or the gods of the Amorites, in whose land you dwell. But as for me and my house, we will serve the Lord.

—Joshua 24:14-15

Joshua, the great field general for Moses, was in the closing moments of his life. He had seen and experienced much, both under Moses' command and by leading Israel himself. He had lived through both the failures and the successes of life in the Promised Land. He himself had been faithful and triumphed in victory; he himself had been prayerless and suffered defeat.

Joshua made a statement so stunning it is still repeated to this day: serving God is a choice, even when you are one of God's chosen people. We all make hundreds, maybe even thousands, of choices each day. You have made the choice to read this devotional, maybe have coffee and breakfast, and brush your teeth (I hope). The rest of the day will be followed by a series of choices spanning lane changes during your commute to what's for lunch. Some may choose to take a class or drop one. Others will choose to call a client or make a delivery.

In the midst of all these everyday choices, you must also choose whether to serve God. You don't have to read your devotional, you don't have to eat your breakfast or lunch, you don't have to brush your teeth. But isn't life better if you do? Choose today to serve God in some way. It pleases Him, impacts others, and makes you the beneficiary of His blessings.

Life is filled with distractions, many of them time stealers used by the enemy. But our God, who has chosen us in His Son, asks us to choose to serve Him.

Choose this day to serve with all your heart, soul, mind, and strength the one who alone is worthy. You will never regret it, nor will you ever feel as though you have wasted the precious gift of time.

January 22

Then Judah said, "The strength of the laborers is failing, and there is so much rubbish that we are not able to build the wall."

—Nehemiah 4:10

Nehemiah arranged the children of Israel into work parties according to their tribes. As they toiled, their enemies mocked and threatened them. One of them, a man named Sanballat, said to his friends, "What are those feeble Jews doing? Will they fortify themselves? Will they offer sacrifices? Will they complete their work in a day? Will they revive the burned stones from the heaps of rubbish?"

The Jewish work parties were not stonemasons; they were just ordinary people trying to do a work for God. The threats and insults of their enemies finally got to them, however, and they said, "There is too much rubbish to continue."

The Hebrew word for *rubbish* is *aphar,* which means "gray dust." You see, years earlier the Babylonians had destroyed Jerusalem and burned the city, including the limestone walls surrounding it. Limestone, when superheated, loses its structural integrity and becomes worthless for building. Additionally, these stones were covered with a film of gray dust, dust that represented a humiliating defeat from the past. Yet it is so like the Lord to take that which once defeated us and turn it—and us—into a fortress of strength.

I have much "gray dust" in my life, things I wish I had never done. For a while, Satan successfully harassed me about those things, and I felt like the Jews, like there was too much rubbish in my life for God to build anything. But the promise of 2 Corinthians 5:17 is mine. I am a new creation in Christ. Old things, including my gray dust, have passed away, and all things have been made new.

Do not let your past rule your present, but let God build a work in you. He can even use the gray dust if He chooses. He has used mine time and time again, even as Satan has tried to convince me that God cannot build upon my failures.

In traveling to Africa, I learned a saying common among Christians in Malawi. It has served as a great reminder for me, and it can serve as a reminder for you too. "The devil is a liar!" the Africans jubilantly declare. That is indeed true. If God can use burned stones covered in gray dust to build a wall around His city, He can build a work from the gray dust of your life too!

January 23

Then He came to Bethsaida; and they brought a blind man to Him, and begged Him to touch him. So He took the blind man by the hand and led him out of the town. And when He had spit on his eyes and put His hands on him, He asked him if he saw anything. And he looked up and said, "I see men like trees, walking." Then He put His hands on his eyes again and made him look up. And he was restored and saw everyone clearly.

—Mark 8:22–25

It is quite amazing to see how life has progressed in the last century or so. Man, who traveled for millennia on foot or on the backs of animals, now traverses the globe in a matter of hours. But man's progress in the information age has led us to believe that "instant everything" is our right. We want fast food and instant downloads. We even want our pizzas ordered, cooked, and delivered in less than half an hour, or we demand to get them for free!

This age we live in has even caused Christians to sometimes expect the same pace from God. We want instant answers to our prayers and instant blessings for our deeds. That is why I have always found the healing of the blind man in Mark 8 so interesting. In this account, Jesus broke from His pattern of instantaneous healing and touched the blind man twice before he could see clearly.

Why would He do this? Some say Jesus did not release enough power the first time and realized the man needed to be zapped again in order to see clearly. But that would in essence deny His deity, for God knows all, and all that God does is good and perfect. To say He didn't release enough power at the first touch denies both of those things. So why the two touches for this one man?

I believe Jesus did this for the benefit of all who would later read this event. I believe He wants us to recognize that God's healing is sometimes a process, not just an event. Sometimes we need to keep asking and keep seeking and not lose heart when it seems as though a setback has come. Our God is awesome and powerful and never needs to touch us twice, but He chooses to do so at times to increase our faith and trust in Him.

Do not make the same kind of demand on God that you do on the pizza guy. God does His will in His way and in His time. He is always right and never does wrong, even in the "instant everything" age!

January 24

For the vision is yet for an appointed time; but at the end it will speak, and it will not lie. Though it tarries, wait for it; because it will surely come, it will not tarry. Behold the proud, his soul is not upright in him; but the just shall live by his faith.

— Habakkuk 2:3–4

Habakkuk was unique among the Old Testament prophets, both in his method and in his message. He was unique in his method in that the book of Habakkuk opens with a question to God: "O Lord, how long shall I cry, and You will not hear?" (Hab. 1:2). He was unique in his message in that he did not simply proclaim judgment upon Israel for its rebellion but also sought justice for Israel from its persecutors.

Habakkuk, much like you and me, was tired of the prosperity of the wicked and the unjust treatment of the righteous. He was a man who longed for the righteous God to act against the evil in the world, which in his case meant the oppressive Babylonians.

The Lord's response to Habakkuk's opening question is quoted many times in the New Testament and for centuries has inspired the hearts of men and women to a greater understanding of the Word of God and the God of the Word. The Lord tells Habakkuk that justice is indeed coming, but for now, the just shall live by faith.

How easy it is to find ourselves consumed with the injustice of the world and our lives dominated by cries of "How long, oh Lord?" How long before wrongs are no longer gotten away with? How long before that conniver at work is exposed? How long before those who call evil good and good evil (Isa. 5:20) are exposed? The list goes on and on.

The Lord answers, "The vision of justice is for the appointed time. It will indeed come to pass, but for now, as a saint justified by the blood of Jesus and set apart for a holy work, your mission is to live by faith." This is a faith that trusts in God even when no change in circumstance can be seen, a faith that is not circumstance driven.

Justice is coming, and faith is our modus operandi until then. With it, we live in hopeful expectation, knowing that all the injustice of this life will not be allowed in the next.

Even so, come quickly, Lord Jesus!

January 25

"No weapon formed against you shall prosper, and every tongue which rises against you in judgment you shall condemn. This is the heritage of the servants of the Lord, and their righteousness is from Me," says the Lord.

—Isaiah 54:17

Don't you wish that this just read, "No weapon will be formed against you"? But the fact is, the fiery darts of the enemy come as an endless stream to those who seek to live by faith. They may impact us and even inflict pain upon us at times, but they will not prosper against us, the servants of the Lord!

In the closing chapters of Isaiah, the word *servant* applies not only to Jews but also to all saints, both Jew and Gentile. The enemy's plans, or weapons, are formed against us all. The word *formed* carries the implication of being specifically designed, with the Hebrew word referring to the shaping of a piece of pottery for a specific use.

Satan designs specific strategies against us as individuals. Yet the one who imputed (transferred) to us His righteousness promises that they will not prosper and even that we can condemn them as servants of the Lord.

We see this truth illustrated in Jesus' testing in the wilderness. Jesus, having not eaten for thirty-nine days, was first tested with the temptation of making bread from stones. Furthermore, Satan offered the world to Jesus in exchange for worship, but Jesus, knowing He was going to die to redeem the world, resisted. Satan specifically targeted events in Jesus' current situation and sought to attack His eventual destination as well.

This, too, is true in your life. Your current difficulties and future ministry are Satan's targets, and he loses no opportunity to exploit them. What is your defense? Jesus used the commands and promises of the Word of God to repel the weapons formed specifically against Him, and that is your defense too.

So be on guard, yet be confident as a servant of the Lord. The promise to you at this present hour is that you will prevail against anything Satan forms against you!

January 26

Now to Him who is able to do exceedingly abundantly above all that we ask or think, according to the power that works in us, to Him be glory in the church by Christ Jesus to all generations, forever and ever. Amen.

— Ephesians 3:20–21

I love how often the Bible seeks to assure us of the longevity and stability of God's promises. Sometimes we read the Scriptures and look at books like Acts as glorious days gone by. We view them with a kind of "back in the day" perspective.

But Paul reminds us that the power at work in us through Jesus Christ, who is able to do above all that we ask or think, is promised to every generation, so be it (amen). So if the power is promised and He never changes, then that means He still can do exceedingly abundantly above all that we ask or think.

So why the seeming power shortage today? Because the power is given in order to bring Him glory in the church—not just the church corporate, but also in the church member or individual saint as well. This means Jesus Christ can do things in and through us beyond anything we could ever imagine!

Jesus can use us to reach others with His gospel, He can use us to strengthen another weary saint, He can use us to speak words of knowledge and wisdom, He can use us to display supernatural discernment. He can do in and through us more than we could ever dream or imagine. All He asks in return is one thing: do all that we do for His glory.

If we understand our mission, we will see more manifestations of His power. He has demonstrated on the cross the lengths He will go to in order to save us, and He will demonstrate through us all the power needed to reach others for His glory. He is worthy of the reward of His suffering! And the reward of His suffering is the rescue of lost souls.

God will do more through you than you could ever imagine if your goal and mission are in tune with His will. So step out and share your faith today. He will do more with one small step of faith than you could ever imagine!

January 27

A fool vents all his feelings, but a wise man holds them back.

—Proverbs 29:11

I have often said there are two 29:11s in the Bible that every Christian needs to remember: Jeremiah 29:11 and Proverbs 29:11. Like the verse in Proverbs, the book of James also talks about our speech. Chapter 1 of the epistle instructs us to be quick to hear and slow to speak, and chapter 3 adds that the person who can control the tongue is able to bridle (control) the whole body.

We have all heard the saying "Think before you speak." The danger in speaking quickly and venting all our feelings is that we often say things we haven't even thought of yet! We do so at the hurt and expense of others. Perhaps that is why God placed the tongue behind two rows of teeth: to guard it from getting out of control!

I love the acronym often used to inspire us to think before we vent all our feelings. Taken from the word *think,* the individual letters stand for what we must consider before we speak: (1) T, is it true? (2) H, is it helpful? (3) I, is it inspiring? (4) N, is it necessary? (5) K, is it kind?

Not everything we think in our minds needs to be said, and as the verse in Proverbs 29 warns, it is foolish to vent all we feel. We have all experienced situations in which something we thought about someone or something was proven wrong. So if we speak true, helpful, inspiring, necessary, and kind things to one another, we will greatly diminish the odds of saying something foolish.

January 28

Call to Me, and I will answer you, and show you great and mighty things, which you do not know.

— Jeremiah 33:3

Jeremiah was shut up in the court of the prison by King Zedekiah of Judah for speaking out against the false prophets who spoke lies to the people of Israel. While he was imprisoned for doing what God had commanded him to do, the word of the Lord came to him.

First, God said to Jeremiah, "Call to Me." We might paraphrase this as "Keep in touch," or "Keep praying." God followed this with the assurance "I *will* answer" and then concluded with "and show you great and mighty things, which you do not know."

Some things can be revealed only through difficulty, but how can God show Himself faithful if we are never in a situation where only "great and mighty" can deliver or sustain us? I believe this encouragement to Jeremiah is appropriate for all of us as well.

God encourages you today, even when you face tough times and especially when they are not of your own doing, to keep in touch with Him. Don't let the prison imprison your faith, but keep calling. He will indeed answer, for there are great and mighty things to be revealed in your difficult situations.

Now I want to be careful here. To be honest, I don't like trials and testing any more than you do. In no way do I mean to belittle the difficulty you may be facing right now. But if God has allowed your current circumstance, there is something great and mighty that can come out of it. It might be a stronger or more compassionate you, or it might be a steadfast and immoveable spirit. Maybe a deeper trust born out of waiting will result.

But remember, no matter the circumstance, the depth of the difficulty, or even the darkness of the hour, call to Him. He will surely answer and reveal great and mighty things to you — right where you are!

January 29

But seek first the kingdom of God and His righteousness, and all these things shall be added to you. Therefore do not worry about tomorrow, for tomorrow will worry about its own things. Sufficient for the day is its own trouble.

— Matthew 6:33–34

It has been well said that 90 percent of the things we worry about never happen. Though I believe that is true, it's the other 10 percent that worries me! But seriously, how much time do we spend borrowing from tomorrow that which influences or even ruins today? Jesus said not to worry, however, and He offers this, not as advice, but as a command.

The Greek word for *worry* means "anxiety," and this is what Jesus is getting at. He isn't telling us to have a robotic and mindless oblivion regarding this life's troubles and concerns, but He is saying that when problems come, we are to keep our focus on Him, remembering to seek Him first.

This means we must not neglect the one thing we can rely on when pressed on every side. We cannot allow trials and struggles to change our focus, but we must keep putting Him and His will first. I realize this is easier said than done. When trouble or trials come, many of us try to seize control in order to get ourselves out of the situation. But Jesus says, "No, keep putting Me first, and we'll deal with this stuff together." After all, we can't see tomorrow, so why disconnect from the one who can?

Never measure the size of the mountain before you until you remember the size of your God! He is never surprised or unprepared for the things you face each day.

So how can you not worry? Keep living like He will enable you to do all things through Him. Keep believing that He knows all and is in control of everything, and do not let the devil trap you in the desolation of isolation. Keep praying, keep reading, stay in fellowship, and serve, just like you do when things are at their best. That is the way to seek God first, and that is the antidote to worry.

January 30

Nor is there salvation in any other, for there is no other name under heaven given among men by which we must be saved.

— Acts 4:12

There are some names that when mentioned create an instant association in the majority of people. Say the name *Elvis* and the "King of Rock" comes to mind, or say *Michael Jackson* and the "King of Pop" comes to mind. The name *Hitler* or *Manson* conjures thoughts of horrible wickedness, the name *Lincoln* makes us think of war and the tragic death of a great man, and the list goes on and on. Just the mention of a name can call to mind things associated with a person's accomplishments or influence.

But there is one name above all others, a name that means "salvation." We know him as Jesus, but in Hebrew His name is *y'hôshûa (Jehoshua)*, meaning "Jehovah saves."

In this age of political correctness, most people are comfortable with the word *God* or the concept of God. People have their own idea about who or what God is, so when you say, "God," an image is generated in their minds in harmony with the being they have created.

But there's one name that always causes a stir, and that is the name of Jesus, the one who saves. Say the name *Jesus* and now you're talking about someone specific: the one who said He is *the* way, the one who said you must be born again, the one who said without Him we cannot see heaven and that loving Him includes obeying His commandments.

There is power in the name *Jesus*. God is a title of the one triune being we know in three persons. But to some, the word *God* can also refer to Zeus, a higher power, a state of consciousness, or even a spiritual essence. To them, God can be part of all matter, and all that exists is included in their concept of God.

But friends, there can be no mistake in meaning when you say the name of Jesus. Speak His name and you will see the power of it even today. It's a name unlike any other, so speak it and see what I mean!

January 31

For the word of God is living and powerful, and sharper than any two-edged sword, piercing even to the division of soul and spirit, and of joints and marrow, and is a discerner of the thoughts and intents of the heart.

— Hebrews 4:12

It is amazing to me the number of people who have never read the Bible yet love to criticize and question it. It is equally amazing that the Bible is actually alive and powerful.

Could you imagine reading *Moby Dick, Tom Sawyer,* or some other classic over and over every day for decades? After a year of that, reading those books would become drudgery and perhaps even feel like punishment. But most important, after a few times through, you would know the book backward and forward and never learn anything new.

Not so with the Word of God! I have been hearing it for over fifty years, and I have been a serious student of it for more than twenty-five years. I have been teaching it regularly for more than twenty years, yet I am still learning and growing and being impacted by it. Though I have taught its books numerous times, each time I study them, they yield different and powerful truths.

The Word of God has no equal—not even a close comparison. It speaks to our hearts right where we are and right at the perfect time. I have never had anyone send me a quote from *Moby Dick* or *Tom Sawyer* to offer me encouragement or direction. But countless times someone has shared the Word of God with me, or I have read it myself and felt like it should have said "Dear Barry" at the beginning, so clearly did it speak to me. No other book is like that! The Bible cuts to the heart when needed and comforts and strengthens where necessary.

I have heard it said, "Seven days without reading the Bible makes one weak." I couldn't agree more. This book I teach from multiple times a week and spend personal time in every day is still revealing things I missed the last time around.

This Bible is no ordinary book we read. It's the living Word of God—read it today!

February 1

Blessed be the God and Father of our Lord Jesus Christ, who has blessed us with every spiritual blessing in the heavenly places in Christ.

—Ephesians 1:3

I have noticed that in some ways Satan is like an illusionist. He distracts our attention with one hand while he does something else with the other. One of his common tricks today is to create the illusion that we must wait for things that we already have, things like spiritual blessings.

Paul told the Ephesians (and you and me) that we have been given every spiritual blessing. So what are spiritual blessings? They come in the form of gifts and fruits. The gifts of the Spirit enable us to proclaim God's truth to the lost, and the fruits of the Spirit are evidence and confidence of the change within us and give us strength and comfort as we use our gifts for God's glory.

So what are we waiting for? If we already have all we need in Christ, then we can step out in the faith He has given us and share His love with others, having the fruits of the Spirit manifested in us while we do. Satan, however, constantly whispers, "You're not ready"; "Look over here at this thing you did the other day"; or "Look at that other person. God can use him, but not you." These are merely distractions from already given blessings. That is not to say you cannot be disqualified from certain ministries by your actions, but that is not what I am talking about here. I am talking about Satan trying to convince you that you cannot be used at all—ever!

It is always so refreshing to be around new Christians. Many times they act as though they have found something so wonderful they are compelled to talk about it no matter what. They act like knowing Jesus has changed everything. Remember those days?

Satan, however, has created the illusion that the zeal of a new saint is a passing thing we grow out of. He tries to convince you that you have to wait for the next wave of feelings to wash over you in order to get fired up again. But that is not true. You have every spiritual blessing in Christ Jesus. You have what you need to do His will, and there is no reason to wait to accomplish it. All you need, you have in Jesus! Don't be distracted by Satan, the deluded illusionist.

February 2

For God is not unjust to forget your work and labor of love which you have shown toward His name, in that you have ministered to the saints, and do minister.

—Hebrews 6:10

We have already established that we have every spiritual blessing in Christ Jesus, and now the author of Hebrews says God is "not unjust to forget your work and labor of love which you have shown toward His name."

The word *forget* is a very long Greek word, *epilanthanomai* (ep-ee-lan-than'-om-ahee), which means "to lose track of" or "to neglect." This means it would be unjust for God to ask us to do great things and then lose track of us or neglect us while we seek to do them. This is a providential promise that God is in all we do for His name's sake and glory.

This is important because it reminds us that when we are in the desert and do not feel God's presence, we must still do what we are called to do. Imagine if we went to work or school only when we felt like it. Similarly, we don't serve God because we feel like it; we serve God because He is worthy of it.

God is with you, and He will not leave you hanging when you step out in His name, no matter how you feel. That would be unjust, and God is not unjust. It would be a conflict of character to be both holy and unjust, so God cannot be unjust. It is not even remotely possible.

I have often told our church that we overcomplicate things far too often, and I have often exhorted them, "If you want to do something for God, then do something for God." He's not unjust; He won't lose track of you or neglect you.

As a secondary blessing, labors of love toward His name are often the cure for dry seasons. In the feelings department, nothing feels better to the saint. When we do these labors of love, we experience the wonderful flood of emotions and feelings that come from bringing Him glory. God is not unjust in the dry times. He is there, and we are secure in Him.

February 3

I will bless the Lord at all times; His praise shall continually be in my mouth.

—Psalm 34:1

David had recently slain Goliath and married the king's daughter. The women of the city had danced in the streets and sung, "Saul has slain his thousands and David his ten thousands." On top of all that, King Saul's own son had become David's closest friend and ally. What a great time for him to write such words!

But the thing is, David did not write these words under those circumstances. He wrote them when he was estranged from his wife and on the run from a king who sought to kill him. In an effort to escape, he landed in a city of Israel's archenemies, the Philistines, acting like he was crazy in an effort to escape from the hands of the Philistine king. It was then that he wrote, "I will bless the Lord at all times."

It has often been said, "Fruit grows in the valleys, not on the mountaintops." The fruit of David's praise in the valley was far richer and sweeter to the Lord than any praise he might have offered on the mountaintop of triumph. David had come to realize that praise is not based on our experiences, but rather on God's worthiness. No matter how things were going for him personally, David knew God was worthy of praise at all times.

So whether today is a good day or a bad day is irrelevant when it comes to praising God. Whether things are going great or you were just treated like a fool, praise the Lord, for He is worthy!

David also wrote in Psalm 32:3, "When I kept silent, my bones grew old through my groaning all the day long." Praise is to the soul what breathing is to the flesh—you just can't live without it.

So praise God today no matter what's going on, for He is worthy. And remember, silence is hard on your bones!

February 4

When you pass through the waters, I will be with you; and through the rivers, they shall not overflow you. When you walk through the fire, you shall not be burned, nor shall the flame scorch you. For I am the Lord your God, the Holy One of Israel, your Savior.

—Isaiah 43:2–3

You have to wonder if more than a century later, three guys named Shadrach, Meshach, and Abed-Nego didn't have this promise in their heads and hearts when Nebuchadnezzar threatened to throw them into the fiery furnace if they refused to bow before his image. It seems unlikely that mere coincidence could explain how the exact thing written actually happened; therefore, it is safe to assume the three Hebrews, who were among the best and brightest of Israel, were well aware of Isaiah's words.

We know at this point Israel had already passed through the waters twice, at the Red Sea and the Jordan River, and now three captives would literally walk through the fire unscorched. What this tells us today is that we can have the confidence not only to know but also to act upon the Word of God.

Note that Isaiah doesn't say "if" we pass through the waters and "if" we walk through the fire—he says "when." We *will* encounter fiery trials, as 1 Peter 4:12 says, and the enemy at times will come in like a flood (Isa. 59:19). But when the fiery trials and flood of the enemy threaten to consume us, we are free to act upon the Word of God, confident that the rivers will not overflow us and the flame will not scorch us.

In other words, because the Holy One of Israel is with us, we can make it through any trial, and we are free to live like we are going to make it through. No circumstance can overcome us when we live with that knowledge as our reality.

So whether it's flood season for you, or you feel like a dartboard for the enemy's fiery darts, you are not alone. "You will make it through!" declares the Lord.

February 5

And you, who once were alienated and enemies in your mind by wicked works, yet now He has reconciled in the body of His flesh through death, to present you holy, and blameless, and above reproach in His sight — if indeed you continue in the faith, grounded and steadfast, and are not moved away from the hope of the gospel which you heard.

—Colossians 1:21–23

Right in the heart of this majestic statement about the reconciling work of Jesus Christ, Paul inserts two little letters (in English translations) that might form the most significant word in all the New Testament as it pertains to the Christian life. He says we were enemies but are now reconciled by the body and blood of Jesus *if* we continue in the faith.

This pretty big *if* is not a qualification, but rather an indication of a life reconciled to God. The thought is much like Paul's instruction to the Corinthians when he urged them to examine themselves to see if they were really of the faith (2 Cor. 13:5). Wouldn't it be reasonable to assume, then, that we might need to know what to look for and what questions to ask to determine if we are really of the faith?

The answer is, those really of the faith will continue in the faith, grounded and steadfast, and not move away from the hope of the gospel and follow other religions or gods. This is what we examine ourselves for. Of course, that does not mean that we will never have momentary lapses of faith or perhaps even a season of prodigal living (I had a long one). But even in those times, the grieved Spirit within will remind us of our conversion, and that too is evidence of a reconciled life to God. (Note: I highly discourage prodigal living at all costs!)

Jesus purchased us with His own blood and gave us the Holy Spirit as a guarantee of our inheritance (Eph. 1:14). So what will the Spirit do in us? He will cause us to continue in the faith, keeping us grounded and steadfast and never moving from the hope of forgiveness and eternal life through Jesus Christ.

To follow Jesus Christ and have our sins forgiven is the most important decision we will ever make. Paul says here there will be supporting evidence that will show us and all others that our conversion is real.

February 6

But you shall receive power when the Holy Spirit has come upon you; and you shall
be witnesses to Me in Jerusalem, and in all Judea and Samaria,
and to the end of the earth.

— Acts 1:8

In Acts 1:4, Jesus instructed His disciples to wait in Jerusalem for the promised power of the Holy Spirit. They then asked Him, "Will you at this time restore the kingdom to Israel?" (Acts1:6). The verse above was Jesus' answer.

The answer the Lord gave implies that the power of the Spirit is not given to rule the world, but rather to change the world with the good news of the gospel. In His answer, Jesus reveals the purpose of the empowering of the Holy Spirit, and that is to give us power to be witnesses. Whether in our own town, the surrounding areas, or anywhere else we might go, the power of the Spirit will enable us to be witnesses.

I personally believe "the end of the earth" mentioned by Jesus in this verse refers to both a time and a place. That means the promised power given to the first disciples is applicable for the rest of us as well. It also reminds me of the frequent questions regarding the power of the Holy Spirit and His work in the church today.

We need to be careful to remember that the purpose of the Spirit's coming *upon* us is to empower us to be His witnesses, while the Spirit *in* us provides assurance, peace, and comfort and aids in our understanding of the Word of God (John 14:26). We get off course when we separate the power from the purpose. This, unfortunately, leads to attributing certain things to the Spirit of God that are clearly apart from the purpose of His power.

Conversely, if you want to experience the power of the Holy Spirit upon you, then fulfill the purpose of being a witness. You will quickly see His empowering. Don't believe me? Then tell someone about Jesus today, and watch what He does through you!

February 7

Blessed be the God and Father of our Lord Jesus Christ, the Father of mercies and God of all comfort, who comforts us in all our tribulation, that we may be able to comfort those who are in any trouble, with the comfort with which we ourselves are comforted by God.

— 2 Corinthians 1:3–4

It was not yet 9:00 a.m. at our home, and the day was already looking like an emotional roller coaster. Our day began with a grieving mom who told us that one year ago this day, she had last heard the voice of her son making plans to visit with his family that very weekend. The next day he was injured in an accident that took his life twenty-eight days later.

Five minutes later, we received a very different message from another mom. Jubilant, she told us the wait for her prodigal child had finally come to an end. "Our prodigal has come home!" were the joyous words she shared.

These two friends were both women who loved God and their families, women who were faithful and consistent in their walks and love for the Lord. Yet the contrast of their two experiences at this moment in time was almost surreal. One woman's time of grief had just come to an end, while the other woman's grief was still in the beginning stages. Yet both, as I had seen with my own eyes, had experienced the comfort of the unchanging God of heaven.

Comfort is available to us at all times and in all circumstances. Whether our time of grief has just begun or has come to an end, God is there with us. He is the same yesterday, today, and forever (Heb. 13:8).

Maybe today you need to remember Paul's declaration of blessing to the God of all mercy and comfort. If you are in an hour of grief or suffering, know that God is there. In the nearness of your God, you can experience a comfort that no words can offer or actions extend. If your heartfelt prayer has been answered and your long-awaited deliverance has come, your prodigal has returned, or your loved one long prayed for has received salvation, do not forget to bless the Lord for His mercy and comfort.

Life is filled with many contrasting experiences, as we so radically evidenced with our two women friends that morning. But our God is with us in and through them all. He is near to those who are of a broken heart, so we can boldly proclaim, "Blessed be God!"

February 8

Let your light so shine before men, that they may see your good works and glorify your Father in heaven.

— Matthew 5:16

In a section known as the Beatitudes, Jesus opened the Sermon on the Mount with nine ways that blessings can come into our lives. In these statements, Jesus addressed actions, attitudes, self-control and contentment, morality of heart and mind, and mercy when persecuted. He confidently asserted blessings can be found in all these things.

Jesus further said that a life lived in accordance with these principles will not be regretted but rather rewarded in heaven. He followed this with the reason it is important that these things "be our attitudes" (beatitudes): we the church are the only preserving and purifying influence on the earth.

The Lord then explained that the beatitude kind of life begins with being a lamp in the home and then spreads outside the home as a lamp set on a hill, meaning the surrounding community. Then He said, "Let this light shine through your good works in such a manner that others glorify the Father in heaven."

I find it interesting that Jesus, in providing this list of attitudes, labeled them as works. This tells us that works are not limited to the cup of cold water and the feeding of the hungry we read about in Matthew 25:35. Visible works that cause others to glorify God also include attitudes, such as being humble, offering comfort to those who mourn, walking in meekness (power under restraint), hungering for righteousness, and being pure in heart. It even includes, as Paul said, being "simple concerning evil" (Rom. 16:19); that is, living in peace when facing false accusations.

This kind of life is a blessed life, and the greatest blessing of all is that it reveals God to others. That is the summary of the great truth of the Beatitudes.

Look around today through the lens of the Beatitudes and you will see more opportunities for good works than you have ever seen before. Through them, you will bring glory to God by leading others to Him!

February 9

I will lift up my eyes to the hills — from whence comes my help? My help comes from the Lord, who made heaven and earth.

— Psalm 121:1–2

You have probably heard it said, "How do you eat an elephant? One bite at a time." This, of course, is a metaphor, but the implied meaning is clear. Some things take time, and not everything happens instantaneously, as much as we would like them to.

I love the way the Bible contrasts our struggles with God's power. Our struggle may look elephant sized, and God's counsel to us as we look at the elephant may seem like just one bite of a giant problem or dilemma. But if we follow God's lead and take one bite at a time toward solving the problem, eventually we will triumph over it.

We can be sure that the psalmist was facing an elephant-sized situation in one of life's valleys when he lifted up his eyes. So often we too face mountain-sized problems, and we begin to feel overwhelmed at the circumstances in front of us. Thoughts begin to creep into our minds like, *How am I ever going to get through this?* or even *Things are never going to change; this is too big.* But as Jeremiah reminds us in his book, "There is nothing too hard for God" (Jer. 32:17).

Things that look overwhelming can be put into perspective with just one simple act of obedience to the Word of God. Are you facing a mountain-sized problem today? God's word to you is to lift up your eyes. This is not some type of magic formula to make your problems disappear, but rather wisdom to keep them in perspective. Yes, life is indeed hard at times, but through the psalmist, the Lord reminds us that heaven is our eternal home. Life may be unfair at times, but heaven never is. Life may bring sorrow, but sorrow is banned from heaven.

The implied mountain of the psalmist is Mount Zion, the New Jerusalem of Revelation 21:2, the city whose builder and maker is God (Heb. 11:10). The Bible is saying to you and me today, when life seems like one long valley, lift up your eyes to heaven. Remember that this life is a vapor and someday will pass away. This won't necessarily make your "elephant" disappear, but it will definitely keep it from consuming you!

February 10

Fight the good fight of faith, lay hold on eternal life, to which you were also called and have confessed the good confession in the presence of many witnesses.

—1 Timothy 6:12

Paul encouraged young Timothy to remember his calling, the good confession he had made in the presence of many witnesses. Paul also reminded Timothy of something we often lose sight of: the Christian life is a battleground, not a campground. A battle rages around us, and as many of us sang growing up, "We're in the Lord's army!"

We wrestle not against flesh and blood (Eph. 6:12), but against the enemy principalities and powers that wage against us. I have often reminded believers that in God's army there is no Secret Service or covert ops. Every Christian soldier is on the front lines of the battle. There are no days when this is not true, just days when we fail to engage in combat. Yet even then, the enemy never rests from seeking to gain ground.

The enemy is spiritual, and so are our weapons (2 Cor. 10:4). We fight him by faith, through prayer, and through the study of the Word to prepare ourselves for battle. Then we engage the enemy by witnessing, listening, and helping those in need.

All around us are those whom the enemy has in his sights. A word of kindness or hope spoken by a Christian soldier can repel the enemy's advances in their lives. All around us are those whom the enemy is advancing upon. Preying on their personal needs and stresses, he fires darts at them tipped with the accusation that God doesn't care.

Engage in the battle today! You are daily surrounded by those being targeted by the enemy, but you are behind enemy lines and have daily opportunities to practice faith, extend hope, and express God's love. Against these three weapons, the enemy is defenseless.

Someone is wounded in battle and needs you today, soldier. So go out and fight the good fight of faith!

February 11

Therefore, to him who knows to do good and does not do it, to him it is sin.

—James 4:17

Paul reminded the Corinthian church that we walk by faith and not by sight (2 Cor. 5:7). We could well expand that to say we walk by faith and not by feelings or any of the other senses. But it is also true that doing the things God has instructed us to do, whether it be changing an attitude or action or doing the good we ought to do, feels really good.

Jesus said it is more blessed to give than to receive (Acts 20:35). The word *blessed* means "happy are they" or "oh, how happy." Could we not then say that a life of giving and doing good feels better than one that does not give and do good?

Sin grieves the Holy Spirit. Since the Spirit dwells in us, it only stands to reason that not grieving the Spirit makes us feel better, and grieving Him makes us feel worse. So often the enemy wants to convince us that we are feeling discouraged or in despair because of the things we do not have. However, the Bible says not doing the good we know we ought to do is more likely the cause.

We are all going to face down days, so I am not talking about living in some type of continual blissful state. What I am talking about is eliminating the self-inflicted wounds that result from not doing the good that feels really good to do. Now again, feeling good is not our motive for doing good, but it is a secondary benefit nonetheless.

So the next time you're visited with one of those "what's wrong with me?" days—maybe even today—ask yourself, "Have I done the good I know I ought to do?" Whether it is gaining ground on a change of attitude or an action you need to take on behalf of another, just go ahead and do it. Either way, it always feels better to obey God, no matter the situation.

So do the good you know you ought to do, and today will be a better day for you and someone else!

February 12

Serve the Lord with gladness; come before His presence with singing. Know that the Lord, He is God; it is He who has made us, and not we ourselves; we are His people and the sheep of His pasture.

— Psalm 100:2–3

I always find it interesting to meet people who seem to think they are self-made or the masters of their own destinies. For a while, I tried being self-made and my own master, but I made a mess out of my life and almost lost my marriage and family in the process. I like God's way and plan better.

I don't even mind that God's Word often compares me to a sheep, a noto-riously dumb animal. In fact, I have done so many dumb things in my day that being called a sheep sometimes feels like an upgrade! But as dumb as I may be, I am still His sheep. He is my shepherd, and I am in His pasture. And the way He has treated me in spite of all "the dumb I have did" (couldn't resist) makes me want to sing of His greatness and serve Him with gladness. He is God. He made me, and His plan for my life is always better than any plan I could ever contrive. This is true for you too!

I don't want to be a self-made man, because self-made men are usually self-serving men. It is better to serve the God who made me than to serve me, myself, and I.

A sheep without a shepherd can get into lots of trouble and is prone to wander and even follow another sheep into danger. For a sheep to be its own shepherd is a recipe for disaster. Sometimes, when we find ourselves having wandered from the Good Shepherd's pasture by doing something dumb, we wonder if He wants us to come back. The answer is unequivocally yes! Come before His presence with singing, for He is God, and God always rejoices over His sheep who come home, no matter how dumb the choices that caused them to wander.

Have you done something dumb today? If not, it's either too early, or the day's not over yet. But if you have, or when you do, remember, you're all His. The voice that whispers in your mind, *You can't go home, you've gone too far, you're no longer welcome there* is the voice of the wolf — not the voice of the shepherd. The Lord rejoices over His people, even when they come home after acting like dumb sheep!

February 13

So he said, "I have been very zealous for the Lord God of hosts; for the children of Israel have forsaken Your covenant, torn down Your altars, and killed Your prophets with the sword. I alone am left; and they seek to take my life." Then He said, "Go out, and stand on the mountain before the Lord." And behold, the Lord passed by, and a great and strong wind tore into the mountains and broke the rocks in pieces before the Lord, but the Lord was not in the wind; and after the wind an earthquake, but the Lord was not in the earthquake; and after the earthquake a fire, but the Lord was not in the fire; and after the fire a still small voice. So it was, when Elijah heard it, that he wrapped his face in his mantle and went out and stood in the entrance of the cave. Suddenly a voice came to him, and said, "What are you doing here, Elijah?"

—1 Kings 19:10–13

I am not sure why, but I have always found something humorous in this account of Elijah's ministry. He had, just weeks earlier, stood up for the name of his Lord before 450 prophets of Baal and witnessed the fire of God consume the sacrifice, altar, and all the water around the altar, while the god Baal did nothing to answer the cries of his prophets. Elijah then had the 450 prophets executed, prophesied imminent rain in the midst of a drought, and was supernaturally empowered to outrun a king's chariot to the city of Jezreel. I would say that Elijah was having a pretty monumental run of events. But when he arrived in Jezreel, he was threatened by King Ahab's wife Jezebel and, despite all that he had seen and done, went into hiding because of her threats.

So here was the prophet of the Lord, the man who had called down fire from heaven, executed hundreds of false prophets, prophesied torrential rains and saw it fulfilled, and outran the king's chariot, hiding in a cave and lamenting, "I alone am left of the faithful prophets, and others are trying to kill me."

Imagine the scene: The wind tore through the mountain, followed by an earthquake and then a fire. I wonder what Elijah expected to hear or see next from God. Maybe a heavenly "You're awesome, Elijah," or "You rock Elijah! You the man!" But what did he hear from God? "What are you doing here, Elijah?" asked the Lord. I believe Paul captured the essence of the Lord's message to Elijah when he said, "For God has not given us a spirit of fear, but of power and of love and of a sound mind" (2: Tim 1:7).

Has something or someone caused you to hide in a cave of silence? Maybe the fear of persecution has silenced you or put your faith in hiding. But God is saying to you, "What are you doing here hiding in fear? Speak up, and do not fear, for I have not given you that spirit." Be bold today and confident in the power of God as you seek to stand fast in a fallen world.

February 14

For God so loved the world that He gave His only begotten Son, that whoever believes in Him should not perish but have everlasting life.

— John 3:16

The stories surrounding the origin of Valentine's Day are many and varied. Some accounts say that the name *Valentine* was common among the martyrs of the early church, and the holiday was an effort to honor their name. Others say it started in an effort to replace the pagan ritual to honor the goddess Juno Februata. In this ritual, the names of young women were put into a box, and young men drew out the names by lot. The matched couples were considered partners for the year.

Whatever the true origin of Valentine's Day, it is indisputably a major holiday. The U.S. greeting card association estimates that approximately one billion valentines are sent each year worldwide, making the day the second largest card-sending holiday of the year, surpassed only by Christmas.

The fact is, despite the many cards and notes expressing love that are widely exchanged on that day, there is another expression of love that exceeds them all. Through the apostle John, the Spirit of God has written the greatest love letter the world has ever known. Interestingly, John, who penned perhaps the most famous and oft repeated words in human history, commonly referred to himself as "the disciple whom Jesus loved" (John 13:23).

You may or may not receive a Valentine's card today, but you have received a love note from heaven that declares God so loved the world He gave his Son to die for your sins. The ultimate expression of love is to lay down one's life for one's friends, and that is exactly what Jesus did.

On this Valentine's Day and every day, we would all do well to emulate John and recognize ourselves as disciples whom Jesus loves. His love is so different from human love, for His love alone can save souls and change lives. This is the message of His heavenly valentine to you and to me: "You are a disciple whom I love!"

Happy Valentine's Day!

February 15

Therefore we also, since we are surrounded by so great a cloud of witnesses, let us lay aside every weight, and the sin which so easily ensnares us, and let us run with endurance the race that is set before us.

— Hebrews 12:1

We have all seen someone compete in a race of some kind. Whether it was a car race, a track competition, or a swimming event, there was one common element in each mode of racing—speed.

Speed is not just the result of horsepower or leg or arm power, but speed is also attained by reduced drag and weight. Race cars are kept as light as possible because lighter cars go faster and farther. Track shoes, too, are designed as light as possible in the hopes of running faster. Even swimsuits are designed with the lowest drag coefficient possible. All this is done in hopes of attaining greater speed and increasing endurance.

This principle is true for our Christian lives as well. Hebrews tells us we must contend with weights and sins detrimental to our endurance. Weights are not necessarily sinful in themselves, yet they drag us down and rob us of our energy and endurance. Sin, however, is exactly that—sin—and robs us of the joy meant to be part of the race.

It is easy to gradually increase our drag coefficient almost without knowing it. As weights are gradually added to our lives, we lose the zeal and commitment required for winning. Undealt with sin slowly wears down our endurance, much as a pulled muscle on a runner hampers efficient performance.

Is something in your life weighing you down and stealing your time and commitment to the Christian race? Remember, this may be something that is not sinful in and of itself. Are you allowing a sin in your life to take your focus off the race and to slowly consume you? If either is true, lay it aside and watch your spiritual endurance increase immediately. Without a doubt, you'll finish well the race set before you.

Most races conclude with a final burst of speed. Runners, swimmers, and cyclists all give a last kick. Sometimes we say they are putting "the pedal to the metal," or, in the case of motor sports, running "wide open." However, if the competitor is out of fuel because of bearing extra weight of some kind, the finish of the race may not be as exciting as it should be.

Run the race to win, and finish well. Lay aside the things that consume your energy and hinder your performance. Then, as you round the last turn of life, you will have plenty in reserve to finish well!

February 16

I beseech you therefore, brethren, by the mercies of God, that you present your bodies a living sacrifice, holy, acceptable to God, which is your reasonable service. And do not be conformed to this world, but be transformed by the renewing of your mind, that you may prove what is that good and acceptable and perfect will of God.

— Romans 12:1–2

I love what the Spirit inspired Paul to say here and how He had him say it: "Present your bodies... be transformed by the renewing of your mind, that you may prove what is that good and acceptable and perfect will of God." In other words, Paul is urging us to be living proof of the will of God. He then states that the reasonable place to begin is with our bodies—our morality, if you will.

In 1 Corinthians 6:9–10, Paul lists a group of obvious sins of the body, or moral failures. Then, in verse 11, he says, "And such were some of you." So Paul consistently communicated that the pattern of a life that is living proof begins by exercising moral self-control, and this self-control is a fruit of the Spirit (Gal. 5:23).

But in our passage in Romans 12, Paul addresses issues of the flesh more difficult to change: those of the mind, or attitudes. He challenges us to effect this change through the renewing of our minds. In this context, the word *renew* may also be translated "renovate." In other words, our minds must be reworked so that the pressures of society and its flawed definition of success are replaced with God's perspective of what is good, acceptable, and even perfect.

I have often thought it interesting that many Christians feel a sense of failure because of the fact that they still battle lusts or worldly desires. But the truth is, the flesh and the spirit are always warring against each other, no matter how long we have walked with the Lord, and this battle will rage until we "put on incorruptible immortality" (1 Cor. 15:53). Victory always begins with the reasonable service of fighting the flesh by presenting our bodies, our moral character, to the Lord. It's only when we stop fighting against the desires of the flesh that we have failed.

So don't stop fighting, and don't start flailing and listening to the enemy's taunts. Remember instead to present your body as holy and acceptable (control your moral behavior) so that you will have hope for a renovated mind.

February 17

For God did not appoint us to wrath, but to obtain salvation through our Lord Jesus Christ, who died for us, that whether we wake or sleep, we should live together with Him. Therefore comfort each other and edify one another, just as you also are doing.

—1 Thessalonians 5:9–11

It's funny—not funny "ha ha," but interesting funny—how often truth can be identified by what the enemy attacks. The coming of the Lord for His bride, or the rapture of the church, is one of those things. We know there is a time of wrath coming on this world that Jesus Himself said no flesh would survive unless those days were shortened (Matt. 24:22). Yet we are also told to comfort and build one another up (edify) with the truth that we the church will not see the day of God's wrath.

Paul told the church at Thessalonica that whether we are alive at that time or die before that day (v. 4), we will ultimately be with Him. So if you are having "one of those days" (or weeks or months), let me comfort and build you up by reminding you that this world is not your home. Though life may be hard, even brutally hard at times, the wrath we deserve for our sins was poured out on Jesus Christ. He Himself kept out appointment with wrath!

A day is coming when the Lord will return for His bride. The enemy, however, often calls this day into question because he does not want us to be comforted and built up by this knowledge. Rather, he wants us to live torn down and discouraged. But friends, there is comfort to be found by keeping our minds and hearts focused on the truth. Yes, there is a day of wrath coming for those who dwell on the earth, but those who know Christ as Lord and Savior will not be here to experience it.

The best is yet to come, Christian. The day is soon approaching when we will be in heaven. Whether death takes us or the Lord comes for us, the wrath of God is not appointed to us. Take comfort in these words today, and offer them to others that they might be comforted too!

February 18

"Behold, the days are coming," says the Lord GOD, "that I will send a famine on the land, not a famine of bread, nor a thirst for water, but of hearing the words of the Lord."

— Amos 8:11

Israel's continual rebellion and rejection of God's warnings concerning its spiritual adultery (idolatry) led to four hundred years without a prophet in the land. This four-hundred-year famine of hearing from the prophets of God spanned the time of Malachi to the coming of John the Baptist. Far worse than a famine of bread and water, it was a famine of the word of the Lord.

It is always interesting to me just how much the church's actions parallel those of Israel. Israel is pictured as the wife of God (Jer. 3:20), and the church is referred to as the bride of Christ (Rev. 21:9). Israel experienced a drought of the words of God right before the coming of the Messiah, and 2 Thessalonians 2:3 tells us that before Christ comes for His bride, there will be a great falling away from truth, a famine of heeding the words of God.

The difference between the two famines is that we have the written Word of God readily accessible to us, whereas the Jews had to rely on the rabbis to teach them the Torah and the prophets to speak to them on God's behalf. So the famine the Jews experienced was one of judgment, while the famine the church and world will experience before the coming of Christ for his bride will be one of choice. It will be knowingly choosing to disregard the Word of God or defecting from its truths.

The point is, there is a spiritual famine today even though the Bread of Life is readily available. In the last days of this earth, there will be a famine of heeding the Word of God. Israel's failure to heed brought on the famine of hearing; the church's failure to hear has brought on the famine of heeding. But it need not be so. Are you feeding on the Word of God daily? Is your church serving up the whole counsel of God? There is a famine today, but it is one of choice, not the result of uncontrollable circumstances or judgment.

Last week I was teaching the Bread of Life discourse in John 6 to a young adults study. We were learning how to avoid a crisis of faith and concluded that we must do what the Bible says, no matter what we think. This will keep us fully fed and in tune with the Word of God — even during a famine of choice!

February 19

But love your enemies, do good, and lend, hoping for nothing in return; and your reward will be great, and you will be sons of the Most High. For He is kind to the unthankful and evil. Therefore be merciful, just as your Father also is merciful.

— Luke 6:35–36

In these verses, Jesus gives a rather difficult command. It is not in our nature to do good to people who hurt us or to love our enemies. It is, however, completely consistent with His character. After all, while we were yet sinners Christ died for us (Rom. 5:8).

In today's Scripture passage, Jesus says, "Do good, and lend, hoping for nothing in return," with the obvious application a financial one. If we lend hoping for nothing in return or expecting no repayment, then we have not really made a loan, but rather given a gift.

I believe we can draw a conclusion here, since Jesus includes the unthankful and the evil with those to whom God is kind. Like the righteous, they too experience the benefits of His mercy. The conclusion is that we are to meet the tangible needs of others, even our enemies. The blessings of rain fall on both the just and unjust farmer (Matt. 5:45), and so must our blessings. In other words, we must not discriminate in our hearts and minds when it comes to helping others.

Isn't it funny how we give to someone and say, "It is more blessed to give than to receive" (Acts 20:35), but if a thank you is not forthcoming, whether verbally or in the mail, we quickly get into a mental huff about how ungrateful that person is? At such times, few of us remind ourselves it is more blessed to give.

The key in the passage above is found in the word *hoping.* In the Greek, the word means "to fully expect." So the core issue at hand is eliminating the expectation of thanks when giving, even from our enemies.

Today's exhortation is quite a challenge and will be a faith and strength builder. Be kind to the unthankful and the evil today, and you will spend the day in Jesus' shoes, walking in the manner He did while on earth. That's all you have to do today—nothing to it! Just make sure to read Philippians 4:13 before you leave!

February 20

But those who wait on the Lord shall renew their strength; they shall mount up with wings like eagles, they shall run and not be weary, they shall walk and not faint.

—Isaiah 40:31

I am sure there are others like me who find waiting in any capacity a great trial. When I am at the local Costco and approaching the checkout area, I find myself engaged in an elaborate scheme to pick just the right line that will afford the shortest waiting time. Not only do I measure the length of each line, but I also take note of the quantity of items in the baskets of each person in line. Then I monitor the efficiency of the checkout person. I find myself looking at the checkers and thinking, *Okay, that one is a talker*, or *That one is indifferent to the customer's time*, as I consider the unavoidable waiting time ahead. Yes, you can pray for my wife, as she is "blessed" with shopping with me!

But after all my careful calculations and estimations, after the "right line" is finally chosen, what do you think happens? The person in front of me writes a third-party out-of-state check needing a manager's approval, and I wait anyway!

In a similar fashion, ordinary life experiences often creep in to our spiritual lives. How often, when waiting on the Lord, do we find ourselves examining the efficiency of how He could or should answer, provide, or deliver? For me, waiting is not my favorite thing, and as I wait, renewing my strength is not usually the first result I experience.

But God often allows us to wait until the waiting renews our strength. The implication here is "rest" and clearly parallels Jesus' words in Matthew 11:28: "Come to Me, all you who labor and are heavy laden, and I will give you rest." The Lord will allow us to wait until we simply rest in Him, but sometimes our attitudes, estimations, and evaluations of what God ought to do only prolong our time of waiting. Having times of waiting is a given in life, but how we wait is a decision.

Are you waiting on the Lord for something? Don't estimate, evaluate, or calculate what God should do or how God ought to handle the situation. Just rest in the fact that His timing is perfect. And when you do, the end of your wait may come sooner than you think!

February 21

Those who regard worthless idols, forsake their own Mercy.

—Jonah 2:8

To many of us, Jonah is the Bible's poster boy for disobedience. God told Jonah what He wanted him to do, but Jonah didn't want to do it so jumped on a ship out of town. That ship was nearly dashed to pieces by the sea because of his disobedience, and then Jonah was forced to jump ship, lest the ship and the entire crew be lost (his presence on board had already cost the crew their cargo).

This statement in verse 8 of Jonah's own record of these events is a portion of a prayer he prayed from the belly of a great fish (sorry, but Jonah wasn't swallowed by a whale, because whales aren't fish). In this most unlikely setting, Jonah prayed insightfully that to regard worthless idols is to forsake the very source of mercy, God Himself.

Jonah's idol was... well, Jonah. The Assyrians' capital city of Nineveh was enemy territory, and later in Jonah we discover why he did not want to go there to begin with. Chapter 4 tells us that after the reluctant prophet carried out his assignment, the entire city of Nineveh repented, and the Lord relented of the disaster He was going to bring on it. This made Jonah angry, and he said to the Lord, in essence, "I knew you were going to do that. That's why I fled to Tarshish. Just take my life now, for I'd rather be dead."

The lessons are many in the journey of this pride-filled, disobedient prophet of God, but I believe the greatest of them is the one most often overlooked: Jonah preached to Nineveh, and Nineveh repented! This affirms Isaiah 55:11 that declares the Word of God does not return void but accomplishes the purpose for which it was sent. That means we are to share the truths of God's Word today, even with an enemy. Someone just might repent—maybe even an entire office or school. It happened in Nineveh, it can happen today, and it can even happen through you!

If God has been prompting you to share with someone, you can be sure He has already been at work there and wants that person to repent. So even if you feel reluctant, step out in faithful obedience and watch what the Lord will do through you!

February 22

If we confess our sins, He is faithful and just to forgive us our sins and to cleanse us from all unrighteousness. If we say that we have not sinned, we make Him a liar, and His word is not in us.

—1 John 1:9–10

At this writing, the closing days of the first decade of a new millennium are right around the corner. The year 2010 is just days away, and as I look around, I am faced with the rather sad reality that humanity is no longer seeking truth. Political correctness rules the day, even within Christianity.

John the Beloved gives us a word of caution in this area as he makes his famous statement in verse 9. By using the word *if*, he lets us know what follows is conditional. John couples "if" with "confess," and *confess* means "to speak or see as the same." Putting the two thoughts together, we might paraphrase John's words to say, "If we agree with God that what He calls sin is sin, He is faithful and just to forgive and cleanse us; but if we redefine sin, we call God a liar and thus reveal we don't know Him at all."

We need to be careful today of much that is packaged as truth. The Bible is neither irrelevant nor antiquated. It is not only current but also necessary for guiding us into the things that are acceptable to the Lord (Eph. 5:10). We cannot allow ourselves to be duped by marketing schemes disguised as the gospel that contradict the moral code of God.

If we see sin the way God does, accept His definitions of right and wrong, and practice the implied repentance, then He is faithful and just to forgive us and cleanse us from all unrighteousness. So if you hear someone say that the Bible doesn't mean what it clearly states concerning a moral issue or that the Bible is not relevant to our day, run for your life. Someone is about to call God a liar!

God's moral code defines the boundaries within which life is meant to be lived. Following it brings enjoyment and blessing to the fullest as we avoid many of the pains and pitfalls of sin's self-inflicted wounds. But it begins by honoring the Word of God as our source of moral and spiritual truth.

The Bible may not be politically correct to some, but it is still very popular in heaven! Live how it says you should live, do what it says you should do, say what it says you should say, and in the end, "Well done, good and faithful servant" will ring in your ears for all eternity!

February 23

But without faith it is impossible to please Him, for he who comes to God must believe that He is, and that He is a rewarder of those who diligently seek Him.

—Hebrews 11:6

This verse is one of those frequently half-quoted verses we are all familiar with. We easily hear part of the verse, but we don't always grasp the entire verse. It is much like reading Romans 6:23. We read and understand, "The wages of sin is death," but we often gloss over the balance of the verse, which says, "But the gift of God is eternal life in Christ Jesus our Lord." In a sense, we hear only the bad news and not the good news.

This is true with Hebrews 11 as well. In this verse, the negative is spoken before the positive: we cannot please God but by faith. Then we are told the one who comes to God must do two things. First, he or she must believe God exists, or that "He is." Next, the conjunction *and* appears to set the second condition, which is believing that God is a rewarder of those who diligently seek Him.

The phrase *diligently seek* comes from the practice of repeating the same Greek word twice for emphasis. Thus the words actually read "seek, seek." It is similar to the way Jesus said "verily, verily" to inform us that what followed was of extreme importance.

This is true in this famous half-quoted verse. Without faith, it is impossible to please God, for he who comes to God must believe in God and believe that He will reward those who are serious about seeking Him. So be a serious seeker today. Search out the deep things of God, and seek to serve Him more today than you did yesterday. Make that your goal tomorrow, and then again tomorrow, and your life will be very rewarding indeed!

February 24

Thus says the Lord: "Stand in the ways and see, and ask for the old paths, where the good way is, and walk in it; Then you will find rest for your souls. But they said, 'We will not walk in it.' "

—Jeremiah 6:16

Israel continually did what much of the church does today (and vice versa): they were influenced more by society and the culture around them instead of influencing the society and culture of the day. Even though the Lord Himself warned them about this through Jeremiah, they said, "We will not walk in the old paths." Those ways seemed too out of touch with society and were inconsistent with the desires of the children of Israel. This was true even though God had told them judgment was coming on Jerusalem but could be averted if they would get back on the old paths.

The church and many Christians today seem to fall into the same trap. We know judgment is coming on this world; Jesus Himself went to great pains to be sure His people would know that (Matthew 24–25). Yet many of us act as though it will not happen, and we no longer worry about walking in the ways of God. After all, that's old school, we say. We need to be more culturally sensitive, and we need to make our message more relatable, we insist. We don't want to offend anyone searching for God, so we certainly don't talk about such unpopular topics as hell and sin.

Though heaven will be populated by people of every tribe, tongue, and nation (Rev. 5:9) and will include people from every station in life, both rich and poor, slave and free, male and female, there is one common denominator that all in heaven will share. Every one of them will be there because the gospel was preached to them. It may have been the heavens declaring God's handiwork (Ps. 19:1) or the faithfulness of a follower of God that spoke to them, but each will be there as a recipient of the gospel of grace.

There are many new ways to proclaim the old truth, but the old path is still the only way to heaven. The "good way" is still the good news of Jesus Christ who came to save sinners. There is no other way, and there is no other path.

Someone today needs to hear about the old path. Quit worrying about offending people by talking about the gospel. The cross is an offense to those who are perishing (1 Cor. 1:18), but it is also the only means through which a person can be saved. So if you leave out the message of the cross, the name of Jesus, the word *sin*, and the threat of hell, what motivation is left for anyone to be saved?

The old path is still the only path, and there are no others!

February 25

And my God shall supply all your need according to His riches in glory by Christ Jesus.

—Philippians 4:19

What a blessed promise from the one who speaks galaxies into existence, (Genesis 1), rides on the clouds (Ps. 68:4), and spans the universe with His hand (Isa. 40:12)! He will supply all your needs according to His riches.

I have often remarked that although Jesus told us it is hard for a rich man to enter the kingdom of heaven (Matt. 19:23), most of us are willing to give it a try! But we need to remember that Philippians 4:19 is not God's PIN number: punch it in and out come the blessings. He supplies according to *His riches,* and His definition of riches is often very different from ours. In fact, His riches are often things money can't buy.

We do know that God blesses financially and promises bountiful provision to the faithful giver, but money is insufficient in more things than it is good for. It can make life easier and even more pleasant at times, but there are other times in life when monetary riches just don't cut it.

But here is God's promise to you and me: what we need from Him today, we shall have. Sometimes it's a definite financial need, but other times it's something intangible, like patience. Sometimes it's contentment, and other times it's strength; but whatever *He knows* we need, He is faithful to provide.

Here too is another great thing about His riches: our bank account fluctuates with our spending, but God's account never dwindles. If you needed strength yesterday and need yet more today, don't worry. You'll never have an overdraft of what God supplies, because His resources are endless.

Yesterday you were encouraged to share the good news of the old path with someone. Maybe you didn't do it. Maybe you needed courage or boldness and didn't have it, or maybe you forgot or were too busy.

Guess what God has for you today? Whatever you needed yesterday to bring glory to Jesus is still available today. It's like a coupon with no expiration date, and you'll never need a rain check. He will always supply all you need to do His will, and He will bless you as you do it!

February 26

Then God said, "Let there be light"; and there was light. And God saw the light, that it was good; and God divided the light from the darkness. God called the light Day, and the darkness He called Night. So the evening and the morning were the first day.

—Genesis 1:3–5

This is one of my favorite subtleties in all of Scripture, but we'll miss this magnificent reality if we are not careful. Here it is: God said, "Let there be light," and there was light on the first day of creation; however, He did not create the stars, sun, and moon until the fourth day of creation.

This tells us two things about knowing God. First, He is the light of the world, and where He is, there is no need for the sun. We see this to be true in heaven, as recorded in Revelation 21:23. The city mentioned had no need of the sun or of the moon to shine in it, for the glory of God illuminated it. The Lamb was its light.

The second thing this tells us is that God is not bound by natural laws. He doesn't need the sun to produce light—Jesus is the light! This is not a metaphor, but a reality first revealed in creation.

These two truths also have significance in the lives of those whom the Light of the World has entered. God is not bound by natural circumstances, and things do not have to be "thus and so" in order for Him to cast His light into any given situation. I have often encouraged those who are praying for a lost friend or loved one that they don't have to see progress for God to be moving. The situation can look hopeless and dark, but then seemingly out of nowhere God says, "Let there be light" —and there is light.

Never lose hope in praying for those you long to come to the Light of the World. Remember, the God you are praying to can light up the universe without creating a single heavenly luminary. That's your God! He speaks and it happens, even when natural law or circumstances say it is impossible. He takes nothing and makes something out of it, just as He did in the beginning of creation.

Tell someone about Jesus today. Find someone in total darkness, someone who seems very unlikely to ever see the light. You never know, the lights might come on right before your eyes!

February 27

Him we preach, warning every man and teaching every man in all wisdom, that we may present every man perfect in Christ Jesus.

—Colossians 1:28

An interesting phenomenon has exploded in the church in recent years, though it has long been with us in one form or another. Paul dealt with it in Corinth when the church there began to divide and fragment over their favorite teachers (1 Cor. 1:12). Unfortunately, we still see this same division rampant in the church world today. Some Christians like to boast about the particular church they attend or the particular person who is their pastor. Although there is nothing wrong with loving your church or supporting and loving your pastor, it is important to remember that Paul wrote this exhortation to the entire church at Colossae, not just to the vocational pastors there.

If you are part of a wonderful, thriving, Bible-teaching church, praise the Lord! But your commission as an individual saint is not to tell people about your church, but to tell people about Jesus Christ. Paul says, "Him we preach," warning and teaching in wisdom so that others may be perfected in Christ.

The fact of the matter is, if the church as a whole were busier with the Father's business, individual congregations wouldn't have so much time to worry about each other! That is not to say there are not things to be careful of and even separate from, but if we spent more time preaching Jesus and less time casting doctrinal stones, the church as a whole would be far more effective than it is.

As you approach this day, remember that Jesus saves not churches, no matter how wonderful they may be or how eloquent their pastors. As I have told visitors at our church countless times, "If you have come here today looking for the perfect church, your search is over, because there isn't one!"

Do the work of an evangelist today and tell someone about Jesus. Then, after you tell them He is the way, truth, and life (John 14:6), after you lead them in prayer accepting Christ, tell them of the place they can go to be with others who know Him—your church!

February 28

Or else, if you will not let My people go, behold, I will send swarms of flies on you and your servants, on your people and into your houses. The houses of the Egyptians shall be full of swarms of flies, and also the ground on which they stand. And in that day I will set apart the land of Goshen, in which My people dwell, that no swarms of flies shall be there, in order that you may know that I am the Lord in the midst of the land. I will make a difference between My people and your people. Tomorrow this sign shall be.

— Exodus 8:21–23

Moses had now approached hard-hearted Pharaoh three times to petition him to let God's people go. But each time Pharaoh made excuses or simply refused. Even as the plagues increased in intensity, he continued to promise to let the people go, but always with limitations, or he would say yes then renege on his word.

I have always found it interesting that the first three of the plagues that came upon the Egyptians were also encountered by the children of Israel. But before the fourth of the ten plagues, God distinguished between His people and the people of Egypt (I believe this is a typology of the rapture of the church).

The lesson for us is clear. We will share in many of the experiences of the people of the world, much as they will share in many of the blessings God pours out on His people (Matt. 5:45), but there are limitations, in both directions. The people of the world can never experience the fullness and richness of knowing God and the wisdom, strength, and discernment afforded us through the indwelling of the Holy Spirit. Because of sin, we will share in many of the tragedies and difficulties of the world, but we will face them differently, for God makes a difference between His people and Pharaoh's (the world).

No matter what we face in life, knowing God makes a difference! We may experience many of the same trials and traumas as the world, and we may even go through some of the results of sowing and reaping as a society, but as the church, we will never experience His wrath (1 Thess. 5:9).

The Lord said to Pharaoh through Moses, "Tomorrow this sign shall be." Friend, someday that "tomorrow" is going to come, that day when God will separate His people from the world. We must be ready, and we must also remember until then that life is different—better—just by knowing Him! The wrath of God is not in our future. It was poured out on Jesus for our sins, and that is the difference between God's people and the people of the world.

One day will be the day when it could be said, "Tomorrow the rapture will happen." Live today like it is that day!

March 1

Trust in the Lord with all your heart, and lean not on your own understanding; in all your ways acknowledge Him, and He shall direct your paths.

—Proverbs 3:5–6

To describe myself as a creature of habit would probably be a significant understatement. I am not one who is prone to losing things, because I tend to put items in the same place all the time. Each day when I come home, my wallet, keys, and the assorted "man stuff" I carry go into the same allotted space in the same drawer.

On my way to a favorite restaurant, I will often say that I am going to try something different this time. But when the server arrives, the same words as usual come out of my mouth, ordering the same thing I always get (recently I have broken this trend more!).

Though being a predictable creature of habit does offer some benefits, it also brings difficulties. Life does not always happen on my schedule, and God certainly doesn't operate inside my box. What I view as obvious resolutions to obvious problems don't always happen how or when I think they should. But if I insist on approaching the ups and downs of life in my own understanding, I am in for a frustrating journey.

The famous proverb above says to entrust our understanding and our paths to God. He is always leading, but we are not always following, especially in circumstances we do not understand or that lie outside the way we think they should be done. But God is in control, and His will is going to be done. However, it will be done in His way and in His time because His ways are higher than ours (Isa. 55:8–9).

God frequently wants us to go outside our comfort zones and into the realm of trust so He can stretch and strengthen our faith. Do not let your habits or even your rituals get in the way of God's will. It's too easy to let your faith get stuck in the rut of what you always do. And remember, as some have said, that a rut is nothing more than a grave with the ends kicked out!

Do something different in your walk with God today. Speak to someone, pray for an enemy, give your lunch away, or let God direct your path without leaning on your own habits or understanding. There are many wonderful encounters waiting outside the box if you will only venture outside the norm once in while.

Try it—you'll like it!

March 2

You therefore must endure hardship as a good soldier of Jesus Christ. No one engaged in warfare entangles himself with the affairs of this life, that he may please him who enlisted him as a soldier.

— 2 Timothy 2:3–4

In an age where the focus of much of the church seems to be on improving life experiences, many have lost sight of the fact that hardship is part of the Christian life. Sadly, in the church today, many are being taught how to avoid hardship instead of how to handle it.

Part of the battle in this life deals with becoming entangled in the affairs of life. Paul warned Timothy not to do that. As he explained it, no good soldier entangles himself in the affairs of life, but instead remains focused on pleasing his enlisting officer, who, in our case, is the captain of our salvation, Jesus Christ (Heb. 2:10). Life's destiny and purpose are all about pleasing Him, not ourselves. Life is about His exaltation, not our accumulation.

It is easy, however, to become entangled with the affairs of life if we begin to listen to things in conflict with the plan and purpose of God. We have all seen pictures or footage of a fish or other animal trapped in a net or snare. The net or snare is the animal's only focus, and all the creature's energy is spent on trying to get free. Paul warns us to avoid this altogether by not getting entangled in the first place, lest the entanglements begin to consume us.

How do we do this? It always begins by remembering that this world is not our home and that nothing in this life is worth having at the expense of pleasing our captain. The Christian life is the best life there is, and the best life is also filled with enduring hardships that may be as simple as living unentangled.

Most traps involve the use of bait to attract a specific animal. What bait does Satan use to entangle you? You can easily identify it by considering the thing you just cannot live without, other than food and shelter, of course. This is the thing that says something about who you are, and this is your most likely point of entanglement.

Be careful of entanglements. If you are not, they will consume all your time and energy and rob you of the privilege of pleasing the Lord!

March 3

For I am persuaded that neither death nor life, nor angels nor principalities nor powers, nor things present nor things to come, nor height nor depth, nor any other created thing, shall be able to separate us from the love of God which is in Christ Jesus our Lord.

— Romans 8:38–39

What a promise! What a banner to hang over our lives each and every day! Nothing can separate us from God's love in Christ Jesus. Not one thing the devil does now or in the future can alter that truth. Neither the highs and lows of life nor any single element in the whole of God's creation can separate us from His love.

That means, at no time, in no place, from any source, is it even remotely possible for us to be separated from God's love. Even the days that are not our most stellar days as Christians, even when we let our guards down or our tempers flare, even when we fail and knowingly do the wrong thing, God's love is there.

Now there is nothing wrong with conviction of the Holy Spirit, to be sure, but when you start thinking things like, *You blew it this time*, or *God has rejected you*, or *You've gone too far*, or *That was your last chance*, be assured that is not the voice of the Lord. Though you may have blown it, though you may have sinned or fallen, His love is still there.

Proverbs 24:16 says, "For a righteous man may fall seven times and rise again." Most of us have heard that the number *seven* in the Bible is the number of completion or completeness. If we apply that thought here, we could interpret Proverbs 24:16 as, "A righteous person may completely blow it, but they can rise again."

Friend, God loves you, and nothing can separate you from that love. If you have fallen, get up and walk in His love again. The voice that whispers, *It's over between you and God* is not His! Take it from someone who was a master at completely blowing it for many years. God's love never failed me; in fact, it was His love that carried me through in my many failures.

Nothing we have ever done could make the Lord stop loving us. The devil knows this, so he continually seeks to squelch our love for God by challenging the verses about His unconditional love. Sadly, it does work on some people because God's kind of unconditional love is so foreign to us. We cannot comprehend a love that is not performance based but is constant, even on our worst days!

Maybe you had a rough day yesterday and didn't exactly represent the Lord well. If that is the case, rise again today because God still loves you and wants to spend this day with you!

March 4

But Daniel purposed in his heart that he would not defile himself with the portion of the king's delicacies, nor with the wine which he drank; therefore he requested of the chief of the eunuchs that he might not defile himself.

—Daniel 1:8

Daniel was a young man who was committed to his commitment! Though he was captive in a foreign land, his commitment to his faith had traveled with him. He purposed in his heart that he would not violate his dietary restrictions, forego abstinence from wine, or eat meat offered in sacrifice to idols. Daniel was not going to let the culture redefine his faith, but rather, he purposed in his heart to stay true to his commitment to the Lord.

The heart, or will, is where commitments are not only born but also maintained. So often when we read Scripture and come across the Bible's giants of the faith, we tend to assume they had something we don't. In our minds, they were supersaints, members of an elite squadron of God's choicest people. But that is not true; these giants of faith were simply men and women who purposed in their hearts to serve God with every fiber of their beings.

The word *purpose* means "to put." Like Daniel, Deborah, Paul, Priscilla, or any other hero of faith, we can put into our hearts the determination to remain committed to our commitment, no matter what goes on around us.

Daniel lived in a foreign land amidst the people who had conquered his homeland and by whom he had been carried away captive to serve in the king's palace (Dan. 1:4). Daniel could have easily gone into survival mode and said to himself, *If I am going to make it through this, I am going to have to make some compromises.* But Daniel purposed in his heart that he would not be defiled by the culture around him. He made a decision to be committed to his commitment.

Something in your world may be trying to take you captive—maybe a delicacy or an opportunity of the world. How can you do the right thing? Put it in your heart that you will do right, and make the decision *before* you sample the delicacy. Then you will be among the Daniels and Deborahs who have remained committed to their commitment.

You don't have to sin if you don't want to!

March 5

And let us not grow weary while doing good, for in due season we shall reap
if we do not lose heart.

—Galatians 6:9

I am sure most pastors would agree that one of the most discouraging and frustrating aspects of ministry is when people make appointments to discuss a problem, but as you share the Word of God with them, you see in their eyes that they are in a far and distant land. You know full well as they leave the room that they are not going to act upon anything discussed and will soon be back. At such times, it is easy to think, *Why did you even come in to see me? You really don't want answers!*

You may have people like that in your life, perhaps friends or relatives you are weary of doing good for because you are tired of seeing them fall into the same hole time and time again. The key to not losing heart in these situations is to remember that all of us, at one time or another, have been that person with the far and distant look in the eyes.

God didn't give up on me in my nearly a decade of prodigal living, even though I dragged His name through the mud I was wallowing in. I am sure I broke His heart a thousand times in those years, but He never quit on me, though I came to Him again and again with empty promises and commitments in my journey back home.

The key to dealing with repeat offenders is to not lose heart. There is a *due season*, a conversation, a moment, an action, or maybe even just patient availability, for the same person doing the same thing over and over again. But one day it will finally be "that day," and all your efforts will bear fruit. At last the lights will go on, and that person will see what was obvious to you all along.

Don't miss the chance to be there for that great moment by growing weary of being there now. Share with the person a hundred times, and listen to the confession of the repeat offender who never seems to learn. Be there for the people around you, and one day, when you are sharing the same thing for the thousandth time, they will finally get it.

Don't miss the moment because it is taking them so long to get there. You will reap in due season if you do not lose heart!

March 6

But it so happened, when Sanballat heard that we were rebuilding the wall, that he was furious and very indignant, and mocked the Jews. And he spoke before his brethren and the army of Samaria, and said, "What are these feeble Jews doing? Will they fortify themselves? Will they offer sacrifices? Will they complete it in a day? Will they revive the stones from the heaps of rubbish – stones that are burned?"

— Nehemiah 4:1–2

Paul tells us in Ephesians 6 that we do not wrestle with flesh and blood, but with principalities and powers. Nehemiah, called to lead the great work of rebuilding the wall around Jerusalem, was continually battling principalities and powers that were using humans as their weapons of discouragement.

The tools and tactics of the enemy mentioned in this passage reveal some of his favorite and most effective weapons. In this example, Sanballat tried to use the past to discourage the great work of God that Nehemiah and the other Jews were doing. First, Sanballat called them "feeble Jews," and indeed those working on the wall were not stonemasons by trade; they did, however, share a burden for the work of the Lord. Then Sanballat mocked them, questioning if they would fortify the city, complete a day's work, and build with stones from heaps of rubbish – stones, in fact, that had been burned.

The unqualified Jews who were trying to rebuild the wall were using stones that had been burned and thrown down the hillside when Nebuchadnezzar destroyed Jerusalem in 586 BC. The walls had been constructed of limestone, a soft stone that loses its structural integrity when superheated or burned. Now the stones were nothing more than rubbish, the remains of the gray dust and ashes left by the fire.

What Sanballat was doing was using the past to discourage the work of God's people in the present. This is how the enemy will attack you too. He says that your past has made you useless, God can't build anything out of you, you're burned, you're rubbish, you are feeble, you'll never make it.

But here is the interesting part: everything Sanballat hurled at Nehemiah was true! The task was impossible, the past was terrible, and the work was too much for these people; but what Sanballat overlooked was the fact that these people had a heart for the work of the Lord.

Do not let the enemy infiltrate your present with past mistakes. When you confess your sins, God is faithful and just to forgive your sins and cleanse you from all unrighteousness (1 John 1:9). Remember, you cannot be disqualified for service by your past, but only by your present. Don't listen to the enemy. You are not rubbish. Your past need not rule you, and you can complete the work the Lord has called you to. The work is the Lord's, and all you do is done in the power of His might.

Discouragement is not from God, so when it comes, even through a messenger of flesh and blood, know that the devil is behind it. You are free in Christ to just keep building. Remember, God builds great things, even out of lives that once were rubbish!

March 7

But may the God of all grace, who called us to His eternal glory by Christ Jesus, after you have suffered a while, perfect, establish, strengthen, and settle you.

—1 Peter 5:10

Peter had just reminded the church of their adversary who roams about like a roaring lion seeking those whom he may devour (v. 8) and urged them to resist him by remaining steadfast in the faith, knowing that this was the experience of all their brothers and sisters in Christ (v. 9). Now, in verse 10, after a reminder of grace and eternal glory, Peter mentions suffering, as though it were a fact for all, not just a possibility for some.

The word *suffering* means "to experience a sensation," with the implication of a painful sensation. Peter follows the reality of suffering with four things that suffering accomplishes. First, it *perfects*, meaning "to complete thoroughly." Second, it *establishes*, meaning "to set fast in a certain direction." Third, it *strengthens*, which means exactly what it says. And fourth, it *settles*, which means "to lay the foundation or to ground."

Life is filled with numerous painful sensations that bring these four truths into our lives, and God wastes not a one of our sufferings. But all of us, at some time in life, still ask the same question: why does God allow suffering? To answer this age-old question, we must consider two things. First, the majority of the suffering in the world today is caused by man's greed and sin, so we need to be careful about blaming God for suffering. Second, we need to consider that the suffering God allows in our lives as Christians is not without purpose. The four companion products mentioned above give it rich meaning.

Suffering alone can teach us not to waver in our faith. It completes us thoroughly, makes us steadfast in our direction, strengthens and grounds us. But it also does one more thing: it refines the body of Christ as it separates those who are truly His from those who are just following Him for the blessings (John 6:26).

One last thing to keep in mind: If you are experiencing a sensation today that is not that sensational, remember, suffering is not allowed in heaven. So no matter what you are going through today, this too shall pass! Hallelujah!

March 8

Then Jacob awoke from his sleep and said, "Surely the Lord is in this place, and I did not know it." And he was afraid and said, "How awesome is this place! This is none other than the house of God, and this is the gate of heaven!" Then Jacob rose early in the morning, and took the stone that he had put at his head, set it up as a pillar, and poured oil on top of it. And he called the name of that place Bethel; but the name of that city had been Luz previously.

—Genesis 28:16–19

This is one of my favorite portions of Scripture for many reasons. First, we see Jacob on the run from his brother, Esau, because Esau had been scammed out of his birthright. Second, Jacob scammed both Esau and Isaac, his father, because he was trying to manipulate a blessing that God had already promised to him (Gen. 25:23). Third—and the best part—God was still faithful to His promise, even though Jacob had acted like a knucklehead (something I do frequently!).

So there was Jacob—on the run, estranged from his family, asleep in the desert with a rock for a pillow. That night he dreamed of a ladder with angels ascending and descending on it, and he was given the same promise of multitudes of descendants that had been given to his grandpa Abraham. In verse 15 of Genesis 28, God said to him, "Behold, I am with you and will keep you wherever you go, and will bring you back to this land; for I will not leave you until I have done what I have spoken to you."

Jacob, in his self-induced suffering, had a rock for a pillow and the desert floor for a bed. But there in that place, he also encountered the promise of God. In response, he said, "This is none other than the house of God" and renamed the place *Bethel*, which means "the house of God." Overcome with reverential fear of the Lord, he declared, "How awesome is this place!"

Are you in a place of self-imposed exile? God will still be faithful to you and keep His promises. Maybe you need to worship Him right where you are, with a rock for a pillow and the desert for a bed. Remember, God didn't transport Jacob back home or out of the desert, but He turned the desert into a place of worship, even the house of God! Worship Him right where you are, and you too can then say, "How awesome is this place; this is none other than the house of God!"

March 9

Now it happened when Sanballat, Tobiah, Geshem the Arab, and the rest of our enemies heard that I had rebuilt the wall, and that there were no breaks left in it (though at that time I had not hung the doors in the gates), that Sanballat and Geshem sent to me, saying, "Come, let us meet together among the villages in the plain of Ono." But they thought to do me harm. So I sent messengers to them, saying, "I am doing a great work, so that I cannot come down. Why should the work cease while I leave it and go down to you?"

—Nehemiah 6:1–3

I have always found it interesting the large number of people interested in magic. Modern magicians today are at least a little more honest about their trade than those of the past. Admitting there is no magic in what they do, they call themselves "illusionists"; however, I think we can take it a step further and call the illusionists "distractionists," because they draw your attention to one hand while doing something else with the other.

Sometimes we forget how subtle enemy attacks can be. Nehemiah had been called to a great work of restoring the walls and repairing the gates of Jerusalem. The opposition to this task, however, was immediate and growing, and more forceful threats were soon to come, even that of death. But the enemy began his assault on the work with the tactic that works best against anyone called to do a great work for God: distraction. The enemies of the project called a meeting in the plain of Ono, to which Nehemiah rightly replied, "Oh no, I am doing a great work, so why should the work cease while I meet with you?"

Distraction is such an effective tool because it diverts your attention to the enemy's tactics and stifles progress in your calling. The right response to the enemy's distractions is always to say "oh no to Ono." You fight the enemy best by sticking to the task at hand and not getting sidetracked from God's will for your life.

Don't let the enemy create the illusion that pulling your hand from the work for even a moment is the right thing to do. Remember, he only wants to do you harm. Why should the good work cease for you to have a meeting with the enemy? Stay the course, fulfill the task at hand, and always say "oh no" to his invitations to Ono!

March 10

Thus says the Lord of hosts: "Consider your ways! Go up to the mountains and
bring wood and build the temple, that I may take pleasure in it and be glorified,"
says the Lord. "You looked for much, but indeed it came to little; and when you
brought it home, I blew it away. Why?" says the Lord of hosts. "Because of My
house that is in ruins, while every one of you runs to his own house.

—Haggai 1:7-9

No matter a person's opinion on tithing as a New Testament principle, the fact of the matter is, God has a plan for us in every area of life, including finances. Some have said that the standard of giving in the New Testament age is whatever we can give cheerfully, based on 2 Corinthians 9:7. There are two problems with that viewpoint. First, using that as a basis for giving takes the Scripture verse out of context; and second, cheerfulness is an emotion, and since when are God's people to be guided by emotion? If a person cannot give anything cheerfully, is that person then exempt from supporting the work of the Lord?

The children of Israel had failed to rebuild God's house while they continued to live in their paneled houses (Hag. 1:4). They continually offered excuses for why it was not yet time to repair the house of the Lord. Finally, the Lord said to the people, "Listen, you're robbing yourselves of My blessing by ignoring My house"; and in verse 6 of this same chapter, He said, "He who earns wages, earns wages to put into a bag with holes."

Ever feel like there is a hole in your checkbook or bank account? Perhaps it's a result of your financial practices. I personally believe that since tithing is mentioned long before the law as a practice of the friend of God (Gen. 14:20), then a tenth is the standard of measure by which we are to support our home church. Offerings, such as Paul addressed in 2 Corinthians, are something God loves to receive when they are given cheerfully.

Is God's house part of your financial plan? It should be. As a matter of fact, God seems to indicate that blessings on the 90 percent we keep is dependent upon the 10 percent we tithe. Yes, some ministries today do abuse believers in the realm of finances, but don't let one person's abuse become your excuse. All that will do is allow a liar to make you into a thief (Mal. 3:9)!

March 11

For God has not given us a spirit of fear, but of power and of love and of a sound mind.

—2 Timothy 1:7

What a great and glorious truth this is! We could well understand this as Satan trying to impose his will on us and God giving us superior weapons to combat him. This reminds us of a couple of great truths. First, we are going to encounter fearful situations in life, yet even then the feeling of fear is not from God. In a word, we could say that knowing God offers us stability at all times and in all situations.

Second, God does allow us to encounter situations that might cause our flesh to fear or worry, but His provision in those situations is not fear, but rather fear's antithesis: power, love and a sound mind. The circumstances that challenge them are often the tactics of the enemy seeking to impose his will on our lives.

Paul indicates that the fear he is speaking of is spiritual. There is nothing wrong with being afraid of a lion, a tiger, or a bear (oh my!); fear of this sort is natural and even healthy. But fear in the realm of the spirit is not from God. Through Him, we can approach the unknown outcomes of life with power, love, and a sound mind. In other words, God has given us the ability not to freak out!

This doesn't mean we won't have concerns—even deep ones—or that we move through life as unfeeling, emotionless blobs. But Paul is saying here that you and I, as Christians, possess a God-supplied ability to meet fearful situations with His power and, because of His love, with a mental stability not available to those who face crisis or difficulty alone.

So when fear creeps in, remember, it's not from God. He has given you power, love, and a sound mind, no matter what you may be facing or are called to endure!

March 12

The Lord will be awesome to them, for He will reduce to nothing all the gods of the earth; people shall worship Him, each one from his place, indeed all the shores of the nations.

—Zephaniah 2:11

Some of you may be thinking, *What's a Zephaniah?* Zephaniah is not a *what* but a *who*, and his name means "hidden in the Lord." Zephaniah was a prophet who warned Israel of Babylonian exile and captivity if they did not repent of their idolatry. While Josiah was king in the seventh century BC, Zephaniah's message did indeed bear impact, and the nation of Judah did indeed experience revival for a time. But Bible history tells us that after King Josiah's death, the kingdom of Judah reverted to its old ways. Only fifty years later, Babylon invaded and destroyed Jerusalem and carried off captive many of the children of Israel.

Zephaniah prophesied, much like Joel and Zechariah, of a day when all the things that people worship, every false religion and idol, are going to be exposed for what they are—nothing! The Lord will be awesome in that day. This is not a "whoa, dude, that's awesome" kind of awesome. No, this is awesome in the sense of a majestic display of divine power that reduces everything people worship other than God Himself to nothing.

We often sing, "Our God is an awesome God," and indeed He is. But that's not written with the intent some seem to sing it with, like "Our God is way cool." What that song really means is that our God will display His awesome power against every false religion and idol and put them on public and permanent display as the "nothing" they really are. And in that day, people will worship Him. Now that's awesome!

You don't have to wait until then to worship Him in all His majesty and glory. You are free to do that right now in this age of false religions and idols all around you. Someday every knee will bow, but you can bow right now because God is awesome to you!

March 13

The law of the Lord is perfect, converting the soul; the testimony of the Lord is sure, making wise the simple; the statutes of the Lord are right, rejoicing the heart; the commandment of the Lord is pure, enlightening the eyes; the fear of the Lord is clean, enduring forever; the judgments of the Lord are true and righteous altogether. More to be desired are they than gold, yea, than much fine gold; sweeter also than honey and the honeycomb. Moreover by them Your servant is warned, and in keeping them there is great reward.

— Psalm 19:7–11

Funny how our flesh responds to terms like *laws* and *statutes* when we read God's Word. Our minds immediately think of boundaries and limitations, though we ought to think of safety and rewards.

David reminds us that God's laws are perfect, and therefore nothing negative is contained in them. When we follow them, we are not going to miss out, but we are going to be blessed. Our life experiences are not going to shortchanged, but they're going to be more fulfilling.

The apostle John reminds us that loving God is expressed through keeping His commandments and that His commandments are not burdensome (1 John 5:3). The rejoicing of the heart, the enlightening of the eyes, the "sweeter than honey" reward of Psalm 19 are the end results of everything from loving your enemies and doing good to those who hate you to not committing fornication and every other command of the Lord in between.

The best and most rewarding way to live is according to God's commands. His way is perfect and leads to rejoicing. The way of sin does not, even though it may yield a moment of passing pleasure (Heb. 11:25).

Has God been speaking to you about an attitude or an action in your life? Do things His way, even if your flesh is protesting it's too hard. If your mind is fixated on the perceived boundaries and limitations, refocus on the rejoicing and rewards that await you after your obedience.

Remember, God's way is not only right, but it's best all of the time. As a matter of fact, His way is the perfect way to live life. So don't view His Word and His commands as boundaries or bondage, because the fact is, they grant freedom from slavery to sin. Sounds like the perfect way to approach life, doesn't it?

March 14

And when they had prayed, the place where they were assembled together was shaken; and they were all filled with the Holy Spirit, and they spoke the word of God with boldness.

— Acts 4:31

Have you ever been in a "place shaken" prayer meeting? I have been in a few. However, I have also been in a few meetings where there was "a whole lotta shakin' goin' on," but I was not so sure that it was the Holy Spirit doing the shaking! How can we know the difference between the two? Quite simply, it is the outcome of the shaking that gives us our answer.

Nowhere in Scripture do we find the moving of the Holy Spirit as something merely meant to make us feel better. The power and presence of the Spirit are for our enabling, not our entertainment. If God is shaking things up, it is, without question, because He wants those He is shaking to get something done for His name and glory. He wants His people to be empowered to speak the Word of God with boldness, because it the Word of God, not the "shakin' of the saints," that does not return void (Isa. 55:11).

Yes, prayer meetings should be powerful and filled with the manifestation of the gifts of the Holy Spirit. But if what happens within the walls doesn't make it outside the walls, then the manifestation was either the result of the flesh or the result of the people's disobedience when they left. Everything God does is specific and for a purpose.

I love prayer meetings where you can feel the presence of God, see Him touching and healing lives and hearts, and hear Him speaking through others. Such experiences are as real as the room you're in. It's a wonderful feeling and experience, to be sure. But remember, friends, church and prayer meetings are simply places where God imparts boldness to His people to proclaim His Word so that when they leave the building, they're bold preachin' and praisin' machines!

Are you using what you have been given for God's glory? If not, today is a great day to be bold in your faith and speak the Word of God. It is God's will for you today, of that you can be sure. So try it today, and you'll see and feel the Spirit of the true and living God working boldly through you!

March 15

Now Sarai, Abram's wife, had borne him no children. And she had an Egyptian maidservant whose name was Hagar. So Sarai said to Abram, "See now, the LORD has restrained me from bearing children. Please, go in to my maid; perhaps I shall obtain children by her." And Abram heeded the voice of Sarai.

—Genesis 16:1–2

Have you ever listened to bad advice then lived to regret it? The passage above must be the pinnacle of all bad advice, as the repercussions of Ishmael's birth reverberate through the history of Israel to this very day. But in all fairness to Abram and Sarai, they were well beyond the season of life for bearing children. It seemed logical and even reasonable to resort to the standard practice of their Chaldean culture, in which a barren woman's maid could bear a child for her mistress as a surrogate. At birth, that child would be delivered onto the knees or lap of the mistress as her own. It was an acceptable practice and seemed like a logical next step for Abram and Sarai, since it was obvious Sarai was not going to give birth to a child... right?

But as I have told my church at times, we need to remember God's promises are true when they're said, not just when they're seen. In other words, when it's said, it's done—when the "say-er" is God Almighty! Has God spoken to you about a situation and told you it will be thus and so? Has He told you the prodigal will come home, the hardship will end, the pain will subside? If so, then what He said is as good as done!

So be careful about even well-meaning counsel that tempts you to try to do what God has promised He will do. Take it from someone who has tried to make God's plan happen on more than one occasion: it is always better to wait on the Lord. It's hard, I know, and it seems like an eternity at times, but better to wait than to live with the regret of following bad advice.

God is faithful, and it is utterly impossible for Him not to be. If He said it, it will come to pass. God's words are true when they're said—not just when they're seen!

March 16

Now therefore, speak to the men of Judah and to the inhabitants of Jerusalem, saying, "Thus says the Lord: 'Behold, I am fashioning a disaster and devising a plan against you. Return now every one from his evil way, and make your ways and your doings good.' " And they said, "That is hopeless! So we will walk according to our own plans, and we will every one obey the dictates of his evil heart."

—Jeremiah 18:11–12

Isn't it interesting how little things have changed since Jeremiah penned these words some twenty-six-hundred years ago? Though we find God's foretelling of the end of all things in both the writings of the Old Testament prophets and in the New Testament book of Revelation, many people today seem to insist, "Nah, that's not going to happen. We'll just keep doing our own thing, and whatever feels good, we'll do it!"

But what God foretells, He fulfills, and we would do well to have the heart of Jeremiah concerning the revelation of disaster we find in Scripture. Eternity is real, judgment and hell are real, and so is God's unwillingness that any should perish.

I have posed this scenario to my church several times: What if somehow God revealed to you that the rapture of the church would occur tomorrow at 11:00 a.m. and that the ensuing time of hell on earth would soon follow? What would you do differently between now and 11:00 a.m. tomorrow? I believe we live in just such a time and must live with a sense of urgency as never before. Like Jeremiah (who is known as the weeping prophet, BTW), we must plead with people to repent and come to the Lord.

I once heard a pastor say, "If you believe that Jesus could come back for His church at any moment, then act like it!" I couldn't agree more. Today is the day of salvation (2 Cor. 6:2), and today just might be "the day"—or maybe tomorrow at 11:00 a.m. Therefore, whatever you would do if you knew that for sure, today is the day to do it!

The Lord has foretold a coming disaster upon this Christ-rejecting world, and all that God foretells, God fulfills. Someone needs to hear about Jesus from you today!

March 17

If My people who are called by My name will humble themselves, and pray and seek My face, and turn from their wicked ways, then I will hear from heaven, and will forgive their sin and heal their land.

—2 Chronicles 7:14

In chapter 6 of 2 Chronicles, King Solomon prayed a very honest prayer that when God's people sinned, God would hear their prayers offered from the temple built for the Lord's name. The Lord replied in verse 15 of chapter 7, "Now My eyes will be open and My ears attentive to prayer made in this place." It is important to see that God set conditions for the healing of the land, and those conditions were repentance of the people and a return to humble prayer.

In a time when our nation is in great moral peril, as are many other nations around the world today, it is important for the church to understand its role in world affairs. The healing of the land is dependent upon the people of God, and though there is not a temple in Jerusalem today, there are temples of the Holy Spirit all over the world. These temples are God's people called by His name.

I believe that God is calling His church back to the ministry of being salt and light in every country of the world. Salt both and purifies and preserves, and that is our calling as Christians in any given country. As a matter of fact, it is the presence of God's people that is essential to the blessings of a nation. As Psalm 33:12 says, "Blessed is the nation whose God is the Lord, the people He has chosen as His own inheritance."

We Christians are chosen by God as His inheritance, and surrendering our heritage of being salt and light is the worst thing we can do for our country. The hope of healing a nation is not in a new government or a fresh set of politicians, but in the humble prayers of repentance from God's people who turn from the wickedness of not being the salt and light they were called to be. The hope for America is not in the White House, but in God's house. Blessed is the nation whose God is the Lord!

Lead the charge today, Christian, into the healing of our land by being salt and light. Our nation is depending on you!

March 18

You are of God, little children, and have overcome them, because He who is in you is greater than he who is in the world.

—1 John 4:4

The "them" that we who are of God have overcome are the "instead of Christ" (antichrist) things in the world. The presence of God in us in the person of the Holy Spirit is greater than anything the devil puts in front of us in place of Christ. This removes, in a very real sense, the words *I can't* from the Christian's vocabulary.

If nothing is too hard or impossible for God to do (Jer. 32:17) and God is in us, then we can overcome every bad habit and wrong attitude because greater is He who is in us than he who is in the world. But it also means, as John reminds us, that we possess power over deception and need not be led astray by "instead of Christ" spirits.

Satan's pride and desire to be worshiped led to his fall (Isa. 14:14), and it is still the thing he covets today. *To worship* means "to prostrate" and "to submit." However, when we think of Satan worship, we often envision it as singing songs of praise to Satan or wearing weird robes and repeating morbid chants. But the fact of the matter is, Satan worship is prostrating and submitting to his will, and his will is for us to bow before anything instead of Christ.

But greater is the Spirit of God in us than anything Satan throws at us. Because we have Christ, we cannot say, "Alcohol is bigger than me," "Drugs are bigger than me," or "Gossip [lying, cheating, or stealing] is bigger than me." I know this is true because many of those things were once part of my life, but through Christ I overcame them.

I can't say "I can't" anymore. Neither I nor any other Christian is perfect, but as I have said many times, "We don't have to sin if we don't want to!" Though we all fail from time to time, we don't have to, but rather we choose to. But we don't have to make that choice anymore, because greater is God who is in us than Satan who is after us!

March 19

And we know that all things work together for good to those who love God, to those who are the called according to His purpose.

— Romans 8:28

I am often amazed at how a small adjective or conjunction in Scripture can make such a great impact on meaning and how small groups of letters can wield great power. Words like *and* and *if* often bear great importance, and here in our text, one of the smallest words in the verse carries the most significant meaning. That is the word *all*.

Could you imagine if this verse read, "Some things work together for good," or "Occasionally things work together for good"? There would not be much assurance in such a statement. But because of the small adjective *all*, we know that God can and will work together for good everything we encounter in life!

Years ago I came under nearly unbearable personal attack in the industry in which I was working. Such vicious lies were told about me that I simply could not believe the things that were being said. Though this happened nearly two decades ago, I have yet to understand why it happened and have not seen anything good come from it. But that doesn't mean it didn't; it just means I haven't seen it.

God has said in His Word that all things work together for good *to* those who love God and are the called according to His purpose. Again two little letters bear great impact on the text. The thought that God works all things together for good *to* those who love Him means that God will somehow use for good all that we experience.

As Christians, we know that there is a "good" that awaits us that is like no other—heaven. But in this life, it may mean that God sometimes uses our pain for the good of another. It may be intended to teach someone else how knowing God changes the way a person handles adversity. I cannot see one good thing that came out of the personal attack in my life; it hurt then and still does today. But I do believe that good came from it somewhere, because God said He would use it to do just that.

Maybe you have had one of those experiences in your life too. Maybe there's something you still can't see any good in, and it still looms in your mind from the distant past. If that is so, remember, sometimes you just have to trust the Word of God when the good remains yet to be seen!

March 20

Now I know that the Lord saves His anointed; He will answer him from His holy heaven with the saving strength of His right hand. Some trust in chariots, and some in horses; but we will remember the name of the Lord our God.

—Psalm 20:6–7

Horses and chariots were the standard by which ancient armies were assessed for strength. The more of each an army possessed, the mightier the army was considered, and rightfully so. As a result, the strategy in confronting an enemy was based largely on the enemy's horse-and-chariot count. But King David had learned that the enemy's size doesn't matter when God is on your side. And obviously, Goliath learned that lesson too!

Nevertheless, for most of us, it is far easier to focus on the enemy's horses and chariots than on an unseen God, even though we believe in Him. But if, like David, we *know* that the Lord saves His anointed, all we have to do is *act* like the Lord saves His anointed. Even in this great challenge, David gives us some great counsel: "Remember the name of the Lord our God."

In our battles, friends, we sometimes feel as though *our* names are on the line, *we* are the ones facing the great challenge, and the battles are *ours* to fight. At those times, it is easy to look at the horses and chariots of our enemies. But those are exactly the times to remember the name of our God. His name is El Shaddai, "God Almighty"; His name is El Elyon, "God Most High"; His name is Jehovah Jirah, "the Lord Will Provide." No wonder David gave this counsel; there is such power in the name of God.

Friends, as you face the horses and chariots of life, proclaim those names. I feel built up just writing them because they remind me that God Almighty sits on high and will provide everything I need to meet this day's horses and chariots. I know the Lord saves His anointed with the strength of His mighty right hand!

And who is seated at the right hand of the Father? Jesus Christ is the one, and remember, *Christ* means "anointed." So measure every enemy tactic against the name of your God, and not only will you know the Lord saves His anointed, but you will begin to act like it too!

March 21

By this all will know that you are My disciples, if you have love for one another.

—John 13:35

Funny how what is given as an indicator can also be an indictment. Jesus says it here, and John repeats it in his epistle: "Beloved, let us love one another, for love is of God; and everyone who loves is born of God and knows God. He who does not love does not know God, for God is love" (1 John 4:7–8).

Love is not a series of emotion-driven actions, but rather acts of obedience stemming from love and respect for God. Love is what we do regardless of how we feel. Jesus, for example, despised the shame of the cross yet endured it (Heb. 12:2). Jesus prayed for another way to deliver humanity from its sins but accepted the Father's way and will (Luke 22:42). Certainly nothing about the stripes on His back or the nails in his hands and feet felt good. The old adage is true: "Nails didn't hold Jesus to the cross—love did."

The same idea holds true for us as well. All will know we are Jesus' disciples when we do what love does. The example of what this love will do and the limits to which it will go are revealed in the fact that He gave His own life for us. Let us ask ourselves this question today: *Would I rather die than disgrace God's love?*

I believe we have been sold a bag of goods in much of today's easy "believe-ism," because there is nothing easy about loving when wronged or doing good to those who hate us. As a matter of fact, it's not always easy to love even other disciples. But it is how we are identified as Jesus' disciples.

So "set aside your feelings and love one another" is the meaning of Jesus' exhortation here. Why? Because love is of God, and everyone who is born of God loves. What does this look like in life? Just remember the stripes, the beating, the ripped-out beard, the crown of thorns, the nails, and the pierced side of Jesus. He endured it all though possessing the power to strike down His enemies with a single word.

That is how to love one another!

March 22

For all things are for your sakes, that grace, having spread through the many, may cause thanksgiving to abound to the glory of God.

—2 Corinthians 4:15

It is amazing how the Word of God consistently interjects hope in much-needed places. Paul had been relaying to the Corinthians that he was hard pressed on every side, yet not crushed; perplexed, but not in despair; persecuted, but not forsaken; struck down, but not destroyed; and delivered to death for Jesus' name's sake. It might seem odd to insert the verse above in the middle of talk about persecution and martyrdom, but I believe Paul was reminding the Corinthians and all who would read this to not lose sight of all the things God has done for us. His grace should always cause a spirit of thanksgiving to well up within us.

Have you ever seen a person worship and praise God in the midst of a trauma or tragedy, even the death of a loved one? I remember a few instances like this in my life, and the grace God bestowed on those in deep and dark trials caused thanksgiving to abound in me to the glory of God.

Praise from the valley of despair is powerful. It brings a legitimacy to the transforming presence of the Spirit of God like little else in life. I find it quite easy to praise God when it's all good, as I am sure you do as well. But my heart is moved, even to this day, when I remember praise issuing forth from someone hard pressed on every side, someone perplexed and persecuted, or someone in the valley of the shadow of death. In those times, God's grace in someone else was so undeniable that I experienced His grace in a deeper way in my own life.

If things are great today, praise the Lord. If things are not so great, praise the Lord. Regardless of the circumstances, offer praise simply because He alone is worthy. And this kind of praise, from the depths of life's traumas and tragedies, can bring change to others that lasts a lifetime. I know, because it happened to me!

March 23

*Beware lest anyone cheat you through philosophy and empty deceit, according to the
tradition of men, according to the basic principles of the world,
and notaccording to Christ.*

—Colossians 2:8

I have always found it interesting that Paul does not qualify his statement here by warning of *bad* philosophy; instead, he speaks merely of philosophy and empty deceit. From Merriam-Webster's online dictionary, the word
philosophy is defined as "a search for a general understanding of values and
reality by chiefly speculative rather than observational means." Paul is saying
here that we need to beware of letting the world teach us things contrary to
what we already know.

The Bible has already told us how things began, has given us a moral code
and compass, and has given us spiritual truths verifiable through reality. The
Bible has even removed any speculation about the love of God. Nonetheless,
many Christians follow the traditions of men that conflict with the truth
claims of God. Paul says such people are being cheated.

Many allow philosophy to send them down the road of, how could a
God of love do thus and so? Friend, that is not a question even worthy of
pondering. The real question worthy of consideration is, how can fallen man
reject the offer of salvation from a loving God?

Don't get cheated by human rhetoric, especially from the speculators of
our day. In the beginning, God created, and man chose sin. All the world's
problems today are man's fault, because man sinned and fell short of the
glory of God (Rom. 3:23).

To look at the condition of the world and from that question God's love is
empty deceit. God is love, and the cross of Christ proves it is so. If God were
unloving, He would have left man in his fallen condition. Do not fall prey to
the speculations of foolish men!

March 24

You shall not take the name of the Lord your God in vain, for the Lord will not hold him guiltless who takes His name in vain.

—Exodus 20:7

This is one of the many areas in which I believe we have not fully grasped the meaning of Scripture. We associate this third commandment with using the name of God as a curse word or as an expression used in place of "oh my gosh." Though we should certainly avoid the flippant use of the Lord's name, this is not the meaning of the verse at all.

The word *vain* in the Hebrew is the word *shâv'*(shawv). It means "to desolate," "to use for evil," "to ruin morally," "false idolatry," and "to use as deception or for vanity." If we want to understand this command fully, we could loosely translate it as follows: "Do not take My name and then empty it of its power (desolate) by using it for evil purposes, while living in immorality or practicing false idolatry, for deceptive purposes, or in spiritual pride." Changes it up a little bit, I would say!

No wonder the enemy wants to reduce this third commandment to merely not using the Lord's name as a slang word. Friends, God wants those who bear His name to walk worthy of His name. Where we fall short, His mercy and grace bridge the gap.

As I said yesterday, philosophies and empty deceits are all around us, and one them in particular is being perpetuated in the name of the church. That is the idea that each Christian is free to do what is right in his or her own eyes. In this view, there are no moral absolutes, and the Christian life is about living life to its fullest, materially and experientially. But God says, "Don't take My name there; I will not hold the one guiltless who does."

I believe that one of the greatest needs of the modern church is the restoration of the fear of the Lord, in the sense of reverent awe. Interestingly, all the giants of Scripture had it, and all those we revere in church history had it. But somehow in the postmodern church era, we think we don't need it. Nothing could be further from the truth, however. We need to fear the Lord just as much as any people in history have ever needed it.

To claim God's name but then live immorally or in idolatry is taking the Lord's name in vain. Instead, we need to have a reverent awe of God restored in our lives. Let us have this godly fear in our day once again—the fear of taking the name of the Lord in vain!

March 25

For I am not ashamed of the gospel of Christ, for it is the power of God to salvation for everyone who believes, for the Jew first and also for the Greek.

—Romans 1:16

Have you ever met one of those people who are witnessing machines? Everywhere they go they share Christ, and doors for the gospel seem to swing open to them all the time. Don't you sometimes wish you were like that?

I will admit that I am more comfortable speaking to hundreds or thousands of people at a time from behind a pulpit than being in the trenches in one-on-one ministry. But just because it's outside my comfort zone, that does not give me a free pass not to witness.

One reason many of those witnessing machines do what they do is that they have experienced firsthand the transforming power of the gospel. Having seen the gospel immediately impact someone or having experienced the thrill of seeing one seed out of the many sown fall on fertile soil and transform a life, they want to do it again.

I have, as most preachers do, taught this text with all the focus on the "I am not ashamed" part; however, I now see the glory of this verse is in "it is the power of God to salvation" part. To paraphrase this part of the verse, "No matter what your nationality or religious beliefs, the gospel of Christ has power—even the power to save!" So if we approach this verse, not just from the "I am not ashamed" angle, but also from "it is the power of God" aspect, we can find great motivation to share our faith more frequently.

I know many Christians who are intimidated by sharing the gospel, but I also know that I have never met a one who was not longing for the power of God to be manifested through them. The great thing is, God has included both His gospel and His power in one package deal.

So if you are looking to walk in God's power, shod your feet with the gospel of peace (Eph. 6:15), and you are in for a power-packed day. Go forward with this confidence: the gospel has power everywhere it is preached. Any lost soul is a candidate, so don't wait for the door to open—it already is. Just go out there and preach it, and see the power of God manifested through you!

March 26

Peter was therefore kept in prison, but constant prayer was offered to God for him by the church. And when Herod was about to bring him out, that night Peter was sleeping, bound with two chains between two soldiers; and the guards before the door were keeping the prison. Now behold, an angel of the Lord stood by him, and a light shone in the prison; and he struck Peter on the side and raised him up, saying, "Arise quickly!" And his chains fell off his hands.

— Acts 12:5–7

I have never been in prison for my faith or bound with two chains between two soldiers. But I have had to endure things that I had no control over, things that kept me up at night. Though they were insignificant when compared to my faith and eternal destiny, the events and circumstances were nonetheless very important to me.

Here in this passage we find Peter sleeping in prison after his arrest by Herod. The evil king had just executed John's brother James, one of the two Jesus had called the "Sons of Thunder" (Mark 3:17), yet here was Peter sound asleep between two guards. I am sure he did not know in advance of the angelic visitation that was about to happen. I am sure he had no reason to expect anything other than the same fate that James had suffered at the hands of Herod.

But the church was offering constant prayer for him, and two things resulted: Peter had peace, and deliverance came. But notice, Peter couldn't see the church praying, and the church couldn't see Peter sleeping; but the God who sees all connected the request and the requirement, and the prayer was answered.

Are we praying for those bound and chained today? Too often we have a "confirmation oriented" prayer life, meaning we want to see the results. However, I can assure you as you read this, there is a pastor in prison in China, a persecuted saint in Iran, or a lonely missionary in Africa who would love for an unseen member of the church to remember them in prayer. Praying even in generalities lets the all-knowing God connect the request with the recipient.

God answers prayer, even when we don't see the answer. So pray for those who are persecuted and held captive. You don't need to know their names or their circumstances — just pray. If you have more information, then by all means, pray specifically, but don't let your lack of information keep you from praying in the first place. And if you are one of those people who need to be more specific in order to feel effective but don't know the name of a missionary or imprisoned pastor, then pray for me. I could always use a good night's sleep!

March 27

My eyes shall be on the faithful of the land, that they may dwell with me; he who walks in a perfect way, he shall serve me. He who works deceit shall not dwell within my house; he who tells lies shall not continue in my presence.

— Psalm 101:6–7

David was seeking to practice some good housekeeping by surrounding himself, not with those who were perfect, but with those who walked in a perfect way (the way of the Lord is the obvious implication). Though we need to be careful about living in a Christian cocoon, we need to be just as careful about what we allow into our homes and whom we allow in our presence. This was obviously foundational for what Paul would later write about not being unequally yoked (2 Cor. 6:14).

The issue for David wasn't—nor is it for us—one of thinking he was better than others. Rather, the issue was about creating an environment that minimized the opportunities to be dragged down by others while maximizing the possibilities to be strengthened by others.

We are not to shelter ourselves from all contact with the world, for the world is our mission field. But like David, we must monitor our close relationships, our confidants. We would do well to measure and guard our fellowship, for at one time or another, we have probably experienced the reality of having a friend who was bad for us. Maybe it was someone fun or someone we just clicked with, but for us as Christians, it is like having fellowship with those we are supposed to be in ministry to.

Are our houses, our hearts, and our minds places where we can dwell safely, or have we surrounded ourselves with opportunities to fail or be pulled down morally or spiritually? Even as I write this, I sense strongly that some have in mind a person who is damaging their walk with God. If that is you, don't abandon the relationship; just change it. Turn it from fellowship into ministry, and watch things change. Either the person will begin to walk with you in the perfect way, or he or she will say, "Things are different in your house now, and I am going another way." Either way, you have done what is best and right as one who follows the Lord.

March 28

No one can serve two masters; for either he will hate the one and love the other, or else he will be loyal to the one and despise the other.
You cannot serve God and mammon.

—Matthew 6:24

Two very key words are present in this verse: *serve* and *mammon*. The word *serve* comes from the Greek word *douleuo* (*dool-yoo'-o*), which means "to be in bondage to." *Mammon* is actually an ancient Chaldean word, *mammōnas*, which means "wealth" or "avarice" (the desire for wealth).

Jesus is saying that you cannot be a servant to both Him and money. He doesn't say you can't serve Him if you have mammon, but He does says you can be a slave to only one master. This is why the teaching that God wants us all to be rich is so strange. Time and again, wealth and the desire for wealth have proven to be wicked taskmasters (1 Tim. 6:10).

What Jesus means is simple: be a slave to things eternal, not to things temporal. At the end of their lives, many people are going to look back and sadly say, "Wealth was my god. It took my time, my energy, and my effort, and there was little or no room for the true and living God." But others will joyfully say, "I gave God my time, my energy, and my effort, and He added all the things I needed because I put Him first."

Serving Jesus first does guarantee that He will supply all your needs according to His riches, but serving riches cannot guarantee what knowing Jesus supplies. In this label-conscious, success-oriented society, we have to stop and ask ourselves, *Who is my master?*

How do you know whom you serve? Is it Jesus or mammon? Who gets your time, effort, and energy? One master can provide everything for you, but the other can provide only money. One you can lose in a down market, while you can never be separated from the other.

It's really quite simple: choose the master who will supply all your needs and whom you can never lose, or choose the master you can never have enough of and can easily lose. Jesus or mammon? Only one can be your master!

March 29

But you be watchful in all things, endure afflictions, do the work of an evangelist, fulfill your ministry.

—2 Timothy 4:5

Imagine if you were to approach one of the great men of faith of whom we all know, perhaps C. H. Spurgeon, D. L. Moody, or Billy Graham, and ask, "How would you summarize the Christian life in one sentence?" This is exactly what we have before us in this one verse. These were the closing words of instruction by one of the greatest men of faith in all of church history to a young struggling pastor.

At the end of his life, knowing that the time of his departure was at hand (2 Tim. 4:6), Paul took the whole of the Christian walk and life and compressed it into four components. First, he urges us to "be watchful," which implies keeping our guard up. Our enemy is relentless, and we must always be on guard doctrinally and morally.

Second, he says to "endure afflictions." The word *endure* means "to undergo," but far too often affliction causes Christians to "go under." But Paul emphatically encourages us that when afflictions come, we must keep going and not let hardship stifle our progress.

Third, Paul says we are to "do the work of an evangelist." The use of the word *work* tells us that reaching the lost requires sacrifice. We understand this to be true in every other worthwhile pursuit in life, and so too is it true in reaching the lost. It requires a sacrifice of time, attention, and even resources to do the work of an evangelist.

Finally, Paul says to "fulfill your ministry." This doesn't mean to merely fulfill a ministry as an evangelist as it pertains to the lost, but it also references our interactions with other saints. Being hospitable, offering comfort, praying and interceding, and exhorting our family in the faith are all vital parts of our ministry in the Lord to His body.

This seemingly complicated life of living for Jesus really isn't that complicated at all. Keep your guard up against enemy attack, keep going when afflicted, sacrifice in order to reach others, and serve others in the body of Christ. That's all you have to do—nothing to it! These four simple instructions will cause your life to be fruitful for God's kingdom.

March 30

Hear, O Israel: The Lord our God, the Lord is one! You shall love the Lord your God with all your heart, with all your soul, and with all your strength.

— Deuteronomy 6:4–5

This is what the Jews refer to as the Shema. It's much like a statement of faith, a summary of beliefs, if you will. In Matthew 22, a lawyer asked Jesus a question in order to test Him: "Teacher, which is the great commandment in the law?" (v. 36). Jesus quoted the Shema in response: " 'You shall love the Lord your God with all your heart, with all your soul, and with all your mind.' This is the first and great commandment. And the second is like it: 'You shall love your neighbor as yourself.' On these two commandments hang all the Law and the Prophets" (vv. 37–40).

As mentioned yesterday, the whole of the Christian life was summarized by Paul in one sentence in 2 Timothy 4:5. But the fact is, if we attempt to follow Paul's instruction as a set of rules, it will soon become very burdensome. But if we approach the Christian life, not as a set of disciplines, but as an expression of love for God and others, we will enjoy a more successful and sustainable Christian life.

We never have to be pushed into doing the things we love. We run to them, we long for them, we make time for them, and we even make them a priority. This is exactly why the Shema was Jesus' response to the lawyer who questioned Him. "It's all about love" was Jesus' answer.

Not that there are no disciplines at all in love, but have you noticed how easy it is to overlook something in someone you love than it is in someone you dislike? Have you noticed how you can accept things you don't understand when it pertains to someone you love as compared to someone you don't?

Love changes things, including your perception and reaction to the actions of others. God does things you do not understand, and at times other Christians do things you dislike. But what should be your response? Love the Lord your God with all your heart, soul, and strength, and love your neighbor the way God loves you!

March 31

No man shall be able to stand before you all the days of your life; as I was with Moses, so I will be with you. I will not leave you nor forsake you.

—Joshua 1:5

Joshua, who was the great field general for Moses, now found himself designated as Moses' replacement. I have to wonder if perhaps he was a little intimidated by the shoes he was asked to fill. Maybe he was thinking, *God was pretty tight with Moses, and after all, Moses was the humblest man in all the earth* (Num. 12:3).

Yet even though there had not been a prophet in Israel who spoke to God face-to-face since Moses (Deut. 34:10), the Lord assured Joshua that He would be with him. Though the person in command had changed, God had not. As He was with Moses, so too would He be with Joshua!

I hope the words spoken here to Joshua strike a chord in your heart as well. They have a rather familiar ring to them, for they are promised to us in Hebrews 13:5–6. It is easy for us to look at the giants of the faith and think, *Well, no wonder the Lord was with them. Just look at them and what they accomplished!* And though it is true some people seem to excel as spiritual giants, it is also true they do not have anything that we ourselves don't have. The fact is, those whom we see as Moses-type figures in any age are merely people who chose to use their gifts, talents, and abilities for God's glory.

As the Lord was with Moses, so too was He with Joshua and the people of Israel. As the Lord was with Moses, so too will He be with you. The greatness we admire in others is not that of their own, but the greatness of God Himself.

Moses chose affliction with Israel over the pleasures of the palace in Egypt (Heb. 11:25), and God was with him. So too will He be with us in every aspect of our lives. When we put Him first, He will show Himself strong on our behalves, even as He did with Moses. Every giant of the faith was a giant because of almighty God, the one who is the same yesterday, today, and forever. Amen!

April 1

Listen to Me, you who know righteousness, you people in whose heart is My law: Do not fear the reproach of men, nor be afraid of their insults.

—Isaiah 51:7

On a day when many Americans try to fool one another, I could not help but think of how many people in our day think you are a fool for following Jesus. Yet Psalm 14:1 says the fool is the person who says there is no God. The Lord speaks through Isaiah some great reminders to those who encounter such a person, one who says no to God and declares you a fool for saying yes to Him. "Do not *fear* their reproach," He says, "nor be *afraid* of their insults."

The word *reproach* means "to shame or rebuke"; the word *afraid* means "to discourage," "to cause to dismay," or "to beat down." God says, "You who know righteousness and have My law in your heart, do not be discouraged, dismayed, or beaten down when others seek to shame or rebuke you as a fool for following Jesus."

Peter tells us that Isaiah's encouragement to Israel applies to us as well. In 1 Peter 4:14, he says, "If you are reproached for the name of Christ, blessed are you, for the Spirit of glory and of God rests upon you. On their part He is blasphemed, but on your part He is glorified." So suffering reproach for the name of Jesus is a blessing. How so? Because someone actually recognized you as a Christian, and that means Jesus is shining through!

So fire away, you who say there is no God and you who call me a fool for following Jesus, because I am blessed by the fact that you can tell I am following Him. My part in that means that Jesus is glorified, showing through and in me.

Today might be April Fool's Day, but if you have said yes to Jesus, you're no fool. And if others can see Jesus through you, that means you're no phony, and that's a blessing indeed. So shine for Him today, and do not be discouraged, dismayed, or beaten down because someone insulted your faith. Rejoice—someone can tell you're a Christian!

April 2

In this manner, therefore, pray: Our Father in heaven, hallowed be Your name. Your kingdom come. Your will be done on earth as it is in heaven. Give us this day our daily bread. And forgive us our debts, as we forgive our debtors. And do not lead us into temptation, but deliver us from the evil one. For Yours is the kingdom and the power and the glory forever. Amen.

—Matthew 6:9–13

Luke's gospel records that Jesus' disciples asked Him to teach them how to pray and that He gave them this model prayer as an example of how to format a prayer. In studying this model, I have found within it what I call the five *P*s of prayer. I believe if we are experiencing dryness in our spiritual walks or emptiness in our prayers, we would do well to examine our prayer lives to see if we are praying as Jesus taught us.

The five *P*s in the Lord's Prayer are as follows: (1) *praise*, hallowing His name; (2) *proclamation*, His kingdom come and will be done; (3) *petition*, give us this day our bread; (4) *promise*, forgive us and help us to forgive; and (5) *power*, His is the kingdom and power and glory forever. Praise, proclamation, petition, promise, and power — these are the five *P*s of prayer.

One *P* in particular, petition, tends to dominate our prayer lives; however, it is the one that received the least attention from Jesus in this model prayer. Here in Matthew, Jesus' prayer is composed of sixty-six words in English, but only seven of them are dedicated to petition, or provision. That indicates that less than 10 percent of our prayer lives should be spent on asking for stuff. Jesus says to limit our petitions for provision to this day's needs.

A restored balance in your prayer life that is aligned with Jesus' model for prayer will effectively enliven your spiritual walk and prayer time. Do you open your prayers with praise? Do you proclaim the authority of His will? Do you limit petition and stand on the promises of His power? Try it and you'll see what a difference it makes to pray how Jesus taught us to pray!

April 3

Through the Lord's mercies we are not consumed, because His compassions fail not. They are new every morning; great is Your faithfulness. "The Lord is my portion," says my soul, "therefore I hope in Him!"

— Lamentations 3:22–24

What beautiful words of joy and encouragement in a book titled Lamentations authored by Jeremiah, a man known as the weeping prophet! Nevertheless, while it may seem on the surface a strange juxtaposition of title and verse, it is fitting that it appears here. Even in our laments, we will not be consumed, for the Lord's mercies are new every morning. In our laments, great is His faithfulness, and He is yet our portion; therefore, there is hope in Him.

Jeremiah's laments resulted from a burden he carried for his people and country. It seemed as though God had been pushed out of the land and that immorality and idolatry ran rampant. Unbelievable as it seems, innocent children were being slaughtered and offered to the god Molech (Jer. 32:35). Jeremiah pleaded with the people and warned them of the coming judgment of God, but the people protested, "That's not going to happen." Instead of heeding his words, they devised plans against him (Jer. 18:18) to silence the word of the Lord spoken through him.

Sounds familiar, doesn't it, in our age where prayer is driven from the schools, fable is taught in place of the facts of creation, and all things Christian are gradually being silenced while all things pagan are promoted? It would be very easy for us to fall into lamenting and lose hope. But like Jeremiah, we must remember the Lord's mercies and resist becoming a Jonah and wishing for judgment.

At times, I feel just like Jeremiah, brokenhearted over the condition of our country. But I also feel like Jeremiah in that I remember the mercies of God and that the Lord is my portion and my hope. So let's not let allow legitimate reasons to lament rob us of the placement and content of these beautiful verses. Great is His faithfulness; the Lord is our portion, and our hope is in Him — even today!

April 4

For if you remain completely silent at this time, relief and deliverance will arise for the Jews from another place, but you and your father's house will perish. Yet who knows whether you have come to the kingdom for such a time as this?

— Esther 4:14

Earlier in this same chapter of Esther, we are told of a law in the Persian Empire that made it a crime punishable by death to enter the king's inner court uninvited. Unless the king extended his golden scepter to the uninvited guest, the prescribed sentence was swift and sure.

In our Bible passage, the wicked Haman had schemed against the Jews to destroy them. The young Jewess Esther, who was queen, had access to the king, but even she could not approach him uninvited. Furthermore, it had been thirty days since she had been invited into his presence. Yet Mordecai, Esther's cousin and former guardian, made a tremendous statement of faith in the face of possible execution. He explained to Esther that the command to exterminate the Jews may have indeed been issued, but God had promised to be faithful to them. God would surely deliver them through someone, he said, and maybe Esther was the one selected.

So too is it true for you and me. God has great works He wants to do, even in perilous times. The promises of God are going to be fulfilled, and His will is going to be done. He is going to incorporate His people into carrying out His plans, so it might as well be you and I!

Mordecai seems to be saying, "Listen, Esther, don't miss this opportunity to be an instrument of God's peace and play a role in carrying out His will. God has a plan for you today, and it might seem perilous. But if it pertains to God's promise and will, it is going to be done; so why not through you?"

Maybe you have come to your job, your campus, or your neighborhood for such a time as this. Maybe God has you in a place where you are the only Christian. Maybe you and I need to remember that one Christian plus God makes a majority and is enough to carry out His will.

Like Queen Esther, you know people who need saving. The wicked one has plotted their deaths, but God is not willing that any should perish. Someone is going to have to step out and tell them of God's saving grace. It might as well be you!

April 5

Salt is good; but if the salt has lost its flavor, how shall it be seasoned? It is neither fit for the land nor for the dunghill, but men throw it out.
He who has ears to hear, let him hear!

—Luke 14:34–35

Most of us have heard some people described as being "worth their salt." This saying dates back to Roman times when soldiers were often paid with salt. Salt was also necessary in preserving stored meat, as meat would quickly go rancid if not packed in salt. When salt lost its preserving properties, it was thrown out into the street and trampled underfoot (Matt. 5:13).

To the listener of Jesus' day, the illustration of salt would be well understood. When salt loses its worth, it is useless. Jesus said in Matthew 5:13 that we are the salt of the earth, and when we couple this with our passage in Luke 14, we learn two things. First, we are the only thing that keeps this world from being completely rotten, and second, if we lose our flavor, men will trample us and throw us out.

So how does salt lose its flavor? By being used. Take, for example, a prime rib roast. Many cooks pack the roast in salt before cooking it. However, after the cooking has been completed, they do not take that salt and attempt to put it back into the saltshaker. It has lost its flavor, or purpose.

The spiritual truth Jesus is teaching here deals with participation in worldly things, things that are rotten. When we laugh at or tell dirty jokes, we lose our purifying influence. When we attend the kind of party that a Christian should not attend or give our money to a movie that promotes sin and blasphemes God, we lose our purifying influence. In either case, the people of the world will trample us underfoot.

You are the salt of the office, you are the salt of the warehouse, you are the salt of the community; but if you lose the purifying and preserving capacities of salt by participation in sin, you have let the world trample you underfoot.

Be worth your salt today. Stand alone, if you have to. Be the only one who says no—or maybe says yes. If you are the only Christian in your sphere of influence, you are the salt of your world!

April 6

I am the true vine, and My Father is the vinedresser. Every branch in Me that does not bear fruit He takes away; and every branch that bears fruit He prunes, that it may bear more fruit.

— John 15:1–2

In this day of homeowner and community associations, it is not as common as it used to be to have one house in the neighborhood that receives little or no upkeep. Still, there are always those dwellings that seem subpar in comparison to the others. Nevertheless, no one ever thinks, *Look at that house. Look at that lawn. Why does that place allow itself to be so unkempt?* No, the house's outward appearance says something about the people inside, not the building itself.

The same could be said of a garden or a vineyard. The unattended vineyard will soon be overrun with weeds and sucker shoots if the vinedresser does not care for it, and the overgrown, weed-ridden vineyard says something about the vinedresser, not the branches themselves. In a spiritual sense, every branch (person) that is in the vine (Jesus) will be tended to and pruned by the vinedresser (the Father). Why? Because it is His name that is associated with the branches.

God will prune the sucker shoots from our lives. These are the things that bear no fruit of themselves but only hinder our ability to produce fruit. He will also prune us so that we will bear more fruit in each season of life. Are you feeling pruned today? Know that it is the careful and loving vinedresser at work in your life. He wants you to bear more fruit and will prune the needless and harmful things that keep you from doing so.

One of the jobs of the vinedresser is to pick up the branches that have fallen into the mud and clean them so that the photosynthetic process may continue. This is what the Lord does for you and me. He keeps us clean so that the Son's work in us can be seen by others. But the work of the vinedresser doesn't end there.

We can understand when God prunes the sucker shoots from our lives, the fruitless things that rob us of time and strength. But we find it harder to understand when God trims us in places where we are already bearing fruit. Why does He do this? So we can bear more fruit! I have experienced this many times in both big and small ways, and the most severe prunings have yielded the greatest fruit, though they were the hardest to endure for the moment.

Has the Lord taken something out of your life, or have you experienced a cutback? That is often God's way of producing more fruit in you. It's not easy to have a fruitful area of your life cut back, but the owner of the vineyard knows just what to do to get more fruit out of you!

April 7

Beloved, do not avenge yourselves, but rather give place to wrath; for it is written, "Vengeance is Mine, I will repay," says the Lord. Therefore "If your enemy is hungry, feed him; if he is thirsty, give him a drink; for in so doing you will heap coals of fire on his head." Do not be overcome by evil, but overcome evil with good.

—Romans 12:19–21

"Let God handle those who do wrong—you just do what's right" may be a way to summarize Paul's instruction on dealing with our enemies. I do have to say my flesh nature is usually stirred when I read these verses, for I, like you, have those who have wronged me and continue to wrong me. In my flesh, I will admit, I would like to heap coals of fire onto their heads. And in this passage, God is telling me just how to do that—only, of course, He is speaking metaphorically while I am not!

But the fact is, the quickest way for any of us to be reminded that we are still flesh and blood battling to walk in the Spirit happens when we are wronged or offended. I remember one time I was out walking our small dogs to the local park, and a carload of teenage boys drove by and yelled out some rather offensive things. They even questioned my masculinity for walking two little dogs. I am somewhat embarrassed to share the scene that played out in my mind as I wondered if I should try to catch up with them at the corner signal. There I was—a pastor—envisioning teaching those "punks" a lesson about who is a man and who is not.

We don't realize how close to the surface that old nature is until we encounter it in someone else. So God tells us what to do: let Him deal with the vengeance department, and let us be people of mercy and grace. The reason this statement is so powerful is that returning evil for evil changes only you, not the ones who did you wrong; it merely causes you to stoop to their level. However, when you do good to those who have done you harm, the possibility exists for them to recognize the wrong they committed against you. But when you react in the flesh, they merely become convinced that they were right, and you confirm it by seeking to retaliate.

The ones who leave vengeance to the Lord and do right touch the consciences of others, and they will have opportunities to tell even their enemies what God has done for them. Those who continually react in the flesh, however, will never enjoy such opportunities.

So if someone drives by and yells obscene things at you, just keep walking. Let God touch their conscience through your returning good for evil!

April 8

And they said to me, "The survivors who are left from the captivity in the province are there in great distress and reproach. The wall of Jerusalem is also broken down, and its gates are burned with fire." So it was, when I heard these words, that I sat down and wept, and mourned for many days; I was fasting and praying before the God of heaven.

—Nehemiah 1:3–4

The "they" of this text were a group of Jews who had visited Jerusalem and then reported to Nehemiah on the condition of the city and people of God who had returned there from captivity in the then-ruling Persian Empire. Upon hearing the report, Nehemiah was distraught and wept, and he mourned for many days while fasting and praying.

The remainder of chapter 1 provides the details of Nehemiah's prayer, but the rest of the book is a record of what Nehemiah actually did concerning the burden of his heart. I cannot read this great book without thinking of the words of the eighteenth-century Bible commentator Matthew Henry, who said, "Fervent prayer is to be seconded [followed by] diligent action." Nowhere do we see this more clearly than in the lives of men like Daniel, women like Deborah, and leaders like Nehemiah, men and women of faith who allowed their burdens to be translated into action.

Each of us has issues that we are passionate about—abortion, hunger, poverty, teen immorality—all issues worthy of concern. We must begin to address these issues as Nehemiah did: with a broken heart and fervent prayer. But our fervent prayers must be seconded by actions. Many today say that Christians need not be concerned with social issues, that it's not our calling. I would remind all of us that Nehemiah runs in some rather elite company in Scripture; he is one of the few of whom nothing negative is written. He is in the company of men like Joseph and Daniel, both of whom God appointed to political positions, because God cares about the plight of His people.

If you have a burden regarding an issue of our day, remember, your primary mission is always the gospel of Jesus Christ. But those doors are often opened by meeting the tangible needs and distresses of others. After all, does Jesus divide the sheep and the goats by their doctrine or by their deeds (see Matthew 25)?

It's great to have a burden, and it's great to fast and pray, but follow Nehemiah's actions and Matthew Henry's words and second your prayer with action!

April 9

Then the Lord answered Job out of the whirlwind, and said: "Who is this who darkens counsel by words without knowledge? Now prepare yourself like a man; I will question you, and you shall answer Me."

— Job 38:1–3

Could you imagine hearing such words from God, even if you were someone like Job? "Now prepare yourself like a man; I will question you, and you shall answer me," He commanded. What follows is a bit of a comparison between a finite human being and an infinite God. I believe every Christian needs to read Job 38 and 39 every once in a while just to keep things in perspective about "who's who." It may be even more beneficial when we feel like life has given us a raw deal and God has allowed it.

In the midst of his suffering, Job issued complaints and made demands of the Lord. In chapters 38 and 39, God reminded Job that he—not the Lord—is the servant. As we move through the chapters, we read God's mighty replies: "Where were you...?" "Have you...?" "Who has...?" "Can you...?" "Do you...?" "Will you...?" Each question is answered with an obvious negative response from Job: "I was not there," "I haven't," "Not me," "I can't," "I don't," and "I won't." Read the chapters and see what I mean.

I think that any person familiar with the story of Job would agree that if ever there was a person who had a right to ask God *why* it would be Job. By God's own profession, Job was "upright in all his ways" (Job 1:8); yet he faced trials like few of us have ever seen. In only a matter of hours, he lost all he had and all he loved. Nevertheless, Job 1:22 says, "In all this Job did not sin nor charge God with wrong."

It seems as though after his wife told him to curse God and die (Job 2:9) and after he received counsel from his friends concerning why all these things had happened to him, Job found it all a bit too much to take and made his case that he had done no wrong. But ultimately, Job was a sinner like you and me, and God put things back into perspective for him in the two marvelous chapters of Job 38 and 39.

God has some questions for us as well in our times of self-justification or even self-pity. These are the times when we ask, "Why didn't you stop this, God?" or "Why didn't you answer my prayer the way I wanted You to?" When you're tempted to ask these kinds of questions, read through Job 38 and 39. There you'll find the holy attitude adjustment that Job encountered and the kind that you need. Take it to heart and apply it to your life, lest God say to you, "Prepare yourself; I have some questions for you!"

April 10

Knowing this first, that no prophecy of Scripture is of any private interpretation, for prophecy never came by the will of man, but holy men of God spoke as they were moved by the Holy Spirit.

—2 Peter 1:20–21

I love the acronym that has been applied to the word *Bible*: Basic Instructions Before Leaving Earth. What a great way to label this magnificent book of truth! We know that we are called to walk in and live by the Spirit (Rom. 8:9; Gal. 5:25), but God has also given us His Word to tell where and how His Spirit will lead.

The Spirit of God will never conflict with the Word of God, and no true prophecy or interpretation of Scripture will ever conflict with another portion of Scripture. When something you hear conflicts with the Word of God, the Holy Spirit in you will reject it as the will of man. Yet many today fail to do the work of the Bereans to search the Scriptures to find out if what they have heard is true. "The pastor said it, so it must be true" has never been a safe approach to understanding the Christian life. Don't get me wrong—the pastor should be "imitatable" (new word!), as 1 Corinthians 11:1 clearly says. But let's not forget, the preaching the Bereans were checking out was that of Paul and Silas. How much more, then, should we check out the words of the pastors and teachers among us!

I do believe we have yet to uncover all the majestic nuances of the living Word of God, but I also believe we have been given a fail-safe in this manual of instructions. For example, the Word of God says that Jesus is God and was with God in the beginning and that all things were created through Him and for Him (John 1:1; Col. 1:15–16). Therefore, if someone says Jesus was an angel, is the spirit brother of Lucifer, or was merely a great teacher among many, we know that is not true. Similarly, if someone claims to have a new revelation that is inconsistent with the balance of the Word of God, then it is not true. No prophecy of Scripture, whether fulfilled or unfulfilled, is of private interpretation.

God will lead us by His Spirit and guard the way with His Word. So when you hear something that doesn't sit well with your spirit, don't accept it just because of who said it. Search the Scriptures and see if it is so!

April 11

In Him you also trusted, after you heard the word of truth, the gospel of your salvation; in whom also, having believed, you were sealed with the Holy Spirit of promise, who is the guarantee of our inheritance until the redemption of the purchased possession, to the praise of His glory.

—Ephesians 1:13–14

One of the most intense debates of the last half millennium has been that of free will versus predestination, or Calvinism versus Arminianism. Much time, a great deal of energy, and many resources have been diverted from furthering the gospel by each side trying to convince the other that it is wrong.

If you forced me to take sides, I would have to say I am a staunch "Calminianist"! One of the points of the Calvinists that I agree with is eternal security. Many pastors shy away from the question of whether someone who falls away from the Lord and dies estranged from Him was ever really saved. I may not be smart enough to avoid the question, but I lean on two Scripture passages for the answer.

The verses here in Ephesians tell us that the presence of the Spirit in our lives is a guarantee of our inheritance. Notice, we do not find the word *unless* in this passage. But Scripture always gives a balanced perspective, lest we wander off into thinking we can live immorally yet expect heaven in the end because our salvation is secure. In the closing of the Sermon on the Mount, Jesus said in Matthew 7:21, "Not everyone who says to me, 'Lord, Lord,' shall enter the kingdom of heaven, but he who does the will of my Father in heaven." Then, to paraphrase Him, some will say, "But Lord, we did a lot of Christian stuff and even used Your name when doing it," to which Jesus will respond, "I never knew you; depart from Me, you who practice lawlessness!"

These two passages taken together say that the presence of the Spirit not only seals us for eternity but also guides us to live in a way that brings God glory. So friend, if you have asked Christ into your heart and been filled with His Spirit, your eternal destiny is secure. Next look at your life. Is it bringing glory to God, even though you may stumble and struggle at times? The presence of the Spirit says you are eternally His; the presence of the Spirit also means others will see Him in you.

So what does all this theological debate have to do with your day? Just this: As a "Calminianist," I believe the only proper approach to living the Christian life is to live each day as though salvation has to be earned, and rest each night as though you can't possibly lose it!

April 12

Blessed be the Lord, who daily loads us with benefits, the God of our salvation! Our God is the God of salvation; and to GOD the Lord belong escapes from death.

—Psalm 68:19–20

David was well acquainted with escapes from death, and as he wrote this psalm, he would have had an archive of references to draw from. These encounters ranged from escaping the javelin of jealous Saul to David's escape from Achish, the king of the Philistine city of Gath, where David played the madman to escape the clutches of the enemy king. So there was much for David to recall as he penned these words.

But it was also true for David, as it is true for you and me, that he probably escaped many other unknown close encounters with death. Once in a while, I feel the need to thank God for all the unknown things He has done for me. I'm sure He has averted from me many unknown encounters with death, intervened to prevent potential tragedies, and foiled countless plots of the enemy that I never even knew had been planned against me.

I have wondered at times if we will know all the things He has done for us when we get to heaven one day. How amazing it would be to learn about the many escapes from death we had, knowing that the enemy who roams like a roaring lion (1 Pet. 5:8) only wants to steal, kill, and destroy us (John 10:10).

We all have times and seasons when life brings things our way that seem to overshadow the many reasons we have to praise Him. If you are in a season like that, a season where your reason to praise feels like a short list, praise and thank Him for all the things you don't even know He has done. As a matter of fact, I do not think it a stretch to say that all the unknown things He's done for you far outnumber the things you do know.

I guarantee that your day today is going to be loaded with benefits. Most of them you won't even be aware of, but praise Him anyway for the unknown benefits, just as you praise Him for the known ones!

April 13

Then Caleb quieted the people before Moses, and said, "Let us go up at once and take possession, for we are well able to overcome it." But the men who had gone up with him said, "We are not able to go up against the people, for they are stronger than we." And they gave the children of Israel a bad report of the land which they had spied out, saying, "The land through which we have gone as spies is a land that devours its inhabitants, and all the people whom we saw in it are men of great stature. There we saw the giants (the descendants of Anak came from the giants); and we were like grasshoppers in our own sight, and so we were in their sight."

—Numbers 13:30–33

The twelve spies that Moses sent into the Promised Land returned with a cluster of grapes so huge it took two men to carry it on a pole. They told of a land flowing with milk and honey and filled with magnificent fruit; and "Oh, by the way," they said, "there are giants in the land." As soon as those words were uttered, the size of the fruit and the richness of the milk and honey no longer mattered. There was a problem in the Promised Land—big problems, people problems.

We know that Joshua was in one accord with Caleb, but look at the focus of the other ten spies. Both Caleb and Joshua said, "Let's do it," but the other ten said, "It can't be done." Notice, Caleb didn't try to convince them otherwise or coerce them to his point of view; he simply stated a fact. Not only were they able, he said, but they were "well able" to overcome the obstacles.

Did Caleb see something the others didn't? Did Caleb not see what the others saw? The fact is, both parties saw exactly what they were looking for. One was looking for what God had promised, and the other was looking for all the problems with what God had promised. All they could see was why the promise couldn't happen, why it wouldn't work, why it couldn't work.

Have you ever approached a promise of God with a "here's all the problems with the promise" mentality? Have you ever told God, "Here is why it won't work," "Here is what is wrong with the people," "This is what is wrong with this place," or "These are all the obstacles"? Friend, don't do that! If God said it, that settles it. Don't let a little detail like giants in the land make you forget the size of the grapes.

Is there something you feel God is calling you to do? Is there someone in your life who is a giant problem? Is something in your land threatening to devour you? If so, then do what Caleb did and proclaim, "I am well able to overcome it!" After all, it's not about you. It's about God's promise to give you the land, even the land of the giants!

April 14

For consider Him who endured such hostility from sinners against Himself, lest you become weary and discouraged in your souls. You have not yet resisted to bloodshed, striving against sin.

—Hebrews 12:2–3

I am baffled by the belief of many Christians today that they are walking like Jesus if they never say anything negative or offensive to anyone. Now I am not saying that Christians ought to be obnoxious, as we have all encountered a brother or sister in the Lord who needed a little tempering. But have you considered that the reason Jesus endured such hostility from sinners was exactly because of the things He said? No one wanted to stone Him for feeding thousands with a few loaves and fish; in fact, they wanted to make Him king. No one called for His death because He healed the sick and raised the dead. Well, no one other than the Pharisees, of course, but even they objected not to what He did but to when He did it, on the Sabbath.

Jesus endured hostility from sinners because of the things He said. To the paralytic in Matthew 9:2, He said, "Be of good cheer; your sins are forgiven you," but in the very next verse, we read that "some of the scribes said within themselves, 'This Man blasphemes!' " John 19:5 says that after Jesus was scourged and brought out to the people, wearing a crown of thorns and a purple robe, Pilate said, "Behold the Man!" In response, the Jews answered in verse 7, "We have a law, and according to our law He ought to die, because He made himself the Son of God."

As Jesus hung on the cross, Pilate had a plaque made to hang over His head that read, "Jesus of Nazareth, King of the Jews." John 19:20–21 says, "Then many of the Jews read this title, for the place where Jesus was crucified was near the city; and it was written in Hebrew, Greek, and Latin. Therefore the chief priests of the Jews said to Pilate, 'Do not write, "The King of the Jews," but, "He said, 'I am the king of the Jews.' " ' "

It is not our goal as Christians to be offensive or obnoxious, but neither can we measure the success of any day by having not been offensive. We are called to say the same kinds of things that caused Jesus to endure the hostility of sinners: that Jesus forgives sins, is the Son of God, came into the world as the King of the Jews, that He is the Messiah.

Consider what Jesus said that caused such a stir of hostility around Him, and say those things too in the course of your day. Then you will find that you have spent the day walking like Jesus, doing good for others without expecting anything in return, and speaking the truth in love that others might know and believe He is the Son of God. Say those things and you are assured of an action-packed day, just like Jesus had!

April 15

Then they sent to Him some of the Pharisees and the Herodians, to catch Him in His words. When they had come, they said to Him, "Teacher, we know that You are true, and care about no one; for You do not regard the person of men, but teach the way of God in truth. Is it lawful to pay taxes to Caesar, or not? Shall we pay, or shall we not pay?" But He, knowing their hypocrisy, said to them, "Why do you test Me? Bring Me a denarius that I may see it." So they brought it. And He said to them, "Whose image and inscription is this?" They said to Him, "Caesar's." And Jesus answered and said to them, "Render to Caesar the things that are Caesar's, and to God the things that are God's." And they marveled at Him.

—Mark 12:13–17

In 1811, the IRS established what would later become known as the "conscience fund," which was a confidential way for those who had cheated on their taxes to come clean. The first year the fund received only five cents. Since then, the fund has received over 570 million dollars, one thousand of which reportedly arrived with this attached note: "Dear Internal Revenue Service, I have not been able to sleep at night because I cheated on last year's income tax. Enclosed find a cashier's check for a thousand dollars. If I still can't sleep, I'll send you the balance"!

Even the Pharisees and Herodians (partisans of Herod) tried to use paying taxes as a weapon against Jesus, hoping to trick Him into saying the Jews should not pay taxes. The plan was to take that information and use it against Him. But Jesus, of course, did not fall for their trick, and Romans 13 further asserts our responsibility to obey the government, for government is an institution created by God. Civil disobedience is allowed, however, when the government infringes upon God's commandments (Acts 5:29).

This event in the life of Jesus ought to remind us of the many different ways the enemy will try to trap us or trip us up. Think of the damage he can do to a person's reputation and a church's effectiveness if he can expose either as a tax cheat or a fraud. After all, he tried it on Jesus, so why wouldn't he try it on us?

Christians should be the most dedicated and honest citizens, a blessing to their country. So let's render to Caesar what is Caesar's and to God what is God's, and our lives and our nation will be blessed as well!

April 16

There is one who speaks like the piercings of a sword, but the tongue of the wise promotes health.

—Proverbs 12:18

We have all known someone at one time or another who might fall under the description of being "sharp tongued." Some are unknowingly sharp, while others are knowingly arrogant, but neither type is pleasant to be around. That's because their words cut and inflict deep wounds in their relationships with others.

There is a saying I like that humorously remarks, "Those who are quick to speak often say things they haven't thought of yet." This is often the case with sharp-tongued people. Their words slip beyond their teeth and gums before their impact has been measured.

We all know someone who fits comfortably under the banner of sharp tongued, but the fact, is we have all been guilty of speaking piercing words at times. The thing is, though, words are not like a sneeze, an uncontrollable involuntary reaction. Words can indeed be controlled, and we can put several important safeguards in place to harness them.

Capturing words while they are still thoughts is one. James 1:19 says, "Let every man be swift to hear, slow to speak," and Galatians 5:23 says that one of the fruits of the spirit is self-control. So it is possible to control the piercing tongue.

Proverbs, however, presents a step beyond the captured thoughts and controlled tongue, and that is to use words to promote health. Now I do not believe in positive confession, speaking and believing things into existence, but I do believe in positive speaking. Sharp-tongued people always put us on edge because we constantly wonder if they are going to hurt us as they "wield their swords." Yet consider those people of whom it is said, "I've never heard them say an unkind word about anyone." What a wonderful reputation to have, all because their words promote health.

If your tongue is frequently sharp or just occasionally sharp, let it be your goal today that not one unkind word will slip from your mouth. As you begin to string together days like this, you will soon develop the reputation of being a person whose words promote health in your hearers!

April 17

And it shall come to pass, as soon as the soles of the feet of the priests who bear the ark of the Lord, the Lord of all the earth, shall rest in the waters of the Jordan, that the waters of the Jordan shall be cut off, the waters that come down from upstream, and they shall stand as a heap.

— Joshua 3:13

The children of Israel were about to end a forty-year period of wandering. All the doubters were dead, and it was now time to move forward into what God had promised (Deut. 1:35). However, even though the doubters had all died in the wilderness, moving forward was still going to require obedient steps of faith.

The words from Joshua at the beginning of this devotional may be prophetic for some of you, while for others, they are confirmation of a learned truth. That would be true regardless of the day assigned to this writing. Some of you today are in that first group and have been considering a step of faith to move into God's plan for you. Like God's people of old, you have been waiting for the waters to "stand as a heap" so you can cross over.

Part of crossing into the land of promise, the place of His perfect will as it pertains to your God-ordained inheritance of service, involves getting your feet wet. I have often had young men tell me they feel a call to ministry, and one of my questions to them is always the same: "What are you doing for the Lord right now?" In essence, are you getting your feet wet?

Every ministry begins the same way, whether a ministry of full-time Christian service, lay ministry at church, or personal ministry in daily life. They all begin with one step into the water, the proverbial getting your feet wet that comes from this verse.

One more important detail: Joshua and company were standing on the banks of the Jordan during flood season, and the river had overflowed its banks (Josh. 4:18). There couldn't have been a worse time to cross the river, but this was God's timing, and this is how He often operates. Furthermore, He didn't stand the waters in a heap first, but He had the priests put their feet into the floodwaters first. Don't wait for the waters to part before you dare to move forward. They will not part until you take the first step and get your feet wet.

I have also told those who have worried about making a mistake in their step of faith to remember that God is just as faithful at telling us when to stop as He is in telling us to go. But you'll never know that unless you take the first step of faith. Get your feet wet today!

April 18

For if you forgive men their trespasses, your heavenly Father will also forgive you. But if you do not forgive men their trespasses, neither will your Father forgive your trespasses.

—Matthew 6:14–15

This is one of those frequently misquoted and misunderstood verses that has left some Christians stifled and others disobedient. Jesus made a statement here that if not understood properly would impose unbiblical conditions on our salvation; namely, that unless we forgive other people for what they have done to us, God will not forgive us for all we have done. Under this interpretation, the work of offering forgiveness becomes a necessary component of salvation.

Let's look at this logically. First, Ephesians tells us we are saved by grace, not by works, and salvation is the gift of God (Eph. 2:8). Second, did Jesus' death on the cross automatically forgive everyone? If so, why will there still be people who go to hell? So then, are we being asked to do something that Jesus Himself did not do? So what *does* this verse mean?

In the context of Matthew 6, Jesus was drawing a contrast between the Word of God and the actions of the hypocritical scribes and Pharisees who said one thing but did another. They were always condemning others for breaking the law though they themselves were lawbreakers. What they didn't realize was that as they condemned others, they were condemning themselves. The meaning for us is clear. We cannot be hypocrites when it comes to forgiveness. Having been forgiven much, we must be forgiving of much.

You don't have to forgive in order to be forgiven, for that would be works. But since you have been forgiven, then be forgiving. "Being forgiving is evidence of being forgiven" would be a good way to understand it. After all, remember the words of the psalmist: "If I regard iniquity in my heart, the Lord will not hear" (Ps. 66:18).

Three times in this chapter Jesus used the word *hypocrite*. This provides the proper understanding of these great verses. Don't be a hypocrite when it comes to forgiveness. You received forgiveness that you didn't deserve, so extend forgiveness in the same manner. Refusing to do so shows you have not fully understood forgiveness, and for some, it reveals they are hypocrites whose prayers remain unheard by the Lord!

April 19

And the word of the Lord came to me, saying, "Son of man, prophesy against the prophets of Israel who prophesy, and say to those who prophesy out of their own heart, 'Hear the word of the Lord!' " Thus says the Lord GOD: "Woe to the foolish prophets, who follow their own spirit and have seen nothing!"

—Ezekiel 13:1–3

The influence of eloquence, even when it is completely devoid of fact or truth, is frightening. The Lord commanded Ezekiel to speak out against and therefore expose those who claimed prophetic vision but had actually seen nothing. He was ordered to pronounce "woe" to such men.

Let's remember a few facts today. First, an apostle is one who has seen the resurrected Lord, according to the Bible's definition (1 Cor. 15:8). Interestingly, we seem to have a resurgence of those who claim to be apostles in our day. That means either Jesus has appeared to them personally, which is impossible, for we are told that when He does return, every eye will see him (Rev. 1:7), or that they have ascended into heaven and seen Him there. That may not be impossible, but it is highly unlikely, and here's why.

Paul ascended to heaven, and when he returned, he said, "And lest I should be exalted above measure by the abundance of the revelations, a thorn in the flesh was given to me, a messenger of Satan to buffet me, lest I be exalted above measure" (2 Cor. 12:7). Those who claim to be apostles today seem to have returned from their alleged heavenly visits with a much different message, even an opposite message. Their message is often that God wants us all to be exalted above measure, limitlessly healthy and wealthy. And thorns in the flesh? We merely speak them out of our lives.

What does this have to do with us today? God instructed Ezekiel to foretell the future of those who lay claim to prophetic visions they haven't really seen: woe awaits them. And if woe awaits them, what awaits those who follow them? Many are prophesying out of their own hearts today, but if they had actually seen the Lord, their message would most assuredly not be one of self-exaltation. Rather, it would be like Isaiah's: "Woe is me, for I am undone.... For my eyes have seen the King, the LORD of hosts" (Isa. 6:5).

What was true in Ezekiel's day in Israel is true in the church today. So be careful whom you follow, friends; eloquence can be a great deceiver. All those who have truly seen the Lord have the same reaction: humility, reverence, and awe—not pride and self-promotion.

April 20

Oh, love the LORD, all you His saints! For the LORD preserves the faithful, and fully repays the proud person. Be of good courage, and He shall strengthen your heart, all you who hope in the LORD.

— Psalm 31:23–24

Over the years, numerous people have told me that they appreciate the fact that I am a humble person. I have always taken great pride in that! But seriously, folks, if pride is something God repays, then obviously He attaches great magnitude to this sin.

It is also worth noting that David here contrasts faith and pride as receiving opposite rewards, and therefore they are opposing attributes. Preservation from the Lord for the faithful and repayment from the Lord for the proud tell us that humility is of the Lord and pride is... well... of the devil.

David also reminds us that the life lived by faith requires courage. This courage is necessary to deal with elements in our day that have always been present, but never quite as flagrant as they are now. In biblical times, pride was often associated with the rich, but pride today is marketed to the rich and poor alike as an essential aspect of getting ahead. We know this is true simply by walking through a modern bookstore and counting the number of rows and shelves containing books under the theme of self-help.

But the Bible tells us, friends, that exaltation is reserved exclusively for the humble (Matt. 23:11). There is no help in self; our help is in the Lord. However, it takes courage to be humble, and it takes courage not to promote self or climb over others on the ladder of success.

The fact is, God hates pride. He says, "Pride goes before destruction and a haughty spirit before a fall" (Prov. 16:18). So there you have pride's reward: destruction and a fall. But conversely, divine preservation, courage, and strength are the reward of the humble.

In this age of self, strength and courage await the humble. Give it a try today and see how you stand out. Also, you'll see just how hard it is to do! But don't return insult for insult, and don't try to climb above others by tearing them down. Be humble today, which simply means, don't exalt yourself. It takes no strength to be proud. Any weakling can do that!

April 21

For the message of the cross is foolishness to those who are perishing, but to us who are being saved it is the power of God.

—1 Corinthians 1:18

I have yet to meet a person who enjoys being disliked or thought a fool. We don't even like being thought a fool when we have acted like one! It hurts, it's demeaning, and it's difficult to be made to feel that way. Yet here we are as Christians commissioned to carry a message that many will think is foolishness. And since most people are unable to disconnect the message from the messenger, we will often be regarded as fools because of what we believe.

If we think about this one element of our flesh, wanting to be liked or accepted, we soon realize that this drives our words and actions far more than we care to admit. We say certain things in order to be accepted, and we do and don't do other things in hopes of being accepted. The sense of loneliness that can arise from being disliked is avoided at almost any cost, and many will do anything to be "in" with those they deem accepted or popular. No one, whether young or old, likes to be the outcast.

This innate human desire for acceptance is something the enemy tries to exploit to his advantage and use against us in hopes of silencing us. Think about it. What is the first thing that comes into your mind when you think of sharing your faith with someone? Isn't it, *What are they are going to say?* or *What are they going to think?* Even though we know the message of the cross is the power that saved us and the message that changed us, we are still guarded when we share it, because of our fear of not being accepted.

So how do we overcome human nature in this area? I don't think we need to overcome it, really. I think we just need a bit of a "peer adjustment." Rather than worrying about being *out* of the in crowd if we share the gospel, why not see our efforts to preach the cross of Christ as putting us *in* the right crowd? That way we wouldn't be so concerned about what others think. When we share our faith, some on earth may indeed think it foolishness, but the fact is, we have put ourselves in with a great cloud of witnesses (Heb. 12:1).

You are not an outcast when people reject you and think you a fool for following Jesus. You are in company with the likes of Paul and Peter, John and James, C. H. Spurgeon and D. L. Moody. You've thrown in with Billy Graham and Billy Sunday. You're running with the likes of G. Campbell Morgan and the Wesley brothers. You're peers with Hudson Taylor and David Livingstone. Funny thing is, no one remembers those who labeled the preaching of these men as foolishness, but now hundreds and even thousands of years later, here we are, still remembering their names because they preached the cross of Christ.

You're not in the out crowd, friend, when people reject you and think you a fool for Jesus. You just joined the in crowd of all in crowds, the one that people still talk about today. Be bold and share your faith, for the cross is the power of God unto salvation!

April 22

In those days I also saw Jews who had married women of Ashdod, Ammon, and Moab. And half of their children spoke the language of Ashdod, and could not speak the language of Judah, but spoke according to the language of one or the other people. So I contended with them and cursed them, struck some of them and pulled out their hair, and made them swear by God, saying, "You shall not give your daughters as wives to their sons, nor take their daughters for your sons or yourselves."

—Nehemiah 13:23–25

Could you imagine something like this happening today? If church leaders responded to Christians who married nonbelievers by smacking them around, pulling their hair out, and cursing them in this manner, the ACLU, NOW, "LMNOP," and every other acronym you could think of would be breathing down their necks so fast they wouldn't know what hit them!

What caused such an extreme reaction from Nehemiah? History. The next two verses read: "Did not Solomon king of Israel sin by these things? Yet among many nations there was no king like him, who was beloved of his God; and God made him king over all Israel. Nevertheless pagan women caused even him to sin. Should we then hear of your doing all this great evil, transgressing against our God by marrying pagan women?"

Nehemiah reminded the leaders of Israel that this was the very sin that had brought down the great King Solomon. Now we might think Nehemiah should have toned it down a bit and had a sit-down with these guys instead of taking it to the next level right away. The fact is, Ezra had addressed this same subject some thirty years earlier (Ezra 9:1–4), but clearly his words fell on deaf ears.

So what is the life lesson in all this? I believe it is clear and simple: the issue is compromise. We tend to measure compromise in degrees. We think there are big compromises, like we see in this passage of Scripture, and small compromises, things that aren't that bad. The fact is, compromise is compromise, and it isn't measured in degrees; there are just varying degrees of consequences.

The reality is, you would be hard pressed to identify a situation in which someone's first compromise of faith was a "big" one. It always begins with what we deem a "small" compromise. But we need to realize that compromise is the problem in and of itself, not the specific manifestation or act associated with it. Big or small, it's still compromise.

The lesson to learn from Nehemiah's actions is to take drastic measures against compromise—any compromise, all compromise. Compromise brought down the smartest and richest man who ever lived, Solomon, and it can do the same to you and me.

Just say no to compromise!

April 23

Brethren, if a man is overtaken in any trespass, you who are spiritual restore such a one in a spirit of gentleness, considering yourself lest you also be tempted. Bear one another's burdens, and so fulfill the law of Christ.

—Galatians 6:1–2

The law of Christ is to love the Lord your God with all your heart, soul, and mind and your neighbor as yourself (Matt. 22:37–39). Many gifts and callings of the Lord that help us do that are specific to individual members of His body (1 Cor. 12:11) and to their roles in fulfilling His plan. Other aspects of being a Christian are applicable to us all, and Paul here reveals one of them: to bear one another's burdens.

We need to be careful not to read something into the meaning of Paul's words when he said "you who are spiritual." This is not referring to people who are somehow more spiritual than others, supersaints, if you will. The word *spiritual* here simply means not carnal, or regenerate. In other words, all who have been born again are privileged with the calling to be a restorer of the overtaken.

In this verse, the word *overtaken* comes from the Greek word *prolambanō*, and it means "to eat before others have an opportunity." Do you remember the rebuke Paul gave to the church in Corinth? They were coming together for a meal, a love feast, but some were arriving early and eating all the food and not sharing it with others. That's *prolambanō*; the trespass in Corinth was greed and gluttony. Putting oneself before others and being indifferent to the needs and struggles of others. So Paul is saying here in Galatians that when we see someone overtaken, we should gently restore that person while keeping in mind that we are capable of doing the same thing.

This keeps us from restoring with a "holier than thou" attitude, and that is the principle to keep in mind here. We may be tempted to approach a fallen brother or sister with a "what's the matter with you?" attitude or a "how could you be so stupid?" mind-set, but Paul warns us this is nothing less than falling into sin while seeking to restore.

Have you a fallen person in your life, one who has erred in the same thing time and again, one you have talked to time and again? *Consider yourself* as you talk to them again, lest your efforts to restore become a temptation to condemn. Bear one another's burdens, and so fulfill the law of Christ!

April 24

Learn to do good; seek justice, rebuke the oppressor; defend the fatherless, plead for the widow.

—Isaiah 1:17

"I don't smoke and I don't chew, and I don't go with girls who do" is an old adage that many people seem to think is an apt definition of the Christian life. We are the people who don't do this and don't do that. It is true there are things God has told us to refrain from, things we are not to do. But if that is how we approach the Christian life, we will encounter only a sense of bondage rather than the joy of liberty.

It is all the things we "do do" (sorry, couldn't resist) that keep the Christian life filled with passion and excitement. It's not just learning not to do bad, but it's learning to do good. Look at the series of verbs used here by Isaiah: *learn, seek, rebuke, defend, plead*. This certainly does not describe an empty life governed by a list of "I can't, I'm a Christian" prohibitions. Only learning not to do bad and not learning to do good, I believe, is one of the leading causes of succumbing to the pressures of the world, especially for young people.

We must consider the lives of those we revere in Scripture. These were all people of action—not inaction. Take, for example, one of the best-known Bible heroes, King David. A mighty warrior for God, David took action, though he was but a youth, when the entire army of Israel was being intimidated by Goliath (1 Samuel 17). This was David's greatest victory.

There is, however, another famous story about David, but this one tells of his greatest defeat: his sin with Bathsheba. In 2 Samuel 11:1, the Bible says, "It happened in the spring of the year, at the time when kings go out to battle, that David sent Joab and his servants with him, and all Israel; and they destroyed the people of Ammon and besieged Rabbah. But David remained at Jerusalem."

David fell into sin when he was "not doing." He was the king, but at the time of year when kings were supposed to go out to battle, he did not go. He stayed behind and let others go, and though he was not physically present on the battlefield, he was the one who fell.

When David was on the battlefield as a boy and Goliath was challenging the army of the Lord, David's older brother said to him, "What are you going to do, you prideful little wimp?" (loose paraphrase of 1 Sam. 17:28–29). David replied boldly, "Is there not a cause?"

Do you have a cause that you are acting on, or is your Christian life merely a list of things you don't do? Don't set yourself up for a fall, but live a life that is full with reaching out to others. Take up a cause for the widows or the unborn. Rebuke those who oppress, and care for the orphans. After all, doesn't Jesus divide the sheep and goats by what they did as well as by what they did not do?

The Christian life is one of doing and not doing. Both are required if we want a life that is rich and full. Learn to do good—not just not to do bad. It will keep you from living a life bound to nothing but "thou shalt not"!

April 25

For we do not have a High Priest who cannot sympathize with our weaknesses, but was in all points tempted as we are, yet without sin. Let us therefore come boldly to the throne of grace, that we may obtain mercy and find grace to help in time of need.

— Hebrews 4:15–16

These two magnificent verses are often quoted separately as single thoughts, but in doing so, we lose some of the majesty of what is said. For those times when we feel alone and as though no one knows or understands what we are going through, we are reminded that our High Priest knows and understands, a beautiful and sound truth. We also know that when we are in need of grace and mercy, the blood of Jesus gives us access to both those things, also a magnificent and comforting truth. This is the way we often hear these verses applied, as two separate though powerful truths.

But let's look at them as a unit and see what is there. If we examine them together, we see that Jesus was tempted in every way that we are yet never sinned, and we can find help when we're tempted by coming before the throne of grace. In other words, there is help for us in times of temptation. This shows us two important things. First, it is not a sin to be tempted, and second, there is help from heaven when we are.

Oftentimes the enemy holds us in his grasp by the mere fact that we are tempted. He whispers things into our ears like, *What kind of Christian thinks things like that?* or *If you were really saved, you wouldn't be battling lust*, or *No real Christian struggles with doubt.* But remember, Jesus Himself was tempted in all points, yet He remained without sin.

So what should you do when you're tempted? First of all, don't listen to the devil, and second, run in prayer to the place where grace is available. I have often told others to do something spiritual when confronted by the desires of the flesh. Pray for the lost, read the Word, ask a friend for prayer, tell someone else you love Jesus and He loves them, help someone in need, and on the list goes. When confronted with the temptation to do something you shouldn't, respond by doing something you should. This is an excellent way to combat temptation.

If every time the devil tempts you, the end result is not only do you not fall for it but you do something that strengthens your faith, reaches out to others, or spreads the gospel, then he will be forced to select another target. When you discover the grace you need in time of temptation, you prove your mastery of that temptation.

So remember, when tempted, head for the throne. There's help there whenever you need it!

April 26

Do all things without complaining and disputing, that you may become blameless and harmless, children of God without fault in the midst of a crooked and perverse generation, among whom you shine as lights in the world

— Philippians 2:14–15

Two small words in this great command change the meaning and magnitude of all that follows. The words are "all things." This command would be a cinch to obey if it read, "Do all things you like without complaining and disputing," or "Do all things with all those you like without complaining and disputing." But Paul says, in the midst of crookedness and perverseness, do all things without complaining and disputing.

The word *complaining* is the Greek word *goggusmos* (gong-goos-mos'), and it means "murmuring" or "grumbling." The Greek word for *disputing* is *dialogismos*, obviously the Greek root for our English word *dialogue*. The word means "deliberating." Stating that the Philippians were to do all things without murmuring deliberation in the midst of the crooked and perverse indicates that Paul's concern was for their witness.

Anyone who is a sports fan knows that every sport has those who quietly excel at their craft. Even when a bad call or the poor performance of teammates influences their game, they place no blame nor make excuses. But we also know those who seem to be constant complainers and blamers, always griping about how they got robbed or someone else was to blame for their poor performance. Athletes who do their jobs without complaining and disputing become leaders both on and off the field or court. The self-promoting constant complainers, however, are looked upon as just that, both on and off the field. The respect for the ones who quietly excel far surpasses any respect for the ever-complaining, self-promoting ones.

Paul is saying to the Philippians—and to you and me—to do all things without complaints and disputes so that our actions will gain the respect of the listening ears and watching eyes around us. Anyone can do the things they like with people they like without complaining and disputing. But the one who does so when surrounded by crooked perversity is someone whose voice is going to command respect when the time comes to speak.

Do all things today without grumbling deliberation, and at the end of the day, you will have been a light in this dark world!

April 27

So when Jesus had received the sour wine, He said, "It is finished!" And bowing His head, He gave up His spirit.

—John 19:30

What glorious words to remember each day: "It is finished!" Access to salvation was made available to all, and all who believe are safe in His hands. It is also worth noting the control, or sovereignty, demonstrated by Jesus here on the cross: "He gave up His spirit."

Many died under the hand of the Roman scourge, and Isaiah prophesied that the Messiah's beating would be so brutal that His visage would be marred more than the countenance of any other man (Isa. 53:14). In fulfillment of prophecy, Jesus was indeed beaten so as to be barely recognizable as a human being, but He did not yet say at that point, "It is finished."

It was necessary for Jesus to go to the cross. Not at the hands of the Roman whip could He give up His spirit, but rather He had to do it on the cross, lest prophecies about His death remain unfulfilled. Had He left even one scripture unfulfilled, the consequences would have been unimaginable. The Word of God would no longer be inerrant, future prophecies would be suspect, and hope would be less secure.

But Jesus said "it is finished," when it was finished. Verse 28 of this same chapter says, "Jesus, knowing that all things were now accomplished, that the Scripture might be fulfilled, said, 'I thirst!' " Then, receiving the sour wine and thus fulfilling the final scripture, Jesus proclaimed, "It is finished." I am sure the words reverberated like the voice of doom throughout the domain of the devil and his demons. Those words unequivocally told him he was finished and remind you and me that the great work of Christ is finished.

I love the saying "The next time the devil reminds you of your past, you remind him of his future." He is finished, and the work of salvation is finished because the Messiah finished that which the Father sent Him to do. Today He is seated at the Father's right hand awaiting the time when His enemies become His footstool and we arrive in heaven (Heb. 10:12).

So remember today Jesus' proclamation of "It is finished" as you encounter the blessings and trials of life. Those powerful words mean the saving work of Jesus is finished on your behalf, and the enemy who seeks to steal, kill, and destroy is finished as well!

April 28

*Hear, O Israel: The L*ORD *our God, the L*ORD *is one! You shall love the L*ORD *your God with all your heart, with all your soul, and with all your strength. And these words which I command you today shall be in your heart. You shall teach them diligently to your children, and shall talk of them when you sit in your house, when you walk by the way, when you lie down, and when you rise up. You shall bind them as a sign on your hand, and they shall be as frontlets between your eyes. You shall write them on the doorposts of your house and on your gates.*

— Deuteronomy 6:4–9

These are the words of the Jewish Shema, often written on a scroll, rolled up, and then placed inside a mezuzah, which is then nailed to the right-hand doorpost of a Jewish home. The top of the mezuzah points inward toward the home, symbolizing the blessings that adhering to the Shema will bring to that home. It is a wonderful ritual indeed, yet the true meaning lies beyond the tradition of literally nailing these verses to the doorpost of a home.

The Lord desires for our homes to be places where His name is mentioned frequently and His ways taught to those who dwell within. The fact that our God is one God manifested in three persons, God the Father, God the Son, and God the Holy Spirit, is to be diligently taught to our children. The knowledge that we are to love God with all our heart, soul, and strength is to be the practice within our homes. Our love for Him should be the dominant topic of our conversations, governing all that we set our hand to and all that we put before our eyes. All who enter through the doorposts of our homes should recognize them as houses of the Lord.

This is the heart and meaning of the Shema and a fitting desire for us Christians today. Our homes must be sanctified, set apart, from all that is of the world. The lust of the flesh, the lust of the eyes, and the pride of life (1 John 2:19) are not fitting inhabitants for the houses of those who serve the true and living God.

Whether we are single or part of a family living under one roof, we must protect the reputations of our homes. They are to teach through actions and words that the Lord our God is one and that we love Him with all our hearts, souls, and strength. That should be evident to those who pass through the doors of our homes. Not that we need to have pictures of Jesus and framed scriptures on our walls, but we do need to remember that what is heard and seen in our homes represents the Lord our God.

What does your home tell the visitor who passes through your doorposts, who happens upon your DVD collection, who opens your refrigerator, or who listens to the conversation within your walls? Is your home one where the Shema is fulfilled?

April 29

Then the Lord *saw that the wickedness of man was great in the earth, and that every intent of the thoughts of his heart was only evil continually. And the* Lord *was sorry that He had made man on the earth, and He was grieved in His heart. So the* Lord *said, "I will destroy man whom I have created from the face of the earth, both man and beast, creeping thing and birds of the air, for I am sorry that I have made them." But Noah found grace in the eyes of the* Lord.

—Genesis 6:5–8

We do not know much about life on earth between the time of Adam and Noah, though we do know from Genesis 5 that people lived a long time. Added to that is the fact that there was no birth control, so suffice it to say, there were a lot of people alive at the time of the flood. Can you imagine life on earth if you were one of only eight righteous people on the entire planet? That's what Noah faced.

In Matthew 24:37, Jesus said, as it was in the days of Noah, so will it be before the day of His return. Very few people walking in righteousness and billions whose every intent and thought are continually evil will characterize the days prior to the coming of the Son of Man.

But grace is still to be found in the eyes of the Lord, even on a planet of more than six billion people, relatively few of whom seek Him. Grace is how we are saved, and grace is how we stay sane in times such as these. God's grace is sufficient (2 Cor. 12:9) for every time and season on earth, including the age that will be as it was in Noah's day.

Consider this: Noah, living among those whose every intent was only evil, was building an ark in the desert one hundred miles from the ocean on a planet where it had never rained. Until then, only a mist had watered the earth (Gen. 2:6). Do you think that possibly Noah was ridiculed once or twice during the hundred years it took to build this great ship? Do you think maybe the few who were righteous were scorned and viewed as fools for doing what God had commanded them to do while everyone else pursued their own desires? How could Noah and his family endure such a time? Grace!

Jesus is coming, friends. Yes, evil is all around us, but evil is no match for the grace of God. So keep building, keep sharing Jesus, keep living like He's coming at any time. Noah acted upon God's instructions and found grace in a time when the righteous were frighteningly few. Just like in Noah's day, God's eyes are still filled with grace for all who look to Him. Keep looking up. Not for rain, but for reign—Jesus' reign, that is!

April 30

But to each one of us grace was given according to the measure of Christ's gift. Therefore He says: "When He ascended on high, He led captivity captive, and gave gifts to men."

— Ephesians 4:7–8

We know the greatest gift of all is our salvation. It is indeed a truth we need to be thankful for all day every day. Yet we also know that along with this greatest of gifts, we have also received spiritual gifts. Without the gifts of the Spirit, we could not face life with the peace that passes understanding (Phil. 4:7), nor could we do the will of the Father (Matt. 7:21). This is why the enemy tries to divide the church over this issue of spiritual gifts. If Satan can keep us debating the gifts of the Spirit, he will succeed at keeping us from using the gifts of the Spirit.

God wants to use us for His glory. Jesus made it clear that without Him we can do nothing (John 15:5) and that the Holy Spirit is here to help us give testimony of Jesus (John 15:26). So regardless of our opinions, the fact is, God gave each of us gifts to bring us peace and to enable us to do His will.

We need to be careful about confusing gifts with talents. The difference between the two is that a gift of the Spirit cannot be used for personal gain or glory, while a talent can be used to promote self and generate income. Singing or playing an instrument, for example, are talents and can be used for self or for God. With a gift of the Spirit, however, God does something in and through us that we lack the natural talent to do. Make no mistake, it is a wonderful and glorious thing to surrender our talents to the Lord for His use. But we must also use the gifts He has given us and not just the talents genetics has provided.

Stepping out to share your faith without the talent of being an eloquent communicator requires a work of the Holy Spirit, and in the end, God receives the glory for it. When was the last time you did something that you were afraid to do, something just for Him, something that would be an absolute mess if He didn't work through you or help you overcome a fear, even for just that moment? In those instances, His gifts were necessary and the reason for whatever success you experienced.

One of my greatest fears in presenting a teaching or a sermon is being unprepared. Yet one of my greatest joys in ministry is when God calls on me to share something without any prior notice. It has to be Him working through me at those times, because the situation freaks me out. My mind says, *I need to study, I need to prepare.* God's Spirit says, "Get out of the way and let Me use you."

God gives you gifts of His Spirit, friend. If this rubs your theology the wrong way, just take the test. Take a step outside your comfort zone and seek to minister to others for God's glory. And see, after He uses you, if you still think it was you.

Try it—you'll like it!

May 1

This Book of the Law shall not depart from your mouth, but you shall meditate in it day and night, that you may observe to do according to all that is written in it. For then you will make your way prosperous, and then you will have good success. Have I not commanded you? Be strong and of good courage; do not be afraid, nor be dismayed, for the LORD *your God is with you wherever you go.*

— Joshua 1:8–9

I love this promise to Joshua! God reminded him that no matter where he went, He would be in command and control. Along with this magnificent statement of His sovereignty, the Lord also gave Joshua a word of instruction about enjoying the benefits of God's perfect will wherever he went. Speak, meditate on, and observe to do all that is written in God's Law, and *then* your way will be prosperous and you'll enjoy good success.

The Hebrew word for *prosperous* literally means "to push forward." The word translated as "good success" is the Hebrew word *śâkal* (saw-kal'), which means "intelligently," "prudently," or "wisely." So let me paraphrase this passage for our understanding and application today. God said to Joshua, "Stay focused on and obedient to the Word, and everywhere you go and everything you attempt will be done intelligently, prudently, and wisely." Now that's a promise, and it belongs to all who trust in the Lord.

The Bible is not an investment guide or a manual for positive thinkers; the Bible is instruction in righteousness (2 Tim. 3:16), which is always the intelligent, prudent, and wise way to live. If we allow the Word to be our guide, the decisions we make in life will be of good success.

As you consider the multitude of decisions in life, consider all that is written in the Word of God. Then you will make your way prosperous and have good success. God will not instruct you to do things that will hinder your walk with Him or infringe upon your commitment to Him.

If you want to push forward into the land of promise, then heed the counsel of the Lord to Joshua. Stay in the Word all the time, and let it be your guide for obedience.

May 2

Therefore, if anyone is in Christ, he is a new creation; old things have passed away; behold, all things have become new.

— 2 Corinthians 5:17

There are some verses that make me want to stand up and shout hallelujah, and this is one of them. The reason this verse means so much to me is because of the "old things" in my life: drunkenness and drugs, abuse and neglect of my wife and family, a life estranged from the Lord I learned about as a child and committed myself to as a young boy. It is a part of my life I wish had never happened. But praise God, in Jesus, it is truly just as if it never did! That old person has passed away, and all things have become new.

We can all use a little reminder and encouragement in this area; I know I still do from time to time. The devil loves to parade through my mind on a regular basis the memories of the old dead man, and I must continually remind myself that the proclamation of 2 Corinthians 5:17 is not poetry, but actuality. It really happened! My past has been crucified with Christ (Gal. 2:20). It's dead and gone, and I am a new creation!

So why would anyone continue to live under the influence of a dead and buried past? The reason, I believe, is that sometimes the person who struggles the most to forgive and forget the past is the one who lived it. As an expert in this, let me encourage you today. Don't keep living in a past Jesus died to kill. I have a million things I wish I could change and twice as many I would give anything to do differently. But here is wisdom: to live controlled by the past is to doubt the sufficiency of the blood of Jesus to bring new life. And that is not about the past; that is about the present.

I have taught others and reminded myself often that like Paul, Peter, Abraham, and countless others, we cannot be disqualified for service by our past, but only by our present. So if you are in Christ, you are a new creation. Your past is dead and your future secure, so live in the present like these things are really true!

May 3

He who is not with Me is against Me, and he who does not gather
with Me scatters abroad.

— Matthew 12:30

One of the many coups of the enemy today comes in the message of religious tolerance and political correctness. I am not saying we should attack people of other religions, but the message of religious tolerance today says that for Christians to claim an exclusive path to eternal life *is* an attack on other religions.

It is also true that this political correctness has penetrated the thinking of the church corporate in many ways. "Don't tell people they're lost and unsaved, because that's offensive," we're told. "Just identify them as unchurched." Or maybe you've heard this one: "Don't say Jesus is the only way, because that's offensive. Just say Jesus is the way for Western civilization and that God has revealed Himself in other ways in other parts of the world."

Statements such as these are not only unbiblical but also directly opposed to the teaching of Jesus Himself. Jesus said the planet is occupied by two groups and two groups only: His friends and His enemies. From the apostles' writings, we know they too shared this mentality. Look what the Holy Spirit spoke through Paul in Colossians 1:21: "you, who once were alienated and enemies."

I am not a proponent of brash methods of evangelism and yelling at sinners that they are doomed to hell, but I do believe we have the responsibility to tell them of their eternal destination if they lack a personal relationship with Jesus Christ. I fear, however, that many today define Christlikeness as that of never offending anyone.

Friends, Jesus is the only way. He is the only truth, and there is no eternal life through any religion or any person but Him. That is what He said, so that is what we should say too. But let's also recognize the fact that if we say what He said, we may experience what He experienced. But that too is part of Christlikeness.

Those who know me know I am not a big fan of the word *unchurched*, which gets thrown around a lot today. I don't care for that word because it gives the impression that people need to "get churched." People need to get *saved*, friends, and hear that they are either for Jesus or against Him. They need to know that Jesus is God come in human flesh and that there is but one God existent in three persons: Father, Son, and Holy Spirit. And they must be told that if they are against Jesus or choose to follow another path, they are enemies of God.

Our goal is not to be offensive, but our message is by definition an offense to those who are perishing (1 Pet. 2:8). The reality of what Jesus says is this: if we preach a message that does not divide, then we have not preached the truth. The sin of man and the love of God are inseparable components of the gospel, and both must be preached.

When Jesus said people are either for Him or against Him, His words offended many people. So for those who are always asking, "What would Jesus do?" I answer, "He would tell the world He is the way, the truth, and the life and that no one gets to heaven but through Him." Even when it isn't politically correct or doesn't demonstrate religious tolerance, it's what Jesus would do!

May 4

Though one may be overpowered by another, two can withstand him. And a threefold cord is not quickly broken.

— Ecclesiastes 4:12

I have used these beautiful and appropriate verses in many weddings, as many pastors do, but the context of what King Solomon wrote here applies beyond the boundaries of marriage. In this chapter, Solomon warned of the downfall of a life absent of interpersonal relationships or, in a word, friends.

Solomon expanded his thoughts on this issue to business relationships and friendships and observed that all aspects of life that share the Lord as a common bond (third cord in the strand) create strong ties. Friends who know and love the Lord can offer strength and encouragement that others cannot. Business partners who know the Lord can keep the relationship and business moving forward even when times are difficult and stressful.

Like Solomon, Jesus also taught this principle when He said, "Again I say to you that if two of you agree on earth concerning anything that they ask, it will be done for them by My Father in heaven. For where two or three are gathered together in My name, I am there in the midst of them" (Matt. 18:19–20).

A Christ-centered marriage enjoys a bond not easily broken. A Christ-centered business partnership also enjoys a bond not easily broken and, might I add, the blessings of the Lord to boot. I cannot count the times I have heard people say, "My church family is closer to me than my blood family." This is what Christ-centered relationships do: they form bonds like no other, one that has Christ interwoven through and through.

It is interesting that the word *threefold* brings to mind pictures of a braid, but the word actually means "to intensify" or "to triplicate." So businesses, marriages, and friendships centered on the Lord are three times more intense than those without that common bond. In this sense, *intense* means "imparting strength."

Beware of isolationism. Build your business, marriage, and friendships on the Lord, and they will be stronger and accomplish more than you could ever imagine!

May 5

"Bring all the tithes into the storehouse, that there may be food in My house, and try Me now in this," says the LORD of hosts, "if I will not open for you the windows of heaven and pour out for you such blessing that there will not be room enough to receive it. And I will rebuke the devourer for your sakes, so that he will not destroy the fruit of your ground, nor shall the vine fail to bear fruit for you in the field," says the LORD of hosts; "and all nations will call you blessed, for you will be a delightful land," says the LORD of hosts.

—Malachi 3:10–12

To me, the issue of tithing is one of the great paradoxes in the church today. Though we believe in a God we have never seen, trust our eternal salvation to someone we have never met, pray fervently to a God we have probably never audibly heard, and act on things we believe He wrote thousands of years ago, we refuse to prove God in the one thing the Bible says we are to prove Him in, and that is tithing. We say things like, "Tithing is part of the law," but Abraham paid tithes and he wasn't under the law. Others say, "We only have to give what we can give cheerfully," so does that mean we no longer walk by faith but by emotion? And if we can't give anything cheerfully, does that mean we are exempt from supporting the work of the Lord? The arguments against tithing just don't hold up.

I will be the first to admit there is much abuse in the arena of finances within the church as a whole, such as those who teach a "give to get" approach. But I will say now what I have said many times before: don't let a liar make you into a thief! The verses preceding the exhortation above equate the failure to tithe to robbing God. But here's the real paradox: who loses when God is robbed? Certainly not Him.

So let's keep a balanced perspective on this issue and not use charlatans as an excuse to be a thief. Tithing is a principle that spans the whole of the Bible; it's not for God's benefit, but for ours. It's not His work that is going to suffer or bear the consequences, but ours. God said, "Try Me in this and watch what I will do in your fields and vineyards and how I will rebuke the devourer for your sake."

Contrary to what you may hear from some, God's work is going to get done whether you tithe or not. But God has said to us all, "If you want Me to bless the 90 percent of what you keep, then you have to be faithful in the 10 percent I have commanded you to give."

May 6

He who has pity on the poor lends to the LORD, and He will pay back what he has given.

—Proverbs 19:17

Many Christians do not recognize the difference between tithes and offerings. We give tithes to support God's house, our home church. As yesterday's exhortation reminded us, tithing is simply giving what is not ours to keep in the first place. The tithe, or tenth, is the Lord's (Lev. 27:30).

We give offerings above and beyond our tithes. Paul often collected offerings for the "poor saints in Jerusalem" (Rom. 15:26), which was the case in 2 Corinthians 9. Additionally, in this same chapter, when Paul noted that God loves the cheerful giver, he was discussing offerings.

As a young Christian, I once gave my tithe to someone in need rather than to my church, but as I searched the Scriptures in my journey of faith, I came to realize that this was not what God had ordained. God loves the cheerful giver because giving an offering to someone in need is a sacrifice, whereas tithing is an act of obedience (not robbing God's house).

Over the years, I have heard many people say that they give their tithes to a parachurch organization because they like what that organization is doing, yet they attend a local church regularly and do nothing to support their home church. This is like eating at one restaurant but going to another to pay for the meal. It doesn't make sense!

He who has pity on the poor lends to the Lord, and the Lord will pay back what he has given. Think about this: if you rob from God's house to give to those in need, what is there for Him to pay back? Tithes are for God's house, your home church; offerings are for the burdens on your heart concerning the poor and needy. No matter the city you are reading this in or the year you are reading it, there are needs all around you. God loves it when you sacrificially meet those needs.

May 7

But you, beloved, building yourselves up on your most holy faith, praying in the Holy Spirit, keep yourselves in the love of God, looking for the mercy of our Lord Jesus Christ unto eternal life.

—Jude 1:20–21

There are many interpretations of what it means to pray in the Holy Spirit, ranging from praying in tongues to groaning in the Spirit. But I believe the point is not so much the method but the manner of prayer. Jude mentions keeping ourselves in the love of God and looking for mercy in Jesus for eternal life.

Along with studying the Word, we can build up our most holy faith another way, and that is by having a truly spiritual prayer time. That may sound obvious, but has your prayer time ever looked much like a to-do list for God or a Christmas wish list for Santa? If so, you're not alone.

I love how the apostle John introduces the Revelation of Jesus Christ he received while on the island of Patmos. John says in Revelation 1:10, "I was in the Spirit on the Lord's Day, and I heard behind me a loud voice, as of a trumpet."

This is the heart of what Jude is saying: in your prayer time, do you hear from the Lord, or do you just drop Him a laundry list of things to do for you? That is not going to build up your most holy faith!

I believe Jude is saying that prayer is a spiritual experience in which humanity and eternity will intersect until we see Him face-to-face. When a time of prayer includes hearing from God and not just speaking to God, then that time will build faith. Prayer takes time, and like most other things, we get out of it exactly what we put into it. Did you wait to hear God's answers to your prayers today or His instruction for the day? Or was your prayer time like mine is at times: *Heavenly Father, do this for me, protect me from that, and give me these things because I ask them in Jesus' name. Amen, see You later?*

Kind of convicting reading it, but it's true for all of us. Can we characterize our prayer times as "in the Spirit"? If not, we are missing out on some good stuff, including getting to know more about God, His love and mercy, and even the glory of eternal life.

Take time to pray is good counsel; take your time in prayer is even better!

May 8

So I will restore to you the years that the swarming locust has eaten, the crawling locust, the consuming locust, and the chewing locust, My great army which I sent among you. You shall eat in plenty and be satisfied, and praise the name of the LORD your God, who has dealt wondrously with you; and My people shall never be put to shame.

—Joel 2:25–26

The children of Israel had invited disaster into their lives by disregarding and dishonoring the law of the Lord and therefore the Lord of the law. As always, God had allowed His people time to repent, and prophets like Joel had given words from the Lord calling the people to turn from their ways. The people, however, did not repent, and disaster struck. Like locusts, a wave of invading armies consumed Israel, and years were lost to captivity.

In the verses preceding this passage, the Lord told the people to rend their hearts, not their garments (v. 13), and they were instructed to blow the trumpet and call for a fast (v. 15). The result would be the restoration of the years consumed by the locusts. Only God could make such a wonderful promise of creating something from nothing.

This is what God can do in our lives as well. He can take a troubled and wasted past and make something wonderful out of it. He can take a life consumed by rebellion and make it into a glorious vineyard for His name and glory. This is a tremendous truth to embrace and a magnificent one to share.

Myriads of people today need to hear a message of hope. Some are still ensnared in a troubled past, while others struggle with an empty past. Some have spent their lives searching for something to believe in, and others have endured years of loneliness. But regardless of the specifics, God can still make something out of nothing and even restore years consumed by locusts. That is the message many need to hear from us Christians today.

Tell someone today that the thing they have been searching for is not a thing at all, but it is Jesus! Joel's name means "the Lord is God"; his name was a proclamation of God's greatness and authority. So too are we called to proclaim the greatness of our God to those who don't yet know Him.

The world today looks much like it did in Joel's day. Open rebellion against God, the diminishing of His Word, and the rejection of His will are found everywhere, even among God's own people. But as long as God is on the throne, there is hope. There is a world around us that needs to hear that message, and they need to hear it from someone whose life has been restored by the true and living God. Make it your mission today!

May 9

He also spoke this parable: "A certain man had a fig tree planted in his vineyard, and he came seeking fruit on it and found none. Then he said to the keeper of his vineyard, 'Look, for three years I have come seeking fruit on this fig tree and find none. Cut it down; why does it use up the ground?' But he answered and said to him, 'Sir, let it alone this year also, until I dig around it an fertilize it. And if it bears fruit, well. But if not, after that you can cut it down.' "

—Luke 13:6–9

I love this parable for many different reasons. It assures me that God never gives up on us and protects us from him who desires to cut us down. But I also discover in this parable that He digs around in our lives to search out the things that keep us from bearing fruit.

God does not want us to simply use up the ground or take up space. A friend of mine in high school wrote under his senior picture the following: "Participated in the space program—took up space." That is not the rich and full Christian life God intends for any of us. As His children, we are meant for much more than just taking up space until we arrive home in heaven.

God desires a vibrant and full life of fruit bearing for each of His children. But it is also true that fruit bearing requires His attention in our lives. Sometimes He must dig up hindrances, and other times He must fertilize, or add to our lives the things that encourage fruit.

Has God been digging around in you lately? He has in me, and He digs up things that I really didn't want to know about myself. He exposes wrong attitudes and indifferences, selfish places and mind-sets that need to be removed. But He also shows me things that I must begin to do in order to bear fruit in all aspects of my life.

Remember, this is a parable, an earthly story with a spiritual meaning. The fig tree is our lives, and the vineyard is the world. The keeper of the vineyard is the god of this world, and the vinedresser is the Father (John 15:1). The fruit is the spiritual fruit of both personal growth and the expansion of God's kingdom.

God's desire is that you grow and bear much fruit. He is not willing to cut you down, even if there has been little or no fruit produced to this point. God is committed to you and to your reflection of Him in this world.

Let God dig around in your life. Listen to what He is telling you about you. Add to and remove the things He reveals. If you do, your life will produce the rich, full fruit that He intended. Yes, it hurts to look at the things He digs up sometimes, but it would hurt a lot more to have as a epitaph at the end of your life "Took up space"!

May 10

You will show me the path of life; in Your presence is fullness of joy; at Your right hand are pleasures forevermore.

—Psalm 16:11

Many people today are in search of happiness and even look to the church to try to find it. To be sure, happiness is a wonderful thing. I like being happy. I like doing things that make me happy, I like seeing others happy, and I like to make others happy. But happiness and joy are two completely different things.

Happiness is an emotion and therefore governed by circumstances. When things are good and go our way, we are happy; but when things are bad and seem to go against us, we are sad. Joy, however, can be experienced no matter what life may bring. A person can be sad yet simultaneously possess joy in the midst of a sad situation. I have seen this many times at the funeral of an elderly Christian. The family, of course, is sad that their loved one is gone, but they take great joy in knowing the person is now safely in heaven.

It is possible to lose our joy, and David indicates how this happens. When we wander from the path of life and distance ourselves from the Lord, we experience a corresponding loss of joy. It's much like the old bumper sticker you may have seen that reads, "If you feel far from God, guess who moved?" His path, His presence, and our proximity to Him are keys to joyful living.

In Psalm 51:12, David wrote, "Restore to me the joy of Your salvation, and uphold me by Your generous Spirit." David had wandered from the path and fallen into sin with Bathsheba. Confronted by Nathan about his sin, David realized that forsaking the path of life had caused him to lose his joy. But God is generous with His Spirit, and joy can be restored by getting back onto the right path.

I like being happy, and so do you, but joy is better and therefore more painful when we lose it. But thanks be to God who told us where joy can be found! It's on the path of life and in His presence.

Everyone thinks they want to be happy, but what most people are really looking for is something that doesn't fluctuate according to circumstances. Happiness cannot be found unless things are good, so that means you have to wait for things to change or something good to happen in order to be happy. Joy, on the other hand, can be experienced right now, even if nothing changes. And even if it seems to be lost, if you get back on the path of life and stay close to God, the generous Spirit of the Lord will restore the joy of your salvation!

May 11

And the lords of the Philistines came up to her and said to her, "Entice him, and find out where his great strength lies, and by what means we may overpower him, that we may bind him to afflict him; and every one of us will give you eleven hundred pieces of silver." So Delilah said to Samson, "Please tell me where your great strength lies, and with what you may be bound to afflict you."

—Judges 16:5–6

Talk about the direct approach! Delilah didn't even try to hide her intentions but told Samson what she wanted to know and why she wanted to know it. "Tell me your strength that you may be bound and afflicted," she brashly declared. We know the following story of Samson's three lies until finally Delilah's wiles wore him down. Giving in to her demands, he told her the truth and lost his strength with his first haircut.

When I read this story, I cannot but think of how the enemy loves to attack not just our weaknesses but also our strengths. Though we often know his intentions in advance and understand the forewarned consequences of his enticements, many of us who are seemingly strong still fall. That's because, as Oswald Chambers says in his devotional *My Utmost for His Highest*, "an unguarded strength is a double weakness." In other words, we cannot say, "That won't happen to me," "That is not my place of struggle," or "I am not tempted by that."

There is never a day off from spiritual warfare. The enemy keeps coming and coming, relentlessly trying to wear us down, just like Delilah did with Samson. The devil attacks strengths and weaknesses alike; therefore, "let him who thinks he stands, take heed lest he fall" (1 Cor. 10:12).

Sadly, the mighty Samson let his guard down, and we know the end of his story. He became a spectacle for the world, put on display as a trophy of the enemy. Similarly, the enemy is going to attack the secret of your strength today and every day in hopes of making a mockery of your testimony. So be on guard—in both your strengths and your weaknesses!

May 12

*And Moses said to the people, "Do not be afraid. Stand still, and see the salvation of the L*ORD*, which He will accomplish for you today. For the Egyptians whom you see today, you shall see again no more forever. The L*ORD *will fight for you, and you shall hold your peace."*

— Exodus 14:13–14

We have all heard the expression often used in retail businesses' three rules for success: "location, location, location." Israel's location at the time of these words from Moses is the key to understanding the magnitude of his words.

In verses 1–2 of chapter 14, we read, "Now the LORD spoke to Moses, saying: 'Speak to the children of Israel, that they turn and camp before Pi Hahiroth, between Migdol and the sea, opposite Baal Zephon; you shall camp before it by the sea.' " *Pi Hahiroth* means "the mouth of the gorges"; Migdol was home to a 250-feet-deep well with water so bitter it was barely suitable for a camel and was known as the "well of bitterness"; and *Baal Zephon* means "master of gloom." Oh, and one more thing—the Israelites had their backs against the Red Sea and Pharaoh's army was approaching in the distance!

Upon exiting Egypt, the children of Israel found themselves with the Red Sea in front of them, the army of Pharaoh closing in behind them, and the mouth of the gorges, the well of bitterness, and the master of gloom surrounding them. In the midst of all this, Moses said to the people, "Stand still, for the Lord will fight for you!" This, in my mind, would fall under the "easier said than done" category—the "standing still" part, that is.

But having studied and taught this passage, I discovered an important lesson we can glean from this event: God may direct us into difficulty for the glory of getting us out! Remember, the Lord was the one who told Moses and the children of Israel where to camp. He was the one who told them to stand still with the Red Sea in front of them, the army of Pharaoh behind them, and the mouth of the gorges, the well of bitterness, and the master of gloom surrounding them. God had His people right where He wanted them. Never for a moment were they in harm's way. It was not even a close call, because the sovereign God was in complete control all along.

I don't think we can slight the children of Israel for freaking out a little bit—okay, a lot. But we also know what they didn't: that because of the spot they were in, God was going to do something so miraculous it would be talked about for thousands of years and even incorporated into hundreds of movies and books.

Though mind and flesh may rebel at the idea, the fact is, God will lead us into difficult places for the glory of getting us out. You might be in a hard place right now, but remember, no matter where you are, it is a place that can bring Him glory!

May 13

Do not be wise in your own eyes; fear the LORD and depart from evil. It will be health to your flesh, and strength to your bones.

— Proverbs 3:7-8

At times, the will of man is a strange and bizarre thing. Nevertheless, man's will is clearly very powerful, even the will of the first man who lived on the earth. Though Adam was given only one commandment to obey in comparison to our ten, he failed at keeping that one.

The will of God for the Christian is simple and clear: do what God says to do, and don't do what God says not to do. Yet our flesh fervently wars against this, as though our way is better than His.

Have you ever met one of those people who look a lot older than they really are? You know, someone who looks seventy but is really only forty. It's the kind of person you look at and say, "They've lived a hard life." I wonder if we don't look like that spiritually at times, like we've lived hard lives.

In a spiritual sense, this comes from being wise in our own eyes and not departing from evil. Such a life robs our flesh of health and wearies our bones. From my own life, I know this is true. When I carried the burden of rebellion to the plan of God, I watched my own health suffer and my strength fade.

God's way is better! It's more healthful and makes you stronger, and it all starts with one simple decision: do what God says to do, and don't do what God says not to do. You won't and can't earn your salvation that way, but you can be a healthier and stronger Christian that way.

Nothing robs Christians of spiritual health and strength like sin. Even though we have been forgiven by God and are blood bought, sanctified, justified believers, sin still is a spiritual health- and strength-killer. The warning from Proverbs about those who write their own definitions of right and wrong, picking and choosing which parts of God's Word are relevant and applicable, still holds true today.

As a former veteran of this kind of rationalizing, let me save anyone reading this devotional a lot of pain and trouble, sickness and weakness. Just do what God says to do, and don't do what God says not to do. It's good for your health!

May 14

Wisdom is better than strength. Nevertheless the poor man's wisdom is despised, and his words are not heard. Words of the wise, spoken quietly, should be heard rather than the shout of a ruler of fools. Wisdom is better than weapons of war; but one sinner destroys much good.

— Ecclesiastes 9:16–18

I remember when car alarms were first introduced into the marketplace and the thoughts that came to mind when you heard one sounding its blaring alarm. Your mind began to race with pictures of car thieves hot-wiring cars and broken glass littering the ground. In the early days, a car alarm would even draw a small crowd of curious onlookers and well-meaning "protectors." When we hear a car alarm today, however, it is merely an annoyance, and we wonder why the bozo who owns the car can't figure out how to shut off the alarm.

This is not unlike the situation here in Ecclesiastes concerning the shout of a ruler of fools and a poor man's wisdom. I have to say, I am amazed at what people will believe simply because of the power and position of the one who says it. Yet those not viewed by the world's standards as successful have little platform to express their views or even have value associated with their opinions. This becomes a problem when the powerful actually lack true wisdom, because one foolish voice in a place of power can destroy much good.

In God's economy, it is not the voice of the masses that we need to hear, but the quiet voice of wisdom that the world tries to drown out with its shouts of foolishness. The popular school of thought is seldom the wisdom of God. In these postmodern times, we need to guard our hearts and minds when we hear the world sounding the alarm of its definitions of right and wrong and its views of success.

So as you are bombarded today by the media's shouts of "This is what success wears," "This is where success lives," or "This is how success eats and drinks," treat it like you would a car alarm. Most of the time, it is nothing more than a cultural annoyance, not a statement of significance. Or as Solomon described it, it's nothing more than the shout of a ruler of fools!

May 15

*When He saw their faith, He said to him, "Man, your sins are forgiven you." And
the scribes and the Pharisees began to reason, saying, "Who is this who speaks
blasphemies? Who can forgive sins but God alone?" But when Jesus perceived their
thoughts, He answered and said to them, "Why are you reasoning in your hearts?
Which is easier, to say, 'Your sins are forgiven you,' or to say, 'Rise up and walk'?
But that you may know that the Son of Man has power on earth to forgive sins" —
He said to the man who was paralyzed, "I say to you, arise, take up your bed, and go
to your house." Immediately he rose up before them, took up what he had been lying
on, and departed to his own house, glorifying God. And they were all amazed, and
they glorified God and were filled with fear, saying,
"We have seen strange things today!"*

— Luke 5:20–26

This is the man whose friends could find no way to get him to Jesus except
by lowering him through the roof. What great friends! But there is another
element to this story that may seem obscure at first but is actually essential to
capturing all that is here.

Jesus told the man his sins were forgiven, an act that only God can do,
as the scribes and Pharisees rightly reasoned among themselves. Although
they were correct, they missed the fact — or, more accurately, simply refused to
believe — that Jesus is God. But the subtlety we need to notice here is not with
the scribes and Pharisees, but with Jesus' command and the paralyzed man's
actions. Jesus forgave the man, and we might expect Jesus would say, "Leave
that rancid old bed behind and go your way!" But Jesus actually said, "Take
up your bed and go home."

What is significant about that? Well, here is what I believe Jesus basically
told the man: "I want you to carry your bed through town all the way home
so that all who see you will recognize you as the man who *was* paralyzed." In
short, Jesus said, "Take your past with you as a testimony into your future."

Our past can be painful to remember, but it can also reveal to others the
glory of God. God allows nothing to go to waste, not even a rancid old bed
where a paralyzed man had lain for years. No, God used it for His glory.
Notice also that this was a direct command to this man from Jesus and is not
necessarily applicable to everyone. But to some of us, God has clearly issued
a command: "Use your past as a testimony to My power."

Maybe you feel as I did, that the past is rancid and better off left behind.
But listen for the Master's command, because He may want to use both what
you were and who you now are to reach others for His glory. He has done that
with me!

May 16

Then I heard a loud voice saying in heaven, "Now salvation, and strength, and the kingdom of our God, and the power of His Christ have come, for the accuser of our brethren, who accused them before our God day and night, has been cast down. And they overcame him by the blood of the Lamb and by the word of their testimony, and they did not love their lives to the death. Therefore rejoice, O heavens, and you who dwell in them! Woe to the inhabitants of the earth and the sea! For the devil has come down to you, having great wrath, because he knows that he has a short time."

— Revelation 12:10–12

Satan is a jerk! Imagine his nerve, accusing us before God day and night — you and me, of all people! The fact is, we often think of the enemy telling lies about us to God, when the reality is, he doesn't have to. He simply takes our sins and failures before the Lord and accuses us with the truth. But thanks be to God, for we have at the right hand of the Father an intercessor (Heb. 7:25), Jesus Christ the righteous, who with every accusation of the enemy says to the Father, "Overcome by My blood"!

Because our sins have been overcome by the blood of the Lamb, we are targets of the enemy, and he increases his wrath against us. But as Revelation 12:12 says, it is but for a short time. I believe this is twofold in its application. For some, the devil's harassment may be the vapor of this life, but for one generation in particular, it means increased attacks because the enemy knows his days are numbered. I believe we are living in that time, the short time before the Lord's coming for His bride and the ensuing hell on earth that will follow, a time known as the Great Tribulation.

We have all heard the question posed, would there be enough evidence to convict you of being a Christian? I like that, but I must also ask a deeper question: if Christians were being arrested, would anyone come looking for you? I have often said, "In God's army, there is no Secret Service," meaning we are all on the front lines. Are you ready for the all-out assault of the enemy? Are you ready to overcome by the blood of the Lamb and the word of your testimony, not loving your life even unto death?

It might sound like the plot of a movie script, but this is a divinely foretold reality of life in the last days. Be bold in your faith in these last days, and love not your life, even as you see the enemy's attacks on Christianity increasing. Jesus the righteous is on your side, and the devil... well, he is a jerk!

May 17

Watch, stand fast in the faith, be brave, be strong.
Let all that you do be done with love.

—1 Corinthians 16:13–14

Nothing to it, right? If we were to read this directly from the Greek text, it would read, "Be vigilant, stationary in the faith, acting manly and empowered, with love." We, especially men, might think, *Vigilant, stationary, acting like a man who is empowered... with love? What is that? Isn't love our soft and gooey side and the other stuff the manly side?* If you are tempted to think this way, you must have never encountered a mother in defense of her children, "mama bears," I call them. These fearless, vigilant women seem to possess superpowers and stand ready to take on anyone who might harm their children.

This was the heart of Paul's exhortation to the church at Corinth. The Corinthian church was surrounded by paganism and philosophy, carnality and promiscuity, and was struggling to be what God had ordained it to be in the first mostly Gentile church of the first century. Paul was describing the actions and motives needed in such a setting.

It is love that transforms ordinary moms into mama bears. It is love that makes them immoveable and empowered and even willing to take on all comers on behalf of those they love. The interesting thing is, they don't have to do anything other than love their children in order to have this kind of response.

In a similar fashion, it is our love for God that is the source of these actions in our lives. If we keep in mind His love for us, the cross that proved His love, and His presence in us that affirms His faithfulness, then when someone attacks Him or His name, we will be vigilant, stationary in the faith, and empowered by love.

So if you are wavering in your faith or succumbing to enemy assaults, try this: Run down the list of all that God has done for you, beginning with sending His Son to die for your sins. Think about all He has given you that you don't deserve, and think of all He hasn't given you that you do deserve. Remember the times you have failed and the mercies that awaited you the next morning. Consider that heaven is your future home and this world a temporary dwelling until you arrive in the Father's house.

Keep these things in mind and you will find your love for God has made you vigilant and stationary in the faith, and like a mama bear with superpowers, you will be emboldened because of what God has done for you!

May 18

Do not be unequally yoked together with unbelievers. For what fellowship has righteousness with lawlessness? And what communion has light with darkness? And what accord has Christ with Belial? Or what part has a believer with an unbeliever? And what agreement has the temple of God with idols? For you are the temple of the living God. As God has said: "I will dwell in them and walk among them. I will be their God, and they shall be My people."

—2 Corinthians 6:14–16

Some of life's greatest blessings are the relationships we develop, but it is also true that some relationships are not healthy for us and can even hinder our spiritual walks and cause a rift in our fellowship with God. Paul uses a very powerful word here as he addresses the issues the Corinthian church was battling both corporately and individually. Corporately, the church had invited philosophy and paganism into its practices. Personally, some Corinthian Christians were finding it difficult to let go of past activities common in their pagan culture, such as sexual immorality, the love of philosophy, and the exaltation of the musings of famous philosophers.

Many other Corinthian Christians, however, did not face this struggle at all, opting instead to just bring all their junk into their newfound faith. Paul likens this practice to having communion with darkness, a comparison likely to grab at the heart of any Christian. Communion was and is a sacred rite, and by using the word here, Paul attempts to better define our interpersonal relationships.

As Christians, we must assess our relationships with those around us. We can have *communion* with other believers, but we can only have *ministry* with those who are not believers. There is a vast difference between the two. Paul reminds the church that past practices and relationships must be measured in accordance with Christian responsibility. Do not have communion when you are supposed to have ministry, and do not seek fellowship in places that you have been called out of.

In the next two verses of 2 Corinthians, Paul reminds the church of the words found in Isaiah and 2 Samuel : "Come out from among them and be separate, says the Lord. Do not touch what is unclean, and I will receive you" (v. 17). And, "I will be a Father to you, and you shall be My sons and daughters, says the LORD Almighty" (v. 18). Ignoring this one principle of Scripture by being yoked to a nonbeliever in a romantic or business relationship has caused more heartache and led to the stumbling of more Christians than I care to remember.

Examine your relationships to see if you are having fellowship where you ought to be having ministry. Are there places of darkness where you are not being light? Jesus said we are *the* light of the world (Matt. 5:14). We're it. But if we don't shine because we are in communion with darkness, we've fallen into the same trap as the Corinthians of allowing the world to influence us more than we influence the world. That's not the communion we should seek!

May 19

*With what shall I come before the L*ORD*, and bow myself before the High God? Shall I come before Him with burnt offerings, with calves a year old? Will the L*ORD *be pleased with thousands of rams, ten thousand rivers of oil? Shall I give my firstborn for my transgression, the fruit of my body for the sin of my soul? He has shown you, O man, what is good; and what does the L*ORD *require of you but to do justly, to love mercy, and to walk humbly with your God?*

—Micah 6:6–8

One of my many pet peeves—and I have a few—is when someone from my past says something about me having "found religion" or that they heard I had become "religious." According to *Merriam-Webster's Collegiate Dictionary,* the word *religion* is defined as "a personal set or institutionalized system of religious attitudes, beliefs, and practices." Though there are attitudes, beliefs, and practices we need to adhere to, that's not what God requires of us. Micah says the Lord requires that we do justly, love mercy, and walk humbly with our God.

Have you ever been around one of those people who make you careful of what you say or do, someone of great respect or importance that you want to make a good impression on? If you are sharing a meal with such a person, you carefully monitor the way you eat and the way you sit. You are on your best behavior and worry about having a piece of lettuce stuck to your front tooth when talking. Or maybe you have been around one of those people who just make you want to be and do better. I am sure we have all had those kinds of encounters.

Micah says what God really wants from us is for us to walk with Him and love what He loves—not observe a bevy of religious requirements. But we so often overcomplicate things and, like the Israelites, add all kinds of stuff to just walking with God.

What does the Lord require of you today? Just to walk with Him, which is quite humbling when you are just and merciful like Him. Don't get all religious today, but just walk humbly in your relationship with Jesus. He wants to walk with you too!

May 20

See, I have inscribed you on the palms of My hands; your walls are continually before Me.

—Isaiah 49:16

The walls the Lord speaks of here are walls of protection, and this means that our protection is a continual concern to the Lord. I like that! That means that what Isaiah wrote a few chapters later about the weapons formed against us not prospering (Isa. 54:17) is true, because God has put a hedge of protection around us. We know the enemy never stops firing his fiery darts at us, but there is an unseen wall of protection surrounding us.

Some might be thinking, *Then why do bad things happen to God's people? Why do some darts make it through if God's wall of protection is always around us?* I do not know, nor does anyone else, why God sometimes allows pain, sorrow, or even tragedy into the life of a believer, but this I do know: the fiery dart of the second death will never penetrate the walls of the true believer. How do I know this? Because we are inscribed on the palms of the hands of our great God and Savior, Jesus Christ!

The one thing that all people ought to fear, death, can never come near us. We can never be separated from the love of God, even through death. God has us in His hands today, and our protection is continually before Him. He will never leave us nor forsake us, (Heb. 13:5), and He upholds us by His righteous right hand (Isa. 41:10). How do we know this for sure?

Nail prints.

The cross is your guarantee of protection from the second death, and nothing can change that. You have been inscribed on the palms of His hands. Someone else needs to know this today, so tell them and watch what the Lord will do for them and through you!

May 21

*And you shall remember the LORD your God, for it is He who gives you power to get
wealth, that He may establish His covenant which He swore to your fathers,
as it is this day.*

—Deuteronomy 8:18

I love the story of the man who invited his rude, brusque boss home for dinner. True to form, the boss was short and abrupt throughout the meal, puffed up with self-importance and showing little appreciation for all that the man's wife had done in preparation for the dinner. As the meal went on, the couple's young son continually stared at his dad's pompous boss. Irritated, the boss finally blurted out to the little boy, "Son, why do you keep staring at me?" to which the boy replied, "My daddy says you're a self-made man." In return, the boss puffed out his chest and replied with a smirk, "Well, your daddy's right. I am!" Puzzled, the boy looked at the boss and said, "Then why'd you make yourself like that?"

I have often wondered what the angels must think as they interact with those the Lord has called His own. Privileged to see God in all His glory, they yet, as Hebrews 1:14 says, minister to us who will inherit salvation. I wonder if we don't sometimes appear to them like the boss did to the little boy. I wonder if perhaps they look at us and ask themselves, *Why do they act like that?*

In Deuteronomy 8, the Lord reminded Israel that which James told the church: "Every good and perfect gift comes from above" (James 1:17). To take credit for anything good that comes into your life is like taking credit for breathing. If you possess a strong mind to understand great things, you got it from God. If you are blessed with a strong back that enables you to carry great loads, you got it from God. If you benefit from a great will and determination to better yourself and the world, that's right, you got it from God.

It is the Lord God who gives us power—period. Pride and pompousness are such ugly things, and we all know and recognize those traits quickly—in others. But let's make sure we are not the ones puffed up with pride, for the fact of the matter is, whatever we have or whatever good we have done, God gets the credit because He is the one who gave us the power to accomplish it. Whether we have gained wealth or become a teacher, an athlete, a financial advisor, a sanitation engineer, or a domestic princess (the toughest job of all), to God be the glory for the great things He has done!

God made a covenant with you and me through His Son, and it was established on the cross of Christ. So let's face today with hearts of thanksgiving, not self-importance. And remember, anything we can do is because of God alone!

May 22

Now Jericho was securely shut up because of the children of Israel; none went out, and none came in. And the LORD said to Joshua: "See! I have given Jericho into your hand, its king, and the mighty men of valor. You shall march around the city, all you men of war; you shall go all around the city once. This you shall do six days. And seven priests shall bear seven trumpets of rams' horns before the ark. But the seventh day you shall march around the city seven times, and the priests shall blow the trumpets. It shall come to pass, when they make a long blast with the ram's horn, and when you hear the sound of the trumpet, that all the people shall shout with a great shout; then the wall of the city will fall down flat. And the people shall go up every man straight before him."

—Joshua 6:1–5

I love this story for multiple reasons. First of all, it's just a cool story. Second, it features the great field general for Moses, the second in command to the hero of Israel, now in charge of the nation and leading it into the Promised Land. What a moment!

The first encounter in the land the Lord had given to Israel was to take place in the city of Jericho. Spies had already been sent in, and they had established connection on the inside with Rahab. In chapter 5, Joshua had a private briefing with the Lord Jesus Himself, and everything was set in place for the battle.

The armed men and rear guard standing ready, Joshua now gathered the priests and all the people. I'm sure a hush fell over the crowd as Joshua lifted his hand and said, "Here's the plan. We're going to march around the city once a day for six days, seven times on the seventh day, and then at the end of the seventh lap on the seventh day, we're going to blow the trumpets and yell! What do you guys think?" (A little liberty taken here for effect!) But do you know what Joshua and the children of Israel did? Exactly what the Lord had commanded! And when they did, the walls of Jericho tumbled down, and the first city in the Promised Land was theirs.

Far too often we want the will of God to make sense to us before we move ahead in obedience. *How can this plan work?* we think, or *Why do You want to do it like that, Lord, when my plans are to do it like this?* Too often we want God to show us the outcome before we take the first step; we want Him to prove His plan will work before we act on it. But God's ways are not ours; they are higher and past finding out (Job 9:10).

So if the plan doesn't make sense to you or seems a bit unorthodox, remember that the Lord your Maker thinks and does things beyond belief as a normal course of action every single day. If God has told you to do something a little unusual or if the outcome of it seems iffy, just do what the Lord says and leave the rest up to Him. His ways are not ours, but they are always better!

May 23

Death and life are in the power of the tongue, and those who love it will eat its fruit.

—Proverbs 18:21

It is often a tragic and sorrowful thing to see the truth of this proverb at work. A child who is never praised, a wife who is beaten down with words, and a man who is never encouraged in his efforts all produce individuals who are alive on the outside but dead on the inside. What a sad thing, and it's all because of someone's use of words.

Have you ever encountered one of those people who are always building up others with a word of hope or encouragement? I had that privilege with a rather well-known pastor. I have read much of what he has written, listened to hours of his teaching, and have greeted him multiple times at conferences and other events. But he impacted me most by a few brief moments we shared just talking one-on-one.

In that brief encounter, I learned a lot, and I left that conversation with a deeper understanding of the power and importance of words. To this day, I remember his words to me, though they were spoken many years ago. This man, whom God continues to use greatly, said some unexpected things to me. He remarked how greatly God was using me, asked if he could pray for me, and commented favorably on our facility, the people of our congregation, and the wonderful things he had heard about our church.

Humbled by his kind words, I realized there was no ulterior motive behind them. The man had nothing to gain from me; his ministry was not going to be advanced by his encounter with me or by puffing me up with compliments. Dumbstruck, I realized, *This is who this man is!* He is an encourager, a man who has chosen to speak life with his tongue rather than the death of discouragement. And I have to say, I enjoyed the fruit of it that day.

I haven't seen this man in almost a decade, but I sure wouldn't mind running in to him again. I have never forgotten his encouraging words, and in turn, I left that encounter with the desire to speak unexpected encouragement to others as had been spoken to me.

Encourage someone unexpectedly today. You'll be blessed, and they're going to love it!

May 24

Ah, Lord God! Behold, You have made the heavens and the earth by Your great power and outstretched arm. There is nothing too hard for You.

—Jeremiah 32:17

One of my favorite realizations about the majesty of God is that to Him, every problem is the same size. They are nothing! There are no big problems or major dilemmas for God. There are no situations where He needs to strategize and formulate a plan. He made the heaven and the earth, and nothing is too hard for Him. Great words of reminder on any day!

Even more interesting is that these words were written when Jerusalem was under siege by the Babylonians and Jeremiah was shut up in the court of the prison. The Lord said that neither the king of Judah nor the city of Jerusalem would be able to stand before Nebuchadnezzar and his armies. King Zedekiah would fight against the Chaldeans but would not succeed, and Jerusalem would be overthrown.

With all this as a backdrop, the Lord then told Jeremiah to buy a piece of property in this land that was about to be overthrown and to secure the deed in an earthen vessel that it might last for many days. Why did God want Jeremiah to do such a thing? Because God had promised that one day the people would return to the land, though for now the land would be overrun by the Babylonians because of the backsliding children of Israel and their worship of false gods.

There is a promised land that has been purchased for us as well by the blood of Jesus, and though it appears as though our land has been overrun with pagan Babylonians, God has promised His return! Thus, like Jeremiah, we can know that all our problems, whether big or small, global or individual, are the same size to God. There is nothing too hard for Him!

Invest in that promised land today. Sow seeds of truth in others, and share the good news of the Lord's soon return. Jeremiah didn't say, "What's the use in investing in a land soon to be overrun by our enemies?" He just said, "God made the heavens and the earth, and that tells me there is nothing too hard for Him." That's a great attitude to have, so why not make it your own today!

May 25

Nebuchadnezzar spoke, saying to them, "Is it true, Shadrach, Meshach, and Abed-
Nego, that you do not serve my gods or worship the gold image which I have set up?
Now if you are ready at the time you hear the sound of the horn, flute, harp, lyre,
and psaltery, in symphony with all kinds of music, and you fall down and worship
the image which I have made, good! But if you do not worship, you shall be cast
immediately into the midst of a burning fiery furnace. And who is the god who will
deliver you from my hands?" Shadrach, Meshach, and Abed-Nego answered and
said to the king, "O Nebuchadnezzar, we have no need to answer you in this matter.
If that is the case, our God whom we serve is able to deliver us from the burning
fiery furnace, and He will deliver us from your hand, O king. But if not, let it be
known to you, O king, that we do not serve your gods, nor will we worship the gold
image which you have set up."

—Daniel 3:14–18

In yesterday's devotional, we read the words of Jeremiah declaring nothing is too hard for God, and here we see those words in action. At the time of this passage, Israel had been conquered, their brightest and finest young men carried away captive to Babylon and trained in the ways of the Babylonians in order to serve in King Nebuchadnezzar's court.

But the king asked the men of Israel to do the very thing that had led to Jerusalem's destruction: bow to an idol. Shadrach, Meshach, and Abed-Nego, along with Daniel, were truly of the brightest and best of Israel because they knew something about their God that Nebuchadnezzar didn't. They knew their God could certainly deliver them from the furnace, but even if He didn't, He was still the only God worthy to be praised or bowed to.

We do not have to bow to the world's demands, friends. Their demands for us to relinquish the exclusive claims of the Christian message must never be obeyed. Our response must be the same as was the response of the three Hebrew boys to Nebuchadnezzar: "We have no need to answer you, for you can do nothing to us apart from God's will. God can deliver from the flame, or He can deliver from this life by the flame. Either way, we're not bowing!"

Now that's living what you say you believe! The world is asking us to bow to many things today, to allow some latitude in what we believe. We are urged to be more tolerant and encouraged to coexist and acknowledge that one person's truth is as valid as another's. But God calls this idolatry — even spiritual adultery. We have no need to answer these things other than by serving our God who is able to deliver, whether from death or through death. Our God alone is the only one we must bow before!

May 26

For the grace of God that brings salvation has appeared to all men, teaching us that, denying ungodliness and worldly lusts, we should live soberly, righteously, and godly in the present age, looking for the blessed hope and glorious appearing of our great God and Savior Jesus Christ, who gave Himself for us, that He might redeem us from every lawless deed and purify for Himself His own special people, zealous for good works.

—Titus 2:11–14

One of the elements of the grace of God that is often ignored is that grace is a practical truth, not just a positional one. *Saved by grace* is a positional truth, but *taught by grace* is a practical truth. Titus reminds us that grace does both: it brings salvation, and it teaches transformation.

If you look at the use of the Greek word *charis*, which translated means "graciousness," you will always find that its use in Scripture refers to the grace to do something. Here in our text, it refers to bringing and teaching; in 2 Corinthians 12:9, to being sufficient; in Galatians 1:15, to calling into ministry; in Romans 5:2, to granting access; and the list goes on of the actions associated with God's grace.

So, in addition to being saved by grace, we are also taught, called, and moved by God's grace. In Romans 12:6–10, Paul wrote, "Having then gifts differing according to the grace that is given to us, *let us use them*: if prophecy, *let us prophesy* in proportion to our faith; or ministry, *let us use it* in our ministering; he who teaches, in teaching; he who exhorts, in exhortation; he who gives, with liberality; he who leads, with diligence; he who shows mercy, with cheerfulness" (emphasis added).

Paul explained to Titus that grace is active in bringing salvation and also teaches transformation through repentance. Paul told the Romans that grace enables the saints through the gifts of the Spirit to carry out the plan of God.

Walk in grace today, both positionally and practically. The positional brings assurance, while the practical calls to action. Let the grace of God be alive in you today as grace empowers you to carry out the will of God for your life!

May 27

*The L*ORD* is slow to anger and great in power, and will not at all acquit the wicked.*
*The L*ORD* has His way in the whirlwind and in the storm,*
and the clouds are the dust of His feet.

—Nahum 1:3

Nahum is listed as a minor prophet in the Old Testament, but this minor prophet certainly had a major message and ministry! Though little is known about him outside of the three chapters of his prophetic book, we might say that he had a follow-up ministry. One hundred years earlier, a man named Jonah had preached to the same city to whom Nahum now addressed his words: Nineveh, the capital of Assyria.

Jonah had reluctantly preached a message of impending judgment to this "exceedingly great city" (Jon. 3:3) that would come in forty days unless the people repented, which they did. An entire city, from the king to the slave, repented, and God relented of the disaster intended for this cruel and carnal city. But in the span of a century, Nineveh reverted to its former evil, and the Lord had to send a follow-up counselor, Nahum, to call the people to repentance once again. But sadly, this time it was to no avail.

There is a great lesson for us today in the way Nahum opened his prophecy by highlighting the majesty and righteousness of God. He eloquently described God as "slow to anger" and "great in power," unwilling to acquit the wicked; yet we know He was willing to send His own Son to die for us that we might be delivered.

We live in an evil time, dear friends, and we must remember the majesty and righteousness of our God, even and especially when the world around us is unwilling to repent. God is righteous, and His justice will not sleep forever. Our magnificent God has His way in the whirlwind and in the storm, and the clouds are the dust of His feet. It is my conviction from the Holy Scriptures that our Lord is coming soon. May His majesty be our comfort and His justice our motivation to preach even to exceedingly great cities caught up in exceedingly great evil.

We may not know much about this minor prophet Nahum, but what we do know is enough. He dared speak of the greatness and justice of our God to a city not interested in his message. Take heart, my friends, as you serve the Lord in these perilous times. Be faithful to proclaim His greatness, for we do this for His glory, whether people receive it or not.

May 28

This is the word of the Lord *to Zerubbabel: "Not by might nor by power, but by My Spirit," says the* Lord *of hosts.*

— Zechariah 4:6

Zechariah lived and prophesied during the seventy-year Babylonian captivity of the children of Israel that had been prophesied by Jeremiah. Interestingly, though they had brought this season of slavery upon themselves by their idolatry, carnality, and forsaking of the Sabbath for 490 years, God still sent them a prophet. Such is the nature of God.

Another interesting note is that the prophet the Lord sent to Israel in their captivity was a man named Zechariah, whose name means "Yahweh remembers." Zechariah's prophecy is rich not only with messianic references but also with promises of renewal and a rebuilt temple, the millennial reign of Christ on earth, and the holy city of Jerusalem as home to His throne. This is the message the Israelites received while under the dominion and oppression of the greatest empire the world had ever known.

So what was the word of the Lord to Zerubbabel, the governor of the first group of returning exiles to Jerusalem, as he wondered what God would do? *How, Lord, is this going to turn around? We're slaves, outside our own land, separated from our families and friends. How, God, are we ever going to get out of this mess?* had to be running through Zerubbabel's mind. God answered him through Zechariah: "It's not your might or power, but My Spirit, that will deliver you!"

Though we all know the Spirit works on our behalves, there is one part of that wonderful truth we all struggle with, and that is, we can't see the Holy Spirit. Over the years, however, I have shared with many people a wonderful truth the Lord has often reminded me of: you don't have to see progress in order for God to be working.

Do you know a captive, love a captive, or maybe even are married to a captive of this world? Don't give up hope. Yahweh remembers, and human might and power are unnecessary when the unseen Spirit of God is at work!

May 29

Now when they saw the boldness of Peter and John, and perceived that they were uneducated and untrained men, they marveled. And they realized that they had been with Jesus.

— Acts 4:13

I am amazed at some of the dumb things smart people believe. For example, many embrace evolution, a scientific impossibility, as though their eternal destination rested on believing it. Other people insist on calling an unborn baby a blob of tissue, though a five-year-old could read an ultrasound of a woman five months pregnant and see a baby. Such people are among those groups who say, "There is no God."

Peter and John were not trained in the rabbinical schools and were unlearned in the estimation of the scribes and Pharisees, but the game changer for them was simple: they had been with Jesus. If that too is our reputation in the world, then we have indeed done well. Even in an age of mockery and intolerance of all things Christian, the highest compliment we can receive is when someone says, "You're one of those born again Christians, aren't you?" No matter how it may be intended, the truth behind those words is that someone can tell when we've been with Jesus.

It is time for boldness and confidence in sharing our message, and it is time to stop being ashamed of the gospel. Remember, a high IQ doesn't make people wise; it just makes them smart, and smart people can be duped into some really dumb beliefs. Knowing Jesus is what makes us wise and exposes foolishness for what it is.

But the reality is, the world's perception of Christians is still much like that of the Pharisees' opinion of Peter and John. When we are bold for Christ, many in the world will derisively say, "Oh, they're uneducated and untrained. They don't know any better than to believe in God and all the propositions of the Bible, including creation and the sanctity of human life."

Let them think what they may, friends. If they can see that we've been with Jesus, then we have done well, no matter their opinion of us. After all, it's who is right in the end that really matters, and if others can see we've been with Jesus, we'll be the smart ones in the end.

Be bold today, and let the world know you have been with Jesus!

May 30

The woman then left her waterpot, went her way into the city, and said to the men, "Come, see a Man who told me all things that I ever did. Could this be the Christ?"

—John 4:28–29

I love the story of the woman at the well for many reasons. First, Jesus was talking to a Samaritan, whom the Jews despised; plus, he was talking with a woman about spiritual things, which was not done in that day. I also like the things Jesus spoke to her about: living water and the worship of the Father in spirit and truth. There are so many other wonderful portraits painted for us in this exchange between Jesus and the Samaritan woman.

The verses above may not be the first that usually come to mind when you recount this story, but they are two of my favorite because they record an aspect of the exchange we often miss. The woman told the men of her town, "Come, see a Man who told me all the things that I ever did." Now we know this statement was not entirely factual; the woman was old enough to have been married five times (v. 18), so the conversation would have had to last days to cover her entire life. I believe the heart of the woman's statement was actually something like this: "Come see a man who told me all the things that continually plague me."

In the first century, a woman like the Samaritan woman would have been the talk of the town. A woman of "reputation," she would surely have regrets from her lifelong pattern of poor decisions and immorality. Jesus spoke directly to these problems, not with condemnation, but with hope and an offer of living water.

Second Corinthians 5:17 is an appropriate reminder here: "Therefore, if anyone is in Christ, he is a new creation; old things have passed away; behold, all things have become new." This is what happens for all of us who believe in Christ, and it is a truth worthy of remembrance every day. We met a Man who knew all that we had ever done but loved us anyway, a Man who put away our old things and gave us living water in place of the dead past.

Jesus died for all the bad things you and I did. I am sure that if we kept this in mind continually, we would find ourselves, much like the woman at the well, compelled to tell someone else to come and meet this Man.

Invite someone to meet Jesus today, remembering He died for all you ever did!

May 31

For since the creation of the world His invisible attributes are clearly seen, being understood by the things that are made, even His eternal power and Godhead, so that they are without excuse.

—Romans 1:20–21

At one time or another, each of us has pondered this question: what happens to people who have never heard the gospel or heard of Jesus? Romans provides an answer by saying creation itself gives testimony to God and His eternal power and Godhead, which speaks of the Trinity.

We do know that knowledge creates responsibility and that God is just and fair. We also know that since the beginning of recorded history, man has formulated thoughts about the universe and its order and man's origins. It is always on man's mind that there must be purpose in all the perfection and order seen in the heavens and on the earth.

Creation itself reveals the attributes of God. His majesty, His order, His omniscience (all-knowing), and His omnipotence (all-powerful) have been visible since the beginning of time. It's no wonder that creation is under such attack from the enemy. God is revealed in creation, so Satan tries to create a race of fools who say, "There is no God" (Ps. 14:1). If there is no God, then there can be no creation and vice versa; the two concepts go hand in hand.

The true heart of the matter is that many do not want to acknowledge a creator and therefore deny that He can be seen in creation. To acknowledge God as the Creator would mean He has rights over His creation, including defining how His created beings ought to live. This is the heart of the issue and explains how some can reject the evidence clearly seen in creation. Our worry need not be the tribal people in jungle areas of the earth; our concern needs to be for those all around us who are buying into the lie that there is no God even while creation itself is screaming, "There is a God in heaven!"

Everything the Bible records surrounding the events of creation are still happening today. Animals are still procreating after their kinds, the hydrologic cycle is still in order, the moon still controls the boundaries of the seas, and women are still bringing forth children with pain. All the things God set in place are still in place, and that is the only truly scientific conclusion that can be drawn if the facts are honestly examined.

"In the beginning God created" is declared every time the sun rules the day and the moon the night. God will care for the isolated tribal people and has indeed revealed Himself through creation. It's those among us we need to be more concerned about, for the knowledge they have is what they will give an account for in the end!

June 1

Finally, my brethren, be strong in the Lord and in the power of His might. Put on the whole armor of God, that you may be able to stand against the wiles of the devil. For we do not wrestle against flesh and blood, but against principalities, against powers, against the rulers of the darkness of this age, against spiritual hosts of wickedness in the heavenly places. Therefore take up the whole armor of God, that you may be able to withstand in the evil day, and having done all, to stand.

— Ephesians 6:10–12

Following this powerful reminder that we are engaged in a spiritual battle is a specific list of the things we are to put on as part of the armor of God. These things allow the Christian to enter the spiritual battlefield fully prepared to meet the enemy's challenges. Sadly, however, far too many Christians walk onto the battlefield only half-dressed. They foolishly venture into the arena without the sword of the Spirit, which is the Word of God (v. 17), and without prayer (v. 18). They even leave behind the shield of faith (v. 16), though it is the very thing needed to quench the fiery darts of the enemy.

Today the enemy will engage you somewhere in the arena of your life. So get dressed before you go out! Paul says twice to put on the whole armor against the unseen spiritual realm of wicked angels and demonic spirits warring against you. You cannot afford to go out half-dressed. A football player would not step onto the field without pads or uniform, and no batter would step into the batter's box without a bat. Hockey players, however, will do anything, so we'll leave them out of our illustration, but you get the point!

Here's another thing. You can't choose not to be in the battle; the enemy is coming at you whether you want to fight or not, whether you have all your armor on or not. Remember, Satan is wicked; he cheats and lies and doesn't fight fair. He kicks us when we're down, stabs us in the back, takes advantage of our weak moments, and loves to see us fall. And most of us who do fall are only half-dressed or even spiritually naked.

Put on the whole armor, and take up the shield of faith. Fiery darts are coming, whether you are ready for them or not. May as well be ready!

June 2

But I will tarry in Ephesus until Pentecost. For a great and effective door has opened to me, and there are many adversaries.

— 1 Corinthians 16:9

Much like yesterday's reading, today's devotional has Paul pairing ministry and adversity almost as casually as though one is never found without the other. That's because one is never found without the other!

I have to say, though, I have encountered far too many Christians over the years who have said that the reason they did certain things was that they "had a peace about it." My standard reply to that is always "Peace is not a fleece." The peace that the Bible promises is a peace experienced *during* adversity, not in the absence of it.

Paul reminds us here in 1 Corinthians 16 that open doors are always opposed. Failure to understand this has stifled more Christian progress than any other tactic of the enemy. Too many Christians want everything to be perfect, with no ripples in the water and a peace in their hearts (meaning they feel good about it), before they will walk through a door of opportunity. But the fact is, we are going to encounter adversity anytime God is guiding us into what He wants us to do and where He wants us to go. So there must be more to moving forward with Him than just having peace about a decision or a direction.

Great and effective doors of opportunity provoke many adversaries. Rather than using "I feel good about this and have peace" as a guiding principle, the more suitable litmus test is "Can any amount of opposition keep me from doing what God has put in my heart?" If the absence of adversity is your litmus test or having peace is your guide, it is very unlikely that the door you are considering walking through is either great or effective.

When a Christian tells me, "I am not sure what to do. Things keep popping up, and a million things seem to be standing in the way," I know that person is likely standing on the threshold of a great and effective door. Even in the midst of all the adversity, a quiet knowing resides inside of them, assuring them that this is the will of God.

That is what a friend of mine calls "stupid peace." It just doesn't make any sense to others around you, but you have it nonetheless. That is the peace that passes understanding, and no amount of adversity can take it away. Great and effective doors are often identified by adversity — not by feeling peace!

June 3

He has made everything beautiful in its time. Also He has put eternity in their hearts, except that no one can find out the work that God does from beginning to end.

— Ecclesiastes 3:11

It is amazing what a tiny seed planted in the dirt and nourished with a little water can produce in time. From the majestic oak tree to the beautiful orchid, from the coffee bean to the banana bunch, all begin with a tiny seed and dirt. But in time, what wonderful things result.

In Ecclesiastes 3, Solomon ponders these wonders, noting that such a process has to be from God. To transform things once ugly and dirty into things majestic and beautiful can only be the work of the Lord.

The wondrous thing about this is that it applies to circumstances and trials in life as well. In time, God takes dark and ugly difficulties and produces beautiful things from them. I have seen Christian after Christian who has faced some of the most unbelievable difficulties in life become majestic oaks of faith and beautiful orchids of hope in the lives of others facing similar trials.

Sometimes life hits you so hard it feels like you're lying in the dirt. Then, to add insult to injury, someone comes along and throws water on you. Now you're not just lying in the dirt, but you're lying in mud. But what magnificent things are produced through just such a scenario! In time, seed, dirt, and water produce an endless array of wonders when the gardener is God, whether in the physical world or in the spiritual.

Times of trial can be hard, lonely, and painful, and we often face them alone. But in time, something beautiful can come from even the darkest of trials. I cannot tell you how many times I have seen a woman wounded early in life by the horrific tragedy of sexual trauma provide comfort to another who has encountered the same thing. In time, one's person's pain became another person's comfort, even if only in the sense of providing the knowledge that someone else knows what it feels like to be hurt in such a way.

Like Solomon, I don't know how God achieves the end results that He brings forth from some people's beginnings, but I have seen Him do it too many times to doubt it. God makes everything beautiful in its time. This is a great truth to embrace today.

June 4

Create in me a clean heart, O God, and renew a steadfast spirit within me. Do not cast me away from Your presence, and do not take Your Holy Spirit from me. Restore to me the joy of Your salvation, and uphold me by Your generous Spirit.

— Psalm 51:10–12

If you're like me, you probably have some favorite Bible verses of difference-making truths that mean so much to you on a personal level. This section from Psalm 51 is one of mine. That God can take a dark, cold heart and transform it into a clean one is a truth worth visiting every day. The assurance of His presence, the possibility of restored joy, and the impossibility of a lost salvation are truths that we need to ponder frequently in our hearts and minds.

These are powerful words indeed from a man who had just been confronted with his sin. King David wrote this from a dark place and moment in his life after being confronted by Nathan about his adulterous affair with Bathsheba and his murderous heart in trying to cover his sin. After all his hiding and rationalizing, David finally came face-to-face with himself and acknowledged his need for the creative power of God in his life.

The content of this psalm in particular records one of the reasons, I believe, that God described David as a man after His own heart (1 Sam. 13:14). David finally arrived at a place where we must all arrive, and that is to see the futility of rationalizing and justifying sinful behavior. He finally allowed himself to be broken before the Lord and to seek a re-created heart, which is exactly the business of our great and awesome God.

Much like David, I have found it refreshing and restoring to face my failures and ask God to fix them. But also like David, I have sometimes lived in denial. When I have refused to face my failures or acted as though I had done nothing wrong, the loss of the joy of salvation became my sure companion.

So whatever it is, confess it, ask God to repair and re-create your heart, and be on your way to restored joy. This is the heart of God, and we are to be people after God's own heart.

June 5

For Jews request a sign, and Greeks seek after wisdom; but we preach Christ crucified, to the Jews a stumbling block and to the Greeks foolishness, but to those who are called, both Jews and Greeks, Christ the power of God and the wisdom of God.

—1 Corinthians 1:22–25

It seems the old adage "The more things change, the more they stay the same" would be a fitting summary of these verses today. The simple message of Jesus dying for your sins and mine is just that—simple. Yet some stumble over that fact, as did the Jews, thinking they don't need some dead carpenter's son to save them. They may be good moral people who try to obey the rules, but they do not see their need for a Savior. Others think, *How foolish! God takes on a human body so He can die for something He didn't do? Any rational person can see the folly in that.*

But the fact is, it really is as simple as Christ crucified. We are the ones who in response to the criticisms overcomplicate the message. We try to help the Bible out a little by engaging in debates and seeking to prove to others that what we believe is true. But our case is actually quite simple: we are all sinners, and we all need a Savior; and Jesus is the only one who meets the qualifications.

One of the reasons we want to push the process along a bit and add our own stuff to the mix is that we live in the "instant" age. We want everything now! Fast computers, fast food, quick fixes, and instant rewards are the norm in our day. But when we add our arguments into the mix of sharing the truth, we are trying to hasten the work that only the Holy Spirit can do. The truth is, as I have heard it said, we don't have to defend the Bible. It's like a lion; if we'll just let it out of the cage, it will fend for itself.

Don't overcomplicate the beautifully simple message of the gospel. Just tell someone today that Jesus is the answer to the emptiness they feel inside. He is the one who by His death filled the void created by sin and who therefore is the only way to heaven. Just let those words out of the cage and watch what they do in time.

The Holy Spirit always blesses His words, so don't entangle them with your own. Just share the simple truths of the Word of God, and then step aside and watch them work!

June 6

And the Lord said, "Simon, Simon! Indeed, Satan has asked for you, that he may sift you as wheat. But I have prayed for you, that your faith should not fail; and when you have returned to Me, strengthen your brethren."

—Luke 22:31–32

I can hardly imagine what it must have felt like for Peter to hear, "Satan has asked for you, that he may sift you like wheat." I also have to wonder if the next words were a bit of a knockout punch when Jesus first said, "but I have prayed for you," and then followed that with, "when you have returned to me." The impetuous Peter, hardly able to believe what he was hearing, boldly declared, "Lord, I am ready to go with You, both to prison and to death" (v. 33), to which Jesus somberly replied, "I tell you, Peter, the rooster shall not crow this day before you will deny three times that you know Me" (v. 34).

I'm sure Peter's heart must have thudded at these words, but there is also a wonderful truth we often miss in reading this account. Too often, in this case and in life, we focus on the words and actions of a person rather than on the words of the Lord. The beauty within this famous exchange is that Jesus prayed that Peter's faith would not fail before Peter's three denials; and since Jesus is incapable of praying outside the Father's will, this means Peter's denials did not cause his faith to utterly collapse.

At one time or another, we all have denied knowing the Lord through our actions or attitudes, and our accuser is always quick to make our hearts thud at the remembrance. But the Lord has prayed for us because He is our intercessor who sits at the right hand of majesty on high (Heb. 1:3).

Of course it is better not to ever deny the Lord, but it is also important to remember the full account of what happened here with Peter. The Lord said to Him, and I am paraphrasing, "Your faith will sustain you even through your denials, and when you return to Me, you will come back stronger than ever and will even strengthen your brethren." This means that God wastes nothing! He takes our doubts and denials, which the enemy uses to condemn and discourage us, and transforms them into areas of strength.

Church tradition tells us that later in life Peter not only refused to deny the Lord under threat of death but also requested to be crucified upside down, insisting he was not worthy to die in the same manner as the Lord. That sounds to me like a man whose faith had matured from weak to immoveable, just like Jesus had prayed.

Don't deny the Lord, friends, in anything. But if you do experience a moment of weakness and fear-based denial, return to Jesus and let Him turn your weakness into a magnificent strength.

June 7

The God of my strength, in whom I will trust; my shield and the horn of my salvation, my stronghold and my refuge; my Savior, You save me from violence. I will call upon the LORD, who is worthy to be praised; so shall I be saved from my enemies.

— 2 Samuel 22:3–4

The enemy David was referring to in this psalm was his boss, King Saul. To make matters worse, not only was King Saul his boss, but he was also his father-in-law. It has often been said we should keep our friends close, but our enemies even closer. But what do you do when a friend or family member is one and the same with your enemy? It is sad how often this is true, but it is exactly how Jesus said it would be in Matthew 10:36.

Saul hated David because he was jealous of the praise David had received for killing Goliath. The same is often true for us. Others sometimes hate us because of our confidence and courage in the God we trust, but when the hatred comes from a close friend or family member, the hurt is much greater and more difficult to bear.

David's situation was a little more literal than most of ours. King Saul had tried to pin him to the wall with a javelin on more than one occasion. Our situations are usually a little less life threatening and more pain related than anything else. I remember the pain my wife and I experienced early in our Christian life together as we endured the reactions of some of our loved ones to our commitment to Christ. To experience reactions like "I am glad you found something that helps you" or to watch relationships change within the family because you "got religion" is often painful to endure.

But like David, we too must continue to trust. Though others may not be trying to kill us, their reaction to our faith may cause us to feel like we are dying. We must know that God will see us through even this great pain and sorrow. If this is your testimony, then call upon the Lord, who is worthy to be praised! And continue to pray for the salvation of those who see your conversion as a crutch or maybe even think you are a fool. Praise will help elevate your heart from this painful time, just as it did for David.

One more side note here: This song of David's became a hymn in all Israel because, like David, his fellow Jews had to contend with many enemies, some of whom were among their families and friends. So keep singing your song of deliverance today, and let your praises deliver you from the enemy of discouragement and despair.

June 8

And not being weak in faith, he did not consider his own body, already dead (since he was about a hundred years old), and the deadness of Sarah's womb. He did not waver at the promise of God through unbelief, but was strengthened in faith, giving glory to God, and being fully convinced that what He had promised He was also able to perform. And therefore "it was accounted to him for righteousness."

— Romans 4:19–22

One of the amazing elements of this great story of faith is the marvelous way in which faith is defined. We are told that Abraham did not waver in faith, yet we know he "heeded the voice of his wife" (Gen. 16:2) and engaged in sexual relations with Hagar in hopes of producing a child. Interestingly, the same phrase, "heeded the voice of his wife," is also used to describe Adam's sin of partaking of the forbidden fruit.

So what does this have to do with defining faith? First of all, it tells us that faith is not just real when we are perfect. Faith is active in the lives of people who fail, people like you and me. The second element of faith revealed here, I believe, is a little more convicting—at least it is to me—and that is Abraham, though he made a dumb mistake, not only believed God *could* give him a son, but he also believed that God *would* give him a son.

Faith is believing, not just what God can do, but believing that He will do what He said He would do. This is why faith and the Word of God are inseparable. People today often try to put their faith in things God did not say in hopes of bringing them about. But as 2 Corinthians 1:20 says, "All the promises of God in Him are Yes, and in Him Amen, to the glory of God through us." Abraham had a direct promise from God, and when God makes a promise, it is as good as done. I have often said we need to remember that God's promises are true when they're said, not when they're seen.

Was God's promise validated the day Isaac was born? Not at all—God's promise was validated the moment He spoke it because it is not possible that God should lie (Titus 1:2). What this means to you and me is that we are free to live according to all God's promises, for in Jesus they are all yes and amen. Faith is not only believing God *can*, but it is also believing God *will* be faithful to His Word.

So if God tells a hundred-year-old man and a ninety-year-old woman they are going to have a child, that means it's time to start decorating the nursery! To all of us, it means we are free to live as though the promises of God's Word are as sure as the God who spoke them. So go out today and stand on the promises of God's Word—every one of them—for they were made to you and to me!

June 9

Ho! Everyone who thirsts, come to the waters; and you who have no money, come, buy and eat. Yes, come, buy wine and milk without money and without price. Why do you spend money for what is not bread, and your wages for what does not satisfy? Listen carefully to Me, and eat what is good, and let your soul delight itself in abundance.

—Isaiah 55:1–2

In Hebrew, *ho* is an exclamation of pity. In this passage from Isaiah, the exclamation and following figurative language are also very timely in our day. Isaiah is basically saying, "Why do you put so much effort into things that cannot satisfy when that which can satisfy your real need is something money cannot buy?"

In this excerpt, the words *wine* and *milk* are metaphors for satisfaction, and the invitation to "come to the waters" speaks of the joy of salvation. There are some things that money just can't buy, such as inner peace, joy, and certainly salvation. Nevertheless, many people today, even some Christians, have lives full of things, but souls that are empty. But Isaiah says to Israel, "Listen carefully to me; eat what is good and your soul will delight itself in abundance."

Have you ever met one of those people who could be described as a "happy soul"? That's the kind of person who just rolls with the punches, and nothing ever seems to bother him or her. Ever wish you were like that? Through Isaiah, God says that this kind of deep inner joy cannot be purchased, but it is a work that takes place deep in the soul in the realm in which only God can operate. However, the truth is, we try to cram all kinds of things into that area of emptiness or dissatisfaction, things that have no power to fill that inner void.

We also need to note that here in Isaiah peace does not come from the absence of effort, but rather from refocused effort. "Buy," "spend," and "eat" are already metaphors for our actions and pursuits, but if we expend our efforts on trying to fill the emptiness with anything other than God, we miss the mark. In effect, we try to do for ourselves what only God can do.

So don't seek fulfillment in the things of this life. Come to the only place where it can be found. Seeking and serving God will satisfy the need of your soul like nothing else can.

Do something to help someone in need today in the name and for the honor of Jesus and see how your soul feels at the end of the day. My guess is it will feel a delightful abundance that money cannot buy!

June 10

And I say to you, "My friends, do not be afraid of those who kill the body, and after that have no more that they can do. But I will show you whom you should fear: Fear Him who, after He has killed, has power to cast into hell; yes,
I say to you, fear Him!"

—Luke 12:4–5

We have all met people who seem to have an attitude that mirrors the bumper sticker of a few years back that read, "Heaven doesn't want me, and hell is afraid I'll take over!" But hell is no laughing matter, and to those who are always saying, "Don't judge me; Jesus said not to judge," I say that the words above are the words of Jesus Himself. According to His words, hell is not a concept or state of mind. It is the eternal home of the devil and his demons and all humans who reject God's only offer of salvation through His Son, Jesus Christ.

Hell is not a frequent topic in much of the postmodern church today. The sad fact is, no one seems to shudder at the concept anymore, and there is certainly little or no fear of hell. The consequences of this are catastrophic, to say the least. First of all, if Christians view hell as merely a description of life on earth without Jesus, then what is our eternal motivation to share the love of Christ? Second, if, as universalism teaches, heaven is the home of all humanity after some time in purgatory or an afterlife purification process, then we have added our suffering to Christ's suffering as a qualification for heaven and in effect made ourselves equal to Him.

Hell is no laughing matter and is to be feared! If God is going to purify and qualify all people for heaven apart from their acceptance of the work of the cross, then why the cross at all? Why would God take on human flesh, live a perfect life, and die a criminal's death but not have finished the work needed to save men's souls?

We have all heard or seen posed the question, WWJD, What Would Jesus Do? If Jesus were on the earth in a physical body today, I know what He would do. He would do just what He did the first time He was here: He would preach and warn us about hell!

Friends, this may not be something we like to hear, but it is something we need to hear and be ever mindful of. People who die without a personal relationship with Jesus Christ will spend eternity in hell. It is not up to us to judge whether that is right or wrong; we are not God. His Son was murdered brutally for our sins, and God is willing to forgive those whose sins sent Jesus to the cross. But He will not forgive those who reject or deny this as the only means of salvation. "Do not fear man, but fear God," is what Jesus is saying in today's passage. May that be our motivation for sharing the only hope for salvation today—the blood of Jesus Christ, shed for the sins of the world!

June 11

He has delivered us from the power of darkness and conveyed us into the kingdom of the Son of His love, in whom we have redemption through His blood, the forgiveness of sins.

—Colossians 1:13–14

Delivered from darkness and conveyed into the kingdom of the Son—what a great truth! But this is exactly the redemption we have through Jesus' blood. Positional statements such as these are great encouragements as we encounter the ebb and flow of daily existence. As good times and hard times roll onto the shores of our lives, the constant truth that we *have* been delivered and *have* redemption yet remains.

In today's passage, Paul employs the common symbolism of light and darkness as references to good and evil and reminds us that the power of darkness is no longer our master. The King James Version of the Bible uses the word *translated* in place of *conveyed* and gives a little better perspective. While *conveyed* might lead us to picture the thought of being on a conveyor and moving from one place to another, *translated* gives the impression of instantaneous deliverance, which is the proper perspective for this passage.

Darkness cannot rule us if we have been translated out of its kingdom and no longer dwell there. Think of it like this: Darkness can prevail only in the absence of light. When a light switch is turned on, the light immediately overpowers the darkness. The darkness cannot impose upon the light, and the room can grow dark again only in the absence of light.

This analogy helps us understand that the blood of Jesus gives us an instantaneous, permanent, and fixed position in His Kingdom and in His love. Here darkness cannot infringe, even when difficulty rolls like a wave onto the shores of our lives.

God is light, and in Him is no darkness at all. And you and I are in Him! This is the only way possible for us to be lights to the world. Shine for Him today. You have been translated into the kingdom of the Son of His love!

June 12

Lord, how they have increased who trouble me! Many are they who rise up against me. Many are they who say of me, "There is no help for him in God." Selah. But You, O Lord, are a shield for me, My glory and the One who lifts up my head. I cried to the Lord with my voice, and He heard me from His holy hill.

—Psalm 3:1–4

David wrote this bastion of truth while running from his own son Absalom, who sought to take his father's kingdom and life. David's "troublers," former friends and counselors, added to his pain by saying, "Not even God can help David now. Absalom will soon have him and his throne." By their words, these people revealed that they were friends of their positions, not true friends of the king. They would back whoever could best assure them of a continued place of power.

Not much has changed in three thousand years. There are still people who will turn their backs on their "friends" in a heartbeat if it will get them ahead. I cannot help but think of how wonderful heaven is gong to be, when writing of realities such as this. But David gives us some sound wisdom here about handling betrayal: remember who God is and what He has done for you.

I am sure we can all relate to David's experience in some form or fashion. Maybe someone we were close to, even a family member, turned on us, and we have added their name to the list of those who would trouble us. This is painful, to be sure, but David tells us how to treat this kind of pain. "Remember that the Lord is your shield, your glory, the one who lifts your head," he says. "So cry out to Him, for He hears you!"

Our Savior knows all too well the feeling that accompanies betrayal. So when faced with betrayal, rather than trying to reason with the betrayer (which we always want to do), cry out to the one who knows how it feels. Remember, He is your shield and your glory and always worthy of praise!

June 13

Grace and peace be multiplied to you in the knowledge of God and of Jesus our Lord, as His divine power has given to us all things that pertain to life and godliness, through the knowledge of Him who called us by glory and virtue, by which have been given to us exceedingly great and precious promises, that through these you may be partakers of the divine nature, having escaped the corruption that is in the world through lust.

—2 Peter 1:2-4

In a single day's devotional, there is no way to even begin to unfold all that is in these three verses. Nonetheless, just reading these verses ought to stir our hearts in thanksgiving for the grace and peace of God in our lives.

Peter opened his second epistle with the customary greeting of the day, "grace and peace," and then moved into how grace brings peace into our lives. His first reminder is that God's divine power has given us all things that pertain to life and godliness, but it is paired with the condition that these things come through the knowledge of Him. From Peter's epistle, we can easily see the importance of knowing the Word of God in order to know the God of the Word.

The Bible is a treasury of exceedingly great and precious promises, and to partake of them obviously demands that we know of them. It is the promises of the Word that give us insight in how to partake of the divine nature as we walk through this lust-filled, corrupt world.

One of the interesting things that many Christians seem to do is to conclude that the promises of God are specific to an elite group of saints and unattainable for the common Christian. Nothing could be further from the truth! Great men and women of the Word are no different from you and me. They simply know God's promises and live as though they are true.

When Peter says God has given "to us," he is referring to the church, the body of Christ—not the apostles. All things that pertain to life and godliness are expressed to us through Jesus Christ, and we—all of us—can be partakers of what Christ has done for us.

The promises of God are true for you today, and the Word of God has an endless supply of promises and truths to take as your own. That means you can have peace in knowing you have escaped this lust-filled and corrupt world, and you do not have to fall prey to temptation or distraction. Just know and remember the promises of God for you!

June 14

Yours, O LORD, is the greatness, the power and the glory, the victory and the majesty; for all that is in heaven and in earth is Yours; Yours is the kingdom, O LORD, and You are exalted as head over all. Both riches and honor come from You, and You reign over all. In Your hand is power and might; in Your hand it is to make great and to give strength to all.

—1 Chronicles 29:11–12

The words of a great king at the end of a forty-year reign as he passed the throne onto his son would be words to be heeded indeed. As King David stood before the leaders and nation of Israel at the coronation of his replacement, his son Solomon, he clearly assumed a reflective tone in his praise offering to God. Though he had lived forty years of highs and lows, victories and defeats, one thing had been constant through it all: God had been faithful. God had been faithful to correct, faithful to commend, and faithful to command. Not once had David been alone.

I am sure that as David spoke these words, he was awed by the fact of what he was doing and that his life was at it closing moments. But no matter the season of life, it is always good to look back at God's unchanging faithfulness and praise Him for it. I can look back in my life now and see that the twists and turns were actually from the leading hand of a faithful God. I would certainly not have chosen much of the means or the course that God chose, but now with a little water under the bridge (that's code for getting older), I can see the pattern of God's faithfulness woven through all the years.

Sometimes, when today is tough, a glance back at God's faithfulness helps the present from becoming too overwhelming. All that is in heaven and on the earth is the Lord's, and He reigns over all. When we look back or even look at the present, we may see that God has not done things the way we think He should have, but He was and is never wrong. He always does what is right and best.

If that is hard for you to believe right now, just take a look back and praise Him for all that you have gone through. At the time, you may have wished you did not have to walk through the difficulty, but the fact that you can look back now proves that He brought you through. In both the tragedies and the triumphs in your life, God has been there, and He has been faithful. So lift up your voice in praise, for greatness, power, and glory belong to the Lord!

June 15

Therefore, having these promises, beloved, let us cleanse ourselves from all filthiness of the flesh and spirit, perfecting holiness in the fear of God.

— 2 Corinthians 7:1

We can hardly venture forward in this text without first looking back to see what are the promises Paul is referencing. They are contained in verses 16 to 17 of chapter 6 of this same epistle: "For you are the temple of the living God. As God has said: 'I will dwell in them and walk among them. I will be their God, and they shall be My people.' Therefore 'Come out from among them and be separate,' says the Lord. 'Do not touch what is unclean, and I will receive you. I will be a Father to you, and you shall be My sons and daughters,' says the LORD Almighty."

In these verses from 2 Corinthians 6, Paul employed quotes from Leviticus 26:12; Jeremiah 32:38; Ezekiel 37:27; 20:34, 41; Isaiah 52:11; and 2 Samuel 7:14. In this way, he reminded the church, both then and now, of its direct connection to the Old Testament Scriptures and that they are not to be ignored or labeled as archaic and outdated. The promises of God laid out in these New Testament verses are filled with conditional truths that some today want to ignore or malign. But God makes us His people and then calls us out of darkness and into holiness. Paul takes the seven Old Testament references and categorizes them into two components: God's call and God's command.

Those whom God makes his own He also calls to come out from uncleanness, and He promises to receive them on this condition. I want to remind us all again that holiness is not works that lead to salvation, but evidence that salvation is at work. However, it is a sad truth today that the moral decay within the church nearly matches that of the world, and that is due, at least in part, to the absence of preaching repentance. Far too many today categorize repentance as works.

But Paul reminds us here that the promises include a call to repentance from all filthiness of the flesh and spirit, perfecting holiness in the fear of God. This is clearly both an inward and outward work, as the flesh and spirit are both mentioned. In other words, legitimate inner transformation always has outward manifestations that could be defined in one word: *holiness.*

Regarding salvation, it has been well said that if there is no change in your personal life, then there has been no change in your eternal destiny. The evidence of this is before us in today's verses. I am also mindful of the first message Jesus preached after the death of John the Baptist. Recorded in Matthew 4:17, it reads, "From that time Jesus began to preach and to say, 'Repent, for the kingdom of heaven is at hand.' "

Do not let the words of those who preach a lesser gospel take you captive. God's presence in a person's life always brings repentance of flesh and spirit. Holiness is not works — just evidence of God at work in you!

June 16

For a day in Your courts is better than a thousand. I would rather be a doorkeeper in the house of my God than dwell in the tents of wickedness. For the LORD God is a sun and shield; the LORD will give grace and glory; no good thing will He withhold from those who walk uprightly. O LORD of hosts, blessed is the man who trusts in You!

— Psalm 84:10–12

It is noteworthy that the authors of this psalm are the sons of Korah, the descendants of the man who sought to lead a rebellion against the leadership of Moses as recorded in Numbers 16. This act of rebellion against the God-appointed leadership of Moses led to God causing the ground to open and swallow alive Korah and those who followed him (Num. 16:31–32).

There are many who seek to detract from God's love and mercy by claiming that the Old Testament portrays God as angry, vengeful, and unconcerned for His people. Yet here we have the descendants of a man who experienced God's judgment directly proclaiming the greatness and goodness of the Lord. Their spirit of humility stands in direct contrast to the arrogance of their ancestor who had said to Moses, "Who made you the boss? I can do what you can do, and so can any of these other Israelite leaders gathered here." Amazingly, years later the sons of Korah wrote of the privilege of being a doorkeeper in the house of God rather than dwelling in the tents of wickedness, perhaps a reference to their ancestor whose tents had been swallowed up.

This brings us to a great reality and also addresses a grave misconception that has been making its rounds in the church today: the issue of generational curses. The sons of Korah were not cursed for the actions of their ancestors, for that would be outside the covenant of God's law. Deuteronomy 24:16 says, "Fathers shall not be put to death for *their* children, nor shall children be put to death for *their* fathers; a person shall be put to death for his own sin" (emphasis added). Korah's descendants realized the error of their ancestor and fell in love with the wisdom and wonders of God demonstrated through His act of judgment.

So blessed child of God, do not get sold a bill of goods that makes you think you have to break some kind of ancestral curse on your family before you can move into the fullness of God's plan and purpose for your life. The curse was broken on the cross of Jesus Christ, and no matter what happened in your family's past, you are free to do what the descendants of Korah did: praise the Lord for His grace and mercy!

No good thing will God withhold from those who walk uprightly, no matter what kind of knuckleheads their ancestors may have been. So praise the Lord today, for the curse of sin's grasp on your life has been broken by the blood of Jesus Christ!

June 17

He who scatters has come up before your face. Man the fort! Watch the road! Strengthen your flanks! Fortify your power mightily. For the LORD will restore the excellence of Jacob like the excellence of Israel, for the emptiers have emptied them out and ruined their vine branches.

—Nahum 2:1-2

We met Nahum some weeks back and were reminded that his is one of two books among the Minor Prophets (the other is Jonah) that focuses, not on Jerusalem, but rather on Nineveh, the capital of Assyria. Though God had used Assyria as an instrument of punishment to the rebellious northern kingdom of Israel, He yet remembered His covenant with His chosen people. In this section of Nahum, God spoke of their restoration to excellence by means of replanted vineyards and beautiful vines filled with clusters of grapes.

The words of the Lord in verse 1 carry a tauntingly sarcastic tone, with God saying to the Assyrians, "Man the fort, watch the road, strengthen your flanks, fortify your power." Despite all their efforts, He would still restore the excellence of Jacob, He declared.

We would do well to remember that the devil is no match for our God. He may plot, plan, and seek to fortify his power against us, but God is for us. All the enemy's plans are nothing against the power of our God!

But notice, though God spoke this word of restoration, He had already set conditions for this victory: "Behold, on the mountains the feet of him who brings good tidings, who proclaims peace! O Judah, keep your appointed feasts, perform your vows. For the wicked one shall no more pass through you; he is utterly cut off" (Nah. 1:15).

Nahum called for a return to obedience as he proclaimed God's greatness over Israel's captors. This is key to our restoration to excellence as well. There is nothing the enemy can do to overpower the promises of God to those who obey Him. However, far too often we want to receive the blessings of obedience without doing the acts of obedience.

Maybe life seems to be a time of captivity for you right now, and maybe you are looking for a restoration of excellence in your life. Here is the prerequisite: "Keep your appointed feasts, perform your vows." In other words, return to obedience, and the Lord will restore and bless!

June 18

And you, being dead in your trespasses and the uncircumcision of your flesh, He has made alive together with Him, having forgiven you all trespasses, having wiped out the handwriting of requirements that was against us, which was contrary to us. And He has taken it out of the way, having nailed it to the cross. Having disarmed principalities and powers, He made a public spectacle of them, triumphing over them in it.

—Colossians 2:13–15

What a fitting New Testament endorsement of yesterday's Old Testament truth! God has disarmed our enemies by triumphing over them on the cross! He has removed all human effort to obtain salvation and has given it as a free gift accessible to all. Our past is dead and our enemies disarmed. The law of Moses has been fulfilled and wiped out by Jesus' life, death and resurrection. That leaves our focus, then, not on getting saved, but rather on living saved.

We have every reason to face this day with an attitude of gratitude, because what really matters in this life has already been handled! No matter what comes our way this day or any other day, the past can in no way infringe on the present, nor must we live a single moment unsure of our salvation. The obedience we mentioned yesterday and the calls to holiness we visit frequently are not efforts to become worthy or acceptable to God, but rather the desire to be pleasing to and effective for God.

The life lived within the boundaries of the Word of God is a life that is rich and full, even when difficulty is a part of the day. So not matter what you face today, remember, your salvation was paid for in blood, and nothing can change that great truth. The past is dead, the eternal future unbelievably magnificent, and all principalities and powers are disarmed. This day has great potential if you will just act like what you say you believe is true.

Walk in the confidence today that God has triumphed over your enemies, including death and eternal separation from Him. If that doesn't put some "glide in your stride," then nothing will!

June 19

A wise man is strong, yes, a man of knowledge increases strength; for by wise counsel you will wage your own war, and in a multitude of counselors there is safety.

— Proverbs 24:5–6

There are times when we are called to stand alone, and there are other times when our standing alone indicates we are someplace we should not be or are doing something to which we are not called. To know the difference requires wise counsel.

One of the most significant difficulties I have encountered in ministry is dealing with those of an unteachable spirit. Those who stand alone for what is wrong are far different from those who stand alone for what is right, but the funny thing is, both are equally passionate.

One of the best indicators of a pastor who has lost his way is the absence of a teachable spirit. So too is this true of the sheep. I am a bull when it comes to the doctrines of the Word of God, but I am also a bull in some things that I should be a sheep at.

Our lives are daily battles with the forces of darkness, and there are times when the enemy attacks with blinding pride and causes us to wander from teachableness. Instead, we are deluded into thinking we have nothing left to learn or can't learn from a particular person who seems to be less mature or is less educated than we are. But I have learned great things from young people just beginning their walks or ministries with the Lord, and I have also learned from scholars and at times even from scoundrels.

I mentioned sometime back the need to be careful about moving forward with our plans just because we have peace. Peace is not meant to be a fleece; peace is a feeling in that sense. There is much to learn from others, and if you are standing alone for what you think, check to see if you are standing against saints or against sinners. If you're standing alone against sinners, you're likely standing alone for truth. If you're standing alone in your doctrine or beliefs against the rest of the church, you're likely standing alone in your pride.

A wise man is strong—strong enough to stay teachable.

June 20

No temptation has overtaken you except such as is common to man; but God is faithful, who will not allow you to be tempted beyond what you are able, but with the temptation will also make the way of escape, that you may be able to bear it.

—1 Corinthians 10:13

That's pretty powerful stuff here about temptation and excuses! Paul had just written to the Corinthians about idolatry, drunkenness, sexual immorality, and complaining against God (vv. 1–9), and he followed that by saying these temptations are common to all people. He also said that in all these common temptations, God is faithful in two specific ways: He will not allow us to be tempted beyond what we are able to bear, and He will provide a way of escape from the midst of every temptation.

One of the ways of escape is simply to exercise the wisdom of not putting yourself in places of temptation to begin with. Don't engage in the flirtatious conversation, and don't go to the party or bar, counting on your commitment to stay strong. The escape hatch is not going to be found in places where stumbles and falls are likely. But there are some temptations you clearly cannot avoid, and God promises escape in these as well. In either situation, avoiding temptation in the first place or facing temptations you cannot avoid, God is faithful to do both the things He promised. He will not allow the temptation to be greater than your self-control, and He will always provide a way of escape.

I cannot tell you how many times I have heard the sad story of an unmarried Christian couple who were snuggling on the couch when things got out of hand and an avoidable fall happened. Paul tells us that every temptation is bearable and escapable, so that means if we fall when tempted, we failed to do what God has equipped us to do or did not take the way of escape.

Some of you reading this today are toying with temptation. You need to remember that temptation is very powerful, but God sets limits on what the devil can tempt you with and provides an escape from them. Don't mess with temptation. Avoid it or escape from it by changing your proximity to its alluring and enchanting powers. In other words, get away from there, for God has made a way!

June 21

But the Lord stood with me and strengthened me, so that the message might be preached fully through me, and that all the Gentiles might hear. Also I was delivered out of the mouth of the lion. And the Lord will deliver me from every evil work and preserve me for His heavenly kingdom. To Him be glory forever and ever. Amen!

—2 Timothy 4:17–18

Paul had just warned Timothy about a man named Alexander, who had done him much harm. Timothy, too, needed to beware of Alexander as well as another man named Hymenaeus, because they were blasphemers (1 Tim. 1:20). I have to wonder how the apostle Paul would be received in our day for naming names of blasphemers within the church.

Blaspheme means "to vilify or speak impiously against God." The application of this today would include those who speak against the integrity and infallibility of the Word of God, for you cannot speak impiously of the Word of God without speaking impiously of the God of the Word. We need to beware of those who fragment or twist the Scriptures to their own gain or in support of their own personal interpretations.

Paul said the Lord would deliver him from every evil work and preserve him, just as He had delivered him from a lion's mouth at some point in his life. I have always found it interesting that in the letters to the seven churches in Revelation, Jesus commended some of the churches for taking a stand and not tolerating those "who say they are apostles and are not" (Rev. 2:2) and condemned the churches that tolerated evil in their midst. To them, He warned that tribulation awaited (Rev. 2:22).

There has crept into the mentality of the church today the notion that it is un-Christian and judgmental to call sin, sin. Nothing could be further from the truth. The Bible has already defined truth and acceptable moral behavior for the children of God. Wrongful judging is to define sin, not to declare biblically defined sin as sin. But the fact is, many don't want to take this stand because they don't want to eat lunch alone or fear repercussions or even jeers from those who would call them judgmental.

The fact is, friends, we do people a grave injustice if we fail to warn them of those who are enemies of God. Of course, we should exercise great caution, because our first priority is to examine our own lives—not become sin sniffers. But friends, it is not a sin to point out sin to those who call themselves Christians but live in drunkenness, idolatry, or some other wickedness. It's a responsibility, even an act of love, to do so. The Lord will stand with you whenever your heart is right and winning your brother or sister is your goal.

June 22

Knowing this first: that scoffers will come in the last days, walking according to their own lusts, and saying, "Where is the promise of His coming? For since the fathers fell asleep, all things continue as they were from the beginning of creation."

—2 Peter 3:3–7

It is nothing unusual for nonbelievers to scoff at what we believe morally, prophetically, or theologically. The real shocker about these verses is Peter's implication that this is what some in the church will be saying in the last days. We know this simply because all the epistles were written to Christians, not unbelievers, and therefore the only possible understanding of this passage is that in the last days, many in the church will scoff at the possibility of Christ's return for His bride.

If we look at the Greek words translated into English as "Where is the promise of His coming?" they would read as follows, if translated word for word: "What announces the near return?" If we read carefully Matthew 24 and 25, we see that Jesus moved through the last-days scenario as a whole, discerning the rapture, the tribulation, and even the great white throne judgment.

When Jeremiah warned the children of Israel of God's impending judgment, they responded, "That is hopeless! So we will walk according to our own plans, and we will every one obey the dictates of his evil heart" (Jer. 18:12). I find this statement to be of particular interest when linked with Jesus' words that when He comes for His bride at the end of days, it will be as it was in the days of Noah. As described in Genesis 6:5, this is a time when the thoughts and intents of man's heart will be only evil continually. That sounds a lot like saying everyone will follow the dictates of his or her own evil heart.

Just as Israel did in the days of Jeremiah, so too will many in the church resist the proclamations of impending judgment. But Jesus clearly said in Matthew 24:7–8, "For nation will rise against nation, and kingdom against kingdom. And there will be famines, pestilences, and earthquakes in various places. All these are the beginning of sorrows."

Friends, Jesus is coming soon, so don't scoff at His return. He warned Noah before sending the flood, He warned Abraham before destroying Sodom and Gomorrah, and he warned the Jews before overthrowing Jerusalem. But on each occasion, most people acted as though nothing was going to happen.

In the past, God always forewarned of His judgment, and in the present, He is doing the same. Don't let anyone talk you out of living expectantly for His return. Whoever denies it, even to protect a particular theology, is denying that the unchanging God has always told man when judgment was coming. The coming tribulation will be no exception, so tell someone about Jesus today!

June 23

The LORD is my light and my salvation; whom shall I fear? The LORD is the strength of my life; of whom shall I be afraid?

— Psalm 27:1

It has been said that 80 percent of the things we worry about never happen, but that doesn't keep most of us from worrying. One of the greatest fears the enemy seeks to exploit in our lives is that of the unknown. *What will happen tomorrow?... Will the plans work out?... Will I meet the right person?... Will I get the promotion?... Will the kids make good choices?* On and on the list goes of valid and necessary life concerns that the enemy likes to turn into fears.

We often limit our thinking of God's strength and protection to the realm of our physical bodies, to His ability to keep us from disaster or trauma. But our God is also the God of the unknown outcome. He is the God of what lies ahead, the God of all the things the enemy tries to turn into paralyzing fears.

David reminds us that we are free to live today like God is in control of tomorrow. Fear need not be a part of our day. That is not to say we carelessly skip through life in ignorant bliss, for God did indeed give us minds to discern good and evil and to help us walk in wisdom. But here is the key in all this: God is in control of tomorrow, whether we live in confidence or fear, so why choose fear? Why not choose confidence in God rather than fear of the unknown outcome?

God is not only in control of keeping us from harm, but He is also concerned about life's ordinary situations that can impose upon our joy. God is our light and salvation. Whom or what should we fear?

June 24

Therefore we also pray always for you that our God would count you worthy of this calling, and fulfill all the good pleasure of His goodness and the work of faith with power, that the name of our Lord Jesus Christ may be glorified in you, and you in Him, according to the grace of our God and the Lord Jesus Christ.

— 2 Thessalonians 1:11–12

It is not uncommon in the Pauline epistles to find Paul praying for the church or city he was writing to, and the church at Thessalonica is but one example. Paul's prayer for the church there was simple yet profound. He prayed that they would live in a manner worthy of God so that Christ might be glorified in and through them. What a magnificent course to chart for each day, to set out each morning to live worthy of God and to bring glory to Christ!

Many of us are "to-do list" people and have lists of accomplishments we hope to fulfill on any given day. If, however, we began each day with the objective of walking worthy of God for the glory of Jesus Christ, how would that impact our lists? What would it subtract, and what would it add? Each of us would do well to ask if walking worthy and bringing Jesus glory is on our list.

I am amazed at how fast a day can fill up and how many things need to be accomplished before I call it a day. I'm sure that it is true for all of us. But each day's to-do list is not complete without having walked worthy of God and brought glory to Jesus Christ. How do we do this? Paul says that works of faith and power fulfill all the good pleasure of His goodness. So before we call it a day, we might ask ourselves, *Have I done something today that required faith and divine power?*

This could be expressed in any number of ways: things you did or did not do, steps you took to express your faith and trust in God before others. It could be things you didn't laugh at or gossip you refused to participate in. It could be speaking well of someone that everyone else was tearing down. It could be doing something that needed to be done, though everyone else considered it demeaning. It could be giving your lunch or lunch money to a homeless person you encountered on the way to work or school.

Paul's prayer for the church at Thessalonica to walk worthy and bring Christ glory is a worthy goal for each day. The simple truth is, if you aim at nothing, you are sure to hit it. So run down your to-do list and see what's on the agenda. Make sure walking worthy and bringing Jesus glory made the list, because if it is not on your list, it probably won't happen!

June 25

He who dwells in the secret place of the Most High shall abide under the shadow of the Almighty. I will say of the LORD, *"He is my refuge and my fortress; my God, in Him I will trust."*

—Psalm 91:1–2

My wife and I are like many other couples in that I am usually hot and she is often cold. This is never more evident than when we do one of our favorite things to do on a day off, which is to walk thorough an outdoor mall near the ocean. On a bright sunny day, you can catch glimpses of the sun shimmering on the water as you walk between the buildings of the mall. Half of the walkway lies in the sun and the other half is in the shade, and—you guessed it—my wife walks in the sun and I walk in the shade. But there are other times when we both appreciate the shade. If we are in the desert or if it is the dead of summer and the weather is extremely hot, shade is a blessing to both of us.

The psalmist tells us that God is a shade when the heat is all around us. He (likely Moses) says it is a secret place that provides a fortress and refuge for all who trust in the Lord. In other words, knowing God brings us shade when all others are searching for refuge from the heat.

The analogy of God as a shadow is both picturesque and purposeful. A shadow changes nothing in the environment, but if it is hot outside, the shadow provides shade and refuge from the heat—as long as you take advantage of it. But spiritually speaking, sometimes we choose to remain in the sun though we could find refuge in His shadow. That's what we do when we face struggles on our own or when we look for an exit in a trial rather than running to Him for shade.

Think about this: if it's really hot outside, what do you look for above all else? Shade! You and I have found it under the shadow of the Almighty. When things heat up around us, we have a refuge in God and are free to invite others to come in out of the heat. There is plenty of room under the shadow of His wings for any who put their trust in Him!

June 26

Now Peter and John went up together to the temple at the hour of prayer, the ninth hour. And a certain man lame from his mother's womb was carried, whom they laid daily at the gate of the temple which is called Beautiful, to ask alms from those who entered the temple; who, seeing Peter and John about to go into the temple, asked for alms. And fixing his eyes on him, with John, Peter said, "Look at us." So he gave them his attention, expecting to receive something from them. Then Peter said, "Silver and gold I do not have, but what I do have I give you: In the name of Jesus Christ of Nazareth, rise up and walk." And he took him by the right hand and lifted him up, and immediately his feet and ankle bones received strength. So he, leaping up, stood and walked and entered the temple with them — walking, leaping, and praising God.

— Acts 3:1–8

I love this story! It is such an apt picture of us as human beings and even as Christians. The man who lay at the gate called Beautiful was not aware of what was available to him, so he asked for what he could not earn: alms. But what God had for him was far better than silver and gold; what God had was healing!

There are so many nuances here to take note of. Take, for example, the way Peter took the man by the right hand and lifted him up. The man had lived an entire life without strength in his legs, so I am sure he had little hope of ever standing on his own. But Peter gave the man's faith a boost by extending his hand to lift him out of his circumstances.

We see also that the man did what we all should do when God does something for us, and that is leap with excitement and praise. I always find it a bit unnerving when I encounter people who are neither excited about knowing God nor passionate about the healing of their souls.

But the real point of application here is that far too often we ask for less than God's best. We focus on asking for silver and gold, and though God is faithful in the financial area, He has something so much better to offer than mere material possessions. Are we asking for His Spirit to give us eyes to discern good and evil? Are we praying as fervently for doors to open for the gospel as we are for a check to arrive in the mail? Are we asking God to increase our witness in our neighborhood or school, even at the expense of rejection and mockery? These are the real treasures in life, things that money cannot buy, things that can be accomplished only by the power of His Spirit.

I am thankful for God's healing of my marriage, and I am still leaping and praising God for what He did in it almost thirty years ago. It was nothing short of a miracle! I believe in asking God for the great and mighty things,

things that often don't make sense or are simply impossible. I don't want my prayer life to be dominated by miniscule things like silver and gold. I want to praise and bless His name, seek His will above my own, and lift up my requests to the God of wonders who does the impossible.

Don't pray little prayers, friend. Ask Him to do in you things that money can't buy, and then watch what He'll do through you!

June 27

Seek the Lord and His strength; seek His face evermore! Remember His marvelous works which He has done, His wonders, and the judgments of His mouth.

—1 Chronicles 16:11–12

In the Hebrew, the term *seek* here is the word *dârash*, which means "frequent," and in our passage, it links the associated actions of asking and worship. So these verses are urging us to "frequent" the Lord and His strength and to "frequent" His face forevermore (the face refers to His nature or attributes). This psalm of David is celebrating the placement of the ark of the covenant in the city of Jerusalem. The entire city rejoiced in the marvelous works and wonders God had done for them and the judgments He had imposed on their enemies.

Some Christians wrongly apply David's prayers for victory over his enemies and even for their destruction. We need to be careful about confusing the prayers of a king about to engage in battle with the prayers of a person who is seeking to live right before God and is surrounded by enemies. Jesus said in Matthew 5:44, "Love your enemies, bless those who curse you, do good to those who hate you, and pray for those who spitefully use you and persecute you." So it is clear that an individual's responsibility toward an enemy is different from the national responsibility of a government leader or king appointed by God to protect the people.

The ark of the covenant was a symbol of the presence of God on earth, and rejoicing accompanied its return. God's presence should always lead to rejoicing. In a sense, we Christians are arks of God because His Spirit, His presence, lives in us. So we must be careful to remember the works and wonders He has done, for this is how we can obey such a monumental command as "love your enemies."

Frequent the Lord and His strength, and frequent His attributes and nature forevermore. Remember the marvelous wonders He has done, and remember that your enemy, the devil, is under the judgment of almighty God. If you frequent the wonderful work of His forgiveness and if you frequent the reality of His faithful nature, it's not so hard to extend what you have received to others—even when that "other" is an enemy.

Forgive someone who doesn't deserve it today. It is the will and nature of God in you!

June 28

The Jews answered him, "We have a law, and according to our law He ought to die, because He made Himself the Son of God." Therefore, when Pilate heard that saying, he was the more afraid, and went again into the Praetorium, and said to Jesus, "Where are You from?" But Jesus gave him no answer. Then Pilate said to Him, "Are You not speaking to me? Do You not know that I have power to crucify You, and power to release You?" Jesus answered, "You could have no power at all against Me unless it had been given you from above. Therefore the one who delivered Me to you has the greater sin."

—John 19:7–11

Though I am a firm and passionate believer in Christians' involvement in the realm of human government, especially in a democracy where the opportunity is open to them, I find the arrogance of some people in governmental positions amusing. As I said, I believe we ought to be involved governmentally to the fullest capacity, but Jesus here reminds us of a great truth in the face of great pomposity.

Pilate laid claim to possessing legislative power that could determine whether Jesus lived or died. In response, Jesus said to Pilate, and I am paraphrasing, "You're just a pawn in the hand of My Father, and you can't do anything He has not allowed."

Friends, I am all for standing up for our rights and fighting within the system to keep us one nation under God, but I also believe, regardless of what government may do, God cannot be legislated out of people's hearts and minds. As I have long said, as long as there are tests, there will be prayer in the schools. Yes, I believe the decline of our school system can be traced back to when prayer was banned from the public schools, but the fact is, friends, I think we would do well to remember that our power is in prayer — not in the right to pray.

No power is granted to anyone unless God Himself allows it, and like Jesus, we don't always have to answer every ridiculous allegation from the world. But when the world starts saying it has the power to do thus and so above the will of almighty God, then it's time to take a stand. You can take prayer out of the schools, but you can't take prayer out of God's people!

Pray in school, pray at work, pray all the time and everywhere; no one can take away your right to pray. Your power is in prayer, not in the government's legislating your right to do so. We would all do better to pray for our schools and in our schools than to protest something that cannot be legislated out of our lives anyway!

June 29

The LORD bless you and keep you; the LORD make His face shine upon you, and be gracious to you; the LORD lift up His countenance upon you, and give you peace.

—Numbers 6:24–26

I am sure we have all heard and maybe even quoted this ancient blessing, but I am also sure many may not be aware of its origin. Numbers 6:22–23 says, "And the LORD spoke to Moses, saying: 'Speak to Aaron and his sons, saying, "This is the way you shall bless the children of Israel. Say to them: 'The LORD bless you and keep you; the LORD make His face shine upon you, and be gracious to you; the LORD lift up His countenance upon you, and give you peace.' " ' "

I cannot help but think of Moses on Mount Sinai receiving the law and how on his return, his face shone from being in the presence of almighty God (Exodus 34). It is also noteworthy that the children of Israel were all aware that anyone who entered the presence of a king or magistrate would never expect the official to look the person in the eyes or even address him. For a king to lift up his countenance in a smile was not only rare but also a sign of acceptance and approval.

God instructed Moses to tell Aaron that the priesthood was to speak this blessing over God's people. They were to be met by the joy of the Lord and blessed and kept by His grace.

I am not a Levitical priest, but I am a pastor called by God to speak to His people. Today I speak over you this blessing: "The LORD bless you and keep you; the LORD make His face shine upon you, and be gracious to you; the LORD lift up His countenance upon you, and give you peace."

Tell someone about Jesus today, and may your face shine from having been in His joyful presence by the grace of God through Jesus Christ our Lord!

June 30

Now no chastening seems to be joyful for the present, but painful; nevertheless, afterward it yields the peaceable fruit of righteousness to those who have been trained by it. Therefore strengthen the hands which hang down, and the feeble knees, and make straight paths for your feet, so that what is lame may not be dislocated, but rather be healed.

— Hebrews 12:11–13

I have gone to a gym for many years now, but I occasionally tweak something in my workout routine. In fact, as I sit here today, I have a rib out of joint that is a continual focus of my attention. I keep stretching my arm over my head, and I have tried lying on the floor and leaning my knees to one side or the other in an attempt to pop the rib back into place. This is not the first time I have had this problem with a rib, but each time it occurs, I can hardly think of anything but how good it will feel when the rib goes back into place.

This is not unlike our lives when they are spiritually out of joint. At such times, we are constantly fidgeting and straining to fix what is dislocated. But many times only the Master's touch will bring relief, and that touch sometimes comes in the form of discipline.

When it is time for parents to apply the "board of education" to the "seat of understanding," they often tell their children it will hurt them more than it will hurt the kids. As a dad, I have certainly found that statement to be true. In a similar fashion, God does not discipline us just for discipline's sake, as though He enjoys it. He is trying to reset the dislocated aspects of our walks so that relief can come to our weakened hands and feeble knees. He wants to heal whatever is hindering our walks with Him and put it back into place so that it is no longer dislocated.

Are you feeling a little discomfort in your walk with God? Maybe He needs to pop something back into place. I can assure you, it is better to get things right before moving ahead, because if you try to continue anyway, nothing but pain awaits. So though no chastening is joyful or pleasant, the sooner you confess and repent from any disjointedness, the easier and less painful it will be to pop it back into place!

July 1

He does not delight in the strength of the horse; He takes no pleasure in the legs of a man. The LORD takes pleasure in those who fear Him, in those who hope in His mercy.

— Psalm 147:10–11

Though the author of this psalm is unknown, the situation surrounding it is not. The Jews had been carried away to Babylon for seventy years of captivity as the result of their continual idolatry and ignoring of the Sabbath year but had now returned to Jerusalem. The horses and soldiers of the current world power Babylon had been no match for almighty God, and He was unimpressed with their military prowess. Though they saw themselves as an unstoppable force, they were nothing more than an instrument in the hand of the Almighty.

God is not impressed with our accomplishments and achievements any more than He was impressed with Babylon's global reputation of military might. What the Lord delights in and takes pleasure in is people who fear Him and find hope in His mercy. Don't get me wrong; God loves us and is delighted when we excel in our gifts and talents and acknowledge them as blessings from Him. But God takes even more pleasure in those who fear Him and hope in His mercy.

The word *fear* in the Hebrew is *yârê'* (*yaw-ray'*). It means "moral reverence," and in some applications, it means "reverent trust." This is what makes the adage "the ground is level at the foot of the cross" so beautiful. No matter our accomplishments or perceived level of success, God is more pleased with our moral reverence and reverent trust. That means rich and poor, the one who cleans the building and the one whose name is on the building, are equal in the eyes of God. He takes pleasure in the morally reverent teacher and student alike.

In their captivity, the Jews learned that obedience is the first step in returning to God's blessings. Similarly, in our lives, the size of the failure or the magnitude of the things that took us away from the Lord do not matter. When we return to Him, He takes pleasure in us as morally reverent and trusting children. He is totally unimpressed and is not intimidated by any human accomplishment or prowess. Bless His holy name!

July 2

For in Him dwells all the fullness of the Godhead bodily; and you are complete in Him, who is the head of all principality and power.

—Colossians 2:9–10

Having warned the Colossians of the empty deceit of worldly philosophies, Paul then drew their minds back to Jesus Christ, the head of all supernatural power. His association of our being "in Christ" with His headship over every principality and power makes it clear that He wanted the church at Colossae to understand the futility of infusing worldly philosophies into Christian theology.

We are complete in Jesus Christ. As it pertains to facing life and its daily challenges, we are completely spiritually ready. I have, however, sometimes tried to fight spiritual battles with my flesh, striving to overcome this habit or urge, hoping to retrain this thought process or that attitude. I have told myself, *I am not going to think like that anymore*, or *I'm not going to have this kind of attitude about that anymore*, only to face the situation again and reap the same results. I ended up thinking the same old things and doing the same old things, despite my best intentions.

The key, then, is not to use the world's self-help methods to handle our spiritual ups and downs but rather to incorporate the spiritual into the realm of our personal struggle or failure. When facing an enemy tactic, do something spiritual to combat it. If you want an attitude to change, don't try to strong arm it through the techniques of the latest self-help guru. No, do something "in Christ" to combat it. Visit the sick and imprisoned, help the poor and needy, go to the aid of the widow or orphan—these things are all "in Christ" and effective in days of enemy fire.

Worldly philosophies are just that—worldly. If you're seeking to increase in worldliness, then they are the weapons of choice. However, if you're seeking to increase in godliness, then only the things "in Christ" will prevail. He is the head of the spiritual realm, and we are in Him. That means we are empowered to do all that is in Him!

July 3

Strengthen the weak hands, and make firm the feeble knees. Say to those who are fearful-hearted, "Be strong, do not fear! Behold, your God will come with vengeance, with the recompense of God; He will come and save you."

—Isaiah 35:3–4

In a world filled with war and terrorism, exploitation and extortion, lies and deceit, and political corruption, it is easy to become disillusioned by the present and take our eyes off the future. However, from the history of Israel, through the existence of the church, and right up to the end, God has always urged His people to keep looking up to Him rather than looking around at circumstances. Here in Isaiah 35:3 and also in Hebrews 12:12 where Isaiah 35:3 is quoted, we read of our responsibility to help redirect others who have started looking around instead of looking up.

That's not to say we move through life ignorant of the times and uninvolved in the world. It means we keep our hearts and minds focused on the reality that this life and this world are temporal and that heaven is our eternal habitation.

God is coming back to the earth, and He is coming with vengeance and recompense. In other words, He will punish and repay those who reject His offer of forgiveness and those who persecute His people. We are not to rejoice in the punishment of the wicked, as God takes no pleasure in their deaths (Ezek. 33:11), but justice is not justice if truth does not prevail in the end.

So if the world seems a bit overwhelming at times, and injustice and unfairness are gnawing at your spirit, don't forget, He is coming to save you! By remembering this, you will be strong and not fear. Your hands need not be weakened or your knees made feeble by the intimidation of injustice.

In old Western movies, when the cavalry was down to its last rounds and all hope was gone, the sound of a bugle signified that help was on the way and the battle was about to turn. Consider this devotional the sound of the bugle today. Help is on the way, and justice will prevail in the end!

July 4

If you are reproached for the name of Christ, blessed are you, for the Spirit of glory and of God rests upon you. On their part He is blasphemed, but on your part He is glorified. But let none of you suffer as a murderer, a thief, an evildoer, or as a busybody in other people's matters. Yet if anyone suffers as a Christian, let him not be ashamed, but let him glorify God in this matter.

—1 Peter 4:14–16

I cannot express with words how grateful I am to have been born in America and how much I love our country and celebrate the freedoms we enjoy. But I, like many of you, have also been saddened to see much of our history rewritten and many of the things the Pilgrims died for and the Founding Fathers fought for slipping from our grasp. In a nation where the Bible used to be the book by which children learned to read, it is heartbreaking to realize that the sacred book is now not even allowed in our schools. And, of course, praying to the one the Bible reveals as the Creator is strictly forbidden in our schools.

It is hard to imagine that Christians in the United States of America could be prosecuted and therefore persecuted for believing and teaching the Word of God. Yet Peter said, if we are reproached for the name of Christ, we are blessed; though others may blaspheme Him, through us Christ is glorified.

Peter also gave a word of warning not to get caught up in the evil practices of the day: do not murder, do not steal, and do not be a busybody. The murderer and the thief are self-explanatory, but the admonition against being "a busybody in other people's matters" means far more than you might think. There is one Greek word for this entire phrase that is nearly as long as this page, so I will spare you its spelling. But the phrase literally means "to meddle in Gentile matters"; practically, it means to get caught up in the things of the world.

As much as I love our country and its history, as magnificent as it is to hear the success stories of immigrants who came to the land of opportunity with nothing, let's be careful to remember on this day, the birth of our nation, why the Pilgrims risked their lives to come here in the first place. Their American dream was not to own a home; their dream was to worship God freely without fear of persecution (though there is nothing wrong with having both).

Happy Independence Day! Live out the original American dream today!

July 5

What does it profit, my brethren, if someone says he has faith but does not have works? Can faith save him? If a brother or sister is naked and destitute of daily food, and one of you says to them, "Depart in peace, be warmed and filled," but you do not give them the things which are needed for the body, what does it profit? Thus also faith by itself, if it does not have works, is dead.

—James 2:14–16

In this great letter of faith, James pushes the envelope and, in the minds of some, encroaches on salvation through grace alone by faith alone. The fact is, nothing could be further from what James is relating to the body of Christ here. In teaching this passage, I have concluded its thought in one summary statement: viable faith is visible faith.

Dead faith never activates a person to sacrificially love others. This kind of love is the fruit of salvation, for in accepting Christ, we assume the label of *Christian*, which means "Christlike." If there is one trait that ought to be obvious in all who follow Him, it is a love-based willingness to sacrifice personal rights in order to help others. This is the idea James is speaking of here. He is not saying that works will acquire salvation, but he is saying that works identify those who are saved.

If we look at the life of Jesus as the model for our lives, we see that He was always teaching and touching others. Sometimes the touching was also the teaching, but regardless, He was continually meeting both the practical and spiritual needs of those He encountered. So if our calling is to be Christlike, then our lives should be lives of teaching and touching. We teach by the manner in which we live distinct from the world, and we touch by sacrificially meeting both practical and spiritual needs.

Living a lifestyle of teaching and touching produces a by-product that cannot come in any other way—joy. A Christlike life that teaches others what Jesus is like and touches them with His love is a life full of joy.

James is calling the church to be truly Christian, or Christlike. That means we embrace sacrificial living and giving that others may know there is a God who cares.

With all you say and do today, let someone know that Jesus loves them!

July 6

*"O our God, will You not judge them? For we have no power against this great multitude that is coming against us; nor do we know what to do, but our eyes are upon You." Now all Judah, with their little ones, their wives, and their children, stood before the L*ORD*. Then the Spirit of the L*ORD *came upon Jahaziel the son of Zechariah, the son of Benaiah, the son of Jeiel, the son of Mattaniah, a Levite of the sons of Asaph, in the midst of the assembly. And he said, "Listen, all you of Judah and you inhabitants of Jerusalem, and you, King Jehoshaphat! Thus says the L*ORD *to you: 'Do not be afraid nor dismayed because of this great multitude, for the battle is not yours, but God's.' "*

—2 Chronicles 20:12–15

The Moabite and Ammonite armies were marching toward Jerusalem with hatred in the their hearts and fire in their eyes to drive God's people from the land of their inheritance. The people of Moab and Ammon had both received mercy when God had brought His people into the land. Understandably, "This is the thanks we get?" was now the cry of the people of Israel.

In response, King Jehoshaphat called for a fast. He cried out to God before all the people, and His concluding words are recorded in verse 12 above: "O our God, will You not judge them? For we have no power against this great multitude that is coming against us; nor do we know what to do, but our eyes are upon You."

God answered through Jahaziel, who was from the tribe of Levi and of the sons of Asaph, and Jahaziel reminded the people that the battle belonged to the Lord. What I find interesting is that Jahaziel was a worship leader, not a military commander. He was a descendant of the sons of Asaph, the psalmists and songwriters of Israel.

It takes but one person to inspire others, one person who remembers that one person plus God equals a majority, one person who will stand and say, "Do not forget, the battle belongs to the Lord." No matter your vocation, you can be an inspiration and reminder to others by taking a stand for the name of the Lord, even if you must stand alone. One thing I have learned over the years is that when one courageous person stands alone, he or she is never alone for long. Others will find the courage to stand too because of that one person's proclamation and reminder that the battle belongs to the Lord!

July 7

Now may the God of hope fill you with all joy and peace in believing, that you may abound in hope by the power of the Holy Spirit.

— Romans 15:13

Paul's epistle to the Romans is a letter that has brought both reformation and revival to the church throughout the centuries. In this portion of chapter 15, he closes by speaking a blessing over the Romans. First, he refers to the Lord as "the God of hope," and then, he expresses his desire that the God of hope would fill the Romans with joy and peace in their believing. Next, he reminds the church of the presence of the Holy Spirit within them. The clear implication of these three thoughts is that since God is a God of hope, and the Holy Spirit is God, and the Holy Spirit is in us, then we too should be people of joy, peace, and hope.

Here is the dilemma: how do we have joy, peace, and hope when strife, contention, and suffering surround us? First of all, we know that God is unchanging, so if He is a God of hope, then He is a God of hope no matter what. Second, if we remember that He is in us, the possibility of actually experiencing joy, peace, and hope in our lives is not remote, but rather our right. So how do we get it?

As I write this devotional, I am thinking ahead to tomorrow night when I will speak to a group of high school students. One of the things I am going to talk to them about is handling peer pressure. One of the things I want to leave with them is an obvious but much needed truth today: whatever we feed our spirits will show up in our flesh.

If we continually feed our physical bodies chocolate, pizza, and burgers (I love all three), then the results of that kind of diet will show up in our bodies. So too is it true with our spirits; if we feed our spirits with things that steal, kill, and destroy joy, peace, and hope, then we create outer persons who lack joy, peace, and hope.

So what's on your spiritual diet today? Ask yourself, *Do I have any joy-killers in my life? Are peace-robbers or hope-destroyers taking up residence within me?* Those things can be moral disobedience. Spirit-filled Christians cannot have the joy, peace, and hope that is rightfully theirs as believers if they knowingly live outside of the will of God and disregard the nudgings of the Holy Spirit.

The old saying is appropriate: "Garbage in, garbage out." So if you seem to be lacking joy, peace, and hope that is unmoved by circumstances, ask yourself this question: did you remember to take out the garbage?

July 8

Honor the LORD *with your possessions, and with the firstfruits of all your increase; so your barns will be filled with plenty, and your vats will overflow with new wine.*

— Proverbs 3:9–10

In Scripture, wine is a symbol of both blessing and judgment. Here in these verses, we find it associated with blessing; but in the book of Revelation and elsewhere, it is associated with God's wrath.

Here in Proverbs, the Word of God clearly tells us that God will bless those who honor Him with their possessions and with their firstfruits, which speaks of the tithe, or a tenth, of all they possess. It has always been a mystery to me why so many people struggle with the concept of tithing or supporting the work of the ministry. I find it odd because many of the same people who resist tithing do not hesitate buy things they want but don't need, even if it means buying them on credit with exorbitant interest rates that drive the long-range cost of their purchases through the roof. But give to support the work of the Lord, which pays eternal dividends? How offensive!

The will of God for us as Christians is what it has always been concerning His people and their finances: God first, then us. Israel was instructed to give the firstfruits of their fields, vineyards, and livestock to the Lord. "Well, that's Old Testament," some might say. Well, that's not Old Testament—it's just good Bible!

In 1 Corinthians 16:1–2, Paul states, "Now concerning the collection for the saints, as I have given orders to the churches of Galatia, so you must do also: On the first day of the week let each one of you lay something aside, storing up as he may prosper, that there be no collections when I come." Paul explains that we are to put the work of the Lord first, which includes caring for poor saints. As our first priority, we put aside for God and others, then store up so we may prosper.

Though this is a touchy issue for many, it shouldn't be. Not many would argue that God is to be first in all things except their pocketbooks. But it is exactly at this point that they balk. The funny thing is, though, not giving as God has instructed us to give accomplishes only one thing: it robs us of His intended blessings. Honor the Lord with your possessions—all of them—beginning with your firstfruits, the tithe, so that your barns may be filled and vats overflow with the promised blessings.

Be cheerful about giving. Remember, tithing is not really giving, but returning something that's not yours anyway. After all, everything you have comes from God. Be a blessing to your church and to the poor by putting God in charge of your finances. I have said it before and I'll repeat it again: God will bless the 90 percent He lets you keep only when you are faithful in the 10 percent He has called you to give. Don't let abuse be your excuse. If you do, the only one who loses is you!

July 9

Because you have made the LORD, *who is my refuge, even the Most High, your dwelling place, no evil shall befall you, nor shall any plague come near your dwelling; for He shall give His angels charge over you, to keep you in all your ways. In their hands they shall bear you up, lest you dash your foot against a stone. You shall tread upon the lion and the cobra, the young lion and the serpent you shall trample underfoot.*

—Psalm 91:9–13

Whether the language is literal or figurative, this psalm of Moses is rich with encouragement, hope, and valor. It is also replete with instruction in that it begins with a key word: *because* (in the Hebrew, *kee*). The use of this word to introduce the sentence makes clear the relationship between action and outcome. It is "because" we have made the Lord our refuge and dwelling place that His angels watch over us, plagues won't come near us, we'll be kept in all our ways, and on the list continues.

However, knowing that over the course of history, great plagues have struck many countries, including ours, and that many Christians have died during these plagues, some might question the validity of these conditional promises. Furthermore, since Moses authored this psalm, what did he mean by the word *plague*? The bubonic plague, plagues of flu, or even the H1N1 virus of our day were not yet known.

Clearly Moses was referring to the plagues God had brought upon Egypt when His people lived as slaves there. In Exodus 8:23, as the plague of flies was about to descend on the land of Egypt, the Lord told Moses to tell Pharaoh these words: "I will make a difference between My people and your people. Tomorrow this sign shall be." The next day, just as God had promised, there were no flies in the land of Goshen, where the children of Israel dwelt, but Egypt was covered with them.

So what does this mean to us today? Because we have chosen to follow God and make Him our refuge, we will be delivered from the wrath that is to come (Rom. 5:9) and will be spared the foretold consequences of rebelling against the plan of God. Let's put it like this: The person who follows the plan of God regarding sexual relations will be spared the consequence of STDs. The person who is generous and remembers the poor will be spared the "piercing through with many sorrows" (1 Tim. 6:10) that the love of money brings. Those who are content with God and their possessions will not suffer the plague of discontentment and the constant nagging fear of always being one step behind the neighbors. Neither will they be devoured by the lion of envy or bitten by the cobra of jealousy.

If we see these conditional promises as literal, they are magnificent and self- explanatory; if we see them as figurative, they are tremendous truths. If we remember that Moses wrote them by inspiration of the Holy Spirit, then we can look back on his life and know that both are true. They are literal and figurative. Nothing can harm us until the Lord says it's time to come home, and nothing can hinder us when we make the Lord our refuge and dwelling place.

Go out with this confidence today as you tell others about our soon coming King!

July 10

*Now in those days, when the number of the disciples was multiplying, there arose
a complaint against the Hebrews by the Hellenists, because their widows were
neglected in the daily distribution. Then the twelve summoned the multitude of
the disciples and said, "It is not desirable that we should leave the word of God
and serve tables. Therefore, brethren, seek out from among you seven men of good
reputation, full of the Holy Spirit and wisdom, whom we may appoint over this
business; but we will give ourselves continually to prayer and to the
ministry of the word."*

— Acts 6:1-4

Because the Jewish law did not grant inheritances to women, the care of
widows was the responsibility of the family or, if a woman had no family, the
responsibility of the community. In this passage in Acts, those who were not
natural-born citizens of Israel felt as though their widows were being ignored
in the communal food-distribution program. Called Hellenists, these people
were of Jewish descent but had grown up outside of Israel and spoke Greek.

The response of "the twelve," a phrase used to refer to the apostles, is
most interesting. They did not say, "Try to find some novice Christians with
nothing else to do who are not yet ready for doing the greater works of God
and give them the job of distributing the food," but rather they said, "Find
seven men of good reputation, mature in the faith, and filled with the Holy
Spirit to take care of this need." Among the seven selected were Stephen, the
church's first martyr, and Philip, who later became known as Philip the evangelist (Acts 21:8).

What is important for us to see is that there is no insignificant task in the
kingdom of God and that great tasks are always assigned to those who have
been faithful in small ones. I have met many a young, self-proclaimed future
preacher who wanted to start behind the pulpit and never considered helping
to clean the pews. I can also say, not a one of those is a great preacher today.

Men and women of good reputation who are filled with the Holy Spirit
are needed in every aspect of ministry, from the humanly menial to the — in
our thinking — spiritually magnificent. It has been well said that God is not
looking for ability, but availability — a willingness not to measure a task by
our definition of success, but on the belief that doing anything for God is
an undeserved privilege, even being a waiter! Stephen and Philip began that
way, and people are still talking about what God did through both of them.

Doing great things for God begins with being faithful in whatever He asks
of you. What opportunities will He put before you today? Look for them.
When they come, don't measure their importance, but remember that all the

great men and women of God began by doing whatever was set in front of them. Only then could God move them on to greater and mightier things.

July 11

The coming of the lawless one is according to the working of Satan, with all power, signs, and lying wonders, and with all unrighteous deception among those who perish, because they did not receive the love of the truth, that they might be saved. And for this reason God will send them strong delusion, that they should believe the lie, that they all may be condemned who did not believe the truth but had pleasure in unrighteousness.

— 2 Thessalonians 2:9–11

One of my favorite preachers, Leonard Ravenhill, once said in a sermon, "Entertainment is the devil's substitute for joy." What a profound truth in our day! Just look at today's TV offerings and you can see that many people derive pleasure from watching unrighteousness. But Paul warns that this practice is a deceptive delusion.

It is no secret in this modern age of neurobiology that the human brain receives a stimulus from the transmission of dopamine into the pleasure center of the brain (basal ganglia) when we do something we deem pleasurable. If we understand that the devil substitutes entertainment for joy, we can see that society is being set up for the coming lawless one. If humans allow their brains to be programmed for pleasure derived from unrighteousness, then lying signs and wonders will be pleasing to them, and a deception that leads to perishing will be the end result.

I am not saying that watching TV is a sin, but I am saying it can be. I am not saying that listening to secular music is a sin, but I am saying it can be. We have enough of a battle against the fleshly nature already, so why, as people who walk in the Spirit, feed ourselves with that which tantalizes and tempts the flesh?

Far too many Christians today seem to have the "ostrich syndrome," stubbornly denying the battle that rages. They refuse to believe that the devil uses the things of this world to lure people into his lair. There is a conspiracy today to promote this view, but that is nothing new. But the truth is, the devil will do anything to hurt, hinder, and harass believers. He knows full well the power of pleasure and the lulling to sleep it brings. He capitalizes on the fact that people feel cheated when their pleasure centers are without stimulation.

One statement that summarizes all I am trying to say is this: should we entertain ourselves with sins that Christ died for? Whether from things heard, seen, or done, how can we derive pleasure from something that sent Christ to the cross?

Entertainment is the devil's substitute for joy. So let's put a God filter on all that we watch and listen to today!

July 12

The L*ORD* *God is my strength; He will make my feet like deer's feet, and He will make me walk on my high hills.*

— Habakkuk 3:19

Habakkuk prophesied in a time when the dominance of the Assyrian Empire was being overrun by the up-and-coming Babylonians. The children of Judah were moving from the influence and oppression of one evil right into another.

The record of Habakkuk's prophecy is primarily a series of petitions, proclamations, and prayers to the Lord under the continual oppression of unjust and evil regimes. Yet in this concluding verse of his prophecy, Habakkuk arrives at a single truth that could well be embraced in any day and age. We could state it like this: God has not destined His children to live *under* the circumstances, but rather *above* them.

Habakkuk uses two names for the Lord to endorse his point. First, he speaks of Jehovah Adonoy, which means "the Lord God is my strength": "He [Jehovah Adonoy] will make my feet like deer's feet, and He will make me walk on my high hills." What great words from a man in the midst of a season where there were few, if any, high points!

But it is so like the Lord to remind His people that life is not to be lived under the circumstances but above them. There are high hills for us to walk on at all times and in all seasons, but the Lord has given us feet that are stable. Even in precarious places, we can walk just as securely as the sure-footed deer on the high hills.

I am not a big fan of heights, and I have learned the truth and effectiveness of the age-old counsel to not look down but to look straight ahead. Nonetheless, I have discovered that it is human nature to look down at potential disaster. This is not God's plan for us, to keep our eyes focused on possible disasters every day of our lives. God, Jehovah Adonoy, says, "Walk on the high hills with confidence. Quit living under the circumstances, but walk above them as I have ordained for you to do." Sometimes this begins by simply no longer looking down.

So put on your deer feet and walk with assurance today on top of your circumstances. Jehovah Adonoy is your strength!

July 13

"Now these are Your servants and Your people, whom You have redeemed by
Your great power, and by Your strong hand. O Lord, I pray, please let Your ear
be attentive to the prayer of Your servant, and to the prayer of Your servants who
desire to fear Your name; and let Your servant prosper this day, I pray, and grant
him mercy in the sight of this man." For I was the king's cupbearer.

— Nehemiah 1:10–11

Nehemiah was about to go before a pagan king to ask for favor on God's people, the same people the king's father had held in captivity after destroying their city. On top of that, Nehemiah was the king's personal valet, an exalted position that was not to be taken lightly or used for personal advantage. This was no small task that Nehemiah was about to undertake.

As we continue to read Nehemiah, we see in chapter 2 that he indeed went before the king but could not hide his burden for his people from him. The problem with this was that according to Babylonian law, it was a crime punishable by death to go into the king's presence with sadness. But Nehemiah could not hide his broken heart for the city and people of God.

There is great insight here for us as Christians. Our hearts need to be broken for the lost in our land to such a degree that we are compelled to action, even at the risk of our own peril. It is this heart like Nehemiah's that has called thousands of missionaries to lands far from homes, friends, families, and even ordinary comforts.

The same heart that caused Nehemiah to go before the king and that causes men and women to forsake all for the gospel calls to all of us as well. Maybe we're not called to cross the globe as missionaries, but maybe we're called to cross the street to share what others may not even know they need. Maybe we're not called to risk our lives, but we are called to sacrifice time and energy for the sake of those whose lives lie in ruin, even as the walls of Jerusalem that broke Nehemiah's heart. Whatever our particular circumstances, the love of Jesus must grip our hearts so that we cannot be silent.

If your heart is not in that place, ask God for a burden for the lost. You can know for sure that a prayer like that is according to His will, and He will grant you exactly what you asked for: a burden, just like His, for lost souls everywhere!

July 14

But the natural man does not receive the things of the Spirit of God, for they are foolishness to him; nor can he know them, because they are spiritually discerned.

—1 Corinthians 2:14

We have all had the experience of encountering either an aggressive nonbeliever or a fanatical cult member ready to defend to the death a false gospel. Many of us have debated Scripture with those who deny the Bible as the inspired Word of God or with those whose doctrines were created by a man or woman claiming revelation that was outside the confines of Holy Scripture. In such cases, arguments erupt and debates heat up, and no one changes their mind or position.

For Christians, this scenario is often a tactic of the enemy to distract us from the matter at hand, which is the person's need for the gospel. I have often counseled zealous debaters of the Christian faith to remember that it is not possible to engage in a theological debate with the unsaved, nor can we argue someone into the kingdom of God. The message for unsaved people, whether they are cult members, atheists, or something else, is not to prove to them that the Bible is true. As a matter of fact, the Bible doesn't even defend itself; it just declares itself as the truth of God.

Nonbelievers simply need to hear the gospel, no matter how many times they have heard it, no matter what they may claim to believe about it. Jesus gave us this model in His encounter with Nicodemus in John 3. Jesus told this religious man and teacher of Israel, "You must be born again."

This is the message for the unsaved and spiritually deluded. The natural man cannot discern the things of God, so how can you convince anyone except with the gospel itself? It is the seed that must be planted in order for anyone to come to Christ. So rather than getting caught up in trying to prove the Bible's record of creation or trying to expose the false teachings of the cults, preach the gospel to lost souls. It is the only message by which people can be saved.

To try and argue people into the kingdom of God is a tactic that never bears fruit. Instead, tell people God loves them and has made a way for them to be forgiven and reconciled to God. That is the seed that takes root and transforms the hardest of hearts time and again. That is why Paul told the Corinthians he knew and preached one thing only: "Christ and Him crucified" (1 Cor. 2:2).

Why did Paul say this? Because unsaved people cannot discern truth until they are born again. So preach the body and blood of Jesus today—someone just might get saved!

July 15

Why do you say, O Jacob, and speak, O Israel: "My way is hidden from the Lord, and my just claim is passed over by my God"? Have you not known? Have you not heard? The everlasting God, the Lord, the Creator of the ends of the earth, neither faints nor is weary. His understanding is unsearchable. He gives power to the weak, and to those who have no might He increases strength.

—Isaiah 40:27–29

The children of Israel were in a place where many of us find ourselves at one time or another. They were not necessarily questioning God's awareness of their plight, but rather His goodness in light of their plight. In this passage, the phrase "just claim" refers to the promises of blessing God had made to Israel all the way back to Abraham and Moses. Some were certainly thinking, *Where are the promises of God?* The implication here is, *Are we hidden from the Lord or something? Does He not remember what He promised?*

The Spirit's answer to Israel's ponderings could be paraphrased like this: "Do you not see the consistency and faithfulness of God, beginning all the way back to creation? Is God's love expressed only through favorable circumstances? Does He not empower the weak and strengthen those with no might? Isn't that the pattern of God in your own history, Israel?" That seems to be the Spirit's probing reply.

It is easy for us to get caught up in the same mind-set as the Israelites, but it is important to remember that God is good—even on our bad days. God is good when times are hard, He is good when we feel like He's not watching, and He's good when His promises seemed to be blurred by circumstances. Isaiah is saying, in essence, that beginning with creation and up to the present day, it is impossible for God not to be good, loving, and kind, regardless of our personal circumstances.

It is not remotely possible for even one of God's promises to fail. No matter what you see around you currently, no matter the seeming impossibility of the situation you're facing, God is watching over you and has everything you need to face your circumstance or weakness. There is zero possibility that He will fail you.

But like Israel, you must take your eyes off the situation and turn them back onto the promises of God. God neither faints nor wearies of strengthening His children in their hour of need—and that includes you! So no matter the situation, remember God's consistency from the beginning of time. Beyond a doubt, that proves it is utterly impossible for Him not to be watching over you!

July 16

By awesome deeds in righteousness You will answer us, O God of our salvation, You who are the confidence of all the ends of the earth, and of the far-off seas; who established the mountains by His strength, being clothed with power; You who still the noise of the seas, the noise of their waves, and the tumult of the peoples. They also who dwell in the farthest parts are afraid of Your signs; You make the outgoings of the morning and evening rejoice. You visit the earth and water it, You greatly enrich it; the river of God is full of water; You provide their grain, for so You have prepared it.

—Psalm 65:5–9

As do many others, I love Psalms, especially the reminders of God's majesty and His absolute perfection and wisdom as evidenced in His creation. It is amazing how often the psalmists and others use nature to point us to God's nature. The bizarre look of the praying mantis, as well as the majesty of the Alps and Himalayas, reveals to us the wonder of God. A clear night under a desert sky proclaims the nature of God and His magnificence. The vastness of the oceans and the faithful rise and fall of their tides show us the divine control of an all-powerful God. Even the fearful power of a mighty earthquake or storm reveals to mankind its frailty and God's majesty.

However, if we focus on man and all he has created, we can lose sight of this great truth. Concrete jungles of corruption and lust, power-hungry men and women climbing over one another up the ladder of success, and the envy of neighbor against neighbor over a new car or room addition are all distractions man has introduced into God's majestic creation. It is so easy to get caught up in and swept away by these things.

When was the last time you just took a look at what God has created and praised Him for His glorious nature? I was driving with my wife recently when we crested a hill and before us sprawled the mighty Pacific Ocean. I stated aloud, "Boy, that's a lot of water!" I can't say she was duly impressed by my grasp of the obvious, but there is actually a lot more behind those words than the obvious understated truth. There is a matchless Creator who put that ocean there, and I see a small fraction of His greatness in it.

Consider today the nature of God displayed in nature all around you. Look at the sky and remember His vastness; marvel at the faithfulness of the sun and the moon in their orbits and let it remind you that He is faithful. God's handiwork is everywhere. Look for reasons to praise Him today. It won't take long to find them if you'll get your eyes and mind off all man's stuff that gets in the way!

July 17

We are hard-pressed on every side, yet not crushed; we are perplexed, but not in despair; persecuted, but not forsaken; struck down, but not destroyed.

—2 Corinthians 4:8–9

I am not much of a "candy coater" when it comes to things, and I am thankful that the apostle Paul wasn't one either. His honest assessment and testimonies of radical Christian living are needed in a day when much of the church has been mesmerized by the promises of wealth and prosperity that are preached from many pulpits. You won't find Paul diminishing the hardship aspect of world-changing Christian living. He warns it is hard in every way, perplexing at times, and may even lead to persecution.

However, in the church today, being crushed with despair or struck down and destroyed is not even mentioned as a remote possibility, even for those living boldly for Jesus Christ. Too much "Christianity Lite" is preached and not enough Paul-like truth, which paints the true picture of being light in a dark world. Because much of what is preached today emphasizes the benefits and privileges of the Christian life, many people are unprepared for the reality of hardship in the Christian life.

In my many years of working with young people, I have always loved talking to the teenagers and twenty-something "tough guys." Often they say something like, "Christianity is weak and for weak people." My challenge to them is always the same. I ask, "So you think Christianity is not for real men?" and their answer is generally the same: "No, Christianity is for the weak."

My next statement to them—and I must admit, I relish and even instigate this type of conversation on occasion—is this: "If you think being a Christian is for the weak, then I challenge you to carry a Bible around all week at school. You don't even have to read it, but just carry it around in front of your friends and others. Just carry that book around for five days of school and then tell me how weak the people are who not only carry it but also live by it!"

Interestingly, I have never had one taker. The fact is, they were all afraid to accept the challenge, knowing what would be said about them. That is because, dear friend, Christianity is not for cowards, but according to Revelation 21:8, hell is!

"Hard-pressed," "perplexed," "persecuted," and even "struck down" does not describe a life for cowards. Christianity is living in absolute and unequivocal opposition to all that is in the world. Don't get sold short of what real Christianity is, but read the words of a man honest enough to tell you how it really is, the apostle Paul. Be bold, be strong, for the Lord your God is with you!

July 18

If you faint in the day of adversity, your strength is small.

— Proverbs 24:10

In light of the developments we see in our world today, it is clear to me that God is calling His people to be prepared. God's people are no strangers to adversity, even as we saw in yesterday's devotional from the life of Paul.

Each Sunday morning as our services open, we as a congregation repeat what we have dubbed the "Calvary Chapel Tustin Manifesto," or the CCT Manifesto to those of us who call it home. This powerful statement of belief was developed while I was teaching through the book of Nehemiah some years back, and it goes like this: "I am a child of God destined to make a difference. I will not doubt or fear in the face of adversity. I am committed to God's will for my life, no matter what opposition may come. I will praise God for every blessing and through every trial, for He will never fail me. I will put God first every day of my life that I may hear Him say, 'Well done.'"

Adversity and opposition are two of the leading indicators that we are indeed in the will of God, and the book of Nehemiah proves it clearly. Yet many faint even at the mention of adversity, hoping to slip into heaven with as little trouble as possible. However, the fact is, only by enduring adversity and opposition do we learn that we can. I don't like adversity and opposition any more than the next person, but when it does come, a little hint of excitement stirs deep in my soul. I know it means God is getting ready to do something magnificent, and the devil is opposing it.

We don't have to like adversity and opposition; if we do, we might need a medical checkup! But neither should we fear it or faint in it. Since our destinies are to make a difference in this world — and that is every Christian's destiny — adversity will certainly come. But if adversity causes us to stagnate, then our Christian lives on earth will be lived with small strength and small results.

That is neither my heart nor my desire for me or any other Christian. I want to be numbered among the faithful, not the fearful; the believing, not the doubting. I believe God wants to use you and me, not because of who we are, but because of who He is.

So praise Him today as you put Him first. Do not doubt or fear in the face of adversity, but commit to His will regardless of opposition. Praise Him for every blessing and through every trial, and at the end of each day, you'll find yourself spiritually stronger than the day before and therefore ready for any adversity!

July 19

And when Simon saw that through the laying on of the apostles' hands the Holy Spirit was given, he offered them money, saying, "Give me this power also, that anyone on whom I lay hands may receive the Holy Spirit." But Peter said to him, "Your money perish with you, because you thought that the gift of God could be purchased with money! You have neither part nor portion in this matter, for your heart is not right in the sight of God. Repent therefore of this your wickedness, and pray God if perhaps the thought of your heart may be forgiven you. For I see that you are poisoned by bitterness and bound by iniquity."

— Acts 8:18–23

It has been said that power corrupts, and absolute power corrupts absolutely. Simon Magus, also known as Simon the Sorcerer, was corrupted by a love of power. Justin Martyr wrote of him in chapter 26 of his work titled *Apology* the following:

> There was a Samaritan, Simon, a native of the village called Gitto, who in the reign of Claudius Caesar, and in your royal city of Rome, did mighty acts of magic, by virtue of the art of the devils operating in him. He was considered a god, and as a god was honoured by you with a statue, which statue was erected on the river Tiber, between the two bridges, and bore this inscription, in the language of Rome: "He persuaded those who adhered to him that they should never die, and even now there are some living who hold this opinion of his.... All who take their opinions from these men, as we before said, call themselves Christians."

Simon did not reject the teachings of Christianity; he simply added to them. He promoted the idea that he was a leader in place of God, and he incorporated the worship of images and statuary into his "church." (Isn't it interesting that the first statue was of himself?) Peter labeled this love of power "poison" and a "bond of iniquity."

Dear friends, beware of those who elevate themselves to positions of equality with God or who seek to gather followers to "private revelations" that distinguish them from everyone else. This is iniquity and robs the glory due only to the true and living God through Jesus Christ our Lord.

How can we recognize such people? They exalt self, not Jesus, yet claim to be a part of the church—a very special part, but a part nonetheless. According to both Jesus and the apostle John, many antichrists will arise in the last days.

How, then, can we know who is who? The first thing to look for is self-promotion and a love of power. Make sure those who influence you in your spiritual life are going in the right direction. Real leaders walk in power and authority, to be sure, but the glory is always given to God.

There are many "Simons" today who are in the ministry for the power it gives. You will know them by their fruits: self-promotion and the exaltation of the signs and wonders they perform. Signs and wonders indeed followed the apostles, but many today are not following the apostles, but following the signs and wonders. Do not go after them!

July 20

Inasmuch then as the children have partaken of flesh and blood, He Himself likewise shared in the same, that through death He might destroy him who had the power of death, that is, the devil, and release those who through fear of death were all their lifetime subject to bondage.

— Hebrews 2:14–15

I have often said that I am not afraid of dying, though I do have some concerns about the method! Like most people, I would prefer to go in the rapture or die in my sleep, but the fact is, the great enemy, the second death, is no real concern of mine.

What many people truly fear, I have no fear of at all. I am not bothered by the question, what happens after we die? I know exactly what's going to happen to me after I die or after the rapture comes: I am going to heaven! I live with no fear or worry about my eternal existence, because Jesus became flesh and died for my sins. In doing that, He destroyed the true power of death — the death of the soul.

I have no fear of going to hell or being rejected by God when I arrive in heaven. I don't worry whether my good deeds have outweighed my bad; I already know the answer to that! But I am not going to heaven because of good deeds or bad deeds, even though my life as a Christian will be examined by fire and tested for purity. I am going to heaven because Jesus tasted death for me. What I deserved, He endured; what I earned as punishment, He paid. That leaves me free to live fearless of what lies beyond the grave.

Dear brother or sister, if that truth doesn't put some "glide in your stride" today, I don't know what will. Go out and face the world today as though your eternal destiny is secure in Christ, because it is! Go out and live in front of others today as though you know that you know that heaven is your eternal home, because it is!

Living like that makes you intriguing to those overwhelmed by this world's pressures and pains. And you never know, your attitude of gratitude just might open a door for you to tell someone else how to be free from man's greatest fear: the question of what happens after death. I know and every Christian knows the answer to that question, and when what we know shows, others are going to want it.

Tell someone today that heaven is your future home and can be theirs too!

July 21

Now the Spirit expressly says that in latter times some will depart from the faith, giving heed to deceiving spirits and doctrines of demons, speaking lies in hypocrisy, having their own conscience seared with a hot iron, forbidding to marry, and commanding to abstain from foods which God created to be received with thanksgiving by those who believe and know the truth.

—1 Timothy 4:1–3

Humankind has an incessant need to practice some form of religion in an effort to feel as though they have somehow played a role in becoming worthy of heaven. Forbidding this and abstaining from that make us feel qualified to be partakers of the heavenly blessings. Clearly the devil has used religion more than any other weapon to lead people astray.

The Holy Spirit expressly, distinctly, says that this tactic will be on the rise in the last days. It is important to understand that the religious activities spoken of are separate and distinct actions, not the collective actions of one group. Some will heed deceiving spirits teaching demonic doctrines, while others with seared consciences will embrace immoral behaviors as acceptable. Still others will seek elevated status through unbiblical self-imposed denials of marriage or foods, returning to some of the erroneous practices of the early church. Paul gives us this prophetic warning, instructing that the Holy Spirit informs us expressly so that those living in the last days will both recognize the signs of the end and avoid getting caught up in the demonic movements that will sweep over the world at that time.

Christianity is today what it was in Paul's day, it is what John the Beloved followed, and it is what Peter practiced. Since Jesus is God and God does not change (Mal. 3:6), then neither does the Christian faith change. But changes to the faith will be rampant in the last days, and when you see these things happening—new age movements, the departure from traditional Christian values, the incorporation of ancient religious rituals into the church—know that it is not the way of the Lord, but the way of deception. When you see these things coming to pass, look up, for your redemption draws near (Luke 21:28)!

July 22

And my speech and my preaching were not with persuasive words of human wisdom, but in demonstration of the Spirit and of power, that your faith should not be in the wisdom of men but in the power of God.

—1 Corinthians 2:4–5

In a culture that revered eloquence and communication of knowledge, Paul wrote to the church in Corinth not to confuse eloquence with accuracy. Though a thought well stated does not make it true, we are often moved by a person's gift of communication and accept as truth something that was merely expressed well. The heart of Paul's exhortation to the Corinthians is to not get carried away from the truth by false things well said.

If he had lived in our media-oriented age, I believe Paul would have written an entire epistle on this subject. We process more information in a day than people in the past would have encountered in a lifetime. We get information from the TV, radio, the Web, e-mail, Twitter, and Facebook. We hear of things happening around the world that people generations ago would have died without ever knowing. This proliferation of information means that our info filter needs to be set extra high, and that filter is the Word of God.

Unfortunately, we have become a lot like the Greeks Paul warned the Corinthians about. Luke tells us that Paul's passion in this area likely stemmed from an encounter he had in Athens, which is described in Acts 17:21. Paul described the Athenians as people who "spent their time in nothing else but either to tell or to hear some new thing." Like the Athenians, many of us today are enamored with information. But we must note what Paul says here, and that is not to confuse the power of speech with the power of God. The demonstration of God's Spirit and power is manifested through us as we touch other people's lives with the power of the gospel.

I love to hear a great speaker as much as the next person, but the fact is, not all information presented or even presented well is true, even in the church. Lots of new things are popping up in the church today, and many of them are communicated well by people gifted with eloquence. But friend, if it doesn't line up with the Word of God, it is just not true, no matter how well said.

As you encounter the deluge of new information coming out of the church today, remember this one thing: if it's new, it's not true; and if it's true, it's not new! This one filter will keep the spam from clogging your system!

July 23

Enlarge the place of your tent, and let them stretch out the curtains of your dwellings; do not spare; lengthen your cords, and strengthen your stakes. For you shall expand to the right and to the left, and your descendants will inherit the nations, and make the desolate cities inhabited.

— Isaiah 54:2–3

I love God's expansion plans! Whether with Israel or the church, God wants the impact and influence of His people to benefit those around them. God's people bring strength to places of moral weakness, and they enlarge the hope in those around them as they live by faith in an unseen God. Their influence will last for generations, and places once desolate will be filled with the blessings of the people whose God is the Lord!

Now we know that these words spoken to Israel were both figurative and literal. It was literal in that God's people did indeed dwell in tents tied with cords fastened to stakes. But it was also figurative in that God was calling them to inhabit the fullness of their inheritance as He gave them vineyards and olive tress they did not plant and cities they did not build (Deut. 6:11).

We too have been given an inheritance obtained by another and given to us as a gift, much like God gave Israel a portion of land. So the question is, are we enlarging in that inheritance? Are we expanding to the right and the left, lengthening our cords and strengthening our stakes? Are we walking in everything that God has given us? If not, God says, "Enlarge the place of your inheritance (salvation) in your life. Walk fully and powerfully in the gift and the joy of your salvation."

The sad fact is, Israel never fully inhabited the land God had given them, but settled in only portions of it. But Christian, God has commanded you to enlarge, to walk fully in His will and plan and to enjoy all that He has given you. So live today as though your future is bright and nothing can change that, because your future *is* bright and nothing *can* change that!

July 24

Pure and undefiled religion before God and the Father is this: to visit orphans and widows in their trouble, and to keep oneself unspotted from the world.

—James 1:27

Though we have all heard that Christianity is not a religion, but rather a personal relationship with God, the word *religion* is appropriate in this verse. The word *religion* here means "ceremonial observance" or "worship." It is the latter of these two meanings that gives us the proper understanding of this verse.

Quite often we dub the portion of a church service that precedes the message as a time of worship. Not to split hairs, but it would be more accurately defined as a time of praise. Worship may include a time of music and singing, but worship, by definition, means to prostrate and submit. This tells us that worship is a way of life, not just a portion of a church service.

Pure and undefiled worship, then, means submitting our lives to helping others while keeping ourselves morally and spiritually pure before God. This can be done every day. So could we not say, then, that worship includes helping people in their troubles? One thing we know without question is that there is unlimited opportunity around us every day.

So as we move forward in this day, let's worship God through praise and by helping those in trouble. Whether we encounter financial, spiritual, or moral trouble, God is well pleased when we do for others what He does for us—help in time of trouble!

Don't wait to get to church to worship. Opportunities abound every day to live pure and undefiled before God.

July 25

Then David spoke to the men who stood by him, saying, "What shall be done for the man who kills this Philistine and takes away the reproach from Israel? For who is this uncircumcised Philistine, that he should defy the armies of the living God?"

—1 Samuel 17:26

On this journey to heaven, we encounter many different types of people, including many types of Christians. Some are more solemn than others, some are more analytical, and some are more vibrant; these are all just different human personalities brought into our lives. But one of my favorite types of people in the body of Christ is new believers. They see God in everything and are righteously indignant about all that is against Him. "Everybody needs to be a Christian" is their mind-set, and many have an attitude like, "You must be nuts if you're not a Christian!" I love their zeal.

At the time of this Scripture verse, David was a newly appointed king. God had already chosen him, but man had yet to acknowledge God's choice. But here we see David, listening to a nine-foot six-inch giant defy the armies of Israel and thereby defy the name of Israel's God. I always like to bring this into our day and look at it as if David were saying, "Who is this clown that defies the armies of the living God?" David was righteously indignant because the name of the Lord was being defiled.

We could use a little of that kind of attitude today. Many things in our world mock the armies of God and discourage us, just as they did in the days of David and Goliath. David, however, displayed a "new believer" boldness that many of us once knew. But sadly, things we once found repugnant have now become acceptable to us, and things we once marveled at, we now view with bored, complacent eyes.

How can we correct this? It's easier than you might think. Just do what you used to do! Stand up for the truth, and speak up for right the way you used to. Be righteously indignant when it is called for. The next thing you know, your spiritual youth will be restored, and you'll be back in the mix again. Your faith will be exciting once more, and maybe even a dry season will end.

David didn't worry about what others thought. He was offended by the challenges against the name of the Lord and did something about it. As the story continues, we find that David's actions offended even his own brothers, who accused him of grandstanding. Well, the end of the story speaks for itself. A young boy with a stick and some stones stood with a giant's head in his hand, and God received great glory. That which defied God was soundly defeated.

Stand up in defense of His name today, and rekindle the fire that once burned within. Try it—you'll like it!

July 26

Being confident of this very thing, that He who has begun a good work in you will complete it until the day of Jesus Christ.

— Philippians 1:6

Though I am admittedly a creature of habit and comfortable in a regular routine, there is a downside to this: monotony and stifled creativity. Over the years, I have found myself losing interest in things, even within my self-appointed comfort zone, that I had first embraced with zeal and passion. That's because the monotony of a routine stifles creativity and fosters boredom.

How glad I am that God is God and I am not! If He got bored or lost interest in people who do the same things over and over again, we would all be in a world of trouble. But God is not like us, and Jesus completes the work He begins in us. Even when we do the same dumb thing over and over, revisit the same pitfall time and again, He never gives up but keeps working on us. And He will continue this process until the day He comes and perfects us all.

Satan wants us to believe the reverse is true. He wants to exploit the feelings of grief and shame that come with repetitive failures and translate them into a loss of interest in us on God's part. But nothing could be further from the truth. God loves us and sent His Son to die for us "even when we were dead in trespasses" (Eph. 2:5), so why would He lose interest in us after we are His?

Don't buy the lie of the enemy. Yes, you might be a creature of habit who needs some new habits, but you are God's creature of habit! What He begins, He finishes, and He is going to keep working on you until you are perfect, which will happen when you are at last in His presence.

But in the meantime, friend, stop falling into the same hole. By the power of the Holy Spirit, create new habits. God is at work in you and hasn't abandoned you. Take captive any thought that God has lost interest in you because you have failed... again (2 Cor. 10:5). It's not from the Lord! What He began in you, He will complete. Even when today's failures look a lot like yesterday's, He will not stop working on and through you. Repent, and times of refreshing will come from the Lord (Acts 3:19).

July 27

Then the sky receded as a scroll when it is rolled up, and every mountain and island was moved out of its place. And the kings of the earth, the great men, the rich men, the commanders, the mighty men, every slave and every free man, hid themselves in the caves and in the rocks of the mountains, and said to the mountains and rocks, "Fall on us and hide us from the face of Him who sits on the throne and from the wrath of the Lamb! For the great day of His wrath has come, and who is able to stand?"

— Revelation 6:14–17

I am bewildered how people can know that God exists yet refuse to repent and surrender to His will or accept that His Son is the only Savior. This tendency will reach its zenith in the heart of the tribulation period. Five different times, Revelation tells us that people will know they are under the judgment of God yet still refuse to repent. This is significant in light of the question people often pose of how a God of love could send anyone to hell or send judgment on the earth.

The fact is, God has done all He can to save humanity without violating the free will He has given us. At creation, it was important that He give man free will, for only by the ability to choose can true love be known. You cannot make someone love you, and God desire's was not to have robotic, mindless followers who had no choice but to follow Him. That's not love, and it is love that God desires from His creation (Deut. 7:9).

How is this important to your day? We all hear accusations levied against God—how could He do this, and how could He do that? Perhaps a good response would be, "People do not go to heaven just because God loves them, but people go to heaven because they choose to love God." God so loved the world that He gave His Son, but that doesn't mean that all the world automatically goes to heaven. God expressed love to this lost and fallen world in the gift of His Son, and those who choose to love God will spend eternity with Him.

Do not let anyone confuse or diminish the love of God by their self-centered arguments. God's love could not be expressed any more clearly than by the sending of His Son, just as man's rebellion cannot be expressed any more clearly than by the rejection of His Son. God is love, and He is not willing that any should perish but wants all to come to repentance (2 Pet. 3:9). So for man to encounter the wrath of God and enter into eternal punishment has nothing to do with whether God is loving, but it has everything to do with whether man chooses to love God.

People use the Bible's teaching about hell as a reason to reject God because they do not want to accept God's plan of how not to go there. It is not even remotely possible for God to be unjust or unfair. Do not let anyone convince you otherwise!

July 28

For many deceivers have gone out into the world who do not confess Jesus Christ as coming in the flesh. This is a deceiver and an antichrist.

—2 John 1:7

It has been said that in the beginning God created man in His image, and in the end man has returned the favor! This speaks of our tendency to create a God that we like while rejecting the God who is.

As I was writing this devotional on a beautiful Saturday morning, two women "coincidentally" knocked on my door. They wanted to tell me about the Jesus they have created, the one who used to be Michael the archangel, a created being of God. But John warned us about that. He clearly said deceivers will go out into the world and say that Jesus was not Christ when He came in the flesh, thus denying the deity of Jesus and His existence as God prior to His earthly birth.

Many religions today have created their own Jesus, and here is why this is important. Acts 4:12 says, "Nor is there salvation in any other, for there is no other name under heaven given among men by which we must be saved."

So if you have created your own Jesus, like the one who is the spirit brother of Lucifer or Michael the archangel, or the one who is merely a great teacher or prophet, that's not the Jesus who saves.

It is of utmost importance for Christians to know what they believe, as there are many who have gone out to deceive. Jesus is God come in human flesh. He did not receive the Christ spirit at His baptism, and He is not the devil's brother. He was never an angel who became a man who then became an angel again. He is God putting on flesh, come to take away the sins of the world!

If you have your own Jesus, a Jesus other than Immanuel, "God with us," then you have created God in your own image. Trusting in that will not save. To believe otherwise is deception; it is antichrist, which means "against" or "instead of" Christ. Do not be fooled by those who want to talk about Jesus but deny His Deity. That's another Jesus, and believing in that Jesus will save no one.

Be confident today. The real Jesus is the same yesterday, today, and forever. Preaching the real Jesus will bring people to real salvation. So stand against deception today as opportunities arise to defeat lies with the truth about the real Jesus!

July 29

It happened in the spring of the year, at the time when kings go out to battle, that David sent Joab and his servants with him, and all Israel; and they destroyed the people of Ammon and besieged Rabbah. But David remained at Jerusalem. Then it happened one evening that David arose from his bed and walked on the roof of the king's house. And from the roof he saw a woman bathing, and the woman was very beautiful to behold.

—2 Samuel 11:1–2

We know how the rest of the story goes. Furthermore, even if we know nothing else about David, we at least know two things: his greatest victory and his greatest defeat. Even nonbelievers know the story of David and Goliath, David's greatest victory, and many know of David's sin with Bathsheba and the ensuing plot to murder her husband. It is interesting that both events hinged on the same decision of battle.

When David faced Goliath, he obeyed his father by taking provisions to his brothers at the field of battle. As a result, he found himself right where God wanted him, and history was made. However, in the verses above, we read that in the spring of the year, when kings commonly went to battle—not when kings sent their generals out to battle without them, but when kings themselves went out to battle—that David remained in Jerusalem. This one decision led to so many grave consequences. First, David slept with another man's wife, and she became pregnant. Then he plotted to have Uriah, Bathsheba's husband, murdered. After Bathsheba gave birth, the child fell ill. The Lord told David the child would die, and he did.

There is no more dangerous place for the Christian than away from the field of battle. When David was where he was supposed to be, the battlefield, he experienced great victory. When he was not where he was supposed to be, again the battlefield, he suffered great defeat. The enemy loves to isolate God's people and draw them away from the rest of the army and away from the battle. Then he will tempt them and talk to them about how they are not needed, how God doesn't care, and how they have a right to better treatment—even pleasure. But it takes only one bad decision to create a lifetime of regret, and one of the greatest errors is to withdraw from the army of God and miss the victory that can be experienced only when gathered with the people of the Lord.

There is a move in the church today that I believe is risky to the health and well-being of all Christians, and that is regularly "attending" church online or via TV. Now obviously, illness, injury, or extenuating circumstances are excluded from this warning, but members of the body need to gather with other believers to encourage and strengthen one another. Attending church in person is much like receiving a briefing as a soldier in God's army. The truth is, if you try to attend the briefing online but have no accountability to the rest of the army, you never know what might happen when you look out your window. David sadly shows us the devastating outcome of even one simple look and resulting wrong decision.

Meet with a family of believers regularly and in person. You need them, and they need you. Do not let the devil isolate you from the rest of the troops.

July 30

From that time many of His disciples went back and walked with Him no more.

—John 6:66

Knowing that chapter and verse divisions were not originally part of the Bible, I still find it interesting that this verse is 6:66, considering what it says! Jesus had just fed five thousand men plus women and children with five loaves of bread and two fish. Furthermore, He had gathered twelve baskets of leftovers, one for each disciple. He then perceived that the people wanted to take Him by force and make Him king, so He slipped away to a mountain to pray while His disciples got into a boat to cross the Sea of Galilee.

While they were at sea, a great wind arose, and the disciples were in a fierce storm. When they were three or four miles from shore, they saw someone approaching them, walking on the water. They were afraid, but as we know, this was Jesus; and John says that when He got into the boat, the disciples were immediately at the place where they had been headed.

The next day the people were looking for this guy who had fed them, but they could not find Him. They jumped into their boats and finally located Him in Capernaum. Gently chiding them for following Him because of the bread they had eaten the day before, he then taught the Bread of Life discourse. In it, Jesus said He was the Bread of Life come down from heaven and that those who follow Him must eat His flesh and drink His blood. This saying was spiritual, not literal, as He explained that He must be their very life and blood if they wanted to follow Him.

Now we arrive at our verse at the beginning of today's devotional. "From that time," the time when Jesus said He must be our everything if we want to be His followers, many went back and walked with Him no more.

What a sad reality that is with us yet today! People want to follow Jesus for what He can do for them, but they do not want to follow when He asks something of them. "Fair-weather followers" might be a good label for this group. I am always pressed in my spirit to remind myself and others that we are God's servants—He is not ours. What He asks of us is best for us, but even more important, it is what He will receive the most glory from.

If God has been asking something of you, if He has been whispering in your heart for you to put Him first, if He has been asking to be your sustenance and your provision, don't stop following Him and don't lose heart. He is asking from you that which is necessary for fulfilling His will and purpose in your life, and it is absolutely impossible for that not to be a blessing. Jesus wants not only your heart, but also your mind and body. He wants to be your everything, and He died for your sins to prove this.

So don't be bummed out if God asks something great of you. Just do it, and you'll never regret it!

July 31

Do not be rash with your mouth, and let not your heart utter anything hastily before God. For God is in heaven, and you on earth; therefore let your words be few.

— Ecclesiastes 5:2

I have often said, "Half of prayer is waiting for an answer," yet as Solomon notes, we often speak an abundance of hasty, even rash, words when we pray. "God, please do this, please fix that, heal them, forgive me for that, see You tomorrow, amen!" it often goes. I must admit, I need to continually remind myself to wait for God to speak in my prayer time. Far too many times, I am guilty of "machine gun" prayers, mowing down my list of needs in a rapid burst of words without a moment's waiting for what God might want to say to me.

So how do we fix this tendency? It may seem odd to some, but I have found that the best way for me, in light of the fact that prayer is talking to God, is to treat my prayer time like a conversation between two friends. I say good morning to the Lord, and sometimes I ask Him how He is today. Then I laugh at myself because I know how He is—He's great! But this simple task of incorporating normal speak into my prayer life has helped me stay focused and, what is more important, real.

Solomon's intent is obvious here. We are to be respectful and attentive when addressing the Lord. But the truth is, we often lapse into hasty and rash prayer times though we don't mean to at all. We love Him and we want to pray, but we're busy and our time talking to Him gets pushed aside and intruded on by everyday life. So the time we do spend in "communion" communication, where there is actually a connect on both ends, needs to be fruitful.

If you're like me and frequently send up prayer flares, slow down and listen. Treat prayer like a conversation with a dear friend seated across the table from you. As I said, I have used this as a tool in my own prayer life. The funny thing is, sometimes when I say, "Good morning, God. How are you?" and then laugh, I sense in my spirit that He is laughing too.

Give your prayer time "time"—time to listen and converse with a God who loves talking with His children!

August 1

But know this, that in the last days perilous times will come: For men will be lovers of themselves, lovers of money, boasters, proud, blasphemers, disobedient to parents, unthankful, unholy, unloving, unforgiving, slanderers, without self-control, brutal, despisers of good, traitors, headstrong, haughty, lovers of pleasure rather than lovers of God, having a form of godliness but denying its power.
And from such people turn away!

−2 Timothy 3:1–5

If we knew nothing of prophecy regarding Israel from Ezekiel, Amos, and the prophets, if we knew nothing of the words of Jesus in Matthew 24 and 25 regarding the days preceding His return, and if we did not have the book of Revelation to provide a time line of church history and the following events of the tribulation, these five verses alone would tell us we are in the last days!

The list certainly reads like a page from the newspaper or a broadcast from the evening news. Each day we hear stories about man's pride, greed, arrogance, and disdain for God and His name; the rebellion of children; the pervasive sense of entitlement; and the lack of love and forgiveness. Furthermore, if it's an election year, we are in for months of slander and mudslinging. From all these things, we see the absence of self-control and the brutality that results from it, the despising of good things and even the redefining of good. You get the point, I'm sure. We are in the last days.

Paul closed this prophetic word of knowledge to Timothy with the reason people would be that way in the last days: "having a form of godliness but denying its power." This phrase is interesting because it could also read that in the last days, men will "formulate a gospel that contradicts its meaning." This too is concrete evidence that we are in the last days and confirms the need to be in a good church that teaches God's truth "truthfully" so we can know which things to turn away from.

Paul's list above is a list of what people who don't know God do. However, Paul tells us in 1 Corinthians 5:9 not to break off relationships with the people of the world, because they're the very ones we need to reach. Paul then instructs us not to keep company with anyone who calls himself a brother who also practices unrepentant sin. This is in line with the sentiment above concerning those who formulate a gospel that contradicts its meaning. From such people, we are to turn away.

It is funny how we sit in judgment of God's Word at times, as though it could be in error. I believe this is the most common form of error in our day. Paul tells us by the inspiration of the Holy Spirit not to keep company with such people in hopes of them coming to their senses. They are on the wrong path and following someone who has contradicted the true meaning of the gospel.

Jesus said in the last days it would be as it was in Noah's day, with the thoughts and intents of men's hearts only evil continually (Gen. 6:5). Sadly, I believe, that is true today, and those who are true believers are relatively few. There are far too many who hold to a form of godliness that robs the gospel of its power. Do we love them enough to turn away from them and not act like everything is okay? That's a hard but sound truth to consider this day.

August 2

Not that I have already attained, or am already perfected; but I press on, that I may lay hold of that for which Christ Jesus has also laid hold of me. Brethren, I do not count myself to have apprehended; but one thing I do, forgetting those things which are behind and reaching forward to those things which are ahead, I press toward the goal for the prize of the upward call of God in Christ Jesus.

— Philippians 3:12–14

I love the subtle manner in which the Bible slips in monumental truths and thoughts with phrases that capture the eye and attention. This, I believe, is applicable to our passage today in Philippians. Note how Paul says "this one thing I do" and then names two things: "forgetting the things which are behind" and "reaching forward to those things which are ahead." Obviously, these are not two things at all, but rather companion truths, a package deal, or even, as some might say, a "twofer."

The marvel of this great truth is that it assures us God does not want us to drag the dead past into our present. The things behind must be forgotten in order to reach forward. Many saints are tormented at times by the memories of forgiven sins, but Paul says that reaching forward and pressing toward require forgetting the past.

I'll be the first to say this is not always easy, especially when the past includes things over which we had no control or choice. But the fact remains, this companion truth is a necessity for those wanting to move forward in spite of the past. One thing I came to realize about my own life is that I had to believe what the Bible said about my past, and I had to accept the fact that God had indeed separated me from my sins as far as the east is from the west (Ps. 103:12). For me to keep reliving my past was to deny what God said He had done for me on the cross.

This is why this "one thing" contains two truths. Reaching forward requires looking forward, and looking forward requires not looking back. If we are His, God has forgiven our sins, and He has provided healing from the past. But we must learn to forget the past, meaning not let it rule the present, so that we can press toward the upward.

Freedom is the word for today — freedom from past sins committed by us and against us!

August 3

No king is saved by the multitude of an army; a mighty man is not delivered by great strength. A horse is a vain hope for safety; neither shall it deliver any by its great strength. Behold, the eye of the LORD is on those who fear Him, on those who hope in His mercy, to deliver their soul from death, and to keep them alive in famine.

—Psalm 33:16–19

Don't you wish we would always learn from other people's mistakes and avoid repeating them? It's too bad this is not true more frequently in our lives, but it seems to be human nature to read things, learn about the consequences, and then do the same things anyway and experience the same outcomes.

The psalmist here is clearly looking back on God's deliverance of the children of Israel against overwhelming odds time and again. Yet the psalmist also notes how easy it is to forget the miracles and go right back to trusting in the visible or known.

God is watching out for you today, friends. He's keeping an eye on you; every day He preserves you from death of the soul. But God is also very practical. He keeps His people alive in famine and hard times. He stretches resources, and He supplies in surprising ways. He never loses track of His children or their needs.

The mistake many have made, and one we should learn from and avoid, is putting their hope and trust in things that can change in a moment. Material things, military might, personal strength—all these are frail and fleeting at best. But God—He never wearies, His power never wanes, His might never diminishes, the odds are never against Him, and the enemy never outnumbers or outflanks Him.

Our God is the mighty God of heaven, maker of all things, and He is our friend, our savior, our provider, and our protector. So why trust in a horse for safety, a man's strength for deliverance, or the power of military might for a sense of protection? Our God is an army of one, and nothing in this life is any match for Him.

So put your hope in the unchanging God, not in fleeting material things. Earthly possessions come and go, and kingdoms rise and fall; but the eternal Lord never changes. His eye is always on you to deliver you from death and keep you alive in famine.

Praise the Lord!

August 4

So the governors and satraps sought to find some charge against Daniel concerning the kingdom; but they could find no charge or fault, because he was faithful; nor was there any error or fault found in him. Then these men said, "We shall not find any charge against this Daniel unless we find it against him concerning the law of his God."

—Daniel 6:4–5

What a powerful testimony of a captive in a foreign land held against his own will in forced submission to a pagan king! No one could find fault against Daniel concerning his work, and neither could anyone call him a hypocrite for failing in his religious convictions. To bring any kind of charge against him, the kingdom officials had to concoct something from Daniel's faith to use against him.

So what did they decide to attack? Prayer. The governors and satraps made it illegal to pray to anyone but the king for thirty days, knowing full well this would not fly with Daniel. The king, being filled with pride, signed the decree into law, and the trap was thus set for Daniel.

But look what happened next: "Now when Daniel knew that the writing was signed, he went home. And in his upper room, with his windows open toward Jerusalem, he knelt down on his knees three times that day, and prayed and gave thanks before his God, as was his custom since early days" (Dan. 6:10). What followed was an event known to this day by believer and nonbeliever alike: Daniel in the lions' den.

The scenario was set into place because Daniel was a man who was faithful in his captivity. He did his job as unto the Lord, and no fault could be found in him. In fact, the only way to affix blame upon him was by making his beliefs illegal. So what did Daniel do in response to a government regulation against prayer? He prayed anyway, in full sight of all, with the windows open toward Jerusalem, as the Jews were supposed to pray. And the miraculous story that followed is now known the world over, though it happened twenty-seven hundred years ago.

Daniel did his job as unto the Lord, and he honored the Lord when his captors legislated a prohibition against prayer. Yes, a lions' den followed, but the Lord handled the lions in response to Daniel's faithfulness to prayer.

Do your job as unto the Lord today, whether you are a student, boss, laborer, or homemaker. At the end of the day, let no charge be found against you concerning your work. If nothing is there, then all your adversaries can do is to try to plot against God, and remember, He never loses a battle!

August 5

Have we not all one Father? Has not one God created us? Why do we deal treacherously with one another by profaning the covenant of the fathers? Judah has dealt treacherously, and an abomination has been committed in Israel and in Jerusalem, for Judah has profaned the LORD's holy institution which He loves: He has married the daughter of a foreign god.

—Malachi 2:10–11

The "holy institution" the Lord loves is marriage! No wonder it is under such attack in our day, for whatever God is for, we can be sure the devil is against. It is almost as though we can identify the things dear to the Lord's heart by recognizing what the devil is attacking in our day.

In this passage from Malachi, marriage is awarded the beautifully poetic label of "the Lord's holy institution which He loves." If the Lord loves it, the devil hates it. So Satan's efforts are to destroy it, redefine it, or belittle it as an unnecessary and antiquated ritual of a generation gone by.

We need to remember that Malachi also said the Lord does not change (Mal. 3:6), so if marriage was the holy institution that God loved in the 400s BC, then marriage is the holy institution God loves in the twenty-first century AD. The reason it is critical that we know and remember this and that marriage remain as God defined it is that marriage is meant to portray Christ's love for the church. If marriage is destroyed by divorce, redefined in its participants, or belittled as an unnecessary ritual of a day gone by, then the idea that Christ's love for the church is unchanging is diminished.

Marriage is God's institution and creation. He loves it and has clearly defined it. He wants us to honor it because it pictures the mystery Paul spoke of in Ephesians 5, which is Christ's love for His bride, the church.

Those who are married must honor marriage as a holy institution loved by the Lord, and all who are in Him must define it as God has defined it. Marriage is under attack today for one simple reason: it portrays the love of Jesus for His bride. If God loves it, the devil hates it; if God defends it, we must defend it too.

If you are married, honor your marriage today, and if you are not married, honor it by standing for God's definition of it. If marriage goes the way the world wants it to, the picture of Christ and His bride will be destroyed, redefined, and belittled. That is a dangerous place for a nation to be, for that nation will find itself fighting against God.

August 6

Let us hold fast the confession of our hope without wavering, for He who promised is faithful. And let us consider one another in order to stir up love and good works, not forsaking the assembling of ourselves together, as is the manner of some, but exhorting one another, and so much the more as you see the Day approaching.

— Hebrews 10:23–25

Though there are many things to consider in these power-packed verses, the first to note is the last one stated. The author mentions that there are some things we will need to exhort one another in more frequently as we see the Day approaching.

The first thing to note is that the Day, the Day of the Lord, can be seen. We may not know the day or the hour of the Lord's coming for His bride, but Hebrews tells us we will see its approach. Matthew 24 and 25 supply us with the details of what to look for, and Hebrews tells us what to do when we see them: hold fast the confession of hope, and do not waver. "Don't follow the current trends in the church" would be a good summary to glean from this instruction. Rather, we must stay on the old paths, where the good way is (Jer. 6:16).

We are next instructed to stir up love and good works. This is a warning against seeing the Day approaching but sitting and doing nothing until it comes. "Be in church a lot as the Day grows near" would be a way to read verse 25. I believe we can conclude from this that we are going to need each other a great deal as the Day draws near. We are going to need to be together more in order to be exhorted more. We are going to have to remind each other more to keep loving and doing rather than hiding and waiting. We are going to need to be encouraged to hold fast, not just to our hope, but to the confession of our hope. "Keep spreading the truth" is a way for us to understand this.

I believe with every ounce of my being that we can see the Day approaching. I also believe we are going to have to exhort one another more and more in the coming days. We will need to be together, pray together, encourage one another, keep those close who are fearful, challenge those who want to disengage, and keep preaching truth as the cost for doing so increases all around us.

Jesus is coming soon, friends. Do not be ashamed to declare it, and do not be moved by those who say, "The church has been saying that for years." The fact is, we are seeing it now with the rebirth of the nation of Israel, a movement toward global governance, and a world rapidly excluding the true and living God.

Encourage someone today that this world is not our home. As was said in the sixties and seventies, "We're just passin' through." Heaven is our home, and soon and very soon we are going to see the King!

August 7

Then the LORD said to me, "Go again, love a woman who is loved by a lover and is committing adultery, just like the love of the LORD for the children of Israel, who look to other gods and love the raisin cakes of the pagans." So I bought her for myself for fifteen shekels of silver, and one and one-half homers of barley. And I said to her, "You shall stay with me many days; you shall not play the harlot, nor shall you have a man — so, too, will I be toward you."

— Hosea 3:1–3

My heart always aches when I encounter a Christian struggling with the assurance of salvation. God asked the Old Testament prophet Hosea to do a difficult thing, and that was to take a wife who played the harlot. This was a woman who would later become the concubine of another man, but whose husband, Hosea, would buy her back anyway.

It is essential to remember that God chose us while we yet chased after other gods and pursued the pleasures of this world. He didn't save us after we got ourselves worth saving; He saved us while we were yet sinners (Rom. 5:8).

In the Old Testament, harlotry often refers to idolatry. In the case with Hosea, however, the meaning is also literal. But God called Hosea to this unlikely marriage in order to paint a picture to Israel and to you and me today.

For those of you who may struggle with feeling as though you have lost your salvation, I ask you to consider: God chose you while you were yet a sinner! Though sin is always a grief to Him and is to be avoided at all costs and consequences, the blood of Jesus did not cleanse you only from past sins, but from all sins. The blood of Jesus is sufficient for even your current failures, and even in those failures, you are still part of the bride of Christ.

Of course, you need to walk carefully concerning such wonderful truths. You do not want to abuse the love of God, as Gomer did Hosea's. But you also need to know, dear friend, if you have fallen, get up and go home! All is not lost. God loves you and wants you to come back to His house and under the covering of His tender care. And not only that, but He has already paid the fifteen shekels, so to speak, to enable you to return home.

God loves you and me with a love beyond human description. He continually gives us that which we do not deserve, just as He did with our salvation. So go out with joy this day, for your groom has paid the price for you to go home!

August 8

For the kingdom of God is not in word but in power.

—1 Corinthians 4:20

As Greeks, the Corinthians loved great orators, but Paul reminded them that words alone are insufficient if no actual power is behind them. This is something we need to keep in mind as we incorporate the Word of God into our lives each day. The things we read in Scripture, the promises we love to hear, are not simply poetic phrases or the musings of a great author or orator. There is power in those words.

The things that we read in Scripture are true and can be acted upon as truth. Many of us have spent at least one Christmas Eve assembling gifts that had to be ready for the next morning. We may have struggled for a while, but once we decided to actually read the directions, things began to come together, and the words and diagrams on the page actually became the product. This is true of the Word of God as well, only on a much grander scale.

If we look at the instructions in the Bible and do what it says, power is manifested in our lives. Consequently, our lives begin to change, and what we read on the page begins to appear in our lives. Jesus said in John 13:17, "If you know these things, blessed are you if you do them." The Word of God is not just words, but the Word of God is power. When we do what it says to do, things happen—wonderful things, amazing things, comforting things!

The book we call holy is just that; it is a holy book like no other. Though it is poetic in nature at times and contains literary eloquence, it is alive! When you follow its instructions, the words on the page appear in your life.

What you read each day in the Bible, do. There is power in the Word of God that is unparalleled by any other writing. It alone has an author who speaks, and everything He says must happen. The kingdom and the book of the kingdom are not just words—they are power. Act on them today!

August 9

And it will come to pass in that day that the mountains shall drip with new wine, the hills shall flow with milk, and all the brooks of Judah shall be flooded with water; a fountain shall flow from the house of the LORD and water the Valley of Acacias.

— Joel 3:18

The Valley of Acacias was the last place the children of Israel camped before entering the Promised Land. These closing words of Joel's prophecy clearly point to the messianic reign of Christ on the earth, but there is also a great lesson for us to glean today. What we can apply to our lives is that God can take even the past, before we began to walk in His promises, and cause it to become fruitful in the present. By that I mean God will frequently take our past hurts and failures and turn them into our ministries.

I cannot count the times God has used my own terrible past to minister to others. Though it is frequently painful to recount and often embarrassing to share, I would not trade what God has done through my past for anything. I do wish my past were different, but the fact is, my past has often become a present ministry.

This is true not only of the self-inflicted wounds of the past, but also of the deepest and most brutal hurts and pains inflicted upon us by others. God uses even those things to reach and encourage others. This is by no means easy for the one who was hurt as a child or suffered from forced pain at any point in life. Sometimes we have to allow our wounds to become scars before we can be used in this way. But a wound is far different from a scar. A wound demands constant care and attention, but over time, the wound heals and a scar forms. The function of the damaged body part has been restored, but the scar remains as a reminder of the injury suffered.

If your past is painful, know that God will and can use it to help others. He will take your pain and use it to bear fruit in others, which in turn bears fruit in you. And the next thing you know, a fountain will flow from your former wilderness, and past pains and failures will become your present ministry.

Let God use all of you today, even if it means reaching back in your BC days to help someone else get out of theirs!

August 10

Praise the LORD*! For it is good to sing praises to our God; for it is pleasant, and praise is beautiful.*

—Psalm 147:1

The words of a people who had just returned home after seventy years of Babylonian captivity were filled with praise and thanksgiving, songs and proclamations to God. As the Israelites returned home to Jerusalem, the songs of praise were inspired by the newfound feeling of freedom—freedom from outside rule, freedom from forced labor, freedom from imposed beliefs and practices. There was reason for praise at this monumental time.

It is also important for us to know what led the Israelites into captivity in the first place. They had forsaken the Sabbath year of the land and not heeded the law of Exodus 23:10–11: "Six years you shall sow your land and gather in its produce, but the seventh year you shall let it rest and lie fallow, that the poor of your people may eat; and what they leave, the beasts of the field may eat. In like manner you shall do with your vineyard and your olive grove."

This command had not been obeyed, and therefore the poor and the beasts of the field had not been allowed to eat from the land that which grew naturally in the seventh year. For 490 years, which included seventy Sabbath years, God's people had ignored this command, and it led to their captivity in Babylon.

Life with all its twists and turns may sometimes bring us to places where praise is not quick to spring to our lips. When we face tough times or encounter tragedy, it's hard to feel like praising, even though all is well between the Lord and us. But as His children, we praise Him anyway, because He is worthy.

There is, however, another time when praise flows freely, and that is when a wrong has been righted in our lives. When we get back into the will of God and under the shadow of His wings, it feels so good that praise comes as naturally as speaking.

Maybe praise has been tough for you lately. Has God required something of you that you have ignored? Is there an act of disobedience He has been calling you to make right? Well, get back home, friend, and praise Him because He is worthy. Then you will rediscover His beautiful and pleasant will!

August 11

And Ezra opened the book in the sight of all the people, for he was standing above all the people; and when he opened it, all the people stood up. And Ezra blessed the LORD, the great God. Then all the people answered, "Amen, Amen!" while lifting up their hands. And they bowed their heads and worshiped the LORD with their faces to the ground.

—Nehemiah 8:5–6

Since I was raised in a very traditional church setting, it took me some time as an adult to allow my outward man to express what was going on in my inner man during worship. I love this scene recorded in Nehemiah as Israel celebrated the rebuilding of the wall around Jerusalem in an amazing fifty-two days. I love the respect shown for God's words. When the book was opened, the people stood in honor of His book. Ezra blessed the Lord, and the people answered in agreement, "Amen, Amen!" with uplifted hands. They bowed their heads and even prostrated themselves before the Lord, physically putting their faces to the ground.

There is no proper posture or position for worship, and worship certainly is not an orchestrated time where all must do this or that at the same time and in the same place. But the scene described above was a genuine spontaneous reaction of the Jews to being in their own city again after having rebuilt the wall. Now, for the first time in a generation, they were reading the word of the Lord together. Though I do not believe that a time of worship ought to be an uncontrolled free-for-all, I do believe that uplifted hands, faces to the ground, and cries of "amen, amen" are appropriate responses to the speaking or singing of God's Word.

I have found this kind of worship particularly significant when I am all alone with the Lord. Something just seems so right about occasionally getting on your face before a holy God, and there is something very appropriate about raised hands and shouts of amen as an offering of praise to our God. Maybe this isn't your church's style of worship, and maybe you would find yourself an unwelcome center of attention if you worshiped like this. But you can worship freely when you're alone. Get on your face before God, bow your head, lift your hands when no one else sees you. For the fact of the matter is, He is the only one that matters.

It's hard to be prideful when you're on your face before a holy God, and it is rather easy to feel humble when you bow before Him. So if you're like me and more reserved in your outward expression, then cut loose and praise Him when you're all alone. That's when your worship is the most sincere anyway.

August 12

I say then: Walk in the Spirit, and you shall not fulfill the lust of the flesh. For the flesh lusts against the Spirit, and the Spirit against the flesh; and these are contrary to one another, so that you do not do the things that you wish.

—Galatians 5:16–17

Many times, I believe, the enemy is able to exploit Christians because they become convinced that only when temptations cease will they truly be spiritual people and good Christians. The fact is, friends, as long as your soul lives in a flesh-and-blood house, there is going to be a war between the spirit and the flesh all the days of your life. It will never subside, and it will never end until your earthly body is replaced with a heavenly incorruptible one.

It's not a sin to be tempted — it's a sin to sin (brilliant deduction, I know)! Jesus Himself was tempted, yet we know He was sinless. The important thing is how we handle the daily assaults of the flesh, or old nature, on our spirits. Paul says the battle is won by walking in the Spirit, and this walk begins by taking thoughts captive, as Paul instructed the Corinthians (2 Cor. 10:5). Identifying temptation in the mind and capturing it there is where the walk in the Spirit begins.

But the walk in the Spirit is also a weapon we can use against temptation. This could be summarized simply as incorporating spiritual things into our day. The Word of God should be a part of our day, of course, but so too should being guided by the Spirit.

Each day we are surrounded by numerous opportunities, and in some ways, our surroundings identify our ministries. If you frequently encounter needy people, then do something to meet those needs, and personal temptations will be overcome by spiritual fulfillment. If you are surrounded by non-believers, then incorporate into your day sharing your faith in some way, and your spirit will be lifted and your flesh and its temptations defeated.

There is never a day when walking in the Spirit is not possible. It can happen through refraining from the office "boss bashing" and instead fasting lunch and praying for your boss. It might be leaving a tract on someone's desk or dropping off something at a local shelter on your way home from work.

Walking in the Spirit is *not* walking with your feet three feet off the ground and talking mystically to others. Walking in the Spirit is daily practical acts that are pleasing to God. Temptation doesn't stand a chance in a life such as that! Temptation won't give up and it will keep coming, but it won't have victory over you if you live spiritually practical each day.

Meet a need, pray for an enemy, read and pray instead of going to lunch, or do something practical today to build your inner man. Then the old flesh and its temptations will soon be conquered!

August 13

Then the apostles gathered to Jesus and told Him all things, both what they had done and what they had taught. And He said to them, "Come aside by yourselves to a deserted place and rest a while." For there were many coming and going, and they did not even have time to eat. So they departed to a deserted place in the boat by themselves.

— Mark 6:30–32

The devil will often use normal and natural emotions and experiences and pervert them into something he can use to our own demise. Nothing has been more perverted in the realm of human emotion than that of loneliness. The apostles here had just returned from an amazing season of ministry where they had been sent out by Jesus to preach and heal the sick. John the Baptist had just been beheaded when the apostles gathered again to report to Jesus all that had happened during their sending out.

In response, Jesus said to them, "Come aside by yourselves to a deserted place." So many people were coming to the disciples that they didn't have enough time to eat. To some, that might sound like a vibrant and exciting time and a great way to live and do ministry. But it is also exactly the time when the Lord will often say, "Come aside by yourself to a lonely place"; that is, a place or time when it's just you and God.

Another point to remember is that the devil seeks to exploit the times when nothing seems to be happening in our lives, the times when we feel alone. People often do not recognize that this is a time to be alone with the Lord. The enemy comes in and says to them, "It's taking too long," "You've been forgotten," or "This isn't fair," and from there he coaxes them into moral failures and crisis of faith. People get tired of waiting for the right person, so they give in to the loneliness and jump into a wrong relationship. People step out — they think in faith — into wrong ministries because "come aside by yourself" is "not how they roll. They are the movers and shakers who insist on doing something — even if it is the wrong thing.

If this is a season of life where you feel forgotten or sidelined, don't let the devil exploit the feeling of loneliness. The Lord might be saying to you, "Come aside to a lonely place where just you and I can recap recent events or maybe talk about a few mistakes. Come aside until you are satisfied with Me as your portion, and then I can move ahead with your meeting the right person." God wastes nothing and even calls His people into lonely places for one-on-one time with Him. Maybe you are the one He is calling right now.

Occasional loneliness is as normal as the sending out and bringing in that we all want the Lord to do in our lives. When it comes, don't let it rob you of alone time with God. Remember, when you're called aside to a lonely place, it's hard to hear the Lord over the sound of your own grumbling!

August 14

Can two walk together, unless they are agreed?

— Amos 3:3

The prophet Amos posed this question to a nation that had experienced a recent renewal of prosperity under King Jereboam II. But the sad truth was, only those close to Jereboam II were prospering. The government was exploiting the working class, seizing their properties and assets and selling some of their citizens into slavery for personal gain. So the Lord sent a working-class man to Bethel, headquarters of Jereboam II, to declare to the pagan king God's love of and demand for justice.

Amos here implied that if the blessings of God were to remain on the kingdom, then agreement with the plan of God would have to be rejoined. The king had been commandeering landholdings that had been in Israelite families for generations, and in God's eyes, this amounted to governmental exploitation.

Amos was a shepherd by trade, and he, much like Moses and David before him, understood the struggles of the common man in running a small family business. It is also interesting that Jesus too was born into a common working-class family. So God sent to Bethel a common man with a message, Amos. "If you are going to continue to exploit the common people," he said, "God will defend justice for His name's sake."

Amos is a book of testimonies and warnings to those who rejected God's love of and demand for justice in the kingdom. On a personal level, we can easily see the implication that when we live in disagreement or even direct conflict with God's love of justice and fairness, we cease to walk in fellowship with God.

There is not a single aspect of life that God does not have a plan and purpose for. Human government is His instrument (Romans 13), and it has boundaries and instructions concerning its exercise. So too is it with business; God has standards of justice and fairness that are to be maintained at all times, lest a business become out of step with God's will. Those who reject His standards and refuse to repent, God will judge.

Thomas Jefferson said, "I tremble for my country when I consider that God is just, and His justice will not sleep forever."

God loves justice!

August 15

Rejoice greatly, O daughter of Zion! Shout, O daughter of Jerusalem! Behold, your King is coming to you; He is just and having salvation, lowly and riding on a donkey, a colt, the foal of a donkey.

— Zechariah 9:9

As we saw yesterday, God is just. Since Jesus is God come in human flesh, then obviously Jesus is just as well. Here Zechariah describes the King of the Jews as just and having salvation, yet lowly and riding a donkey, not a kingly stallion. We know Zechariah was foretelling Jesus' triumphal entry into Jerusalem, the first time He would receive open and public worship as the Messiah (John 12:13–15). I would think that this event alone would have opened the eyes of the Jews as to who Jesus really was, yet we know that was not so. The events that followed a mere seven days later remind us of the adage "There are none who are so blind as those who will not see."

I once heard an old country preacher say, "We don't need more light; we need sight. What good is more light to a blind man?" If you're like me, maybe from time to time you have thought, *Oh Lord, if You would do this, then others would see the light,* or *Oh Lord, if you would just open that door, the light would come streaming into our city.* More light isn't going to help anyone who cannot see. But at times we all think if God would only do this or that for the people in our lives, then they would "get it." But they can't get it if they can't see it.

One spring day in AD 32, a prophecy was so radically fulfilled that it would seem anyone could have seen it. Yet seven days later, Christ was hanging on the cross while the same crowd that had just yelled "Hosanna!" was now yelling "Crucify Him!"

Light has come into the world, friends, and His name is Jesus. More light is not needed, more miracles won't make someone believe, and winning the lottery won't prove God's love to anyone. Nothing can change a person's heart unless God grants them sight.

I believe this is important for us all to understand so that we might simplify our prayer lives. We can move away from a list of things God ought to do to save our loved ones to simply asking Him to open their eyes to what He has already done. This simple prayer does two things: it keeps us praying according to God's will, and it increases the number of people we can pray for each day.

When Jesus read a portion of Isaiah 61 in the temple, this is what He read: "The Spirit of the Lord GOD is upon Me, because the LORD has anointed Me to preach good tidings to the poor; He has sent Me to heal the brokenhearted, to proclaim liberty to the captives, and the opening of the prison to those who are bound; to proclaim the acceptable year of the LORD" (vv. 1–2).

Our world doesn't need more light—it needs sight. Let's ask God to restore sight to those we love that they may see Jesus!

August 16

I, therefore, the prisoner of the Lord, beseech you to walk worthy of the calling
with which you were called, with all lowliness and gentleness, with longsuffering,
bearing with one another in love, endeavoring to keep the unity of the
Spirit in the bond of peace.

— Ephesians 4:1–3

It has always amazed me that Paul the prisoner was so burdened for those on the outside. Despite the slew of imprisonments and beatings he endured, he continually expressed his love and desire for the fullness of the Lord to be experienced by those in the places he had visited. This can only be the work of the Lord in a man's heart, for none of us would have blamed Paul for defending his innocence. Had he asked those to whom he had ministered to organize a defense on his behalf and collect a defense fund for him, we would have understood. But that was not what he did. To the apostle Paul, prison was a pulpit—not a pit.

Look at his exhortation to the Ephesians from his prison cell: Walk worthy, with lowliness, gentleness, and longsuffering, which means to withhold wrath. Bear with one another, and endeavor to keep unity. The word for *endeavor* implies promptness, so Paul is telling the Ephesians to be quick about the unity of the Spirit in the bond of peace.

Every time I read such accounts from Paul, I find myself convicted about how I handle my trials. I have never been beaten with rods, I have never been imprisoned for my faith, and I have never spent a day and a night in the sea; but I have been consumed by my circumstances, and I have focused on the unfairness of the treatment I have received, whether real or perceived.

But Paul gives us a great secret to dealing with trials, and that is simply to minister to others and stay focused on expanding the kingdom of God. This is without question the most effective tool for handling persecution and trials, but it is also one of the least frequently adopted practices. The devil likes nothing more than for us to lose focus on the big picture and be consumed with our own injustices.

If you have been wronged, help someone else in distress. If you have been cheated, do something to help the poor. If you are being persecuted, endeavor to keep unity with the Spirit, and be quick to stay connected spiritually to the will of God. The enemy knows well that the quickest route to the old flesh nature is often through injustice. Injustice grates against us because it is wrong and unfair, but for Christians, it should not be unexpected.

So if you feel like your circumstance is the pits, turn it into a pulpit and watch how you change—even if your situation doesn't!

August 17

This is a faithful saying: If a man desires the position of a bishop, he desires a good work. A bishop then must be blameless, the husband of one wife, temperate, sober-minded, of good behavior, hospitable, able to teach; not given to wine, not violent, not greedy for money, but gentle, not quarrelsome, not covetous; one who rules his own house well, having his children in submission with all reverence (for if a man does not know how to rule his own house, how will he take care of the church of God?); not a novice, lest being puffed up with pride he fall into the same condemnation as the devil.

—1 Timothy 3:1–6

You might read this passage and ask, "I do not desire the office of a bishop or pastor, so what does this have to do with me?" Quite a lot actually. The word *blameless* here can be translated as "without glaring defect," which we could well understand as "having overcome basic sins." These are sins that are generally overcome simply through spiritual maturity, and a list of them follows this word *blameless*.

The gist of what Paul is saying is that in order to be effective as a bishop, a person must have attained a certain level of spiritual maturity. But this truth is not limited to the pastorate; it is true for every saint. The more effective we desire to be for God's kingdom, the more we will have to conquer or overcome.

The root of all the vices listed here is contained in a single word Paul mentions at the end: *pride*. I have seen this play out time and again in the lives of young men who come to Christ and immediately decide they are being called to the ministry. They learn a few things about the Bible, and being novices, they are soon filled with pride and become unusable, having yet to overcome basic sins. Pride was the sin that led to the devil's fall from heaven, and it has been the cause of the fall of many a Christian with great potential but an unwillingness to start at the beginning and master the basics.

On any given day, these verses are a worthy visit to set the course for that day by identifying the things the devil will use to tempt us. They are all rooted in pride. This is why the Bible reminds us time and again that we are servants. Servants have but one job, and that is to do the will of their masters.

Set a course today with the intention of overcoming the basic sins common to all. Then watch the doors of opportunity fly open for you to do even greater things for the Lord!

August 18

But you, Bethlehem Ephrathah, though you are little among the thousands of Judah, yet out of you shall come forth to Me the One to be Ruler in Israel, whose goings forth are from of old, from everlasting.

— Micah 5:2

In light of yesterday's devotional, today's verse provides a fitting reminder that God is looking not for the magnificent, but simply the willing. That thought is expressed here in the birthplace of the Lord Jesus Christ. God did not choose a palace in Rome or a castle in bustling Corinth. He did not even choose the city on which He had placed His own name, Jerusalem. He selected obscure, forgettable Bethlehem as the birthplace of the world's Savior, His only begotten Son.

It is fitting on so many levels that God chooses the meek things of the world to put to shame the mighty (1 Cor. 1:26). God moves in this manner because it assures that He receives the glory. He sent His Son to be born in a little city in humble circumstances to a common family with ordinary struggles and difficulties. That is great news for you and me because it means God wants to use the ordinary to accomplish the extraordinary.

So many times Christians feel like "I am not this" or "I can't do that." That's not to say that God does not use the gifts He has already given us for His glory, but it is also important to see that when He does something through us that we are not normally capable of or gifted at, the glory is all His! Too often we limit ourselves to doing what we know we can do and never venture outside our preset boundaries to experience what God can do through a willing vessel.

Now here is a lesson I have learned more than once: you have to be willing to fail in order to step out and let God use you. God will often test and refine this resolve. But far too many Christians step out in an area and when it doesn't go the way they expected, they never attempt another step of faith.

If this has been your story, take it from someone who knows, and step out again. Yes, you might fail again, but if you do, just step out again. Each time you go through this cycle, you realize your flesh is still far too involved, and a piece of you dies. And that's good. Because the more you die to self, even through humbling situations and failed attempts at ministry, the more usable you become.

Remember, God only uses failures. He has to, because we have all failed! But remember this as well: God uses failures who will not give up but are determined that though they be little in comparison to others, God is going to receive much glory through them!

August 19

For violence against your brother Jacob, shame shall cover you, and you shall be cut off forever. In the day that you stood on the other side — in the day that strangers carried captive his forces, when foreigners entered his gates and cast lots for Jerusalem — even you were as one of them.

—Obadiah 1:10–11

Talk about a family feud! The prophet Obadiah wrote this stinging word of judgment to the nation of Edom for their aiding Judah's enemies, specifically the Babylonians. The amazing thing about this is that the Edomites were the descendants of Esau and thus related to Judah of Jacob. Fifteen hundred years later, the descendants of the two brothers were still going at it.

Amazingly, this all started over a bowl of stew. We know there was much more behind the story than just that, but the catalyst for all the trouble was Esau's hunger after returning home from hunting and the subsequent selling of his birthright to his conniving brother, Jacob (Gen. 25:31). How ugly family feuds can be and over such seemingly small issues! Based on his foreknowledge of the man Esau would become, God had already chosen Jacob, so Jacob did not need to connive in order to obtain what God had already promised. Nevertheless, he did, Esau regretted his rash act, and the feud between the two brothers began.

It is clear that today's verse is a message of judgment against Edom for siding with Judah's enemies. Judah was family, and the principle holds true to this day. Unresolved issues spawned by jealousy, envy, or past injustices should not be allowed to divide families, especially Christian families. Sadly, however, we have all heard of feuds that lasted so long no one even knew what started the whole thing. All the feuding family members knew was that they were supposed to hate certain other members of the family, but they had no clue as to the reason.

Some hurts and pains from early in life may provide legitimate reasons for cutting off a relationship. Abuse and abandonment are hard things to recover from and may require certain boundaries to ensure protection. But do you have a feud over a "bowl of stew" that has simmered for a good while in your family? If so, bring it to an end, for it is shameful to perceive the most prized people in your life as enemies. Remember, "I'm sorry" are two little words that can change everything.

Humility begins at home and within your own family. Don't let your family become Edom and Judah, fighting for years over something that happened a long time ago!

August 20

Therefore, when we could no longer endure it, we thought it good to be left in Athens alone, and sent Timothy, our brother and minister of God, and our fellow laborer in the gospel of Christ, to establish you and encourage you concerning your faith, that no one should be shaken by these afflictions; for you yourselves know that we are appointed to this.

—1 Thessalonians 3:1–3

At the time of this writing, Paul was being chased from town to town by a group that had opposed him in Thessalonica then followed him to Berea and on to Athens. With the heat on in these cities, Paul ended up back in Corinth. From there, Paul sent word to the Thessalonians through Timothy that they were not to be shaken by his trials or by the trials they would soon be forced to endure.

In essence, Paul reminds us that Christians are appointed to affliction. In other words, it's par for the course. I will admit, injustice is a hard concept for many people, including me, to understand. It's hard to accept, even knowing that in the end every injustice will be righted and the memories of this life will fade as we enjoy heaven for all eternity. There, at last, injustice will not even be possible, for we will all be like Jesus (1 Cor. 15:53).

But for now, it is hard to see God's people endure suffering. It's hard to read of the persecution of Christians in Sudan and Nigeria. It's hard sometimes not to wonder, *How long, oh Lord, holy and true?* But the fact is, God wants to save those who are committing injustice.

Even knowing that, it's just flat-out hard to pray for our enemies, especially those who have harmed us or other Christians. But that is our appointment: to endure affliction and to pray for those who afflict us. Jesus did it, and Stephen, the church's first martyr, did it. Thousands upon thousands of times since then, God's people have faced persecution and died with a prayer for their persecutors on their lips. With that in mind, I guess I can bear the minuscule ways in which I experience persecution. Millions have gone before me who have endured far worse, so I will not let myself be shaken.

Brother or sister, this world is not our home, and our visit here, in comparison to eternity, is but for a moment. So let's not be shaken by what we see happening to others or even to ourselves. Let's pray for our afflicters and join the millions who have endured far worse than most of us ever will. Let's face our persecutions with prayer on our lips!

August 21

Let no one despise your youth, but be an example to the believers in word, in conduct, in love, in spirit, in faith, in purity. Till I come, give attention to reading, to exhortation, to doctrine. Do not neglect the gift that is in you, which was given to you by prophecy with the laying on of the hands of the eldership.

—1 Timothy 4:12–14

Paul had earlier referred to Timothy as a "son in the faith" (1 Tim. 1:2), and now he displayed his fatherly love for the sometimes-timid young man. Offering words of encouragement, Paul reminded the young pastor that the gift in him was a gift from God and not to be neglected.

In these verses, Paul is not only an instructor but also an example for us to follow. In him, we see the beautiful picture of older, more seasoned saints encouraging the younger saints, and the younger saints seeking instruction and encouragement from the older examples.

It has been well said that the church is always one generation away from extinction. This reminds us of our sober responsibility to preach the gospel. But it is also true that within the church exists the constant danger of generational disconnect, or, as it has been labeled, a generation gap. This is a two-way street, and a generation gap can be avoided only if both generations participate in open dialogue. The older members must be willing to the reach the younger ones, and the younger ones must be willing to learn from the older. But the reverse is true as well, in that the older must be willing to learn from the younger. Older members may not need to be taught the great precepts of the faith, but rather the struggles and concerns that plague the hearts and minds of the younger generation.

Is there a younger person in your life that you can impact today? Reach out to them, talk to them, encourage them. Young men and women, is there someone who has a little "snow on the mountaintop" (that's code for gray hair) whose life's lessons you can learn from? We all need to remember the devil is the one who promotes statements like "I just don't get this younger generation" or "The older generation just doesn't get it; things are different today." The fact is, the gospel is no different today than it was on the day of Pentecost.

Paul gives us an example of how the truths we hold dear can span the generation gap. Encourage one another and learn from one another, he says, for there should be no generation gap in the family of God. But rather, generation to generation should be passing on great truths in love from one to the other.

Find someone to encourage today that you may not normally see eye to eye with. Learn something new from that person, and also take the time to be an encourager in the faith!

August 22

I appeal to you for my son Onesimus, whom I have begotten while in my chains, who once was unprofitable to you, but now is profitable to you and to me. I am sending him back. You therefore receive him, that is, my own heart, whom I wished to keep with me, that on your behalf he might minister to me in my chains for the gospel. But without your consent I wanted to do nothing, that your good deed might not be by compulsion, as it were, but voluntary.

—Philemon 1:10–14

Here we see the transforming power of the gospel and a foundation for the old adage that the ground is always level at the foot of the cross. Onesimus was a runaway slave. Now before anyone asks, "Why would Paul send a slave back to his master?" it is important to understand that slavery was closer to an employer-employee relationship in Roman times than to our picture of slavery today. People often sold themselves into slavery in order to pay off debt or to simply survive, and it was not uncommon for someone to willingly become a bond-slave. Such a person was free from obligation but chose to remain in servitude out of love for his master.

Onesimus had, in essence, stolen something from his master, and under Roman law, he could be put to death for his crime. Paul, however, appealed to the unity that Christ brings to all, even between master and slave. Paul asked Philemon to willingly receive his runaway slave as a brother, as Onesimus had now become part of the family of God.

The issue at hand could be deemed cross-cultural ministry, though in this case the cultural differences were that of status rather than race. It is amazing what knowing Christ introduces into our hearts and lives. I have been in many places around the world where I did not speak the native language and they did not speak mine, but the sense of family in the faith was undeniable. I have heard "Amazing Grace" sung with words I could not understand, yet I could share the moment with brothers and sisters who had been touched by the same amazing grace, and we were in unity.

Knowing Jesus pulls down all racial and cultural prejudices, and this is what Paul is exhorting Philemon to act upon here. We would do well to heed his advice and help the church to be as it was meant to be. As many of us have sung since childhood, "Red and yellow black and white/They are precious in His sight/Jesus loves the little children of the world." And, might I add, Jesus' children are to love His other children, just as He does.

Do not let old prejudices creep into your faith. The church is made up of many people of different colors and stations in life, but we are all one in Christ. In the melting pot known as America, we need to beware of church becoming a place where everyone is the same skin color or of similar financial status. If so, prejudice may have crept in, and cultural differences have yet to die. We are one family in Jesus Christ, and our bond is our faith—not cultural similarities!

August 23

"Now, therefore," says the LORD, *"turn to Me with all your heart, with fasting, with weeping, and with mourning." So rend your heart, and not your garments; return to the* LORD *your God, for He is gracious and merciful, slow to anger, and of great kindness; and He relents from doing harm.*

—Joel 2:12–13

At this writing, our country is deeply divided. Much like ancient Israel, we are encountering the direct result of denying God and dismissing His commandments from day-to-day life. The book that once taught students to read is now banned from schools, along with prayer. The biblical message of creation is barred from the classroom, while an unproven theory, evolution, is taught as fact. Babies are murdered in the womb to the tune of millions a year, and the biblical institution of marriage between a man and a woman is under constant attack.

The symptoms in our day might be somewhat different from Israel's symptoms at the time of Joel's writing, but the root problem is the same: God has been pushed out of everyday life and replaced with the desires of men's hearts. Since the root problem is the same for us as it was for Israel, then the solution is the same. As Joel says, "Rend your heart and not your garments."

The rending of garments was an outward expression of grief for God's people, but it wasn't the outward that needed to be torn. The inward, the heart, was the source of their problem and the source of ours as well. I am all for Christian involvement in the political arena; after all, human government is an institution of God according to Romans 13. But we need more than outward expressions of grief for the downward spiral of our nation; we need broken hearts for the core problem. America has forsaken God, and we need to pray that people return to Him.

Friends, participate in the process, cast your vote, and write your leaders; these things are all well and good. But let's not get so distracted by the symptoms that we forget the disease. Our country needs Jesus, and do not let your political party's rhetoric replace the truth that America needs to hear. The truth for our country and its people is summed up in John 3:16: without a personal relationship with Jesus Christ, we will perish.

We must rend our hearts, not our garments, which are merely the symptoms of the sin disease that is destroying the world. The rending we need is a heart broken for those headed for hell unless they repent!

August 24

And why do you look at the speck in your brother's eye, but do not consider the plank in your own eye? Or how can you say to your brother, "Let me remove the speck from your eye"; and look, a plank is in your own eye? Hypocrite! First remove the plank from your own eye, and then you will see clearly to remove the speck from your brother's eye.

— Matthew 7:3–5

Few things seem to stir up the Lord's anger as much as hypocrisy. He was constantly in the face of leading Jews about their double standards, and His feelings about the use of His Father's house as a place of merchandise were clear. The reason Jesus took such a strong stance on hypocrisy was that when our professions of belief and actions do not align, we drag His name into the mix.

The particular form of hypocrisy Jesus was addressing here was that of accusing others of something though being guilty of the same thing yourself. Interestingly, sometimes the sins that people attack most harshly in others are the very ones they are guilty of themselves.

Based on this text and others, many Christians have wrongly concluded that we are never to say anything about someone else's sins or errors in the faith. But that is not what Jesus taught. Jesus taught what the Bible always teaches; He instructed us to examine ourselves first and remove that which is not of the Lord before we try to help others with their issues. As a matter of fact, I believe the Lord actually gives us a bit of a perspective check as He instructs us to view others' sins as specks and our own as logs.

Hypocrisy is like a dirty pair of eyeglasses. You certainly wouldn't want your doctor doing surgery on you while he or she was wearing dirty, smudged glasses. So too is it true with helping one another to overcome sins and failures that reflect on the name of the Lord.

This passage is not a prohibition against calling out someone who is in sin; it's an instruction on how to do it. So clean your lenses today, and see your own failures as big as logs and others' shortcomings as small as specks. Then, should a word of correction be needed, your heart will be in the right place to give it.

August 25

But at midnight Paul and Silas were praying and singing hymns to God, and the prisoners were listening to them. Suddenly there was a great earthquake, so that the foundations of the prison were shaken; and immediately all the doors were opened and everyone's chains were loosed. And the keeper of the prison, awaking from sleep and seeing the prison doors open, supposing the prisoners had fled, drew his sword and was about to kill himself. But Paul called with a loud voice, saying, "Do yourself no harm, for we are all here." Then he called for a light, ran in, and fell down trembling before Paul and Silas. And he brought them out and said, "Sirs, what must I do to be saved?"

— Acts 16:25–30

When we read of this event, we often quickly latch on to a few things: singing hymns at midnight while bound in chains, chains being loosed through the power of praise, the salvation of the Philippian jailer, and much more. This passage is packed with great sermons. But there is also a subtlety here we don't want to miss.

The jailer had drawn his sword because death was the penalty under Roman law for a guard who allowed a prisoner to escape. But Paul stopped the man and told him, "Do yourself no harm, for we are all here." Here is the question I find interesting: was the earthquake God's provision, an open door out of injustice? We might quickly assume it was, but two things come to mind. First, not all the prisoners were innocent, and second, Paul knew well the consequences for the jailer should the prisoners escape.

To me, this is a clear reminder to be careful about thinking, *If God's in it, it'll be easy.* I have seen many Christians stifled because of this one thing. When things became difficult, they quit pursuing God's plan, assuming that anything from God will be easy. *Earthquakes will open all the doors, and I'll walk right into God's plan and His will,* they think. *He will have everything ready for me every step of the way.*

God will provide, to be sure, but His way is not always the easy way. Paul could have seen the earthquake as merely God's provision for escape, but Paul was more concerned about other people's souls than with his own safety and freedom. Paul's simple act of staying put when he could have run led to the salvation of not only the jailer, but also, as Acts 16 says, his entire family.

Does God seem to have you in a hard place right now? Don't look for the easy way out. Your hardship has within it many opportunities to praise at midnight and to stay put when others might run. In the end, it may lead to the question any Christian would love to hear from a lost soul, "What must I do to be saved?"

Praise from a prison cell has great power!

August 26

Yet indeed I also count all things loss for the excellence of the knowledge of Christ Jesus my Lord, for whom I have suffered the loss of all things, and count them as rubbish, that I may gain Christ.

— Philippians 3:8

Paul had just listed his spiritual pedigree, beginning with his birth into the tribe of Benjamin and continuing through his life accomplishments and exalted position among the Jews. But then he said he counted it all rubbish, that he might gain Christ.

We might understand this as Paul saying any personal accomplishments pale in comparison to knowing Jesus. He equates them with rubbish, and that is indeed a fitting comparison. Knowing Christ is what gets us into heaven, and not one single accomplishment will mean anything unless it was done for God's glory.

The Bible does not forbid or even diminish the importance of setting goals and accomplishing things in this life, but it does continually remind us of their proper place, which is always second to our faith. Pursuits of education, careers, and family are all very time consuming, and it is easy to become spiritually disproportionate. We would do well to check our lives in the midst of the pursuit of personal goals to make sure that our faith and our spiritual walk have not been relegated to back-burner positions.

Life is a wonderful blessing from God, and I believe that we Christians ought to live life more joyfully and fully because of the one truth Paul expresses here. In comparison to knowing Christ, every life accomplishment is rubbish. But when the goals and pursuits exceed their proper places and are exalted above faith, and when those goals and pursuits experience the normal ups and downs of life, you are forced to ride the high and low tides of whatever you have fixed your hope on. Jesus, however, never changes. If your walk with Him is always your top priority and your goals are in their rightful places, life will be much more balanced than when you ride the ebb and flow of life's changes.

As a Christian, your eternal destiny remains the same every day of your life. On easy days and hard days alike, in both good times and bad times, heaven remains a constant. Anything and everything else is subject to change without notice. If you have exalted anything other than Christ to top priority, a wave of disappointments inevitably awaits you.

Everything accomplished in life is rubbish compared to knowing and serving Jesus Christ. Tell someone today how wonderful He is!

August 27

It is honorable for a man to stop striving, since any fool can start a quarrel.

— Proverbs 20:3

Meekness is not weakness, as some seem to perceive it. We have all experienced getting drawn into a war of words with someone who did not know when to quit. (I was going to say "shut up" but wanted this to sound more spiritual!) It is easy to allow our proverbial feathers to get ruffled by an antagonist, no matter the subject. But Solomon tells us that the honorable thing to do is to stop striving, which indicates both choice and control.

The church my family and I were a part of for many years held annual large-scale evangelistic crusades. Every year protestors gathered outside the event venue, spouting ridiculous comments about our pastor and the event. Just as surely every year, some well-meaning Christians engaged in quarreling with these people, which inevitably led to the conversation getting quite heated at some point. The end result was always smug and satisfied protestors and frustrated and irritated saints who entered the stadium angry instead of expectant and joyful.

Those who have antagonism as their calling know full well, even if subconsciously, how to lure passersby into their web. They tug at our flesh with their words and seek to engage our defenses and even tap into that which lies deep inside all of us, the desire to win the exchange or have the last word. It is honorable to avoid such contentions.

To meekly walk away from contention is honorable and even admirable, but it is a difficult thing to do, to be sure. It takes far more power to exercise restraint than it does to engage the argumentative. We have a choice, and by the power of the Spirit, we possess the self-control to stop striving. As Scripture says, any fool can start a quarrel.

Do you have an antagonist in your life, someone whom, when you see, you think, *Oh brother, not them*? Do the honorable thing; stop striving and choose not to quarrel. You'll be the better for it, but more important, God will be honored by it!

August 28

Delight yourself also in the LORD, and He shall give you the desires of your heart. Commit your way to the LORD, trust also in Him, and He shall bring it to pass.

— Psalm 37:4-5

Many have taken these magnificent verses to mean "Delight in the Lord and He will give you whatever you desire." That is not the meaning at all, but rather we should understand this passage as "Delight yourself in the Lord and He'll give you new desires." How else could we commit our ways to Him? If God granting us anything we desire is the proper understanding, then what about when we want something that is not good for us or not His will for us? Do we get it anyway because God gives us whatever we desire? No, a better understanding is that God will plant godly desires in our hearts, and one of them, in a life that is led by the Spirit, is to commit to the ways of the Lord.

As I look back on my life, I see that after I came to Christ, new desires, new goals, and new priorities were birthed inside me. I committed to those ways and have spent the last twenty-five years watching them come to pass. This required seasons of trust, in which I failed miserably at times.

But God is faithful to bring to pass that which He places in our hearts. He alone knows best, and His will exceeds any plans and desires of our own. Our journeys as saints include a continual revealing of new desires, things we wish to change about ourselves that we know are not His will for us.

The longer we walk with Him, the deeper He probes into our souls to bring to the surface things that need replacing. And when He pinpoints attitudes or actions that are not His best for us, a desire to change begins to form. From that, a commitment to change is made, and then God slowly but surely brings it to pass. Then He does it again and goes deeper, and He does it yet again and goes deeper. He is constantly creating desires in us for things that both please Him and allow us to reflect Him more clearly.

What is His desire for you today? What has He been digging up in your soul in order to create a new desire in you? It may not be too hard to identify; it may be that thing about yourself that you often wish you could change (a spiritual thing obviously). That's the desire. Now commit it to the Lord, pray that the desire will translate into action, and watch God bring it to pass. Then do it again and again and again — until the day when you see Him and are finally like Him!

August 29

"The Spirit of the Lord *is upon Me, because He has anointed Me to preach the gospel to the poor; He has sent Me to heal the brokenhearted, to proclaim liberty to the captives and recovery of sight to the blind, to set at liberty those who are oppressed; to proclaim the acceptable year of the* Lord.*" Then He closed the book, and gave it back to the attendant and sat down. And the eyes of all who were in the synagogue were fixed on Him. And He began to say to them, "Today this Scripture is fulfilled in your hearing."*

—Luke 4:18–21

Just reading it kind of makes you want to stand up and shout, doesn't it? Today—not tomorrow, not some distant time in the future, but today—there is good news for the poor, healing for the brokenhearted, liberty for the captives, sight for the blind, freedom for the oppressed, and proclamation to all that the day of the Lord is at hand! Today this beautiful passage of Scripture has been fulfilled, and Jesus is seated at the right hand of the Father, having finished all that was needed to prove these things so.

As Jesus stood and proclaimed those words, I'm sure quite a murmur rolled through the room. As Luke says, all who heard Him marveled and said—and I'm paraphrasing here—"Isn't this Joe and Mary's son?" The implication was clear: "How can He fulfill these things? He is one of us, the son of a carpenter, just a common man."

Amazingly, the same questions are still asked about Him today: What makes Jesus special? How is He different from any other religious leader? Why would anyone think He was God in human flesh? The answer to those questions is that after Jesus claimed to fulfill the Scriptures, the poor did receive good news, broken hearts were healed, blind people received their sight, many of those oppressed by the law were set free, and the day of the Lord was proclaimed. In other words, Jesus fulfilled all that Isaiah wrote about the Messiah.

Has the Lord changed? Is He still the same yesterday, today, and forever? Yes, He is the same, and that means He still does today all that He came to earth to do. I am always a little frustrated with those who argue that the miracles surrounding Jesus and the apostles were only signs to prove Jesus was the Messiah and to endorse the apostles as sent from God so people would heed their message. This is a problem because it implies Jesus healed people, not because He cared or because their situations and problems mattered, but only to prove He was who He said He was. And that, friends, is totally inconsistent with the nature of God and the rest of the Bible.

That day in the synagogue, what Jesus said was fulfilled was indeed fulfilled: the one sent from heaven had come, and all He was sent to do was now set in motion. There is still healing, freedom, and liberty for all who are in Christ Jesus. Don't let anyone use their brand of theology to talk you out of what Jesus offers. There is freedom from oppression and addiction and freedom from blindness, both spiritual and physical. God is still doing what He has always done, though we may not always understand His decisions regarding those whom He heals and those whom He calls home.

One thing we know for sure is He is the same yesterday, today, and forever. What He fulfilled then, He is still doing now!

August 30

The LORD will guide you continually, and satisfy your soul in drought, and strengthen your bones; you shall be like a watered garden, and like a spring of water, whose waters do not fail.

—Isaiah 58:11

Continually is such a beautiful word set in the midst of this verse of promise. Drought and weakness are met with divine refreshing and strength—continually! That means that though God may have had to refresh you in a dry season once before, He is willing and able to refresh you again. It means that though you may have fallen prey to an area of weakness before, He is willing and able to strengthen you in that area again.

One of the things I am most thankful for about the nature of God is that He is not like us. He does not tire of us and our needs, even when we need refreshing time and again. He does not weary of helping us in our repeated struggles. He does not say to His children, "You made your bed—now lie in it." Instead, He says continually, "Let Me help you up. Let Me help you through. Let Me be your strength and vitality continually."

It is also wonderful to remember that His spring of water does not fail; there is nothing to save for later. When you dip into His strength or refreshment, there is just as much there as was present before you tapped into His resources.

God does not weary of hearing from you, beloved saint. As a matter of fact, He loves to hear from you. He loves for you to cry out to Him, to recognize Him as your ever-present help in time of need. Are you tired and weary? Tell your Father about your day. Just talking to Him will give you strength. Are you dry from the battles of life? Tell your Father how you are feeling. Time spent with Him in prayer is always refreshing when you understand His "continual-ness." (I know it's not a word, but it works!)

God will guide you continually into strength and refreshment. All you have to do is ask. Don't face life dry and weak, because strength and refreshment are an abundant and limitless resource. Even if you needed it yesterday and might need it again tomorrow, God is willing and able to strengthen and refresh you as often as you need it. He never tires or wearies of doing so.

Been a while since your last refueling? Check in with your Father—He has what you need!

August 31

There is no fear in love; but perfect love casts out fear, because fear involves torment. But he who fears has not been made perfect in love. We love Him because He first loved us.

—1 John 4:18–19

In an age where there is much to be concerned about personally and globally, it is reassuring to know that our future is secure, that this life is temporary and heaven is eternal. Fear of the Lord is a wonderful thing, for it means to be in reverent awe. Fear of life and man is not a wonderful thing, but a torment that a holy God has delivered us from.

The word *perfect* means "mature" or "complete." And the fact is, the more mature our love, the more we fear the Lord and the less we fear life, even the great fears of life such as global war, earthquakes and tornadoes, or personal loss and tragedy.

We need not live in fear even though fearful things invade our lives from time to time. "There is no fear in love" does not mean the removal of anything that could cause fear, but rather a reverent awe of God in the midst of fearful situations. God loves us, and always should we expect from Him only what's best for us. All day and every day, circumstances change, and difficult life events come and go. But God is our constant in all these things. He is constantly loving, constantly faithful, constantly merciful, and constantly gracious, even when fearful things come our way.

Although it is true that 90 percent of the things we worry about never happen, it is also true that 10 percent actually do. But God is God over them both. That means we don't have to live in fear of what may be, and we don't have to live without the fear of the Lord in what is. God's love alone is perfect; it never fails us when we need it the most. People will fail us and even bail out on us when we need them the most, but God never does. His love is perfect and unchanging.

Don't borrow from tomorrow worries for today. This is the day the Lord has made; let us rejoice and be glad in it. This day His love for you and me is perfect—just as it will be tomorrow!

September 1

Their sorrows shall be multiplied who hasten after another god; their drink offerings of blood I will not offer, nor take up their names on my lips.

—Psalm 16:4

This pretty much eliminates the argument of the universalists who believe all roads eventually lead to God. David says, "I will have nothing to do with those who run after false gods. I will not offer sacrifices to their idols or even mention the names of their gods." David, writing under the inspiration of the Holy Spirit, reminds us that sorrows are multiplied to those who hasten after other gods. For them, a life of sorrow on earth is followed by an eternity of sorrow, for there is no god but the God of the Bible.

How sorrowful it is to see people trust in fables and lies and even place their eternal destinies in the hands of religions and beliefs contrary to the Word of the true and living God. This kind of life is followed by eternal separation from God for rejecting His offer of salvation, and this is the multiplied sorrow that David speaks of here.

I am continually pressed by the reality of hell that awaits those who reject Jesus as Lord and Savior. No one is more pleased by the absence of hell from today's sermons than the devil; neither is anyone more pleased than he is by the growing concept that one religion is as sound as another as long as a person is sincere.

David said the thoughts and actions associated with idolatry and false gods are not even worthy of being on our lips. Friend, as Christians we have a calling and responsibility to speak of the true and living God and not allow false religions to be spoken of as acceptable. An eternity apart from God in a place of weeping and gnashing of teeth awaits those who die believing in other gods.

You have the truth others need to hear, so do not fall prey to the growing universalism of our day. There is but one way to heaven, and that is through a personal relationship with Jesus Christ. Anything else is sorrow upon sorrow. Love the lost enough to tell them this today.

Also remember, you haven't found something that works for you; you have found the only way to heaven as a follower of Jesus Christ. All those who have chosen other gods are headed for eternal sorrow. So tell them of the way, truth, and life found only through Jesus Christ. That—not "respecting" their religion—is the most loving and kind thing you can do for them.

September 2

He uncovers deep things out of darkness, and brings the shadow of death to light. He makes nations great, and destroys them; He enlarges nations, and guides them. He takes away the understanding of the chiefs of the people of the earth, and makes them wander in a pathless wilderness. They grope in the dark without light, and He makes them stagger like a drunken man.

—Job 12:22–25

Job was a man who knew a bit about deep things and darkness. He knew something about forces outside of his control intruding upon his life. Yet in the face of his detractors, he exalted the sovereignty of God over nations and rulers. God both raises rulers up and destroys them, Job observed. God can take the understanding of great rulers and make them wander and stagger like a drunken man, should He so choose. (Nebuchadnezzar comes to mind!) The armies of Satan, the armies of the world, and the greatest of kingdoms or superpowers are all subject to the word and will of almighty God.

Job's statement here could be summed up in one simple sentence: God is in control! Whether it is kings or kingdoms, powers or armies, or even principalities and powers (which were the direct cause of Job's suffering), all are subject to God's sovereignty. I do not know the system God uses to determine what to stop and what to allow (I don't really believe He has one), but I do know the poster boy for suffering boldly declares that nothing is outside the watchful eye and powerful hand of almighty God. Those are pretty amazing words, considering the source.

There is nothing hidden from our God. The enemy can launch no surprise attacks that God didn't see coming. There are no unexpected outcomes that catch God unaware and unprepared. All that Job encountered was God filtered.

I will be the first to say I do not want God to allow into my life what He did in Job's. But regardless of what happens, I do know the devil is never going to slip something past God, because God is in control. He is ever watchful, and in His providence and sovereignty, He sometimes allows my free will to get me into difficulty. Other times He spares me from trouble by altering the direction I was going. He may even allow unexpected things to come into my life, but they were unexpected only by me—He was ready for them.

Here's the thing to remember today: God is your Father. Whatever is best for you—even the hard stuff—is what He will allow to come into your life. The way you handle that tells the world He is there and for His children!

September 3

If then you were raised with Christ, seek those things which are above, where Christ is, sitting at the right hand of God. Set your mind on things above, not on things on the earth. For you died, and your life is hidden with Christ in God. When Christ who is our life appears, then you also will appear with Him in glory.

—Colossians 3:1–4

We have all been told at various points in life that we can do just about anything we put our minds to. This old saying, like many others, actually has a biblical root. For example, "What goes around comes around" is another way of saying "Whatever a man sows that shall he also reap" (Gal. 6:7). Though the world may have borrowed the concept, the principle remains a constant.

That is also true for what we set our minds on as Christians. Setting our minds on things above does not mean we think about streets of gold and gates of pearl, the wonders of heaven and what it will be like. Though these things are wonderful to remember continually as we journey through this dark concrete jungle of a world, the principle is to set our minds on things that matter to God, not on the things that matter on earth.

In recent sermons I have preached, I have frequently reminded the church not to confuse the American dream with the will of God. It may or may not be the will of God for you to own a home or business, and it may or may not be the will of God for you to strike it rich. But it is without question the will of God that you tell others about Him and live a life that reflects what knowing Him truly means.

Again, as I have mentioned in past devotionals, little words carry such great meaning in some of these monumental verses. In today's passage, it is the word *set*. This indicates a fixed position, so when Paul urges us to set our minds on things above, that means we are to continually focus on the things of God. After all, we can and will do whatever we set our minds to do.

Christ is our life, and our old natures have died with Him. Too often, however, we allow that old man to come back to life by feeding him a barrage of thoughts about what we need or desire, what we want to do or have. There is nothing wrong with things, even nice things, but if our minds are set on them, then our actions will follow suit. The result is a life aimed too low, a life that settles for second best, a life full of things below the best things, the God things, the eternal things.

Raise your thought standards today and think about how to serve and please God. You can do it, if you will only put your mind to it!

September 4

Whenever the living creatures give glory and honor and thanks to Him who sits on the throne, who lives forever and ever, the twenty-four elders fall down before Him who sits on the throne and worship Him who lives forever and ever, and cast their crowns before the throne, saying: "You are worthy, O Lord, to receive glory and honor and power; for You created all things, and by Your will they exist and were created."

— Revelation 4:9–11

In the New Testament, crowns are symbols of our rewards. Thus the verses above are some of the greatest motivational verses for serving God with great effort and zeal, even being spent for the sake of the gospel as Paul mentioned in 2 Corinthians 12:15. I believe that upon our arrival in heaven, as we stand amazed before the Lord, we will find ourselves in awe of the one who purchased us that we might be with Him forever. I believe in that moment of amazed gratitude, we will all wish for more to cast before His throne in thanks for what He has done for us.

Our Lord is worthy, and it is right to seek to excel at bringing Him honor in this life and to do all that we can to lead others to Him. It is right to want to have many rewards to cast at His feet on the day we enter the heavenly scene. I do not want to stand before Him wearing only the crown of life, for that crown is given to all who believe and is based solely on what He did for me, not on anything I did for His name and glory. I want to wear the "soul winners" crown. I want to wear the "remembered the poor" crown. I want to wear the "visited the sick" crown and the "went to those in prison" crown. I want to have much to cast at the feet of the one who created all things and by whom all things exist!

I do not want to stand before Him empty handed when He has already told me to do His business until He comes. When He comes for me, I want to show a profit from investing what He gave me to use for His glory. And when — and this is so God — He rewards me for what He did through me, I want to cast that crown at His feet in thanks and say, "Lord, these crowns of reward rightfully belong to You!"

I believe this is the desire of many of you as well. So what now? Make it a priority to serve Him today. Do something sacrificial, something that costs you time, effort, or even money. Tell someone what Jesus has done for you today — it's very rewarding!

September 5

Your words were found, and I ate them, and Your word was to me the joy and rejoicing of my heart; for I am called by Your name, O LORD God of hosts.

—Jeremiah 15:16

What tremendous words penned by a man whose preaching and prophecies had yet to yield a single convert, a man who in his fifty-plus years of ministry never saw one single Israelite turn to God and away from idols! It wasn't that Jeremiah was never discouraged; it was that he was always sustained by the Word of God.

What a precious jewel the Word of God is to us today! In a time much like Jeremiah's, where the idolatry around us can be depressing and discouraging, we can see the world and our country moving further and further away from God. But like Jeremiah, we too have God's Word as a source of joy and rejoicing. We too can remember that both a new day and a new world are coming. We too can remember that we are called by the name of the Lord of Hosts. We are His children, His family, His purchased possession.

We are the joy that was set before the Lord that caused Him to endure the cross and despise the shame. We are the ones who can never be separated from His love. We are the ones He will never leave or forsake. We are the ones who can do all things through our strength in Christ. We are the ones who can take all these reminders in His Word and let them be our food, food that brings joy and rejoicing in heart, though hearts all around us are hard and will not heed the call of God.

Thank the Lord for His Word today. Have some for lunch and see how it changes the rest of your day. Listen to it, read it, pray it, just stay connected to it. This simple "up look" will change your entire outlook. It did just that for the man known as the Weeping Prophet, and it will do the same for you!

September 6

I will seek what was lost and bring back what was driven away, bind up the broken and strengthen what was sick; but I will destroy the fat and the strong, and feed them in judgment.

— Ezekiel 34:16

It is important to remember that when God makes statements regarding Israel, such as the promise of binding the broken and strengthening the sick, there are always two things to consider. First, some of the promises to Israel are specific and apply only to the nation of Israel. Second, other promises made to Israel are promises that simply reflect God's nature and are thus applicable to us all. The binding and mending of brokenness, the strengthening of the sick, the calling back of that which the enemy or even disobedience has driven away, and the destroying of those made rich off the demise of God's people are all promises consistent with God's nature.

The first of the elements of God's nature mentioned here is His seeking of that which is lost. Some of you today need to remember that the implanted word in the prodigals in your life is going to draw them home. Second, *binding brokenness* is a phrase that means "to wrap firmly" or "to gird about." God is still in the business of fixing broken people, and therefore there is hope for the broken people in your life. The word *sick* in the Hebrew means "worn out," "wounded," or "in travail," and those worn out by life's trials and wounds can expect God, who restores and heals, to be there for them through a relationship with Jesus Christ.

This is why it is so important for us to constantly communicate the hope and healing found in Jesus Christ. Knowing Him still mends the broken and strengthens the sick and worn-out. He is the hope for their salvation and, at times, even for their sanity. We must therefore tell the world of God's promises available through Jesus Christ that are just in His nature to do. We have the answers, friends, or we know the one who does.

This great promise to Israel is a promise consistent with the nature of God. He loves setting captives free, He loves healing broken hearts, He loves giving people a reason to live and a hope to live for. He is exactly what people need today, friends, and He is what you need today as well.

Sometimes as we mature in our walks with God, we distance ourselves from the simple gospel message of Jesus Christ. But remember, the very things that drew you to Him are the same things available to you today. The right to go home if you have wandered, the right to have what is broken in your life girded, and the right to go to Him for strength when you are just plain worn out are all promises based on the nature of our unchanging God.

September 7

The woman left her water jar beside the well and went back to the village and told everyone, "Come and meet a man who told me everything I ever did! Can this be the Messiah?" So the people came streaming from the village to see him.

—John 4:28–30

I love the story of Jesus' encounter with the woman at the well for many reasons, not the least of which are these two: First, Jesus was talking to someone that most Jews would not have spoken to. Second, in John 4:4, the Bible says Jesus "needed" to go through Samaria, a region that other Jews avoided at all costs, to meet a woman that everyone else avoided whenever possible. The fact that the woman was at the well at noon in the heat of the day tells us that she too was hoping to avoid running into someone, her being a woman of "reputation." But Jesus needed to meet her because she needed to meet Jesus.

After the unusually bold and forthright exchange between Jesus and the woman, in which Jesus supernaturally revealed her sordid past, the woman instantly went to find others to bring to Him. But being the woman that she was, she had to sweeten the pot in order to get them to listen to her. So she said, "Come meet this man who told me everything I ever did." Now we know this is not technically true, but I believe there is truth in it. I believe the woman was in essence saying, "Come meet a man who told me everything I always worried about." This woman's past was her nemesis in her present.

The Samaritans, who were at odds with the Jews, were no more accepting of this woman's behavior than were the Jews. The woman was an outcast—and an outspoken outcast at that. But Jesus needed to meet her to address her past and therefore change her present. He identified what was plaguing her mind, I believe: how she had lived, how she was currently living. To her, a woman of poor reputation, Jesus offered living water. She was so thrilled by this man with supernatural revelation who offered her eternal salvation that she just couldn't hold it in; others had to know, and she had to tell them.

I cannot help but think of people who consider themselves too far gone, who think they have done too much to be forgiven. Jesus needs to meet them. He will go to the places no one else will go in order to reach the people no one else will seek in order to offer them what no one else can give: freedom from a past that haunts them every day.

I am so thankful for this story, because Jesus needed to meet me at this same place. At various times in my sordid past, His servants offered me living water, and after staying away from the well for nearly a decade, I finally drank again. When I arrived at the well, I found Jesus already there, waiting to wash away my past, just like He did for the Samaritan woman, a woman no one else wanted to be around, in a place no Jew would go. He needed to meet me, and He did.

Tell someone today about the man who gave you living water and forgave all that you ever did so that they can meet Him too!

September 8

Look among the nations and watch — be utterly astounded! For I will work a work in your days, which you would not believe, though it were told you. For indeed I am raising up the Chaldeans, a bitter and hasty nation which marches through the breadth of the earth, to possess dwelling places that are not theirs.

— Habakkuk 1:5

This fearful pronouncement of the coming invasion and conquest by the Chaldeans was a forewarning that should have brought about the repentance of the nation Israel. The children of Israel had become infatuated by materialism and had lost all concern for the law of God. Nevertheless, Habakkuk was perplexed at the Lord's use of pagan nations to judge His sinful yet chosen people.

The term *Chaldeans* is generally a synonym for the Babylonians, but I believe the use of the term is also specific and intentional. A great warning for the church today can be found in this verse. We too are faced with a very materialistic society, and the message of materialism has crept into the church far more than most of us realize. Sacrifice and suffering for the sake of the gospel have largely been pushed out of many of today's sermons and replaced with messages very similar to those of the self-help crowd that infatuates the world.

But the term *Chaldeans* has more meaning than as a mere identifier of those from the Babylonian Empire. When used to describe an individual, it meant an "astrologer." Today, not only are we deluged with the message of materialism and prosperity, but also many people seek the stars, or astrology, for guidance. Many of these people do indeed receive messages from the spiritual realm, but it's not from the "good guys." Astrology is not a means through which God communicates. God speaks by His Spirit and through His Word; He does not communicate through mediums, spiritists, or taro-card readers.

The warning in Habakkuk is as relevant today as it was in Israel's. God's people must not be bound by materialism or astrology; those things lead only to the bondage of pagan nations. Friend, don't check your horoscope today, but look to the Word of God for direction. Following the stars and the words of spiritists will only lead you to a place that will leave you utterly astounded and unable to believe God. The devil is behind materialism and astrology, and to follow them is to play into his hands.

Leave these things alone — they are not of the Lord!

September 9

Therefore whoever hears these sayings of Mine, and does them, I will liken him to a wise man who built his house on the rock: and the rain descended, the floods came, and the winds blew and beat on that house; and it did not fall, for it was founded on the rock. But everyone who hears these sayings of Mine, and does not do them, will be like a foolish man who built his house on the sand: and the rain descended, the floods came, and the winds blew and beat on that house; and it fell.
And great was its fall.

— Matthew 7:24–27

It is amazing to walk by a construction site where a skyscraper is being erected, especially at the beginning of the process. The pit below the building is enormous and deep enough to reach the bedrock upon which the building will stand. Geologists are brought in, and before a single beam is set into place or even before the foundation's construction begins, the foundation of the foundation must first be approved.

I love Jesus' practical illustrations. He puts things in such a way that deep and eternal truth is understandable by all. This familiar story is a great example of great truth simply explained. But the key that is often glossed over is the twice repeated phrase "whoever hears these sayings of Mine" followed by the doing or not doing of what Jesus just said. It is not the knowing that makes the foundation secure when the storms come, but the doing of the things Jesus has commanded. The commands of Jesus, including loving the Lord with all our hearts, souls, minds, and strength and loving our neighbors as ourselves, are things for us to do, not just know (Matt. 22:39).

James 1:22 tells us to be doers of the Word, not hearers only. Now you may be thinking, *I thought faith comes by hearing and hearing by the Word of God?* (Rom. 10:17). Indeed it does, but consider this: If you step off the curb and someone yells a warning to you about an approaching vehicle, is hearing the warning going to keep you from getting run over? No, you have to act on what you heard.

Through James, both Jesus and the Holy Spirit are saying that we have to do what we hear in order to remain steadfast in the storms of life. Doing what we hear from the Word of God needs to be foundational in our lives *before* the storms come, because a foundation cannot be laid once the storm has arrived. As I'm sure you have noticed, construction sites are closed during storms.

Now that's not to say the Lord is not there for you in the storms, but it is to say it is far better to be ready than to be crying for help neck deep in floodwaters. The Lord will be there, but I would just as soon not need the rescue because of having laid a foundation by doing what I heard from the Word.

Be what Jesus said we should be and do what Jesus said we should do, and the next storm you encounter will not be able to topple your house!

September 10

Cast your bread upon the waters, for you will find it after many days. Give a serving to seven, and also to eight, for you do not know what evil will be on the earth.

— Ecclesiastes 11:1–2

The phrase *casting bread upon the waters* is a metaphor for sowing seed. Solomon reminds us that after many days, we will reap the seed sown in the form of grain or fruit. In other words, we may not see instant results from our sowing, but they will come in time.

Solomon also uses a common literary practice to indicate continual increase when he says "seven, and also to eight." This defines generosity as the topic being addressed. The conclusion, therefore, is that generosity will always yield fruit eventually. Consistently Scripture reminds us to keep a light grip on the things of this world and to sow abundantly and generously into the lives of others. And yes, this includes financial generosity.

Another conclusion we could draw from this wisdom of Solomon is the need to grow in generosity, for we do not know what evil lies ahead. But the generous person who has sown bountifully will harvest in difficult times the fruit and grains of their generosity, both spiritually and materially.

Be generous with what you have, for the truth is, everything you have is the Lord's anyway; everything you earn comes only through the strength and wisdom He gave you to obtain it. So why keep a death grip on what He has granted you the privilege to enjoy?

Over the years, I have loved watching my wife give away certain of her items that others expressed interest in. To keep such a loose grip on things is a reward in and of itself. It also keeps us from being bound to this world and its pleasures and pursuits. The seeds of generosity sown in this life reap eternal rewards in the next. God loves when His people are cheerful in generosity; it catches His eye, if you will.

So be generous, and let it be said that you are generous to a fault. The fact is, that statement is actually a great compliment in the realm of the Spirit. God has been generous to us far beyond anything we could ever deserve, so for us to be generous is only another opportunity to be more like Him!

September 11

Come to Me, all you who labor and are heavy laden, and I will give you rest.

—Matthew 11:28

At the writing of today's devotional, I am in my office on a Good Friday morning. I cannot help but consider the cost of the rest offered to you and me through the body and blood of our Lord and Savior Jesus Christ. I am also thankful that the verse above is not an allegory but a wonderful reality.

True rest can be found only in Jesus. The Greek word for *rest* here literally means "recreation." Now we generally view this word *recreation* as a time of fun away from work, but look at the word carefully. "Re-creation" is the true meaning.

Jesus says, "Come unto me you who labor and are heavy laden, and I will re-create you." This reminds us of Paul's words in 2 Corinthians 5:17 that those who are in Christ are new creations. Paul also tells us why labors and heavy loads are exchanged for rest: "old things have passed away; behold all things have become new." This is such a wonderful truth to keep in mind each day. We have put off laboring while heavy laden with the past because we are new creations—re-creations—in Christ!

I am thankful today God does not abandon the work He begins. Have you ever started a project and left it undone or lost interest in something halfway through it? Thankfully, God is not like that with us. Since He is faithful and unchanging, the rest we enjoyed at the outset of our journey with Him can be experienced all the way to the end. God is continually re-creating us in the sense that there is always more to be learned about Him and always more to be revealed about us. There is nothing more refreshing and more "re-creative" than becoming more like Him in another area of life.

Jesus said, "Come, this rest is yours," and these words apply not just at the beginning but also in the middle and to the end of your journey home. Thank You, Jesus, for Your invitation to come, and thank You for the cost You paid to purchase our rest.

Let your life be a continual *thank you* for the rest Jesus purchased with His own blood!

September 12

Now faith is the substance of things hoped for, the evidence of things not seen.

—Hebrews 11:1

At the outset of this great chapter known as the Hall of Faith, we see *faith* clearly defined. Faith is the substance and faith is the evidence of an unseen work of God manifested in a life of hope. In other words, faith has substance, is evidence, and can be seen.

What follows in this great chapter is a list of names reading like a Who's Who of the Bible. Though the experiences range from building an ark, as Noah did, to being sawn in two, as Isaiah experienced, the common thread among these giants of faith is their hope in an unseen God involved in every aspect of their lives. Faith dictated their actions, because their faith had substance. Faith enabled them to stand alone and choose affliction, as Moses did, or spend a night in the lions' den, as Daniel did. The one thing we know of those listed in this great Hall of Faith is that they all lived by faith's definition given here in verse one. Their faith had substance and was evident. It showed in their lives.

Too often we reduce faith to simply believing or having an awareness of something. But true faith is visible. If we have faith that the laws of gravity are true, we will exercise caution on a mountain road or express thankfulness for the guardrail on the edge of a cliff. Faith is evidenced in actions, and those actions are the substance through which our faith is seen.

Live out a visible faith today, and through it others may see you have a hope they are looking for. Let your actions be motivated by faith, and let your faith define the way in which you travel through life, just as gravity defines how you drive the mountain road. This is what faith is: visible knowledge and beliefs that are unmoved by lions' dens and unimpressed with the passing pleasures of sin.

Set a course today for faith. Give the rest of Hebrews 11 a read before you set out. See how others have lived by faith, and know that your name too can be added to the list!

September 13

For I know the thoughts that I think toward you, says the Lord, thoughts of peace and not of evil, to give you a future and a hope.

—Jeremiah 29:11

Some things you never tire of hearing, and this verse is one for me. From it, many rightfully focus on the parts "peace and not of evil," "a future and a hope." But my simple mind gets stuck on the first part: that God is thinking about me! I matter to Him, my life is important to Him, and all I encounter today is His concern. He wants to be involved in my life all day every day, and He never tires of thinking about me. Oh, I am sure He occasionally thinks about you too. Well, actually, our all-knowing God can simultaneously think about all of us at all times!

God guards our steps and undergirds us when the path includes difficult times and seasons. He has mercy at the ready each morning whenever we need it. He has thought of everything! But often we wonder things like, *Why have I encountered evil? Why have I been hurt? Why am I in sorrow?* or *Why is my loved one suffering?* Are these things in conflict with the great and encouraging words of Jeremiah? Not at all! They are completely consistent with them.

After all, isn't it great to know that God is thinking of you when you are in dire need or when tragedy has struck? We need to be careful about letting our thoughts wander into *If this were true, I would not be experiencing what I am experiencing today.* God is there for you today and every day. His thoughts are of peace and not of evil, even when evil seeks to destroy your peace. His thoughts are of a future filled with hope, even when the present tries to rob the future of all hope.

God is thinking about you, and that has been true since before the world began. He knew what you would encounter in life, and His thoughts are on how to get you through. He knew that dark days would come into your life, but He gave you the hope of a glorious future to remember.

I love this verse and never tire of hearing it. It always reminds me that God is thinking about me, even when I don't understand what has come my way. God is thinking about you too, friend, so don't let a moment of life rob you of that great truth!

September 14

For to me, to live is Christ, and to die is gain.

— Philippians 1:29

Twelve words that say it all! Paul encapsulates the whole of our existence in this simple yet profound statement: to live is Christ, but to die is gain. At the time of this writing, Paul was under house arrest and chained to a Roman guard night and day. He knew his days on earth would soon come to an end, yet he was neither consumed with the thought of death nor fretful or fearful over his circumstances. Later in this same chapter, he would say that he was hard pressed between remaining on earth and going to heaven, heaven being a far better option, he said.

Oh, that we would live with such a perspective, constantly remembering and acting as though the best is yet to come! How that would change our pursuits and perspectives! Paul also would later say that for him to remain here on earth was more needful for the church. To live was Christ, Christ's mission, Christ's message — Christ was Paul's all in all.

I think this passage provides us with a rather significant reminder that life should be lived hard pressed between heaven and earth. A constant longing for heaven is not abnormal and should not be minimized, as many seem to do today. I long for the day when righteousness reigns and truth is the norm. I long for the time when abortion, pornography, rape, and violence cease to exist. I cannot help but think of the place where all that will happen, and that place, of course, is heaven.

But I also think we need to be hard pressed in recognizing that it is better for others if we remain here on earth. We are God's chosen means of reaching the world with His truth of the wonderful place called heaven. So maybe we could just say that Christians are to live with a continual sense of longing, longing for our heavenly home and longing for the opportunity to tell others how to get there. The fact is, it seems as if the two things are inseparable companions. If we truly believe in heaven, our outlook on earth will change as we realize that our presence here is needful.

Don't shut down and just wait for heaven, and don't ignore heaven and just live for the earth. Live hard pressed between the two. People around you need you today, and heaven awaits you in the future. The latter is far better than the first, but the first is where you are needed now.

God has a plan for your day — don't overlook it!

September 15

He who walks with wise men will be wise, but the companion of fools will be destroyed.

—Proverbs 13:20

I am always stirred at the majesty of the Word of God. I often consider how different the world would be if one particular verse alone were obeyed by the whole world. What if no one ever committed sexual immorality? How different would our world be if just that one thing were obeyed globally! What if no one ever coveted, stole, murdered, or lied? Pick any one thing, and if only that one thing were obeyed, the world would be a different place.

That is also true of the verse for today. If kids would not hang out with bad influences, if husbands or wives would avoid that flirtatious person, if the ones battling addictions would change their environments, how much personal self-inflicted disaster could be avoided today!

From time to time, it is always good to assess our relationships and to classify them into one of two groups: the fellowship group or the ministry group. We do not need to be isolationists, but we do need to be "identificationalists" (not an actual word, so use publicly with caution!). We would avoid much grief if we didn't blur the lines between these two groups.

Of course, there will be a blending of the two groups when we meet with family members, but I'm talking about our friendship choices. We need to identify those in our lives to whom we minister, which are the nonbelievers, and those in our lives with whom we fellowship, which are other believers. That is not to say we cannot have casual friendships with nonbelievers, but we do need to make sure that every relationship with a nonbeliever is ministry oriented.

We also need to guard against relationships that are bad for us. I cannot count the times I have counseled those with unhealthy relationships at the core of their current problems. These kinds of relationships divide homes, hinder the participants' spiritual walks, and many times even lead to a fall. Sadly, in these cases, if only the Christians involved had performed relationship checks, their families and lives would not have been destroyed.

Take inventory of your relationships today, and make sure that your life is full of both ministry and fellowship friends. But also make sure you know who is who. One thing you can know for sure is that just as the Lord uses people to carry out His will, Satan also uses people to carry out his!

September 16

All Scripture is given by inspiration of God, and is profitable for doctrine, for reproof, for correction, for instruction in righteousness, that the man of God may be complete, thoroughly equipped for every good work.

—2 Timothy 3:16–17

I like the phrase "God breathed," which is an acceptable understanding of the word translated *inspiration*. Scripture, then, becomes the life breath of God. Even as the Lord breathed into Adam the gift of life (Gen. 2:7), so too the Lord breathes life into every person who is a new creation in Him through His Word.

Have you ever tried not breathing for a whole day? I've never heard of anyone fasting breathing, giving it up for Lent, or even wearing a patch so they could quit! As silly and absurd as that is, so too is trying to live a new life in Christ without the whole counsel of God. We need to know the doctrines of the Word of God so we can be reproved when needed, corrected when necessary, and instructed when ignorant so that we can carry out every good work. Does it not then stand to reason that if we cut and paste Bible passages as to which portions we deem relevant, we will not be ready to carry out every good work?

In today's information age, we are bombarded with a constant stream of information. We are even fed information from pump-top TV at many gas stations, which feeds our minds and in turn our hearts with definitions of acceptance and success that may be in direct conflict with the Word of God. But how will we know the full counsel of God if we read only Psalms, Proverbs, and Jesus' words in red? How will we know the life-changing truths of the Word if our minds shut off whenever we read something we don't understand or, as is the case with many today, don't agree with? But as I have told my congregation many times, if your opinion does not line up with the Word of God, you need to get a new opinion!

Let the Word, not the world, form your beliefs and opinions. Then, if the whole world holds an opinion contrary to the Word of God, you can stand in confidence against the whole world. But if you don't know what's in God's book, you won't recognize the opinions that conflict with it.

The useless and even harmful information assaulting our minds today must be combated with a steady stream of God-breathed doctrine, reproof, correction, and instruction. Only in that way will we be equipped for everything that comes our way each day. As it has often been said, "If you find a Bible that's all worn out, it belongs to a Christian who isn't!"

September 17

For the love of Christ compels us, because we judge thus: that if One died for all, then all died; and He died for all, that those who live should live no longer for themselves, but for Him who died for them and rose again.

—2 Corinthians 5:14–15

The word *compels* in our text could also be translated "hold together," as in a bond. From that perspective, the breadth of this truth is truly amazing. The love of Christ not only holds us together in the sense of keeping us from falling apart, but it also creates a bond without barriers. When two Christians meet for the very first time, though they may have differences in theology, a bond of spiritual unity is present and recognizable. That bond is their love for Jesus Christ.

No matter the language or cultural barrier, the Christian bond is undeniable and unified in its manifestation. Those for whom He died in turn die to themselves. I will never forget the times when I have been in other countries—places where to say the people were impoverished would be an upgrade from their actual condition—and the people gave lavishly of themselves and their meager resources to make sure that their visiting guests were cared for in a manner above the hosts' own normal standard of living. I have learned, as hard as it is to do, to graciously receive the meals and honored-guest treatment on such occasions. To refuse a host's graciousness would be a major insult, no matter how uncomfortable I feel as the recipient of such generosity.

But this is the love of Christ in action. It binds together people who have never before met, people who cannot verbally communicate with one another, people with vast cultural differences. The common bond of loving Jesus, however, makes them the same. I want to be one who is that extension of unity in Christ, who no longer lives for self but for Him who died for me. I pray that is your desire as well.

Today you will undoubtedly be faced with unlimited opportunities to be salt and light, but you may also have the opportunity to be one in Christ with a brother or sister in the Lord who needs to sense that unbreakable and boundaryless bond that comes from knowing Christ. Be an encouragement to a fellow believer today. Go out of your way to do so, and seek out the opportunity. Give of your time, your effort, and even your resources, if necessary, for this is what Christ has done for you and me.

A brother or sister in Christ may need to be blessed today or even reminded of the eternal bond we share in Christ. The enemy cannot sever that bond, and a word fitly spoken might just lift that person from the mire. We've all experienced that blessing before, I'm sure, but let's make sure we are sometimes extenders of the blessing and not just receivers!

September 18

But Ruth said: "Entreat me not to leave you, or to turn back from following after you; for wherever you go, I will go; and wherever you lodge, I will lodge; your people shall be my people, and your God, my God."

—Ruth 1:16

Yesterday's exhortation is illustrated so beautifully for us here today. Naomi's two sons had died and left behind two widowed daughters-in-law, whom Naomi was sending back to their families. Orpah, one of the two, kissed her mother-in-law and departed with tears. Ruth, however, could not do so. Naomi had something that Ruth was unwilling to live without, and that was Naomi's people and, most important, Naomi's God.

Ruth was a Moabitess, a descendant of the incestuous relationship between Lot and his older daughter. Yet even in this dark and sordid family history, we find a story of the love and beauty of God's plan. Ruth fell in love with Naomi and in turn with Naomi's people and Naomi's God. Ruth later met a man named Boaz, who fell in love with her and as a kinsman-redeemer paid the price to redeem her and take her as his wife. Ruth and Boaz later had a son named Obed, who later had a son named Jesse, who in turn had many sons, one of whom was named David, from whose lineage Jesus was born.

The lessons here are too many for one day, but suffice it to say, there are two of great significance. First, may we live in such a way that others will fall in love with God's people and therefore our God. Second, we cannot let life's beginnings dominate the present. God can do anything and can bring great blessing into the lives of any who diligently seek Him. God has a personal plan and destiny for you, and you do not have to be governed by your past or your family's past. You are free to live in a manner that makes other people fall in love with your God and His people.

Don't let the devil hold you back with threats of generational curses, friend. God does not punish one person for the sins of another. Step out in faith, live in your personal forgiveness, and watch others fall in love with your people and your God. There is nothing more refreshing to nonbelievers than believers who are assured that the past is dead and the future bright, and who live like they know God can bring something out of nothing, even as He made Adam in the garden.

Live in such a visible manner of loving God that others might say, "I want what you and your people have. Your God will be my God." Remember, if you aim at nothing, you're sure to hit it. But if you live your love for God out loud today, just see what happens!

September 19

Let the words of my mouth and the meditation of my heart be acceptable in Your sight, O Lord, my strength and my Redeemer.

— Psalm 19:14

I mentioned the phrase *kinsman-redeemer* yesterday, and in today's verse David mentions the Lord as our Redeemer. The word's principal meaning is "the defender of family rights." The Lord is our strength and defender of family rights, and David prayed that his words would be "delightful" to the Lord (that is what the word *acceptable* means here in the Hebrew). The implication is that the words and meditations of our hearts should be filled with gratefulness, which is delightful to the Lord.

It is easy to let a day pass with neither a generic thanks to the Lord nor any thanks at all. Sometimes it seems as though our hearts and mouths are filled only with our needs and what we want from the Lord. This is not generally an act of a malicious heart and mind, but the end result of a rushed and complicated life. Phrases like "stop and smell the roses" are social indicators recognizing that we are indeed a busy people.

To have a delightful flow of words and heart meditations to the Lord, therefore, will require a conscious decision. At the time of a great victory or in the supply of supernatural provision, praise easily flows from our lips for what God has done. But for the majority of our days, life marches on, and nothing other than the normal day-to-day routine faces us. What happens then? That too is the time to offer delightful words and meditations to the Lord.

Take time today to tell the Lord how grateful you are for your salvation. Look back on your walk with Him, and thank Him for all the times you failed Him but He did not fail you. Look back on all the times when you did not fail Him and He used you, and thank Him for that.

Give thanks to the Lord with a grateful heart today. Start with the fact that He is your Redeemer, and then take it from there. Name specific instances of His faithfulness in your life, and you will quickly discover your prayer time has become a delight to both Him and you!

September 20

But in a great house there are not only vessels of gold and silver, but also of wood and clay, some for honor and some for dishonor. Therefore if anyone cleanses himself from the latter, he will be a vessel for honor, sanctified and useful for the Master, prepared for every good work. Flee also youthful lusts; but pursue righteousness, faith, love, peace with those who call on the Lord out of a pure heart.

—2 Timothy 2:20–22

I once heard an old country preacher named Vance Havner say in a sermon, "We don't need to pray that God uses us. We need to pray that God keeps us usable, for God wants to use us, and He will even wear us out!" This is the heart of Paul's exhortation here: stay usable. The "latter" Paul speaks of cleansing oneself from is dishonor. The principle Paul is addressing is sanctification, to set aside or set apart for a holy work.

Although it is important to recognize that salvation is of faith and not of works, it is also important to recognize that great works stemming from sanctification are an extension of faith. In other words, we come to Christ and are saved by faith alone through grace alone. Our service to the Lord, however, is predicated upon our separation from dishonorable things.

I will always remember a man who once approached me in a huff after a service, angry that his music was not being used by our church or any of the other churches he had tried to introduce it to. I had never before met this man, but my nose told me he was a heavy smoker. I asked him if he thought perhaps his gift was being hindered by his habit. This did not go over very well, and he instantly categorized me with all the others who had brought that issue up: I was a legalist.

Friends, the issue wasn't legalism; the issue was usability. Some see nothing wrong with smoking, while others view it as a sin because it damages the body. But if smoking hinders your use of a gift God has given you, why defend it? Why not just give it up? I know this is easier said than done, but the point is not about smoking per se, but about usability.

Paul says sanctification is a prerequisite for becoming a vessel of honor. Fleeing youthful lusts in exchange for a pursuit of righteousness, faith, love, and peace is a good place to start. Is there any habit or pattern in your life that others could view as dishonoring to God? Be it gossip, alcohol, foul language, ill humor, or anything else that could disqualify you, flee from it! Nothing this world offers is more fulfilling or inspiring than serving God. And serving requires sanctification, setting yourself apart from that which potentially dishonors God.

Nothing in life is worth that. So take inventory today and check your usability index. See if you need a tune-up, and don't tune out to what the Lord reveals. God will use you in every area where you remain usable. He will even wear you out!

September 21

Now it happened, as we went to prayer, that a certain slave girl possessed with a spirit of divination met us, who brought her masters much profit by fortune-telling. This girl followed Paul and us, and cried out, saying, "These men are the servants of the Most High God, who proclaim to us the way of salvation." And this she did for many days. But Paul, greatly annoyed, turned and said to the spirit, "I command you in the name of Jesus Christ to come out of her." And he came out that very hour. But when her masters saw that their hope of profit was gone, they seized Paul and Silas and dragged them into the marketplace to the authorities.

— Acts 16:16–19

I have often wondered why Paul didn't rebuke this demon on day one instead waiting for many days. I have also been amazed at the words this demonic spirit of divination spoke through this girl. The spirit didn't tell lies about Paul and Silas; it spoke the truth. They were indeed servants of the Most High God, and they did proclaim the way of salvation. However, we need to note an interesting fact here. Though the truth was spoken, it was spoken through a spirit of divination and used to promote fortune-telling, a practice the Bible forbids (Lev. 20:27; 1 Chron. 10:13).

It has been said that when the devil saw he couldn't defeat the church through persecution, he joined it. That was the scenario in today's passage of Scripture. The enemy, who is the father of all lies, sought to join himself with the truth and align fortune-telling with the gospel. But darkness and light have no fellowship, and Paul rebuked this spirit even though it spoke the truth.

Be careful of those who want to join occult practices with the work of the Lord. Chanting and meditation in hopes of achieving altered states of consciousness are not of the Lord. That holds true even if the words in the chant are true or the target of the meditation is God. Yes, the Bible teaches to meditate on the Word, but the word *meditate* does not imply any association with Eastern meditation practices. The word *meditation* in Scripture means "to ponder" or "to study."

There are no biblical grounds for incorporating Eastern mysticism into the pondering of God's Word. As a matter of fact, everything we need to know about God's views on the marriage of occult practices and His truth is answered right here in this passage. Even though the young girl's words were true, her practices were false. Paul, therefore, rebuked the demon, and the spirit of divination left the girl. All that remained was a young girl speaking truth. This resulted in Paul and Silas being beaten with rods and locked in prison, but a Philippian jailer was there who would be set free from his sin!

September 22

The thief does not come except to steal, and to kill, and to destroy. I have come that they may have life, and that they may have it more abundantly.

—John 10:10

Funny how often we dabble with things that can do nothing but steal, kill, and destroy. I love how Jesus puts it here: it's the only thing the devil comes to do! It is the end result of all his tactics and temptations. It is the only possible outcome of following his allurements, since they can accomplish only what he intended them to accomplish. So why is it we so often act as though it won't happen to us, like we are exceptions? Why do we involve ourselves with things that can only steal, kill, and destroy but then are shocked when our relationships are stolen, our hopes killed, and our witnesses destroyed?

Jesus says Satan has come to do nothing but steal, kill, and destroy, but He came that we might have life more abundantly. The word *abundantly* means "super abundantly" or "superior in quality." So Satan offers the exact opposite of what Jesus offers, because he can do nothing else.

Insanity has been defined by some as doing the same thing over and over but expecting a different outcome. Yet many Christians do exactly that. They continue doing all those things that steal, kill, and destroy life and testimony yet expect a different result each time they do them.

I know I beat this drum a lot, but I must say again that Christians are to avoid sin. That, my friend, is not legalism—it's wisdom. It is insane to play with fire yet expect not to get burned. It is insane to dabble with pornography but not expect sexual perversion to result. It is insane to engage in flirtatious conversations without expecting to be found out or, even worse, destroying your marriage. Dabbling with sin is insane living; a holy and pure life is safe.

Satan does not come except to steal, kill, and destroy. That is the end result of every one of his tactics and temptations, and not a one is the exception. The life that is pure and obedient to the commands of God is a life abundant with blessing. Friend, there are only two teams in the game of life: one comes only to steal, kill, and destroy, and the other offers life and that more abundantly. Living according to one but expecting the outcome of the other is insane. There is no other possible outcome.

Sin is our enemy, and the abundant life is never found by following it. Sin only steals, kills, and destroys lives, sometimes even from those forgiven and going to heaven. Treat sin for what it is—of the devil!

September 23

He who loves silver will not be satisfied with silver; nor he who loves abundance, with increase. This also is vanity.

— Ecclesiastes 5:10

In his day, Solomon was kind of like Bill Gates and Warren Buffet combined, as far as riches were concerned. His wealth and kingdom were legendary, and the queen of Sheba even traveled to see his kingdom (2 Chron. 9:6). When another monarch of great wealth in her own right comes to see your kingdom, you're rich! But interestingly, Solomon said, "It's vanity." An observation like this from a pauper wouldn't carry much weight, but when the man who is the richest man in the world makes such a statement, you can take it to the bank (sorry, couldn't resist)!

It is amazing, I think, how things we lived without even a decade ago have now become so important to us. For example, I could not imagine not having a cell phone. Leaving it at home accidentally is like being in a time warp back into the Stone Age. We also apply this same attitude to things we desire but do not yet have. We think, *Life just won't be the same for me if I don't have _____,* and then when we do get it, a newer and better one soon comes out and we're right back where we were in the first place. Only seeking and serving the Lord will never leave us unsatisfied or empty.

To be sure, it is a battle to keep the desires of the flesh in check, especially when it comes to silver and increase, but those kinds of things will not satisfy; they only create an appetite for more. We have been given all things to enjoy, and life is meant to be rich and full, but we don't have to be rich in order for life to be full. So if you are striving for silver at the expense of your family, remember that silver offers little consolation to your family when they reap the results of your physical absence or love of material abundance.

I cannot tell you how many men I have had to remind over the years that things can never replace their physical presence. I know kids want to keep up with the latest styles and trends, but not at the expense of parental absence. I have never heard a child say, "I wish my mom and dad were gone more. I wish they worked two jobs so we could live better." But I have heard plenty say, "All my parents do is work, and they have no time for me."

Riches and wealth are not evil; they are inanimate and inherently neither good nor evil. But the choices we make in order to obtain or maintain them are where regret and sorrow can creep in. Listen, friend, your eternal home has streets paved with gold, so don't work too hard to obtain a substance that heaven uses for pavement. As Solomon says, this is vanity, and it is costly to your family as well. Parents, you are far more important to your children than a vacation home or the latest shoes. If you don't believe me, just ask them. Solomon learned the true value of riches the hard way. You don't have to!

September 24

Therefore, since Christ suffered for us in the flesh, arm yourselves also with the same mind, for he who has suffered in the flesh has ceased from sin, that he no longer should live the rest of his time in the flesh for the lusts of men, but for the will of God.

—1 Peter 4:1–2

I like how the New Living Translation phrases the end of verse 1: "For if you are willing to suffer for Christ, you have decided to stop sinning." If we were to look at the whole of Scripture, we would be amazed at how often the mind is brought into the equation of living for God. This tells us that the life of walking in the Spirit begins in the mind. We can be Spirit filled yet still need to make up our minds that we are going to be Spirit led. Being indwelt by the Holy Spirit does not make us some kind of zombie-like follower of God; we still must choose to be led by the Spirit *and* decide in our minds that we are going to follow the Spirit.

Peter here identifies a major area in which the mind plays an important role, and that is the area of suffering. We cannot ignore the link between suffering and ceasing to sin. I think we all would be stunned if we recognized how often peer pressure is involved in leading us to sin, whether it is doing something wrong or not doing something right. The reason is that the flesh longs for acceptance and never chooses rejection. But if we are armed with the same mind as Christ, we will suffer for standing against sin when necessary. Whether that means being the outcast at school or the wacko at work "who thinks he is better than everyone else" (in other people's words), we must be willing to choose suffering if we are going to be like Christ.

The type of suffering Peter was referring to here is far greater than anything most of us have ever endured; it was the suffering of torture and death for living openly as a Christian. That kind of puts a little ridicule and not being part of the in crowd in a different perspective, doesn't it?

We must awake each day with the decision to follow the Spirit and live by the Word regardless of the response this elicits from others. Deciding not to sin will generate suffering, and we need to know that and be willing to accept it. It all begins with the mind-set of not living for the lusts and desires of unsaved men and women.

Make up your mind today that sins of commission and sins of omission are not going to be your master. Don't join in the talk about the boss, and don't fall prey to the pressure to attend the party. Make the decision to suffer the consequences of doing right rather than the consequences of doing wrong. Live today for the will of God!

September 25

I marvel that you are turning away so soon from Him who called you in the grace of Christ, to a different gospel, which is not another; but there are some who trouble you and want to pervert the gospel of Christ. But even if we, or an angel from heaven, preach any other gospel to you than what we have preached to you, let him be accursed. As we have said before, so now I say again, if anyone preaches any other gospel to you than what you have received, let him be accursed.

—Galatians 1:6–9

Paul was dealing with the fact that some in Galatia were preaching a gospel of salvation through works of the law, especially circumcision. This was completely contrary to the wonderful grace of God that had appeared to all men in the person of Jesus Christ. Thus the pure gospel was being perverted. In this context, the word *pervert* means "to become its opposite," and the law was certainly the opposite of grace.

Paul elevated the gospel of grace above the identity and reputation of the teachers who were preaching the law and soberly warned, "If we, or an angel from heaven, preach any other gospel..., let him be accursed." Paul delivered this dire warning twice to underscore the seriousness of perverting the gospel message.

Paul's hypothetical situation of angels revealing messages in conflict with the Bible has become an actual reality in our day, and there are people who actually embrace this. However, the reality is, following a false gospel leads to the same destiny as preaching a false gospel—being accursed. I have never been accused of being politically correct, but thankfully, neither have I ever been accused of watering down the Word of God.

Many religious movements today embrace angelic revelations contrary to the gospel of Jesus Christ. But, dear friends, this passage means exactly what it says. We are not doing anyone any favors by trying not to hurt their feelings. Sincerity will not get anyone into heaven; you can be sincerely wrong—and millions are.

If we truly love those who follow false religions, we must love them enough to tell them the truth. "Isn't that judging?" some might ask. Friends, judging is to define right and wrong and to claim the ability to know someone else's motives. The Bible, and therefore God, has already pronounced judgment upon messages received by angelic revelation that conflict with the Word of God.

Islam, Mormonism, and many other religions boast of angelic revelations as their source of direction and enlightenment, and they all conflict with the message of the Bible. Love people enough to tell them the truth. All roads do lead to God, in one sense, but the real question is, where will you go to spend eternity after you meet Him? According to the Word of God, there is no other gospel, only other ways to lead people into everlasting destruction under the guise of a revelation from God.

Love people enough today to speak the truth in love—but speak the truth!

September 26

God is not a man, that He should lie, nor a son of man, that He should repent. Has He said, and will He not do? Or has He spoken, and will He not make it good? Behold, I have received a command to bless; He has blessed, and I cannot reverse it.

— Numbers 23:19–20

Having seen the great victories of Israel and fearful of being next on the list of their conquests, Balak, a Moabite king, hired a prophet to curse Israel. But every time Balaam, the profiteering prophet, tried to curse Israel, God would only speak blessing over His people. The words in today's passage were spoken the second time Balaam tried to curse Israel. In accordance with Balak's desire and guidance, Balaam changed locations, as though there might be a crack in God's covering. It was as though Balak thought, *If you can't curse Israel from over here, try it over there.*

But after the failed second attempt at cursing Israel, Balaam told Balak, "I cannot reverse the will of God." Bless the Lord and shout hallelujah, reader, for the Lord does not change! If the will of God could not be reversed in Balaam's day and the Lord does not change, then the will of God cannot be reversed in our day. God's intention for His children is blessing — not cursing!

God is not a man that He could lie, and neither is He the son of a man that He could repent. His will is irreversible. Like Balak and Balaam, the enemy may keep coming at you from every angle or direction, but he cannot reverse the will of God. If he could, then that would mean God had either lied or changed, and neither is even a remote possibility.

God's desire for you, friends, is to live a blessed life. But God's definition of a blessed life is not always consistent with ours. According to His definition, a blessed life does not necessarily include fast cars and fat bank accounts. We do not need these things to live a blessed life — we need Him.

There may be plenty of Balaks and Balaams coming at you today from every angle. They may try to curse you and strive to quench your victories or postpone their own defeats. But don't forget, it is not possible for God to lie or change His mind as it concerns you, friend. No one can curse that which God has already blessed. Ask Balaam. It didn't work then, and it won't work now.

Go out this day with confidence in your God!

September 27

Therefore I exhort first of all that supplications, prayers, intercessions, and giving of thanks be made for all men, for kings and all who are in authority, that we may lead a quiet and peaceable life in all godliness and reverence. For this is good and acceptable in the sight of God our Savior, who desires all men to be saved and to come to the knowledge of the truth.

—1 Timothy 2:1–4

I cannot help but see a little humor in Paul's exhortation to Timothy here. He seems to say, "Pray for all people, even the government, for God desires that even they would be saved!" I cannot help but see the irony in this as there is such political polarization in our day as members of each political party demonize the other. I have witnessed this even among Christians! But I wonder what would happen if members of both political parties began to pray for one another. I wonder what would happen if we prayed for those we oppose who are in office. Unfortunately, the quiet, peaceable life in godliness and reverence that would follow such actions is a far cry from much of what we see in our nation today.

Now I am all for Christians participating in government. As a matter of fact, I prefer Christians as our leaders because they possess a distinct advantage over nonbelievers. They have a resource of wisdom available that those who do not know God lack. But I must say, I prefer Christian leaders and Christian activists who actually act like Christians! Quiet, peaceable, godly, reverent people who pray for all people would be a nice addition to the political arena of our day. Please note, however, I am not talking about pacifism, but godly, reverent activism.

It has been said there are two things friends should not ever discuss: politics and religion. That is because quiet, peaceable godliness often flies out the door as soon as either subject is broached. But no matter your party affiliation, remember, your first responsibility is to your faith and the behavior and attitudes that reflect your faith. If you disagree with the opposing party, pray for them, vote against them, and even encourage others to do the same. But let it not be said of you that you cannot discuss religion or politics without your Christian attributes flying right out the window!

September 28

The Lord is my shepherd; I shall not want. He makes me to lie down in green pastures; He leads me beside the still waters. He restores my soul; He leads me in the paths of righteousness for His name's sake. Yea, though I walk through the valley of the shadow of death, I will fear no evil; for You are with me; Your rod and Your staff, they comfort me. You prepare a table before me in the presence of my enemies; You anoint my head with oil; my cup runs over. Surely goodness and mercy shall follow me all the days of my life; and I will dwell in the house of the Lord forever.

— Psalm 23

Normally *I* and *me* are words that would be problem indicators when it comes to a person's Christian perspective, but not here. I love how David and so many other Bible authors personalize God's love and care. The apostle John, for example, referred to himself as the disciple whom Jesus loved. Was John really loved more than the others? I don't think so. I think John just knew how much Jesus loved him.

In Psalm 23, David takes this same tone. He opens with a statement of great humility and respect for the Lord that softens the *I*s and *me*s to their rightful and reverent places. He says, "The Lord is my shepherd," which implies that David is His sheep. David says, "I am not my own master; I serve another, and He is the Lord."

Had this most famous of psalms been absent of this opening phrase, it may well have carried a different tone, and the *I*s and *me*s would have seemed a little presumptuous or even arrogant. But because of how David opened this psalm, what follows is not presumption, but rich promises. "The Lord is my shepherd, and this is how He treats His sheep all the way through life until they dwell in His house forever" would be one way for us to read this.

Ponder the words of this great psalm today. There is much more to it than just "Yea, though I walk through the valley of the shadow of death." There is much more there than just a shepherd who sustains His sheep in difficult times. Read it closely, and insert your name in place of all the *I*s and *me*s. There you'll find a list of promises for all who claim the Lord as their shepherd!

September 29

So shall My word be that goes forth from My mouth; it shall not return to Me void,
but it shall accomplish what I please, and it shall prosper in the thing
for which I sent it.

—Isaiah 55:11

It has often been said, "Seven days without reading your Bible makes one weak." I couldn't agree more! Yet as frequently as today's verse is quoted and as majestic as it is, I think we often overlook one aspect of it that anchors the whole verse: the will of God. The Word of God is where we find the will of God, and this is why we must not weaken ourselves by ignoring God's Word. The Word of God tells us what God wants to accomplish in and through us and how we can prosper (the word means "to push forward" or "advance") in the things for which the Word of God was sent.

This great chapter from Isaiah opens with an invitation to the idolatrous children of Israel to come back under the will and blessings of God. In verse 1, the Lord said to the children of Israel, "Come to me for what money cannot buy," and then these things are described as "abundance of the soul" and the "sure mercies of David." Isaiah pleaded with God's people to "seek the Lord while he may be found" and to "let the wicked forsake their way," for God "will have mercy and abundantly pardon." All these things lead up to today's majestic verse.

"Get back under the covering and direction of My Word" is the Lord's exhortation to the wandering heart. Don't just read it or hear it, but allow it to advance in your life. God's thoughts are not our thoughts and His ways are higher than ours, verses 9 and 10 say, so how are we going to know them if we don't read His Word?

God may be calling some of you to get back to His ways as described in His Word. He may be calling some to bring back under His covering their pursuits and desires. God may be asking some to surrender a relationship that is outside His will as defined in His Word. He may be asking some to engage in service to Him and His church as prescribed in His Word. He may even be calling some out of moral darkness and into His marvelous light as depicted in His Word.

God's ways are not only higher, but they are also the only place where sure mercies and abundance of soul can be found. Feeling weak lately? What's the reading on your "Wordometer"? Are you on empty from lack of refueling, or do you perhaps feel empty because of lack of repenting? Either way, sure mercies and abundance of soul await all who return to Him for that which money can't buy: the wisdom and blessings of His Word!

September 30

Therefore we also, since we are surrounded by so great a cloud of witnesses, let us lay aside every weight, and the sin which so easily ensnares us, and let us run with endurance the race that is set before us, looking unto Jesus, the author and finisher of our faith, who for the joy that was set before Him endured the cross, despising the shame, and has sat down at the right hand of the throne of God.

—Hebrews 12:1–2

I remember a time in high school when I went to a state invitational track meet. It was obviously an honor to be there, and my races were the sprints, short distances. On our arrival, we learned that rather than the normal 100-yard and 220-yard sprints, one of the races would be a 330. (This was back in the days when races were still in yards, not meters.) My coach assigned me to run the 330, so I began to prepare myself mentally for the longer race.

Race time soon approached, and I was ushered to the starting area. I will never forget the feeling that swept over me when I first saw the track. The 330 was not run on the usual oval track, but rather on a straight track. That 330-yard straightaway looked longer than anything I had ever seen in my life. It looked like the finish line was in another zip code. By the time the race started, I was so psyched out that I lost the race before I ever ran it; and when the race was finished, I was closer to the back of the pack than to the front.

So many people have exactly this perspective on the Christian life. "I can't do it. It's too hard, and it's too long," they protest. "Look at the goal; it's unattainable," they insist. But Hebrews encourages us to endure the race by looking to the one who has already won it for us.

Imagine preparing to run the 330 but being told before the start of the race that you're definitely going to win, and imagine being told this by God Himself. What's that going to do for your perspective, even if the finish line looks like it's outside the city limits? It's going to change everything: how you think, how you run, your level of confidence.

But there is also another important piece of information here in Hebrews: you will enjoy the race much more if you don't carry along weights or sins. Your endurance will be greater, and you'll not weary quickly, as some runners do. As I mentioned, I lost the race in my mind before I ever stepped foot onto the track. At the 220-yard mark, I was out of gas because I had already weighed myself down with doubt and convinced myself I couldn't do it.

You can do it, friend! Jesus has finished the race of faith, and you are running toward Him. He is your finish line, your goal, your prize. If you choose, you can run weighed down by cares or hindered by sin, but those are not good strategies for finishing well. Keep your eyes on Jesus as you run today, and listen to Him as your coach.

In all my years of running track, I never raced wearing army boots. Every runner carries as little gear as possible. Similarly, if you try to run with sin in your life, partying for pleasure instead of training for the course, you will run weighed down, and finishing will be that much more difficult.

Don't focus on how hard or long it is between here and the finish line. Keep your eyes on the one waiting to greet you at the end of the race—Jesus, the author and finisher of your faith race!

October 1

And God will wipe away every tear from their eyes; there shall be no more death, nor sorrow, nor crying. There shall be no more pain, for the former things have passed away.

—Revelation 21:4

As I write these devotionals each day, I have a master list of 365 verses that I work from. I have been amazed to see how the Holy Spirit weaves one day's thought into the next, and I grow excited knowing that He is going to say something special to someone at just the time they need to hear it.

As I have written the devotionals, my kids' birthdays have come and gone, as well as birthdays for two of my three grandchildren and other family members. Obviously, I thought of them as I wrote that day's devotional. But this day, October 1, is my wedding anniversary, and I read with great interest the verse preselected for this day.

Today's verse has provided comfort for many people throughout the years. Like all those before me, I too am eager for that day when the regrets, failures, sorrows, and losses of earthly life will be mercifully wiped away by the hand of almighty God. But this verse has added meaning for me, because it also beautifully describes what happened in my marriage more than twenty-five years ago.

In a moment's time, the heartache of a dead, painful, tear-filled relationship was wiped away, and the "former thing" passed away. My wife Teri and I often talk of that moment—and it was just that, a moment—when everything changed for us. Yes, we had given our lives to the Lord, we were doing better as a couple, we had purchased a home, I was sober, I had a good job, and we had made progress in our marriage. But we both knew we were not yet where we needed to be.

But one day after a counseling session in which we both had aired our grievances, Teri and I stepped outside the pastor's office and looked at each other and said, "Let's stop this, and let's let go." We did, and in that moment, the tears, death, and sorrow of the past instantaneously and simultaneously melted away. No, it isn't that we never disagreed again or have skipped through "happy land" our entire marriage, but the past died that day, and we had a fresh start.

Because of my personal experience, I will not accept it when anyone comes into my office and announces they are trapped in a hopeless marriage—especially if the person is a Christian. I know what God can do. If He can take the death and sorrow that was in my marriage and transform it into what Teri and I enjoy so much today, He can do it for anyone.

But here's the key: you have to let the former things pass away. You might need to talk some things through with someone, but the past must die, and you must begin again. God can do it; I have seen it with my own eyes. Should the Lord tarry and I have more October 1s in my future, I can confidently say to my beautiful bride, "Happy anniversary," and know that it really is.

God heals marriages!

October 2

A father of the fatherless, a defender of widows, is God in His holy habitation. God sets the solitary in families; He brings out those who are bound into prosperity; but the rebellious dwell in a dry land.

—Psalm 68:5–6

One of Christianity's richest blessings in this life is a church family. I have seen Psalm 68 come alive time and again as people with no family or people who were the only believers in their families found a place of belonging in church. This is why 1 Peter 4:9 reminds us of our call to *hospitality*, the word meaning "having a love for strangers." God has set among us orphans, widows, the destitute, and people with no family and expects us to care for them as loved family members.

As you read today's devotional, keep in mind that the holiday season is right around the corner. Now might be a good time to look for a solitary person to include in your plans. Let your home be a place of ministry for those who are struggling and lonely. This is what the psalmist means when he says, "He brings out those who are bound into prosperity." The abundance referred to is the love of a family related not by blood but in spirit.

Family holiday traditions are wonderful and beautiful, and there is nothing wrong with honoring them, as long as they are honorable traditions. But giving them a rest every once in a while doesn't hurt either, as Teri and I discovered a couple of years ago. That year we spent Christmas Day with strangers in a convalescent home. It was an amazing day, filled with tears and a profound sense of fulfillment.

It might seem odd to you to be reading about the holidays in early October, but if you accept the challenge to expand your concept of family, you will need time to plan, prepare, and even rearrange some traditions. But remember, God's people, in a very real sense, are His hands and feet. Someone lonely needs a person to listen, a hug or a hand to hold. The simplest thing can turn someone's lonely existence into a prosperous day. I have seen it happen time and again, and I have heard repeatedly from those who have given their time to someone in need that it was one of the most rewarding things they had ever done.

How terrible it is when those God has placed in a church family continue in solitude, though they are surrounded by people. Find someone today that you can extend hospitality to. Smiles are contagious; why not pass some out today and see what you get in return?

October 3

If you confess with your mouth the Lord Jesus and believe in your heart that God has raised Him from the dead, you will be saved. For with the heart one believes unto righteousness, and with the mouth confession is made unto salvation.

— Romans 10:9–10

Quite often we Christians overcomplicate things and present a very complex gospel to the world though it is actually quite simple. The word *confess* means "to see or speak as the same" or "to agree." So agree with God that you are a sinner, and believe in your heart that God has raised Jesus from the dead, and you shall be saved. Paul reiterates here what Jesus had already said in Matthew 12:34: that out of the heart, the mouth speaks. When you believe, confession is made, or your mouth speaks what your heart believes.

As I was talking with our young adults last week, we made the observation that only Christians share their ugliest sins and failures with others in hopes of glorifying God and bringing others to Him. This is the mouth speaking out of the heart. What most people try to hide about themselves, Christians share openly because their hearts have been changed and they truly believe.

Christianity has its complexities, to be sure, but the gospel has none. It's simple, easy, and understandable. "God changed me when I gave my life to Him" is an irrefutable statement for sharing your faith. But some Christians, unfortunately, try to argue the complexities of Christianity in hopes of convincing nonbelievers of Christianity's claims. This often results in cyclical arguments that never lead to anything but frustration. However, "Once I was blind, but now I can see" — who can argue with that?

You may have an antagonist in your life who wants to argue about a God of love allowing suffering or any of the other issues people have with God. It's always best to keep it simple. "I gave my heart to Jesus and believe He is the only Savior, and you can know Him too" is about as complex as you need to get. Now that's not to say that sharing your faith should never go any deeper than that, but the majority of the time, it will be enough for those whose hearts God has already prepared. You are never the pioneer when it comes to reaching others with the truth. The truth is, God sends you to people He's already been working on.

So keep it simple with nonbelievers. They can argue all day about Jonah in the whale, the parting of the Red Sea, or any other issue they have with the Word of God. But what can they say to someone standing right in front of them who says, "I know Him and believe He died and rose again for me, and knowing Him has changed everything for me and even about me"?

Be careful about arguing the Bible with people who don't believe it. If they don't believe the stories of the Bible, tell them yours instead. No one can argue with a changed life!

October 4

"Be angry, and do not sin": do not let the sun go down on your wrath, nor give place to the devil.

—Ephesians 4:26–27

I have to say, I am often surprised at the number of Christians who believe that anger is a sin. Psalm 7:11 says that God is angry with the wicked every day, and Jesus was angry when He drove the money changers out of the temple. Regarding anger, sin comes into play only when we let anger control us or get out of control.

Paul's quotation here from Psalm 4:4 is a reminder that among the fruits of the Spirit is self-control, and the implication is not to let anger fester, but rather to resolve matters quickly. When we disregard this instruction, we give the devil place in our lives and are likely to stew for weeks before eventually exploding over the unresolved matter.

Like many of you, I have discovered the rather significant reality that when we are angry with someone and stew over the issue for weeks or months, we are the only ones ripped off in the end. Quite often the ones we are angry with don't even know they did anything to upset us. This is more frequently the case in friendships or in working relationships than it is in marriages. Married couples usually have their ways of letting their mates know when something is wrong—even if it is by the silent treatment.

So many people have allowed anger to become sin simply by not going to the other person and saying, "This hurt me," or "That insulted me." Consequently, the relationship becomes strained, and gossip and evil thoughts creep in. But if we let it be known when we are offended, much of the time the other person will offer a quick apology and the matter can be put to rest. However, the sad truth is, we often want to punish the other person instead of forgive them. *He ought to know he hurt me*, we think. *He ought to come to me*, we rationalize. But the person who doesn't even know he hurt someone is not the one in sin; the person who chooses to be angry for weeks and months without saying anything is the one committing sin.

There is much to be righteously indignant about in our day, and there is a place for our anger about many things. But when it comes to interpersonal relationships, weeks and months of festering anger is the devil's playground. Most often, the only one miserable is you.

If you have been legitimately wronged—and I want to emphasize *if* you have been legitimately wronged and aren't just being a baby—do not let the sun go down on your anger. Settle the matter quickly if at all possible. Ugly things grow out of unresolved conflicts, and they usually grow in angry people, not in the objects of their anger.

October 5

Indeed it came to pass, when the trumpeters and singers were as one, to make one sound to be heard in praising and thanking the Lord, and when they lifted up their voice with the trumpets and cymbals and instruments of music, and praised the Lord, saying: "For He is good, for His mercy endures forever," that the house, the house of the Lord, was filled with a cloud, so that the priests could not continue ministering because of the cloud; for the glory of the Lord filled the house of God.

−2 Chronicles 5:13−14

The dedication of Solomon's temple was the scene here as the ark of the covenant was placed in the Holy of Holies. The scene was both solemn and surreal. At last the ark had a home in the city of David, a cause for great celebration.

Over the years, I have often used these verses to remind worship leaders and Christian artists of their mission as musicians unto the Lord. The key is in verse 13, and I paraphrase: "When the band and the singers were united in the purpose of praising and thanking God," then the house of the Lord was filled with His glory. We might well say that when the people were united in the right purpose, then God joined in the service. What a lesson for us today!

God desires that we remember our purpose in life is to bring Him glory. All the division and distraction that we introduce into praise and thanksgiving keep us from the fullness He wants us to enjoy as those united in Him. When a church that practices one style of worship attacks a group that is either more contemporary or more traditional than they are, this detracts from the true purpose of worship, which is to give thanks and praise to God.

This division, I believe, is the leading cause of not seeing the Lord's glory in His church today. Far too often Christians divide over just about anything, from style of worship to the color of the building. I have a style of worship music that I prefer, but that doesn't mean every other form is wrong or "of the devil." But the fact is, worship has little to do with singing anyway; it is more about unity than the actual music. Being one as we lift praise and thanks to God is what God wants from us.

I have often said that churches are like toast: some people like it dry, others like it with a little butter, and still others want butter and jelly. But regardless of what accompanies it, it's still toast. Now that's not to say anything goes in a church service and that we are to unite for unity's sake alone. But it is to say we are not to divide over matters of taste but rather should unite in praise and thanksgiving to God. That's the kind of church the Lord wants to be a part of and His glory will settle on. That's the kind of church so filled with His glory that the priests (pastors) cannot minister and the Lord of heaven becomes the center of attention!

October 6

In the beginning God created the heavens and the earth. The earth was without form, and void; and darkness was on the face of the deep. And the Spirit of God was hovering over the face of the waters. Then God said, "Let there be light"; and there was light. And God saw the light, that it was good; and God divided the light from the darkness. God called the light Day, and the darkness He called Night. So the evening and the morning were the first day.

—Genesis 1:1–4

One rather startling fact about the first day of creation is usually over-looked, and that concerns when God said, "Let there be light," and there was light. However, a careful reading of Genesis shows that God did not create the sun, moon, and stars until the fourth day. So there was light without the sun!

This observation is particularly interesting in light of several other passages in Scripture. First John 1:5 says, "This is the message which we have heard from Him [Jesus] and declare to you, that God is light and in Him is no darkness at all." Revelation 21:23 says of the city of heaven, "The city had no need of the sun or of the moon to shine in it, for the glory of God illuminated it. The Lamb is its light." John 8:12 states, "Then Jesus spoke to them again, saying, 'I am the light of the world. He who follows Me shall not walk in darkness, but have the light of life.' "

This makes clear that in creation there was light without luminaries, and this could be true only because God is light. Since Jesus said He is the light of the world, then doesn't this logically mean He was declaring that He is God? I am always amazed that some alleged Christians say Jesus never claimed to be God. From Genesis to Revelation, that fact is woven throughout Scripture time and again. From Jesus as the Creator of all things as mentioned in Colossians 1:15–16 to the light references mentioned above, the Bible con-tinually proclaims the Trinity, or "Tri-unity," of God. The Father is light, the Son is light, and the Spirit is light, and there is no need for other lights.

Could we not then arrive at two conclusions from this one great truth of the Trinity? First, the God of the Bible is the only light we need, and second, the God of the Bible is the only light there is!

The Bible is a book that records the whole of time and life as we know it. From beginning to end, the message of man's sin and God's offer of salvation are woven throughout it. The Bible is the book on how to get to heaven and maintains there is but one way. Jesus is the only illumination we need! The Bible declares it from beginning to end.

October 7

But let all those rejoice who put their trust in You; let them ever shout for joy, because You defend them; let those also who love Your name be joyful in You.

—Psalm 5:11

I recently had an interesting experience at one of our Wednesday night services. After opening with prayer, I often instruct the congregation to greet one another, and I say something like, "Tell someone you have never met you're glad they're here." This particular Wednesday night, however, I said, "Before you sit down, tell someone near you that Jesus is coming soon." It was stunning and beautiful how just the reminder of that great truth shifted people's thoughts from their busy weeks to a blessed future hope. In a room full of people in the middle of all their normal weekly stuff, smiles and tangible joy bubbled forth.

There is a progression here in this psalm we don't want to miss. We shout for joy because we trust in Him, knowing He is our defense. Just the mention of His name or even His return causes us to be joyful in Him. So if you are in the middle of a mess or just the normal busyness of life, remind yourself that your hope and your trust are in God. The immoveable, unchanging almighty God is the one you trust in. So shout for joy—He is your defense. Be joyful in Him—He can be trusted.

God will never fail you, and just the mention of His name, His cross, His return, His provision, His protection, or anything else that He does is cause for joy. But the greatest thing about this is that when you look at life and all is not well, when your life is a mess or possibly even tragic, when maybe you feel like heaven is all you have to look forward to, remind yourself of God's care and faithfulness, and rejoice in that.

Heaven is something to look forward to, and I believe that Jesus is coming for us all very soon. That will put a smile on all of our faces. I know, because I saw it happen right before my eyes. Tell people today that Jesus is coming soon. They may not have smiles on their faces, but it will certainly keep one in your heart!

October 8

And I give them eternal life, and they shall never perish; neither shall anyone snatch them out of My hand.

—John 10:28

The "them" of this verse are the sheep Jesus came to lay down His life for. I am thankful for this verse because eighteen verses earlier, in John 10:10, Jesus revealed the existence of a thief who would try to snatch us out of His hands by stealing, killing, and destroying. However, Jesus assures us, in essence, "He can try, but he will fail." So eternal life cannot be taken from us, nor can we be snatched from His hand of protection.

Of course, that doesn't mean the enemy doesn't try. I find it odd that he keeps trying to accomplish something he cannot possibly succeed at, but it is true, nonetheless. He tries to steal, kill, and destroy our salvation, but He has no weapons capable of defeating Jesus' nail-scarred hands. He cannot make the accusation that we got away with our sins, for Jesus was punished for them. He cannot say we are imperfect creatures and thus do not meet the entrance qualifications for heaven, for we are in Christ, the one who is perfect. He cannot say that our failures since salvation now disqualify us, for Jesus sits at the right hand of the Father as our intercessor and advocate.

The scars on Jesus' hands are the reason we cannot be snatched from them. As long as those marks remain on His precious hands, the devil's efforts to snatch us from them will fail. As it has been said, the only manmade thing in heaven will be Jesus' scars, but by them Jesus gave us eternal life. If we could be snatched from His hands, then the life He gave was not eternal. If we could lose that which He gave, then it was only temporary.

This is such a wonderful truth for all who feel like they have lost their salvation. Be assured, if you ever actually had it, you can't possibly lose it! So if you know that you are His and that you definitely gave your life to Him at a certain point in time, then nothing can snatch you from His hands.

I do want to say, however, that feeling unsaved usually comes from acting unsaved. Whether through disobedience or disengagement, the feeling of being unsaved will change with a change of actions. But being snatched from His hands can never happen. The scars on those hands prove it to be so!

October 9

*When a man's ways please the Lord, He makes even his enemies to be
at peace with him.*

—Proverbs 16:7

Not one single aspect of life is unaffected by knowing God, including the one stated in this great proverb. Solomon makes an interesting implication that pleasing the Lord is not always pleasing to others. Our desire to live for the Lord and honor Him in all that we do often creates animosity in those who are antireligion and blame all the world's problems on organized religion.

In a very real sense, pleasing the Lord can make enemies for us, but exactly how does this apply to our lives? It means when we try to please God, we will always encounter spiritual opposition, but obedience to the Lord provides protection that disobedience robs us of. We must not wander outside of God's love, but we must rather remember He loved us enough to send His Son to die for us while we were yet sinners (Rom. 5:8). When we walk in obedience, we remove our enemies' opportunities to inflict on us the consequences of sin. They will keep coming, but God makes them be at peace with us.

Our enemies can indeed be military enemies, as Solomon alluded to, but they can also be the lust of the flesh, the lust of the eyes, and the pride of life. When we walk in the Spirit and do not fulfill the lusts of the flesh, we live free of the painful consequences of sin, and therefore our enemies are at peace with us. There is nothing for them to shoot at, if you will.

Living to please the Lord is the way to enjoy life at its best. Sin, however, always robs us of peace, because we cannot live in peace and guilt at the same time; we can have only one or the other. So seek to please God today in all that you do and say, and the enemies of the flesh will be at peace with you. And at the end of the day, you will have nothing to look back on and feel guilty about. The enemies of the flesh will have no opportunity to create guilt, because you conducted yourself in a way that honored the Lord.

Guilt-free living is the best, and the way to have it and therefore be at peace with the enemies of the flesh is to remove all opportunity for the flesh to prevail. Easier said than done, to be sure, but there is great reward even in trying.

Let your ways please the Lord today. He'll be honored, and you'll be blessed!

October 10

There is therefore now no condemnation to those who are in Christ Jesus, who do not walk according to the flesh, but according to the Spirit.

—Romans 8:1

This is a favorite verse of many, to be sure—well, at least half of it is! I have often said, when considering Romans 8:1, that you have to make sure you get to the "who do" of the verse. Many people, however, quote only the first half, leaving the "no condemnation" portion absent of the following qualifier. We also need to be careful of misreading the verse as a whole even when we do include the "who do," lest we somehow think we are condemned on the days we don't do well and walk in the flesh.

There is only one way to walk in the Spirit, and that is to be filled with the Spirit. There is only one way to be filled with the Spirit, and that is to be born again. That is where the "who do" begins, but that is not where it ends. Those who are filled with the Spirit are not going to be led by the Spirit into things that gratify the flesh—worldly things, ungodly things, things that shame us, our faith, and therefore our God.

This is why the whole verse is so important. Some have used it as license for their sinful liberty, saying as justification that no matter what they do, there is no condemnation because they are in Christ Jesus. While it may be true that Christians fail morally and fall prey to the flesh at times—and this is a great promise to remember at those times—it is also true this is not a "get out of jail free" card, like some seem to think. "I can do whatever I want and not worry about being condemned" is not something the Spirit teaches. That is the expression of a carnal mind, and it is of the flesh. It may be good for such a person to take the self-examination test of faith that Paul talks about in 2 Corinthians 13:5.

What are you walking in regularly and habitually: the flesh or the Spirit? If the flesh rules you and your life looks more like those in the world than those in the Bible, then you might need to get to the "who do" of Romans 8:1 and rethink your understanding of biblical truth. Yes, there is no condemnation for those who are in Christ Jesus, but those in Christ Jesus are those who do not walk according to the flesh but according to the Spirit.

Grace is not cheap, friends, and it is not a license to sin. When you read there is no condemnation for those in Christ Jesus, be sure to include the "who do"!

October 11

But it displeased Jonah exceedingly, and he became angry. So he prayed to the Lord,
and said, "Ah, Lord, was not this what I said when I was still in my country?
Therefore I fled previously to Tarshish; for I know that You are a gracious and
merciful God, slow to anger and abundant in lovingkindness, one who relents from
doing harm. Therefore now, O Lord, please take my life from me, for it is better for
me to die than to live!" Then the Lord said, "Is it right for you to be angry?"

—Jonah 4:1–3

At first glance, we might be stunned that one of God's prophets would be angry with God because of His grace and mercy extended to a city. It is true that the Ninevites, or Assyrians, were a wicked and violent people and had done great harm to the Israelites. But God is not willing that any should perish—even when they are our enemies (2 Pet. 3:9)!

Jonah's attitude might seem shocking, but we are often more like Jonah than we care to admit. Yes, the Assyrians were guilty of heinous crimes against many nations. Yes, they skinned people alive and murdered women and children. And yes, Jonah wanted the Assyrians to get what they deserved. This is where we can be very Jonah-like at times.

Have you ever wanted someone who hurt you or a loved one to "get what they've got coming"? I will admit, I have sometimes found this to be true in my own life, but I have always been brought back to the same place: Do I want what I've got coming? Do I wish God would have treated me like I deserved when I was yet a sinner? Hardly—I wanted grace, mercy, and longsuffering!

This is why Jesus said in the Sermon on the Mount, "You have heard that it was said, 'You shall love your neighbor and hate your enemy.' But I say to you, love your enemies, bless those who curse you, do good to those who hate you, and pray for those who spitefully use you and persecute you" (Matt. 5:43–44).

We too have some Jonah in us, and like Jonah, the first place it shows up is in an attitude that reveals the core issue of bitterness in our hearts. The reason that Jesus gave the command to pray for and do good to our enemies is that most of the time, these actions will cure the wrong attitude and the bitterness behind it. When we pray and do good, we are reminded of the mercy and grace we have received, and though we may not be murderous Assyrians, we realize we are sinners just the same.

Has someone hurt you, even badly? Pray for them, and do good for them. You may not ever see what it does for them, but you will definitely see what it does for you!

October 12

Enter by the narrow gate; for wide is the gate and broad is the way that leads to destruction, and there are many who go in by it. Because narrow is the gate and difficult is the way which leads to life, and there are few who find it.

—Matthew 7:13–14

I was talking with the young adults at our church about the many in the church today who try to make God more palatable to people who reject the narrowness of the Christian message. Nothing could be a greater disservice to the Great Commission than to try to market God by making Him more attractive. It is almost as though—and I have heard things like this from some of today's prominent church leaders—we think we have to employ the old bait-and-switch approach to reaching the world for Christ.

"Draw people in by offering one thing, and then reveal the whole truth after you get them in" seems to be the idea. But when we fail to share the whole of the exclusive claims of Christianity or teach seekers half-truths and fables, we are selling false bait from which there is no switch! This is why we must be faithful to proclaim the whole counsel of God.

We do not need to be ashamed of God and His gospel; neither do we need to make the Christian message more palatable so that more people will want to be saved. The work of saving souls is the Lord's. It is His Word that does not return void (Isa. 55:11). We don't need to apologize for or minimize His standards, and we don't need to worry about chasing people off with our message. And we certainly don't need to switch the truths about our God by offering people the bait of an "anything goes" God who accepts any sincere person.

Narrow and difficult is the road to life, and few find it. We are not going to increase that number by changing the message to something the world wants to hear. Tell the people you know about the true and living God who loves them so much that He sent His Son to die for their sins. That tells them they are sinners and that God is a loving Savior, two essential parts of the message for light-bearers. And to those who come to Christ as Lord and Savior, tell them there is a way He wants them to live and things He wants them to do. Tell them that though these things may be narrowly defined and difficult to fulfill, they are truth.

Tell someone about Jesus today, and speak the truth in love. You don't need to try to sell Him to anyone; just tell them they need Him and He is there for them, but they must come on His terms—not their own. Some will reject it, but a few will receive it. And those who receive it will join you on the path of righteousness because they accepted the truth at the outset—not because they were marketed into the kingdom!

October 13

You therefore, beloved, since you know this beforehand, beware lest you also fall from your own steadfastness, being led away with the error of the wicked; but grow in the grace and knowledge of our Lord and Savior Jesus Christ. To Him be the glory both now and forever. Amen.

—2 Peter 3:17–18

What the reader knew "beforehand" is found in the previous verses where Peter was discussing those who twist the Scriptures to their own destruction. His comments now are a reminder of what the faithful study of God's Word will bring into our lives: growth in the grace and knowledge of our Lord Jesus Christ.

We have all heard the saying "You are what you eat," and it is definitely true physiologically. What we put on the inside certainly shows up on the outside in one form or another. But the same is also true from a spiritual perspective, and a woman once shared with me an example from life that bears this out. This woman told me that she and her family had been a part of a church movement that was more experience based than Bible based. Her eyes were opened to the fallacy of this perspective, however, as she watched countless people whose Christian lives had been built completely on spiritual highs depart from the faith when hard times came. Having been fed no solid biblical truth, spiritual highs could not sustain them and left them with nothing to stand on when they faced life's trials.

The Word of God is essential to our steadfastness in the faith, and it keeps us from wandering into error morally or doctrinally. It tells us how to grow in the grace and knowledge of Jesus Christ. The Bible has no equal, and its influence and abilities are unmatched. No experience or spiritual high can sustain us like the Word of God can. Though spiritual highs are wonderful experiences, they are the by-products, not the primary products, of our journey to heaven.

Good days and bad days, spiritual heights and spiritual depths, are best traversed with the Word of God as our guide. There is no substitute. Far too many Christians, however, want to live an energetic, power-filled Christian life on a meager spiritual diet. They dine on the Word of God once a week, and even then only in a watered-down portion, yet expect to remain spiritually strong and healthy. Our physical bodies could not survive if we treated them that way, and neither can our spiritual walks with God.

Eat a hearty meal today and let the Word of Christ dwell in you richly! Read your Bible, listen to some sound teaching, and talk about what you have learned from the Word of God. The next thing you know, you'll look in the mirror and see someone who is growing in the grace and knowledge of our Lord Jesus Christ!

October 14

Therefore if the Son makes you free, you shall be free indeed.

—John 8:36

According to John 8:31, Jesus was talking to a group of believing Jews who didn't understand this talk about freedom and even said to Jesus, "We are Abraham's descendants, and have never been in bondage to anyone. How can You say, 'You will be made free'?" (John 8:33). I have always found a bit of irony in that statement since the Israelites had been in bondage many times in their history. They had been in bondage to Egypt for 430 years, in bondage to Babylon, and in bondage to the Persians to a degree. Even at the time they made this statement, they were not free, but under the hand of the Roman Empire.

I find it interesting that many people today have the same attitude about freedom as did the Jews in this passage. "I'm not under bondage to anyone or anything," they insist. "I do as I please." They make that statement because they do not understand the bondage Jesus was talking about: the bondage of sin. In verse 34, Jesus made this clear when He said, "Whoever commits sin is a slave of sin." Yet how often people today view freedom from sin as a form of Christian bondage. Some seem to think living a holy and pure life makes a person a slave to religious disciplines, but Jesus says clearly that's not true at all!

As someone with a past that I would do anything to change, I assure you that the long list of things I no longer do is what my freedom is all about. One of the greatest things about being free is living without regrets for actions done the night or day before. Don't misunderstand me; I still do stupid things at times that I later wish I hadn't done, but they are not the things that used to be my master. No longer do I have regret for the actions or words of a drunken tirade. No longer do I live in fear of getting caught for something I did wrong. I am free indeed!

If God has been talking to you about some form of slavery, don't take the attitude of the Jews or the many today who say of their vices, "I can quit anytime I want. I am not in bondage." Friend, if God has been speaking to you about something yet you keep thinking, *I can do this and still be a Christian,* you are a slave to whatever that thing is. But God wants to set you free, and believe me, you will never regret surrendering anything that the Lord says is hindering your walk or harming your witness or body.

He who the Son sets free is free indeed! Doing what He wants and not what you want is true freedom. No habit or practice can bring you that kind of freedom, no matter the liberty you may think it provides. Do what God says to do in His Word, and freedom from regret will be your joyous course in life. Take it from someone who knows!

October 15

O God, You are my God; early will I seek You; my soul thirsts for You; my flesh longs for You, in a dry and thirsty land where there is no water. So I have looked for You in the sanctuary, to see Your power and Your glory. Because Your lovingkindness is better than life, my lips shall praise You.

—Psalm 63:1–3

One Sunday evening at church, I was impressed to break from my normal course of study with the young adults and to have instead an "open mic" night to let some of the young men and women share their testimonies of how they had come to faith in Christ and what the Lord was currently doing in their lives. I was a bit concerned that the fear factor of speaking publicly would be an issue, so I had arranged for one of our pastors to open up the time, as an icebreaker. An hour and a half later, we had heard some of the most amazing and heartwarming testimonies of the love and faithfulness of God.

That night was water to my soul and refreshed many others as well. As the young adults spoke of His goodness, His power and glory were made known in that room, and we all left, I believe, knowing that His lovingkindness is indeed better than life! The things God used as tools to draw these young men and women to Him ranged from tragedy and depression to the emptiness of drug abuse and violence. Our conclusion at the end of the evening was that no one who is still drawing breath is outside God's capability to reach.

As you are seeking Him early this day (or whatever time you are reading this devotional), ask Him for open doors and boldness to tell someone what He has done for you. The great thing about telling someone your story is that they can't argue its truthfulness. They can debate the authority and inspiration of Scripture all they want, but they cannot tell you that what God did in your life did not happen—not when you were the dry and thirsty soul that was watered by His salvation and presence. No one could tell the blind man or the lame man that Jesus healed that they couldn't really see or walk, and no one can argue with you about your own testimony of God's faithfulness and love. You know it's true!

Here is why this is important: people are often convinced by confidence. When you cannot defend what you believe, others don't think it's even worth investigating. But a confident assurance that God is alive and at work today and a testimony offered as evidence create a longing in others that spurs a spiritual search.

Don't feel up to the task of sharing Bible verses and stories? Then tell others your testimony. It too is a Bible story, the story of how the God of the Bible loved you and saved you!

October 16

Finally, brethren, whatever things are true, whatever things are noble, whatever things are just, whatever things are pure, whatever things are lovely, whatever things are of good report, if there is any virtue and if there is anything praiseworthy — meditate on these things.

— Philippians 4:8

I could not even hazard a guess as to the number of times I have heard someone say, "I can't watch the news; it's too depressing." In the information age in which we live, we are bombarded with information from every direction, and not all of it is good. It's hard to watch TV today without feeling "slimed" by some commercial, even when you have tried to monitor what you watch. In certain public settings, it's sometimes difficult not to overhear conversations full of words you would rather not hear and certainly don't use as part of your vocabulary. It's hard not to be impacted by the continual barrage of bad news and inappropriate communication.

In short, it is hard sometimes to find anything just, pure, lovely, of good report, or virtuous to meditate on. So what do we do in a world such as ours? How do we keep our minds pure and focused on praiseworthy things? The word *meditate* is our key. That does not mean to go into a trancelike state or to contemplate your navel from a mountain peak. The word *meditate* is the Greek word *logizomai* (log-id'-zom-ahee), which means "to take inventory."

Maybe you're surrounded by bad news right now, or maybe life has dealt you some horrific blows. Maybe things are financially tough for you, and your mind is consumed with discouraging thoughts. Even so, there are just, pure, lovely, and virtuous things to meditate on in every circumstance and during every season of life. They are the things of God. No matter what else is going on, His word is pure, He is just, and He is praiseworthy. You are going to heaven when you die, and nothing can separate you from the love of God. No weapon formed against you will prosper, and sickness, death, and sorrow are not allowed in heaven. These are the things you need to take inventory of when inundated by a barrage of bad news.

Take inventory of all that God has done for you, including the things yet to come. When you feel like you don't have anything to be thankful for, start with this: because of your relationship with Jesus, you're not going to hell! Take inventory of that, and then count all the things Christ endured to make that true for you. That's how you fill your mind with things worthy of consideration.

Jesus died for you, and because of His death and resurrection, heaven is your future and eternal home!

October 17

Therefore, as the elect of God, holy and beloved, put on tender mercies, kindness, humility, meekness, longsuffering; bearing with one another, and forgiving one another, if anyone has a complaint against another; even as Christ forgave you, so you also must do.

—Colossians 3:12

Nothing is more stifling to the growth and joy of a Christian than unforgiveness. It is so unlike Christ and therefore conflicts with the new nature. One thing important to understand is what forgiveness is not. Oftentimes people seem to think that forgiveness is acting as if you were never wronged or something didn't happen, and treating those who hurt or harmed you as though they did nothing. But that is not its true meaning.

Forgiveness means "to lay aside" or "to put to rest." I have often tried to illustrate forgiveness like this: Imagine that a man in the church is arrested for embezzling millions from the company where he worked and goes to prison. After he serves his time and is released, do you have to appoint him church treasurer in order to prove forgiveness? Silly, I know, but it makes the point that forgiveness is not acting as though something never happened, but being merciful and kind with meekness and longsuffering, just as Christ has done for us.

The reason this is such an important truth for Christians to grasp is that unforgiveness always holds the "unforgiver" captive, not the "unforgivee." This is why Jesus commanded us to pray for our enemies and those who spitefully use us (Matt. 5:44). It is hard to go before God, the one who forgave us, if we are holding unforgiveness in our hearts toward others. Praying for our enemies, then, is as much for us as it is for them.

The phrase "as the elect of God, holy and beloved" tells us Paul's focus is Christian-to-Christian forgiveness. Certainly this truth ought to be practiced most excellently among the forgiven. So if a Christian brother or sister wrongs you, lay the matter aside; it's best for both of you. Do you have to then move forward in the relationship as though nothing has happened? No, that is not always possible, but you should be kind and humble and extend tender mercies to the offender, remembering how you have been forgiven of your sins.

You can forgive some hurts, yet the pain from them remains. The presence of the pain doesn't necessarily mean you haven't forgiven. The reason this is critical, I believe, is that many Christians have been told they need to forgive and forget in order to be forgiven themselves. But that is not true, because that would be a works-oriented salvation, and we are not saved by works.

However, it is Christlike to lay aside the wrongs committed against you, even by those closest to you. So if you have someone in your life who has wronged you, lay the matter aside, and treat that person as Christ has treated you.

October 18

So Joshua ascended from Gilgal, he and all the people of war with him, and all the mighty men of valor. And the Lord said to Joshua, "Do not fear them, for I have delivered them into your hand; not a man of them shall stand before you." Joshua therefore came upon them suddenly, having marched all night from Gilgal.

—Joshua 10:7–9

I have to say, this is one of my favorite Bible stories. A group of people known as the Gibeonites had heard of Jericho's fall and the Lord who fought for Israel. Wanting to protect themselves from conquest, they lied to Joshua and tricked him into entering a covenant with them. Joshua vowed not to destroy them but instead put them under contract as Israel's allies. Hearing of this covenant, a marauding king, Adoni-Zedek, decided to invade Gibeon by joining forces with four other kings and their armies. In this setting, the Gibeonites sent word to Joshua that they were under attack and needed help.

Now comes the part of the story that I like. In one night, Joshua ascended from Gilgal, which lay at an elevation of twelve hundred feet below sea level, and marched forty miles to Gibeon, which sat at an elevation of three thousand feet above sea level. Joshua marched uphill for forty miles just to fight on behalf of a people who had lied to him! No wonder Joshua is considered a type of Christ in the Old Testament. Isn't that much like what the Lord did for you and me: fought our enemy of sin and death while we were yet sinners (Rom. 5:8)?

I also believe this is a great reminder of the effort we must put forth to reach the lost and how God will grant us the strength to do so. Joshua and his army marched uphill for forty miles with a rise in elevation of forty-two hundred feet and then engaged five other kings and their armies and fought all day until they secured the victory—again, for people who had deceived them! Verses 12 and 13 of this same chapter tell us that as the battle was raging and the day was waning, the Lord caused the sun to stand still so that Joshua and his army could finish the battle at hand. Again, all this was so Joshua could defend a people who had lied to him and manipulated him.

This is a wonderful reminder of the Great Commission to go to all the world and preach the gospel. It may not always be easy to get to the battle; it may even require an uphill climb for forty miles all in one night to get to the place where God wants to use us. But after we have made such efforts, the Lord will cause the sun to stand still, if need be, to enable us to accomplish what He has called us to do for His name and glory.

Doing what God has called us to do is not always easy, and sometimes it is a fight just to get to the people He wants us to reach. But oh, what God will do on behalf of those who lay it all on the line for the sake of others! This is why I love this story.

Go out of your way today to reach someone. Not every divine appointment happens conveniently on your way home. For some of them, you may need to march uphill all night just to get to the place where God wants to use you!

October 19

And have no fellowship with the unfruitful works of darkness, but rather expose them. For it is shameful even to speak of those things, which are done by them in secret.

— Ephesians 5:11–12

Paul exhorted the church in Ephesus to maintain its purifying influence in a putrefying city, to be, in Jesus' words, salt and light. I believe the same exhortation is much needed in our day as well, and it begins with having no fellowship with "the unfruitful works of darkness." This is a statement that carries with it great insight and instruction.

First of all, the phrase clarifies there are indeed things that can hinder our ability to bear fruit by our association with them; and second, it implies that fruitlessness is a work of darkness. The topic is too great for a single devotional, but the heart of the matter is this: there are things that we Christians should not be a part of, and those things are identified as unfruitful to our walks.

I have often wondered what the movie industry in our day would be like if just the Christians would quit going to R-rated movies. I have to wonder what the music industry would be like if only the Christians stopped buying music that glorifies immorality and violence. I have to wonder what the world would be like if Christians stopped having fellowship with the works of darkness — not the people trapped in darkness, but the things associated with it.

I believe Paul is drawing on Jesus' words in Matthew 5 where He warned us of putting our lamps under bushel baskets. In other words, He warned us against hindering our ability to shine as lights in a dark world. Being a light speaks of our witness, and this is the matter at hand. Do not fellowship with things that hinder your witness for Jesus Christ. Your life as a Christian is not yours, but His. He bought you back from sin and death, and your mission in life is to reflect Him.

Over the years, including recently, I have heard testimonies of people who cleaned out their music and movie collections — and their language too — after getting saved. They stopped associating with the things of darkness and started being lights. Is there something in your life that hides your light under a bushel? Is there a fellowship with darkness — perhaps a secret sin — that hinders your fruitfulness as a Christian? Remember, secret sin is open scandal in heaven, and no one hides from the Almighty.

Ask the Lord to examine your life today and reveal if there be any wicked way in you (Ps. 139:24). If so, cast it aside so that all fellowship with darkness that causes unfruitfulness may be broken. God wants you to shine for Him today — even through what you don't do!

October 20

But you should not have gazed on the day of your brother in the day of his captivity; nor should you have rejoiced over the children of Judah in the day of their destruction; nor should you have spoken proudly in the day of distress.

—Obadiah 1:12

The Lord here was addressing a family feud that spanned hundreds of years. The feud between Jacob and Esau had become the battle between their descendants, Judah and Edom. The book of Obadiah was actually written to the Edomites and is a word of rebuke to Esau's descendants for aiding the Babylonians in the overthrow of Israel.

The Lord said to Edom, "You should not have stood by in the day of your brother's problem. You should not have rejoiced in his calamity, nor should you have spoken in pride because this didn't happen to you." The point is, God was displeased at Edom's rejoicing over Judah's demise, just as He is displeased when we perpetuate family feuds. Later in verse 15, the Lord ominously warned, "For the day of the Lord upon all the nations is near; as you have done, it shall be done to you; your reprisal shall return upon your own head."

Absolutely nothing good can come from long-standing feuds or arguments. The only thing that happens is that other people get sucked into them and learn to despise others who have done them no wrong. Just because they belong to a group or family someone in the other family had a problem with, the descendants take up the battle. Sad to say, this type of infighting sometimes happens even in Christian families.

Proverbs 24:17–18 says, "Do not rejoice when your enemy falls, and do not let your heart be glad when he stumbles; lest the Lord see it, and it displease Him, and He turn away His wrath from him." As Christians, we are going to have enemies, but we are to pray for their salvation—not for their destruction! Though some will refuse the mercy and grace of God and be lifelong enemies of the cross and cause of Christ, the Lord still does not want us to rejoice over their demise.

Esau's bitterness became his descendants' heritage and eventually consumed them, as bitterness always will. So be careful about perpetuating family feuds. Instead, be quick to forgive, and do not rejoice in another's demise. To do so is not pleasing to the Lord.

Is there some patching up that needs to take place in your family? Take the steps to do so quickly, lest the offense take root and bitterness spring up. By it, many will be defiled (Heb. 12:15), as was the case with Edom!

October 21

O God, You are more awesome than Your holy places. The God of Israel is He who gives strength and power to His people. Blessed be God!

— Psalm 68:35

I love being in the sanctuary at church. I prepare for sermons there, I pray there, and sometimes I just go and sit in there when no one else is around. When I have been gone for a couple of weeks, it always feels so good the first time I walk into that room. It is a holy place. It is where God has touched lives and healed broken bodies and souls, and it is where marriages hanging by a thread have found hope and direction. In that room, searchers have found long-sought spiritual truth. I love being in the sanctuary!

I say this as a reminder of how easy it is to fall in love with a place, people, or ministry to such a degree that the holy place becomes more of a focus than the Holy One. Some time ago, the Lord spoke to me quite clearly on this very matter. Those who call our church "home" refer to it as CCT, and as I was walking through the room, the Lord spoke to my heart a reminder: "I called you to serve Me, not CCT." I understood perfectly and instantly that He was reminding me that He had called me to serve *Him* at CCT. He was the one I was serving even as I served His people.

God is more awesome than His holy places. His power is not limited to a facility, and He gives strength to His people wherever they are. The point in this is to remind us to remain in an ongoing and intimate relationship with God and not to let even good people and good places become our primary focus. The Lord is the one who is awesome. He will not take second place to anything or anyone, including the places and people He calls us to serve. The Lord wants first place in our lives and does not want to be crowded out, even by good things.

God is the one who is awesome. There is no such thing as a powerful church—only a powerful God. So let's be careful about worshiping places and people, as awesome as they may be, for the Lord is more awesome, and He alone is worthy of such devotion. Serve Him where and how He has called you, but serve *Him*!

I often tell the dear people at CCT—and it is sometimes hard to say as a pastor—not to tell people about their church, but to tell people about their Savior. He is more awesome than any holy place. Tell someone about Jesus today!

October 22

Now may the Lord of peace Himself give you peace always in every way.
The Lord be with you all.

—2 Thessalonians 3:16

I love Paul's benedictions as he closed his letters. A word of encouragement or an expression of love and thanks were often accompanied by a list of people to greet or those who were sending greetings. We might well say Paul was always speaking blessings over other people's lives. I believe this would be a great practice for us to incorporate into our daily lives. It would do two things for us. First, it would keep the name of the Lord on our lips, and second, His majesty and grace would therefore be kept on our minds.

The Thessalonians were under heavy spiritual attack, and a benediction of peace probably sounded pretty good to them at the time they received this letter. I am sure if we knew others who were under enemy fire, we might call their names or faces to mind rather quickly. I am also sure that the ones who came to mind would find our words of encouragement rather encouraging!

Today will be filled with opportunities to encourage someone, perhaps in ways other than directly sharing your faith. Though sharing your faith is a form of offering encouragement, encouraging others doesn't have to be grandiose or superspiritual. It can come in the form of a question or even a statement of blessing, as Paul did with the Thessalonians. Asking someone how they are doing is encouraging. Following up with someone about a difficult circumstance they shared with you is encouraging. Talking to the person no one else wants to talk to is very encouraging.

Look for opportunities to encourage someone today. Remember, you can't find what you're not looking for, but if you look for opportunities to encourage, you will see them all day long. Over the years, I have had people say to me, "I know you hear this all the time, but that message you spoke was just what I needed to hear, and it encouraged me." That's what encouragement does; it's kind of a twofer: two people blessed by words of encouragement.

You never know what goes on behind the scenes in people's lives. Sometimes a word of encouragement can end up being a word of knowledge from the Lord, even an answered prayer to cries of "God, are you there? Do you see my situation?" Your voice could be His voice to that person, a sign that God hears.

Be an encourager today, and speak the Lord's blessings over others!

October 23

And the Lord said: "I have surely seen the oppression of My people who are in Egypt, and have heard their cry because of their taskmasters, for I know their sorrows. So I have come down to deliver them out of the hand of the Egyptians, and to bring them up from that land to a good and large land, to a land flowing with milk and honey, to the place of the Canaanites and the Hittites and the Amorites and the Perizzites and the Hivites and the Jebusites."

— Exodus 3:7–8

What a great picture of what Christ has done for us! He has seen our oppression and come down to free us from our taskmaster of sin and its sorrows. During the time of Israel's slavery in Egypt, the taskmaster was the one who applied the whip to the backs of the Israelites. But according to the Lord's promise, the oppression and sting of the taskmaster's whip would be replaced by a land flowing with milk and honey, a good and large land.

Isn't it amazing how some people, even today, choose oppression and the taskmaster's whip over deliverance? They choose bondage to sin over freedom from it, all the while claiming that Christians are the ones in bondage and they themselves are truly free. Stunning! But it happens every day.

One of the most difficult aspects of any believer's life is to watch people that God could do so much for choose bondage over His forgiveness, all the while thinking they are free. What do we do in these cases? I believe Exodus gives us our answer. Moses later told the resistant Pharaoh that death would visit every home where the blood of a lamb was not applied to the doorposts and lintels (Ex. 12:23) This translates to our openly, honestly, and lovingly speaking the truth and letting people know that the blood of the spotless lamb, Jesus Christ, is the only means by which they can obtain true freedom.

We have to remember that the power of the gospel is in the message, not in the method of presenting it. We do need to know what we believe, and we do need to be concerned enough to share the truth, but it is the faithful presentation of the truth itself that is going to take root into people's souls and visit them in the night hours. That truth — not our witnessing skill or techniques — will cause them to ponder if the things we said are true.

Tell people of heaven and hell, and tell them that Jesus Christ is the only way to attain heaven and avoid hell. Tell people God loves them so much He made a way for death to pass over them; but that way is through Jesus Christ alone, and we are either for Him or against Him. Don't try to make the message more acceptable or God less fearful. God has seen the oppression and affliction of sin, and He, in the person of Jesus, has come down to deliver His people and take them to the promised land.

Speak the truth in love today, friend, but speak the truth—even to those who think they are free and you are the captive!

October 24

And because you are sons, God has sent forth the Spirit of His Son into your hearts, crying out, "Abba, Father!" Therefore you are no longer a slave but a son, and if a son, then an heir of God through Christ.

—Galatians 4:6–7

To take such a familiar tone and refer to the Father as "Abba" was unthinkable and even disrespectful to the Jews of Paul's day. *Abba* is a term we might translate as "Papa" or "Daddy," and to approach God in such a manner was a tough pill for many believing Jews to swallow. But this is the very transition Paul sought to bring into the minds of both Jewish and Gentile believers, that through Christ they were no longer slaves to sin or the ceremonial law of Moses.

Paul also gives us a great though subtle detail about this new dimension of life. When he says the Spirit of His Son cries out, "Abba, Father!" he paints a beautiful picture of all three members of the Trinity and additionally reveals that the Holy Spirit in us cries out to the Father, not as a slave, but as an heir, a son or a daughter of God.

This provides us with a very helpful tool in discerning the voice of the Lord. If a voice within us cries out condemnation, telling us we cannot approach the Father because of what we have done, or if we sense in our hearts that the Father is through with us and does not desire further fellowship, that is not the voice of the Holy Spirit, but rather the voice of the flesh or the enemy. Yes, we may experience a sense of guilt for having done the wrong thing or not having done the right thing, but that is exactly the time when the Holy Spirit will remind us that we can go to God as any child goes to its father.

You will not find the word *unadoption* in the Bible; first of all, because it's not a word, but most of all, because it is not a biblical truth. The Spirit in us will always draw us to the Father, but the flesh and the enemy will always seek to drive us away. We can incorporate this knowledge into so many aspects of life. If something pushes us away from the Lord, be it service, fellowship, or ministry, then it isn't from Him. On the other hand, if something draws us closer to Him, be it service, fellowship, or ministry, then it is from Him. Now that is not to say that God doesn't sometimes guide us from one place of service, fellowship, and ministry to another, but it does mean that God will not take us from something fruitful to put us into something empty.

The Spirit of Christ in us will always draw us toward a deeper, more family-like understanding of the Father. He will never push or draw us away from that!

October 25

But as it is written: "Eye has not seen, nor ear heard, nor have entered into the heart of man the things which God has prepared for those who love Him."

—1 Corinthians 2:9

"You have no clue what God has for you" might be a way to paraphrase this verse Paul wrote to the Corinthian church. The purpose for this quote from Isaiah 64:4 was to remind the church what the presence of the Spirit meant practically in contrast to the prophetic revelation of times past.

Paul says that the same Spirit that spoke to and through the prophets now lives in us, and in verse 12, he says, "that we might know the things that have been freely given to us by God." In essence, Paul is saying, "Things are different now. What was once spoken by only a few can now be known and experienced by all."

Yet even with the presence of the Spirit in us, the words of Isaiah still stand. It is impossible to know all that God has for us. Life isn't long enough, and eternity itself isn't long enough to learn all the majestic things of God. This naturally leads us to a thought-provoking question: are we still probing the heights and depths of His majesty and grace, or have we taken what we know and become satisfied with that?

Could you imagine winning a 100-million-dollar lottery tax free (that takes a lot of imagination!) and then never spending any of the money? Who would do such a thing? The matchless, fathomless God has things beyond number for us to learn and do for Him, yet we often settle for merely possessing our salvation. That's like having a 100-million-dollar check and never cashing it.

God has things to teach us about Him, His will, and His ways, all day and every day. We learn some of these things through ordinary life, others through steps of faith, and still others through great steps of faith. There are not many things categorically true about every Christian, but as it pertains to God and His plans for you, I can categorically say, "You ain't seen nothing yet!" There is more, and every time you learn or do something new in His kingdom, there's more after that and more after that.

Don't sit around with an uncashed check, so to speak. Make it your aim to learn more about Him today. Then, before you go to bed tonight, make it your aim to know more about Him tomorrow, and then tomorrow, do it all over again!

October 26

Or do you despise the riches of His goodness, forbearance, and longsuffering, not knowing that the goodness of God leads you to repentance? But in accordance with your hardness and your impenitent heart you are treasuring up for yourself wrath in the day of wrath and revelation of the righteous judgment of God, who "will render to each one according to his deeds."

— Romans 2:4–6

At times I feel like a guitar with only one string or as though I keep banging on the same drum, but the fact is, you cannot separate a just God from righteous judgment. If we cannot separate this from His person, then we cannot eliminate this from our message about Him. God is a just God who will judge with wrath those who reject His goodness, forbearance, and longsuffering and fail to repent.

I recently spoke on the phone with a young man who was a "newbie," an infant in the Lord. A Christian friend had shared with him some details of current events and how they lined up with end-times prophecy. Hearing about the coming tribulation freaked this young guy out, so he called my office and left a message asking if he could speak with me. When I returned his call, an excited voice on the other end of the line said he was afraid of what was coming and had started investigating some of these things on his own. Finding them to be true, he had then shared them with his unbelieving sister, who started to cry, "I need to find God!" to which her brother replied, "I think you should!"

It was a very wonderful conversation, and I assured this young believer that God has not appointed us to wrath (1 Thess. 5:9). Then I shared with him how to minister to his searching and fearful sister, telling him how to share the gospel and lead his sister in prayer. The next thing I heard was an abrupt "Thanks, pastor; see you Sunday" and then a click as he hung up the phone. At the time of this writing, I have not yet heard what happened, but I cannot help but remind us all of where this started: with a conversation about God's justice and wrath.

We do not need to apologize for God being a just God. We do not need to try to make Him seem more loving, nor do we need to make Him into someone that people will like and want to get to know, in hopes of drawing them to Him. God is loving, wonderful, gracious, and merciful, and people need to hear all those things, to be sure. But God is also a just God who hates evil, and judgment and wrath are a part of His plan as well.

I don't think that judgment and wrath need to compose the whole of our message, but let's make sure we don't leave it out, because it's true. Yes, God is good, forbearing, and longsuffering, but He will pour out His wrath on those who reject His offer of salvation. So again, speak the truth in love, but speak the truth today!

October 27

He who covers his sins will not prosper, but whoever confesses and forsakes them will have mercy. Happy is the man who is always reverent, but he who hardens his heart will fall into calamity.

— Proverbs 28:13–14

Some people in law enforcement have said that when people are arrested and put into jail, you can often tell whether they are guilty or innocent by how they sleep at night. The guilty ones sleep soundly, knowing they have been caught and the chase is over. The innocent ones, however, toss and turn all night, knowing they have been wrongfully accused.

There is something undeniably wonderful about getting something off your chest when you have done wrong. The confession leads to great rest, a sense of relief that we have all experienced at one time or another. But Proverbs gives us the rest of the formula for continuing in that rest: forsake the thing that needed to be confessed, and live in reverence. However, hardening your heart, as evidenced by doing the same thing again, will lead to calamity.

Acts 3:19 asserts the same principle: "Repent therefore and be converted, that your sins may be blotted out, so that times of refreshing may come from the presence of the Lord." Repentance, which involves confessing and forsaking our sins, is very refreshing.

There are, without question, times in our Christian lives when we hit the spiritual doldrums. We feel empty, deaf, and alone though nothing is dreadfully wrong. These are faith-building times that all of us encounter. There are other times, however, when the dryness, emptiness, and loneliness are the result of unconfessed sin. The sin may not be one of the "big sins," things like getting drunk, taking drugs, or stealing, but a "little sin" that causes an uneasy feeling because we are not doing the things we ought to do.

I have found that God has an amazing way of bringing to my attention things that need to change: attitudes, actions, and thought processes. I have also found that when I ignore His proddings, uneasiness and restlessness begin to creep into my spirit.

Whatever may come to your mind in this regard, confess and forsake it. It will be quite refreshing, like finally getting something off your chest. The end result could be that evasive good night's sleep that comes only after you finally get caught and know the chase is over. But when God catches you and convicts you, the confession doesn't leave you imprisoned — it sets you free!

October 28

Rejoice always, pray without ceasing, in everything give thanks; for this is the will of God in Christ Jesus for you.

—1 Thessalonians 5:16–18

It is the will of God that we rejoice, pray, and gives thanks without ceasing and that we do so in everything. I am thankful for the Holy Spirit's careful choice of words as He inspired Paul to pen this passage. He tells us to rejoice always and to give thanks *in* everything as we face all that life brings.

I have heard some say that we need to thank God *for* everything that comes our way. According to them, we need to thank Him for illnesses, cancer, the death of loved ones, financial trials, and anything else that happens to us. But that is not the heart or intent of Paul's exhortation here. What Paul actually said was for us to give thanks *in* everything, including the things we may not be thankful *for*.

Rejoicing always, praying continually, and giving thanks in everything are the will of God for anyone in Christ Jesus. Being in Christ means we are heirs with Him. It means we are empowered by His Spirit, and our eternal destiny is secure. Giving thanks for these things will keep us in an attitude of rejoicing prayer as we encounter everything life throws at us.

Life may bring some things your way that you may not and need not be thankful for, but nothing can change the very real things you can always be thankful for. You can always rejoice that you are in Christ, that you are a new creation, that your record of sin has been washed in Jesus' blood and by that blood you have been cleansed and made whole.

If your current season of life is not a cause for rejoicing, then rejoice in prayer for the unchanging reality of your position in Christ. Be thankful for that in times and seasons you may not be thankful for. Rest assured, from dark and difficult times, God can bring good. But until that day arrives, the day when your former difficulty becomes a current ministry opportunity, rejoice, pray, and give thanks that you are in Christ—for this is the will of God for you!

October 29

When the wicked came against me to eat up my flesh, my enemies and foes, they stumbled and fell. Though an army may encamp against me, my heart shall not fear; though war may rise against me, in this I will be confident. One thing I have desired of the Lord, that will I seek: that I may dwell in the house of the Lord all the days of my life, to behold the beauty of the Lord, and to inquire in His temple. For in the time of trouble He shall hide me in His pavilion; in the secret place of His tabernacle He shall hide me; He shall set me high upon a rock.

— Psalm 27:2–5

David was a man who knew about war; he knew what it was like to have enemies without and within, to face times of trouble and to be outnumbered. David also knew about being confident and not troubled during such times. In this passage from Psalm 27, David laid out his battle strategy and said it all hinged on one thing. Then he listed four components of the one thing: (1) seek the Lord, (2) dwell in His house, (3) behold His beauty, and (4) inquire in His temple.

What David is saying here is crucial for us today, though the words are three thousand years old. David is telling us to take time to commune with the Lord, no matter what is going on around us. We must set aside time just for the two of us. To seek Him, dwell with Him, behold His beauty, inquire of Him — this will keep us in times of trouble. David is saying to stick close and not allow the times when we need Him the most to become the times when we seek Him the least.

The Hebrew word *seek* used here means "to search out through worship and prayer"; the word *dwell* means "to remain or tarry"; *behold* means "to contemplate" or "to gaze at mentally"; and *inquire* means "to plow" or "to break forth." With this understanding, we might well summarize David as saying, "When times of trouble come, search out the Lord through worship and prayer and remain in a mind-set of worship and prayer until you break forth." This instruction is then followed by a promise of being hidden in His *pavilion*, a word that means "tabernacle." We are kept in the secret place of His tabernacle, the Holy of Holies, and He will set us on a high rock.

All these things are pictures of Jesus Christ as our refuge and strength. He "tabernacled" among us (John 1:14), He is the entrance into the Most Holy Place (Heb. 10:19), and He is our rock (1 Cor. 10:4). So in other words, in times of trouble, stay focused on Jesus, for He will get you through.

Tell someone about His impact on your life today. Share how He has sustained and strengthened you and that He longs to do that for them too!

October 30

Then Jesus went about all the cities and villages, teaching in their synagogues, preaching the gospel of the kingdom, and healing every sickness and every disease among the people.

— Matthew 9:35

Does God still heal today? Absolutely! Is God still doing miracles today? Yes, now more than ever! I don't know of a Christian today who has not thought that if the Lord would do now what He did back then, more people would believe. Yet the truth is, those who saw all that Jesus did were the same ones who had Him nailed to the cross.

This past Sunday as we examined the words of Paul in Ephesians 2, I had the opportunity to remind the church there is no greater miracle than salvation. In Ephesians 2:1, Paul refers to those "He made alive who were dead in trespasses and sins." Since people are daily getting saved all over the world, and there are more people on the planet now than at any other time in history, we know that God is doing more miracles now than He ever did in the book of Acts.

The problem often lies with the kinds of miracles we want to see Him do. Jesus went about teaching and preaching the gospel; this was His first priority, and the healing of sickness and disease came afterward. It is important for us to remember that not one single person who was healed by Jesus when He walked the earth is living today. Though these people all received great physical healings, they all later died. But we also know that every person who is made alive in Christ is going to live with Him in heaven forever.

In an age when many are seeking movements of the Holy Spirit, we need to be careful about looking for signs in the flesh and overlooking the signs in the Spirit. The greatest miracle of all is still spiritually dead people being made alive. Those who followed Jesus because they saw Him raise the physically dead missed the true miracle of why He came: to make dead men alive in their spirits. We must not make the same mistake.

I am all for church being exciting and sensing the Lord's presence in a gathering, but let's make sure we are seeking what the Lord desires in a house of worship. There is a difference between a place that is lively and a place where people are made spiritually alive. If people are flocking to a place because of what they see happening to dead flesh, and dead men are not being made spiritually alive, then the danger exists of ignoring the teaching and preaching of God's Word and following only the signs and wonders. And this does not lead to the salvation of those who are healed or those who see it happen.

Remember, the greatest miracle of all is dead people being made alive, or people getting saved. Yes, God heals the flesh, even today. Yes, but just like in Jesus' day, physically healed people all later die. So the greatest miracle of all is when dead men are made alive eternally. That's something to be a part of, for that is truly the greatest miracle of all.

God wants to use you in that process. How? By preaching the gospel to every creature and seeing dead men made alive!

October 31

Whoever guards his mouth and tongue keeps his soul from troubles.

—Proverbs 21:23

We can learn much from our bodies just by noting some basic things. For example, the ear-to-mouth ratio tells us we should listen twice as much as we speak. We can also learn something about the times we do speak by noting that God has placed the tongue in a cage between two rows of teeth to guard it and bite it if it gets out of control!

There is a saying that the danger for those who talk too fast is they often say things they haven't thought of yet! I am sure all of us have had words get away from us that we wish we could reel back in. But the fact is, unguarded words cannot be taken back. We can make apologies for them and further explain them, but we can never recall them.

In the Hebrew, the word *guard* means "to protect" or "to hedge about." To protect the tongue from taking over, the Lord put the tongue under guard. The exhortation here is to avoid self-inflicted soul wounds by saying things we did not think through. We need to remember that not everything we think needs to be spoken under the guise of just being honest or speaking our minds. Obviously, there are appropriate times to speak up, but that is not our subject here. Our subject is using words to our own spiritual detriment, troubling our own souls.

We have all said things we wish we wouldn't have said. As a very young and stupid Christian, I wrote a letter to my pastor correcting him for what I perceived as error on his part. I told him the direction he should take the church and where he had gotten off course. That letter, written over thirty years ago, troubles me to this day, and I often wish it would have gotten lost in the mail—or better yet, had never been written. Whether it is words on a page or words spoken by the tongue, remember how that little member of the body can cause big trouble (James 3:1–12) and thus needs to be kept under guard.

I love the saying "You can talk about me all you please, and I'll talk about you on my knees!" If you want to talk about or to someone, talk to the Father first, and keep your own soul from being troubled!

November 1

Therefore, beloved, looking forward to these things, be diligent to be found by Him in peace, without spot and blameless; and consider that the longsuffering of our Lord is salvation – as also our beloved brother Paul, according to the wisdom given to him, has written to you, as also in all his epistles, speaking in them of these things, in which are some things hard to understand, which untaught and unstable people twist to their own destruction, as they do also the rest of the Scriptures.

– 2 Peter 3:14–16

The things we are to look forward to are the new heavens and the new earth in which righteousness dwells. Peter then tells us how we are to wait for that day: without spot and blameless, which means keeping ourselves untainted from the world. He reminds us that the Word of God includes some things hard to understand, so we must be careful whom we listen to concerning the deep things of God.

Twisting Scripture seems to have become an art form in our day. When you couple twisted Scripture with an eloquent, gifted communicator, and on top of that you throw in some passion, you have the recipe for deception. So how can we know what to believe in this age of multiple interpretations of the Word of God?

There are three simple things to remember when answering this question. First, the Bible will never contradict itself. Second, false teachers will usually claim special revelations from God that cannot be confirmed (visits to heaven, angelic appearances, etc.) and are inconsistent with the Word of God. Third, those who twist the Scriptures do so for some form of personal gain, using the Bible as a promotional tool to elevate themselves.

Keeping ourselves unspotted speaks of our own spiritual walks and how we live our lives. In short, we are to live holy lives as we await the new heavens and the new earth. We also need to be spiritually responsible and diligent students of the Word, lest we be deceived by false teaching. We must be on guard against those who twist the Scriptures by isolating verses and taking them out of context and then gathering a following of people who want their words to be true. Peter warns this leads to destruction.

Remember, dear friends, it is the next life that holds our reward. We need to be careful of seeking that which is promised in the next life as our reward in this one. When a message is inconsistent with the whole counsel of God and promotes a life different from the one described in Scripture, then that teaching is destructive.

Scripture twisters are easily identified if we'll take the time to put their teachings to the test!

November 2

For we walk by faith, not by sight.

—2 Corinthians 5:7

A Sunday school teacher once asked her class if someone could tell her what faith is. One young boy answered, "Faith is believing in things you know aren't true!" I think we Christians sometimes feel the same way about walking by faith, as though faith is having hope even when we know things are not going to work out.

Paul gives us a much needed insight here about faith. It is a walk, or in other words, it is a progression in which the outcome remains unseen. Faith is not believing in things untrue, but it is exactly the opposite: faith is acting upon proven truth. Faith is moving forward and trusting that God is who He says He is and does what He has always done and that you are not the exemption to what God has always said and done.

Faith is not walking blindly into an unknown outcome. Faith is walking when the outcome is not yet seen—not when it is unknown. By faith we know that all things work together for good for those who love God (Rom. 8:28), and we need to walk forward in faith as God works things together for good.

Now there is some wisdom we need to apply here. We cannot jump off a cliff and say, "I believe this is going to work together for my good." It is important to understand that faith is acting on proven truth; it is not jumping from cliffs, though at times it may feel like it. Walking by faith is allowing the Holy Spirit to be our guide and the Word of God our guard, for the Spirit will never lead us outside the boundaries of God's Word.

If you feel like you just can't see how things are going to work out, keep progressing in your walk with the Lord until the outcome is seen. Be careful of acting on your own impulses, thinking, *God hasn't answered, so I'll take a leap of faith.* Keep trusting, keep praying, keep serving, and keep sharing. Walk forward in proven truth as you await things working together for good, even when you can see no way for it to happen.

God is not limited to what we can see or the possible outcomes we can project. So keep walking with Him while waiting on Him, and He'll prove Himself faithful time and again!

November 3

And this I pray, that your love may abound still more and more in knowledge and all discernment, that you may approve the things that are excellent, that you may be sincere and without offense till the day of Christ, being filled with the fruits of righteousness which are by Jesus Christ, to the glory and praise of God.

— Philippians 1:9–11

The word *discernment* here can also be translated "judgment," which will help us understand the context. Paul was praying for the beloved saints to have discernment between the things that are excellent and the things that are offenses so that their sincerity would be fruitful to the glory and praise of God. Paul also prayed for consistency and constancy as believers await the day of Jesus Christ. This clearly indicates that this instruction applies to us as well as to the Philippians, since the recipients of the letter are long dead.

Discernment will cause us to approve the things that are excellent and without offense. *Approve* means "to allow" or "to try," and *without offense* is from a single Greek word that means "not leading to sin." So when we put this all together, we see that Paul was praying that the church's abounding knowledge of the will of God would cause them to discern between the things that are excellent and the things that lead to sin so that they could be fruitful in righteousness to the glory of Jesus Christ.

I find it quite interesting that Paul prayed about not approving things that may lead to sin. That means he prayed for the believers to have discernment to avoid things that may not be sin in and of themselves. Such things in life are not sinful per se, but they can lead to undesirable consequences. For example, are you going to places that could entice you to sin, or are you engaging in conversations with a person of the opposite sex that could lead to temptation and a fall? Again, these kinds of things are not necessarily sinful but present great opportunities for sinful possibilities.

I think we could well understand discernment as recognizing our own weaknesses and potential areas where sin has an opportunity to creep in. As you face this day, consider areas that have stumbling potential for you. Remember, though they may not be sins in and of themselves, they can lead to sin in you. This was Paul's prayer for the Philippians and mine for you!

November 4

Behold, I stand at the door and knock. If anyone hears My voice and opens the door,
I will come in to him and dine with him, and he with Me.

— Revelation 3:20

A towering pinnacle of Scripture, to be sure! The Son of almighty God is knocking on the door of every human heart, the very hearts He Himself created. It is also interesting that Jesus says He will come in and dine with those who hear His voice and open the door, meaning He will have fellowship with them and they with Him.

There are so many things to see here. What a beautiful picture of the patience and longsuffering of God that He would knock on the door of the human heart as He lovingly and kindly asks each person to let Him in! But I also cannot help but recognize that we, the body of Christ, are the ones commissioned to be the hands that knock and the voice that speaks.

This verse is also a picture of our manner and method of reaching others. We do so with patience and longsuffering, and we do so with His Word. How I wish Christians would trust in the power of the Word today and remember that the Word of God does not return void (Isa. 55:11) while our words often do!

A pastor shared at a conference recently that early in his walk with the Lord, the Lord clearly said to him, "Available." He wasn't exactly sure what that meant, but after a few minutes, he realized it was actually more of a question: "Are you available?" He heard this for a few days until he realized he was to make himself available for God's use every day. From that point on, each day he looked for that particular person he was to be available to.

God desires for you to be His voice today and share His words. The Holy Spirit will guide you to those on whose doors He has already been knocking.

Available?

November 5

Therefore be imitators of God as dear children. And walk in love, as Christ also has loved us and given Himself for us, an offering and a sacrifice to God for a sweet-smelling aroma.

—Ephesians 5:1–2

That's all you have to do today: imitate God—nothing to it! Why doesn't the Bible just tell us, then, to be perfect? Oh wait, it does (Matt. 5:48)! Before you mentally throw in the towel, take a moment to consider more carefully these great verses from Ephesians.

These verses, I believe, are one of the greatest evidences of the necessity of the deity of Jesus Christ. Here we are given a very lofty and humanly unattainable directive: imitate God. How are we going to do that and not confuse the roles of playing God and imitating God? We need an example to follow, and Paul gives us one in the person of Jesus Christ.

Imitate God, Paul says, and then he tells us how: walk in love as Jesus did. Therefore, Jesus is God, since He is cited as our example of how to walk and whom to imitate. Paul then tells us exactly how to imitate this love: by giving ourselves to others as an offering and sacrifice to God for a sweet-smelling aroma.

This is how to imitate God: walk in sacrificial love. Go out of your way to express it. Do so at great personal expense, and deny your own rights and liberties for the sake of others. This is what we are called to do as Christians. Most of us, however are far too shortsighted, and all too frequently temporal things consume all our love and sacrifice. But when those things are sought for our benefit rather than the benefit of others, they do not produce a sweet-smelling aroma to God.

Paul's call to imitate God is hard, and I am not very good at it much of the time. But in my heart of hearts, I do want to imitate God, and my example of how to do so is Jesus, the epitome of sacrificial love.

I challenge and encourage you today to do something sacrificial for the sake of someone else. Sacrifice some time, sacrifice some money, or sacrifice your personal goals in order to communicate the love of God to others. You might have to miss your favorite TV show, skip lunch, or give away some of your resources, but put forth the effort to meet the emotional, practical, or spiritual needs of others. Do this, and at the end of the day, your life is going to look a lot more like Jesus' than ever before.

Imitate God the Son who walked daily in sacrificial love!

November 6

Pride goes before destruction, and a haughty spirit before a fall. Better to be of a humble spirit with the lowly, than to divide the spoil with the proud.

—Proverbs 16:18–19

Nowhere is the modern worldview in greater conflict with the precepts of Scripture than in the realm of pride versus humility. The world tells us pride is a virtue, while the Bible says the key to exaltation is humility (Luke 14:11). Now we know that to a degree the world recognizes the ugliness of arrogance, but the pride mentioned here in Proverbs is the kind of pride the world admires and promotes. This is the pride of self-accomplishment or self-sufficiency. I like to call it "I trouble."

"I trouble" was Satan's sin, as seen in Isaiah 14 when he said, "*I* will ascend into heaven; *I* will exalt my throne above the stars of God; *I* will also sit on the mount of the congregation on the farthest sides of the north; *I* will ascend above the heights of the clouds, *I* will be like the Most High."

"I trouble" is also the sin mentioned here in Proverbs that leads to destruction. The word *destruction* means "to break or fracture," and the word *fall* means "to ruin." Thus we could well understand this part of the passage as saying that pride breaks and ruins us. We are then told that humility and fellowship with the lowly are better than being broken and ruined.

To us in our day, I believe the instruction is to be careful about getting caught up in the world's definition of success. All day long the media bombards us with its image of success. We are told where to shop, what to wear, which car to drive, and even how to eat in order to show the world that we have made it. But here in Proverbs, the Holy Spirit warns us that this mindset breaks and ruins people. It breaks and ruins marriages, it breaks and ruins families, it breaks and ruins ministries, it breaks and ruins testimonies. How much better it is not to be a part of that than to get caught up in it!

I know how easy it is to get sucked in, however. I remember well not wanting my kids to have anything less than the best and how it troubled me when I could not provide the latest and greatest to my young family. But seeing, both here and in various parts of the world, the richness in a family that loves and cherishes one another though they may not have many material possessions, I rethought my priorities. The quality of life in that kind of family far surpasses anything experienced in a family that chases after things that break and ruin.

Don't buy into the world's definition of success. God's way is better. It brings blessings, but the world's way brings fracture and ruin.

November 7

Then David said to Ornan, "Grant me the place of this threshing floor, that I may build an altar on it to the Lord. You shall grant it to me at the full price, that the plague may be withdrawn from the people." But Ornan said to David, "Take it to yourself, and let my lord the king do what is good in his eyes. Look, I also give you the oxen for burnt offerings, the threshing implements for wood, and the wheat for the grain offering; I give it all." Then King David said to Ornan, "No, but I will surely buy it for the full price, for I will not take what is yours for the Lord, nor offer burnt offerings with that which costs me nothing."

—1 Chronicles 21:22–24

David had sinned, and his sin had caused a plague to break out among the children of Israel. As a result, seventy thousand men of Israel died. Although we might be tempted to wonder why David's personal sin caused a plague to come upon the entire nation, we must remember that the people had rejected the lordship of God when they demanded a king. God had forewarned the people of the possible actions of a king and its impact on their lives, yet they demanded an imperfect king as ruler rather than the perfect and holy God (see 1 Samuel 8).

Many of us have heard David's words in verse 24 approached with a sense of nobility that he would not offer to the Lord that which cost him nothing. But there is so much more to the story than this one well-known statement.

Seventy thousand people had died because David, in his pride, had taken a census. When the plague fell, David said, "Was it not I who commanded the people to be numbered? I am the one who has sinned and done evil indeed; but these sheep, what have they done? Let Your hand, I pray, O Lord my God, be against me and my father's house, but not against Your people that they should be plagued" (vv. 16–17). The Lord's response was for David to erect an altar on the threshing floor of Ornan, and in response to this command, David made the familiar statement that most of us have heard.

There are two things we can learn from this. First, one person's sin can have broad impact, so we need to avoid thinking things like, *I am only hurting myself.* That is never true. Second, though David's gesture was noble, it was still a small price in light of the great consequence already endured by the people. Nevertheless, God accepted it! The threshing floor of Ornan later became the site for Solomon's temple and then Herod's temple, and it will be the location of the temple built during the tribulation.

David's purchase of the land was a humble act of obedience. Although his statement simply noted that it was required of him to own the land to offer the sacrifice, God responded in a huge way. This is a great mystery to me, how

God takes our meager efforts and offerings and does such magnificent things through them, even when we have sinned and hurt ourselves and others. As I have said so many times, God always rewards repentance.

How great is our God—tell someone about Him today!

November 8

For God is not the author of confusion but of peace, as in all the churches of the saints.

—1 Corinthians 14:33

In the summary conclusion of Paul's three-chapter discourse on the person, work, and gifts of the Holy Spirit, the apostle concludes with this simple statement. The word *confusion* really says it all, as it can be translated "instability" or "disorderly commotion." God the Holy Spirit is not the author of disorderly commotion in any church. If we understand this, we can better pray and seek the Lord's will and work in our lives by the power available in Him.

We might well understand the work of the Holy Spirit by simply remembering that His power is what enables us to be used by Him. Therefore, when considering what is of the Holy Spirit and what is not, we could well ask ourselves this simple question: *Is this action or experience stopping with me, or is it flowing through me to benefit others?* Examine whether it is just experiential commotion or whether He is flowing through you to bring peace to others.

It is a sad commentary that churches today are often categorized by the place they give to the person and work of the Holy Spirit. Paul says the Spirit works the same way in every church; therefore, every church ought to be sharing the same perspective on the Holy Spirit. But we know this is not the case, and there is much confusion on this subject.

So in the midst of all the commotion today, let's remember one thing, John 15:26: "But when the Helper comes, whom I shall send to you from the Father, the Spirit of truth who proceeds from the Father, He will testify of Me." The Holy Spirit empowers God's people to give testimony of Jesus in the way they live, act, and do church. So rather than putting ourselves in one camp or the other or taking sides on the issue, let us unite as Christians on the side of the Holy Spirit. Let's not get sidetracked by a denominational stance or a nondenominational perspective, but let's get back to the true purpose of the Spirit's power: to tell the world about Jesus.

You will have all of heaven behind you and the Holy Spirit's power within you when you step out to bring the peace of God to a lost sinner already drowning in the midst of great commotion. This is the work of the Holy Spirit in every church and in every saint. The rest is just commotion!

November 9

Then Job arose, tore his robe, and shaved his head; and he fell to the ground and worshiped. And he said: "Naked I came from my mother's womb, and naked shall I return there. The Lord gave, and the Lord has taken away; Blessed be the name of the Lord." In all this Job did not sin nor charge God with wrong.

—Job 1:20–22

It pains me to admit it, but I cannot say I share this testimony. I have questioned things that God has allowed, and I have accused God of not doing what He should. At times I have felt that God did not do what was best for me or did not answer my prayers when or how I thought He should. I may not have said it directly with words, but the doubts, frustrations, and questions harbored in my heart resulted in the same thing—charging God!

I know I am not alone in feeling like this. But for us all, Job is such a shining example of faith. In a very brief span of time, he received four shocking waves of news that he had lost everything he owned and all those he loved, except for his wife, who, by the way, was a very poor counselor indeed (see Job 2:9)! Yet in all this tragedy, he did not sin or charge God with wrong.

Unlike Job, most of us are guilty of sometimes charging God with wrong in one form or another. But what is the remedy? How do we keep trials and traumas from causing us to charge God? I believe the answer is wrapped up in one word: proximity. The remedy to our doubts and accusations against God's faithfulness is to change our proximity to Him; that is, to draw closer to Him through prayer and worship, to learn more about Him through His Word. The closer we get to Him, the more His love and grace become apparent. That's what Job did, and that's what he learned.

Do you remember how this whole thing started? Satan went before God and when asked what he had been doing, he answered, "From going to and fro on the earth, and from walking back and forth on it" (v. 6). Then, in verse 8, the Lord said, "Have you considered My servant Job, that there is none like him on the earth, a blameless and upright man, one who fears God and shuns evil? " Job was intimate with the Lord; the Lord Himself revealed the closeness of their relationship. Job was blameless and upright because he feared the Lord, and when trouble came, that intimacy is what carried him through.

I wish I could say I have never questioned God's decisions, but I can't. I wish I could say I have never questioned something He allowed or have never felt like He should have done something I asked Him to do, but I can't. But this I know for sure: the longer I walk with Him, the more I learn of Him and the less I question Him in my heart and mind. I have learned more and more of how much He loves me and that the absence of trials and traumas is not how he proves His love for me.

When we are faithless, he remains faithful. He cannot deny Himself (2 Tim. 2:13). So bless His holy name today, for He is worthy of praise, worthy of trust—He is just worthy!

November 10

This is the message which we have heard from Him and declare to you, that God is light and in Him is no darkness at all. If we say that we have fellowship with Him, and walk in darkness, we lie and do not practice the truth.

—1 John 1:5-6

John's epistles can only be described as straight up and to the point. I have always found the urgency in his words quite telling in light of the fact that he wrote his three epistles after he received the revelation of humanity's future and even had a glimpse into eternity. In that revelation, John had seen which groups went to heaven and which went to hell, and he knew why each received its particular destiny.

This is what led John to write so urgently, so powerfully, and, as some might say, so bluntly. John opens his thunderous epistle by stating that which he had heard from Jesus: "God is light and in Him is no darkness at all. If we say that we have fellowship with Him, and walk in darkness, we lie and do not practice the truth." That tells us words alone are an insufficient claim to knowing God. If a person claims fellowship with God but lives a life that denies it through fellowship with darkness, that person's words are a lie.

This epistle, which later says that God is love (4:8), opens with this tremendous declaration about light and darkness. That also tells us love is not silent about the darkness, but rather cares for others enough to warn them of walking in it. According to what John said he heard from Jesus, the testimony of fellowship with God is a changed life.

I have heard it said that the world needs to know what we are for, not just what we are against, and I agree with that statement. However, it is also important to note that in the letters to the seven churches in Revelation, Jesus commended two of the churches for their stand against fellowshiping with darkness and rebuked three of the churches for tolerating darkness in their doctrines and fellowship. The two churches that received only commendation were Smyrna and Philadelphia, the suffering church and the loving church.

This tells us that loving people enough to warn them of false fellowship will likely lead to suffering in our lives. Some will grow angry with us, and others will call us legalists. Some will even accuse us of adding works to salvation by grace through faith alone. But friends, Jesus clearly instructs us to warn against, not embrace, walking in darkness as a continual manner of life.

God is light, and if we are in Him, we will walk in the light and not in the darkness. We may slip, and we may fall; we may sin, and we may fail. But we will not call walking in darkness fellowship with God.

Love someone enough today to tell them what John heard from Jesus. Salvation and repentance are a package deal; one is never found without the presence of the other.

November 11

Since you have purified your souls in obeying the truth through the Spirit in sincere love of the brethren, love one another fervently with a pure heart, having been born again, not of corruptible seed but incorruptible, through the word of God which lives and abides forever, because "All flesh is as grass, and all the glory of man as the flower of the grass. The grass withers, and its flower falls away, but the word of the Lord endures forever."

—1 Peter 1:22–25

We discovered in John's epistle yesterday an exhortation to walk in the light, but it is good for us to remember that we are not capable of doing this in our flesh. Walking in the light is the work of the Spirit. It is not a goal attainable through personal self-discipline, though self-discipline is involved to a degree. The self-discipline needed is not beating ourselves into submission, punishing our bodies into fearful, lifeless masses of flesh. The self-discipline involved is self-denial, not self-mutilation. It is dying to self that the Spirit may flow freely through us, looking to the Word of God to explain the life of self-denial and then dying to the things inconsistent with a purified soul.

The Spirit of God is the incorruptible seed now living in us. This means His desire is not just to give us a list of things not to do, but to replace our desires for the things we used to do. This is a product of the new reborn nature, a love for the things of God, a love for the ways described in His Word. Therefore, obeying the truth is a work of the Spirit as defined in God's Word.

Yes, there are indeed things that Christians ought not to do, but if that is the emphasis of our Christian lives, we will struggle with a negative perspective on the will of God. However, if we look at the Christian life as a series of things we can now accomplish by the power of the Spirit within us, then the old things we used to long for will seem undesirable. That is because walking in the Spirit is an unmatched majestic manner of living that makes everything else seem substandard.

I used to drink and get high—a lot. But I have never experienced anything greater and more fulfilling than knowing that God has used me. It makes the things I once longed for look dark and ugly, and I find myself amazed that I once thought I was "livin' large." If we allow the incorruptible seed to grow in our lives, we will soon have no room for the things that corrupt. I have often said, "A life emptied from its past is still empty," meaning we need to be filled with the works of God done through the power of the Spirit.

So don't look at walking in the light as "You better or else," but rather as "I can by the Spirit who lives in me." There is nothing better than living for Jesus as defined in the Word and being empowered by the Spirit. Don't look at today as a day where you better not do thus and so, but look at today as a day where you can do all things through Christ (Phil. 4:13). Then the "thus and so" won't even have time to happen in your day!

Being a living sacrifice is a great testimony that God is alive in you. When you live like that, others can see Him, not through the things you don't do, but through all the things you do do!

November 12

Out of the same mouth proceed blessing and cursing. My brethren, these things ought not to be so. Does a spring send forth fresh water and bitter from the same opening? Can a fig tree, my brethren, bear olives, or a grapevine bear figs? Thus no spring yields both salt water and fresh.

—James 3:10

Nowhere is the battle between old and new natures more evident than in our tongues! James even says in verse 2 of this same chapter that taming the tongue is essential to controlling the whole body. The illustration James uses here is key to understanding this great battleground of flesh and spirit. A freshwater spring cannot send forth salty water any more than a fig tree can produce olives or a grapevine produce figs. It's all about the source, and so too is it with our words.

If we were going to label this phenomenon, we might well say that with salvation comes a "sanctified tongue." This is a tongue set apart from its old life of profanity, criticism, gossip, and slander and embracing a new life of pure words of blessing, hope, encouragement, and praise. Many times, however, Christians struggle to allow the Holy Spirit to cleanse their tongues and set them apart from past habits and patterns.

I once heard the story of a pastor with a woman in his congregation who was a terrible gossip. One Monday she called the office to inform the pastor— again— that she had left her tongue on the altar, to which the pastor replied, "Were you able to fit the whole thing there?" Though that is a humorous story, it does illustrate that proper control of the tongue requires a cleansing deep in the heart. We can try leaving the tongue at the altar, but unless the source of its words is cleansed, it cannot yield good fruit any more than a saltwater source can yield fresh water.

The tongue is the means by which we sing praise, give testimony, share witness, offer encouragement, speak forth prayer, and proclaim exhortation. This little member of the body has a great role to play in our lives, so let's be sure it is sanctified by giving the Lord the source of our words, the heart. Then our hearts will yield a fountain of refreshing words to everyone we encounter.

Give your tongue to the Lord today. Ask Him to purify the source of your words so that your tongue may not be what it used to be, but rather what He desires it to be—a sanctified vessel!

November 13

Now the serpent was more cunning than any beast of the field which the Lord God had made. And he said to the woman, "Has God indeed said, 'You shall not eat of every tree of the garden'?" And the woman said to the serpent, "We may eat the fruit of the trees of the garden; but of the fruit of the tree which is in the midst of the garden, God has said, 'You shall not eat it, nor shall you touch it, lest you die.' "

—Genesis 3:1–3

I have often said jokingly to husbands that the original sin was not Adam and Eve's eating of the fruit, but Adam's leaving his wife alone to talk to some snake. "God is not fair. He's holding out on you, and He's not treating you right" might be how we could read the motive behind Satan's words in the garden.

The exchange between Satan and Eve is subtle yet significant. Satan initiated the conversation by asking Eve, "Has God indeed said?" This implies an air of unfairness on God's part as Satan sought to twist God's words, much as he does today.

Before we go further with this thought, let's look back at Genesis 2:15–18. The passage reads, "Then the Lord God took the man and put him in the garden of Eden to tend and keep it. And the Lord God commanded the man, saying, 'Of every tree of the garden you may freely eat; but of the tree of the knowledge of good and evil you shall not eat, for in the day that you eat of it you shall surely die.' And the Lord God said, 'It is not good that man should be alone; I will make him a helper comparable to him.' "

Interestingly, Eve was not present when the prohibition concerning the tree of the knowledge of good and evil was given. We can thus conclude that Adam was responsible to communicate this aspect of the will of God to her. Of further interest, where do you suppose Eve got the idea that she and Adam were not to touch the tree? The assumption that they shouldn't put themselves in close proximity to temptation was logical, of course, but where did she get this idea? Did Adam add this to what God had said to him, or did Eve pick up on Satan's indictment of God and try to explain His actions? The reason this is so important is that from it we can see how one small addition or subtraction from the Word of God can be deadly to understanding and communicating truth.

Proverbs 30:5 says, "Every word of God is pure." That means it needs nothing added and nothing taken away from it; it is exactly what we need. But just like he did with Eve, Satan still whispers to those who will listen that God's Word is unfair, His commands unjust, and His promises untrue. "Has

God indeed said?" is still being used to sow seeds of doubt in the minds of all who will listen.

The Word of God is pure and needs no filtration. Do not listen to voices today that say, "Is this really what the Bible says? Is that really what it means?" Those who pose such accusations have been hanging out with a snake!

Twisting the Word of God is the enemy's oldest tactic, still employed to this day. Beware of any and all who would do so, and trust in the words of God as written.

November 14

But as many as received Him, to them He gave the right to become children of God, to those who believe in His name: who were born, not of blood, nor of the will of the flesh, nor of the will of man, but of God.

—John 1:12–13

It has been well said that God has no grandchildren, only sons and daughters. This reminds us, of course, that each person must come into his or her own relationship with God because we are not saved by association. But it is also true that God has no stepchildren, those who live in his house but aren't really his by birth. If you have received Christ as Lord and Savior, you are God's child, and all the privileges that come from being born into a royal household are yours.

We have all heard or read stories where the children of presidents gave the Secret Service responsible for their protection a run for their money. I am sure most of us have put our guardian angels on overtime more than once, but that doesn't make us any less the children of the King.

Too often, however, we live our Christian lives based on performance instead of promise. That's not to say we are to live as we please, but it does mean we need to remember that even when children disappoint their parents, they are no less their children. When we fail the Lord in some way, we may feel as though we have been divorced from God or disinherited from the family, but that is not so. If we were born of the will of God, meaning born again, then we are unequivocally His children, and our Father wants us to live as members of the royal family who have been sent to a distant land to represent our Father, the King.

You might be away from the castle (heaven) right now, but it makes you no less His child and therefore a representative of the royal family. You have the right to live in a manner that fulfills the King's wishes, even though you may have given the "Secret Service" a run for their money at times. As a member of the royal family, you still bear the great responsibility to convey the will of the King to all who dwell in His kingdom.

As a royal heir, you've been commissioned by the King to tell others, "The King is coming again!" Do so today, and you will have all the kingdom of heaven behind you, because you are part of the royal family!

November 15

Now when Peter had come to Antioch, I withstood him to his face, because he was to be blamed; for before certain men came from James, he would eat with the Gentiles; but when they came, he withdrew and separated himself, fearing those who were of the circumcision. And the rest of the Jews also played the hypocrite with him, so that even Barnabas was carried away with their hypocrisy.

—Galatians 2:11–13

We could well title this portion of Scripture "Peer Pressure and the Apostles." This event recorded by Paul reminds us just how powerful peer pressure can be. Though we often talk about it in relation to young people, it is still a factor for adults. It never really changes as we age; it just takes on new forms.

Peter, afraid for his fellow countrymen to observe his freedom from the dietary restrictions of the law, went back to eating only from the kosher table with fellow Jews and snubbed the Gentiles he once ate freely with. Paul labeled this an act of hypocrisy, though Peter's actions may not fit what we commonly regard as hypocrisy. We well accept such a definition of one who claims to be a Christian yet is regularly unfaithful to his or her spouse or who is drunk continually. But the actions of Peter and Barnabas were no less hypocritical, because they communicated something that was untrue and directly contradictory to the tenets of Christianity.

Galatians 3:28 says, "There is neither Jew nor Greek, there is neither slave nor free, there is neither male nor female; for you are all one in Christ Jesus." This is why Paul used such a strong word as *hypocrisy* when discussing succumbing to peer pressure. Division and elitism in the life of the Christian are hypocrisy, for we are all one in Christ. It is always sad to see Christians who will not associate with and even attack those who hold a different view on the subject of last-days eschatology. The pre-trib people won't eat with the post-trib people, and the mid-trib people shun them both. This is hypocrisy!

Hypocrisy can also be a racial thing, as it was here with Peter. That's not to say Peter was a racist, but the peer pressure he struggled with was absolutely a result of his heritage. Racial division in the church is thus hypocrisy. Churches should not be divided by color or ethnicity. Churches may be composed of like-minded people regarding a style of worship, a method of preaching, or even language. But for a church to be restricted to only English-speaking people of the same color ethnicity denies the oneness Christ died to create in His bride.

This past Sunday's message at our church was titled "One God, One Gospel, One Church," and I must say, I was blessed to look out and see every shade of color in the congregation. That, I believe, is what God desires to see in His body on earth.

Is Christ divided? No, so that means division is hypocrisy. Let's not allow adult peer pressure to make us into hypocrites!

November 16

Finally then, brethren, we urge and exhort in the Lord Jesus that you should abound more and more, just as you received from us how you ought to walk and to please God; for you know what commandments we gave you through the Lord Jesus. For this is the will of God, your sanctification: that you should abstain from sexual immorality; that each of you should know how to possess his own vessel in sanctification and honor, not in passion of lust, like the Gentiles who do not know God; that no one should take advantage of and defraud his brother in this matter, because the Lord is the avenger of all such, as we also forewarned you and testified. For God did not call us to uncleanness, but in holiness. Therefore he who rejects this does not reject man, but God, who has also given us His Holy Spirit.

—1 Thessalonians 4:1–8

Straight to the point and without wiggle room, Paul lays it out regarding sex and the Christian. Only in marriage between a man and a woman and only with your spouse is it permissible. All other sexual activity is uncleanness and carries with it forewarned judgment.

I have often considered the various commandments of God and the impact on our world if just one of them were obeyed by everyone. Could you imagine the lives spared throughout the centuries if the first commandment, to have no other gods but Jehovah, had been obeyed? So many wars would have never been fought, and millions of lives would have been spared if the first commandment had been obeyed.

Imagine our world today if God's commands regarding sex were obeyed. There would be no AIDS, no STDs, and no broken marriages because of adultery. Abortion would be curbed, and teen pregnancy would end, to say nothing of the billions of dollars in medical costs that would be saved and used for research or treatment of other unavoidable health problems. (By the way, AIDS was originally called GRIDS, Gay Related Immune Deficiency Syndrome, so yes, it is an STD.)

But greater than all the benefits that our world would enjoy if just this one command of God were heeded, the real issue for the Christian is that sexual immorality is not pleasing to God; in other words, it is sin. There seems to be a movement today to defraud people in this area through silence on the issue and out-and-out promotion of sexually immoral lifestyles that God has forbidden. Paul says those who reject God's definition and parameters for sexual activity haven't rejected man, but God.

Don't let anyone fool you through fraud. Only God can define safe sex, for He created the human sex drive and alone has the right to define its boundaries.

If you are a Christian, your body belongs to the Lord, and your mission is to walk in a manner that pleases God — even sexually!

November 17

A good name is better than precious ointment, and the day of death than the day of one's birth; better to go to the house of mourning than to go to the house of feasting, for that is the end of all men; and the living will take it to heart. Sorrow is better than laughter, for by a sad countenance the heart is made better. The heart of the wise is in the house of mourning, but the heart of fools is in the house of mirth.

—Ecclesiastes 7:1–4

Solomon here provides a great reminder of the importance of living our lives so as to make each day count. He reminds us that times of mourning, even more than times of feasting, can teach us much about life. That's because in times of feasting, people often lose sight of their need for God, but in times of sorrow and mourning, they seek after Him, longing for His comfort. It is in these times of mourning that we learn more about who God really is.

I like the significance some have attached to the dash between a person's date of birth and date of death. That one little symbol summarizes the whole of one's life. Solomon says, in essence, "Live every day in consideration of the dash. Make your life count." As Christians, we must consider that our opportunities for serving God are limited in one sense and unlimited in another; that is, we have limitless opportunities for a limited time only.

Verse 4 of Ecclesiastes 7 says that the heart of a fool is in the house of mirth. *Mirth* speaks of festivals, or "partying" might be the way to understand it in our day. The implication is that the one who lives in constant pursuit of pleasure will not leave much of a legacy. The day of that person's death will not be much to remember. But for those who live each day to make it count for God's kingdom, the day of death will be better than the day of birth. In other words, the dash on their tombstones will symbolize much more than just pleasure-seeking and partying.

We have limitless opportunities for a limited time only. Make today count for God's kingdom!

November 18

And I thank Christ Jesus our Lord who has enabled me, because He counted me faithful, putting me into the ministry, although I was formerly a blasphemer, a persecutor, and an insolent man; but I obtained mercy because I did it ignorantly in unbelief. And the grace of our Lord was exceedingly abundant, with faith and love which are in Christ Jesus. This is a faithful saying and worthy of all acceptance, that Christ Jesus came into the world to save sinners, of whom I am chief.

—1 Timothy 1:12–15

In this age of political correctness where words like *sin* and *hell* have become offensive to many both inside and outside the church and therefore abandoned, I find Paul's words quite refreshing. I find it particularly encouraging that the letters to Timothy were his later writings, and 2 Timothy was his last. So here we have a veteran of the faith and ministry commenting with the quiet and humble recognition of his own sinful state. Keep in mind this was a man whom God had used to reach the known world with the gospel; a man who had started multiple churches (and also riots); a man who at this point had penned epistles like Romans, the two letters to the Corinthians, and even the flagship of Christian theology, Ephesians. Nevertheless, Paul knew it was only by God's grace, mercy, and abundant love that he was in the ministry. What a healthy perspective!

I cannot help but think of Paul's words to the church in one of his earliest writings in 2 Corinthians 2:7: "For godly sorrow produces repentance leading to salvation, not to be regretted; but the sorrow of the world produces death." I believe that the longer we walk with the Lord, the more we will encounter this kind of godly sorrow. This sorrow is not regretted but brings us to the place, even after many years of knowing and serving Him, of recognizing that we are the chief of sinners. But remember, this is not a condemning sorrow, but rather a longing sorrow. It is the realization that because of His mercy, grace, and love, He has put us into His ministry in spite of our own personal "althoughs."

Friends, there is nothing improper or incorrect about using the words *sin*, *sinner*, and *hell*. It doesn't drive people away from Jesus, but rather it produces a sorrow that draws them to Him. The better we come to know Him, and the longer we walk with and serve Him, the more evident this is going to become.

I understand fully how Paul felt, for whenever I read these words, I feel like saying, "Move over, Paul. There's a new chief in town!"

November 19

But we command you, brethren, in the name of our Lord Jesus Christ, that you withdraw from every brother who walks disorderly and not according to the tradition which he received from us. For you yourselves know how you ought to follow us, for we were not disorderly among you nor did we eat anyone's bread free of charge, but worked with labor and toil night and day, that we might not be a burden to any of you.

—2 Thessalonians 3:6–8

Some in Thessalonica were using the excuse that since the Lord was coming soon, they didn't need to work. Instead, they expected other church members to feed them. Paul, however, firmly reminded them that when he was among them, he worked day and night to supply his own needs.

In this passage, Paul, employing a military term, "commanded" the church to break fellowship with those who were acting in this way. He called them *disorderly*, which means "moral irregularity." The word of the Lord here as written by the hand of Paul thus equates such actions to moral irregularity, or immorality, abnormal actions for members of the body of Christ.

We note also that Paul called those "brothers" who were walking in this manner, and he employed the same command and consequence he did in Corinth when a man in the congregation was involved with his father's wife (1 Cor. 5:1). So the church's response to someone not working and expecting others to feed him was to be the same as in the case of the man sleeping with his stepmother. This tells us clearly that both of these actions were considered morally irregular, or immoral.

We have all heard stories of those who have headed for the hills to await the Lord's return and withdrawn from society in order to do so. We must remember that we are not called to isolation, but to infiltration. It is immoral to lead people in such a direction, and it is immoral to follow such a person's lead. The command is to withdraw from those who walk in this disorderly fashion.

All members of the body are called to do their share (Eph. 4:16), and not doing so is disorderly and disruptive to the body of Christ. Paul commands us to withdraw, or break fellowship with, those who refuse to live by this principle. I cannot count the stories I have heard of those who were duped by someone with a "special revelation" from God that caused them to withdraw from fellowship and labor with the body of Christ and even their own families. Paul, by inspiration of the Holy Spirit, commanded the church to break fellowship with those who do such things.

Don't run to the mountaintop to wait for Jesus' return while expecting others to care for your needs. Run into your neighborhood and tell people Jesus loves them and is coming again. Labor and toil all night and day to do so!

November 20

Wives, submit to your own husbands, as is fitting in the Lord. Husbands, love your wives and do not be bitter toward them. Children, obey your parents in all things, for this is well pleasing to the Lord. Fathers, do not provoke your children, lest they become discouraged.

—Colossians 3:18–21

The Bible never tells the wife to love her husband but continually calls the husband to love his wife. Wives, in turn, are called to submit to their husbands and respect them (Eph. 5:33). Husbands who are also fathers are called not to provoke their children, *provoke* meaning "to stimulate with anger," lest they become discouraged ("beaten down" would be a good way to understand this).

What we have before us is God's order for the home and the necessity of honoring one another's God-ordained roles within it. Wives whose husbands love them as Christ loves the church don't need to be told to love their husbands, for they will love being loved that way. Children, though all have moments of rebellion, will have a greater likelihood of obedience when not stimulated with anger; that is, when they are not continually demeaned and belittled.

The word *submit* means "to come under arrangement." God has an arranged order for the home, and it hinges on the love of the husband for the wife and begins to break down when this first link in the chain is weak or broken. Wives are called to respect their husbands' role. That means they should let their husbands be men, recognizing that they have God-given responsibilities to fulfill, including loving their wives like Jesus loves His bride.

I have often told the church that my feminine side is seated in the congregation. My wife is my feminine side; I don't have one, other than her. She is called by God to let me be a man, and I am called by God to love her like Jesus and put her needs above my own. But I don't have to be in touch with my feminine side in order to fulfill that role. I only need to look to Jesus as my model for loving my wife and see all that He gave for the sake of His bride. Though I am not always good at this, my wife has never had a problem submitting to me loving her as Christ loves the church.

Husbands, love your wives as Christ loves the church. Wives, let them do so. Then, your kids, if you have any, will carry that pattern of obedience modeled before them into their own relationships when they come.

God has arranged the home, and though we may rearrange the furniture in it, we are not to rearrange God's plan for it!

November 21

And it came to pass, when Joshua was by Jericho, that he lifted his eyes and looked, and behold, a Man stood opposite him with His sword drawn in His hand. And Joshua went to Him and said to Him, "Are You for us or for our adversaries?" So He said, "No, but as Commander of the army of the Lord I have now come." And Joshua fell on his face to the earth and worshiped, and said to Him, "What does my Lord say to His servant?" Then the Commander of the Lord's army said to Joshua, "Take your sandal off your foot, for the place where you stand is holy." And Joshua did so.

— Joshua 5:13–15

There are so many things I love about this passage! I love the response of Joshua to the man with the drawn sword; he immediately prepared himself to engage in battle as he asked the man to identify his loyalties. I love the Lord's response to Joshua's question "Are you for us or for our adversaries?" The Lord answered no then identified His position as the commander of the Lord's army. I love that all of this reminded Joshua of two things: the battle is the Lord's, as he would soon learn in Jericho, and on the eve of battle, worship is the appropriate response.

This account is clearly an Old Testament appearance of God the Son. Worship is reserved exclusively for God, and the command for Joshua to take off his shoes was an act of reverence for God. We know the rest of the story, the rather interesting strategy the Lord gave Joshua to bring down the walls of Jericho. He was ordered to march around the city once a day for six days in complete silence; then on the seventh day, he was to march around the city seven times and on the seventh lap blow trumpets and shout. After that, the walls would topple!

I have often wondered how the briefing with the troops unfolded as the great field general of Moses shared this strategy as the new leader in Israel. Surely some wondered if perhaps Joshua had stayed out in the sun too long or maybe took one too many blows to the head in battle. When you face a situation where the walls (the problem) seem to be impenetrable yet God tells you to stay silent, keep marching, and pray, it's easy to wonder what's going on. But the plan of God obviously worked for Joshua. The walls came down, and they took the city, just as God said they would. His plan for you will work as well.

If you have a battle looming or one that is ongoing, worship the Lord, for you're on holy ground. Also remember, God's ways are not your ways; they are higher. So regardless of what God tells you to do, though it may seem unusual or even useless, you will prevail if you will just do it.

God's strategy ensured that the Israelites would know who brought the walls of Jericho down. In a similar fashion, God may ask you to employ some battle plans that will show you and others that God alone won the victory.

November 22

See then that you walk circumspectly, not as fools but as wise, redeeming the time, because the days are evil.

—Ephesians 5:15–16

"Watch your step, for the days are evil" would be a way to understand Paul's words here. He adds to this the admonition to redeem the time, which means to rescue it from loss, or as we might better understand it, "Don't waste your time." If we put this all together, we could rephrase it as "Watch your step and walk wisely, not wasting time, for evil is on the rise." In the midst of evil times, we must take each step in life with careful and prayerful precision. Time is short, life is a vapor, and time wasted can never be regained.

Paul opens this great chapter with the admonition to "be imitators of God as dear children" (v. 1), and then in verses 10–11, he urges us to find out what is acceptable to the Lord and not to have fellowship with darkness. This requires us to walk precisely through the minefield of the evils in our day. Just one misstep and huge blocks of time can be stolen from our lives and testimonies. As it has often been said, it takes a lifetime to build a testimony, but only a split second to lose it. With just one misplaced step, years of testimony can be lost and years of recovery forced to begin.

Great falls and personal failures are often prefaced by comments like "That's not a temptation for me," or "That doesn't cause me to stumble." Paul, however, soberly warns us to watch our steps, for the days are evil. He urges us to have no fellowship with the unfruitful works of darkness and to find out what is acceptable to the Lord and to walk in those things and only those things.

As the time draws closer to the Lord's return for His bride, it is especially important that we watch where we step, because we know that in the last days evil will increase and temptation will grow stronger. I am not a proponent, but rather a strong opponent, of Christian isolationism, pulling away from all things non-Christian. To do this makes us a secret society rather than an invading army. Nonetheless, we must walk circumspectly through life. We must take precise steps and watch where we are walking, lest we damage our testimonies and subsequently waste our time trying to recover our Christian reputations.

We are in this world, but not of it. The enemy lays traps in hopes of catching off guard careless Christians and those who think they are not subject to failure. It is an evil day we live in, and we must watch where we are going.

If you find yourself thinking or saying, "I can handle this," or "This isn't a temptation for me, though it might be for others," be careful. This is the first indication that you are not watching where you are going.

November 23

So when the woman saw that the tree was good for food, that it was pleasant to the eyes, and a tree desirable to make one wise, she took of its fruit and ate. She also gave to her husband with her, and he ate. Then the eyes of both of them were opened, and they knew that they were naked; and they sewed fig leaves together and made themselves coverings. And they heard the sound of the Lord God walking in the garden in the cool of the day, and Adam and his wife hid themselves from the presence of the Lord God among the trees of the garden.

—Genesis 3:6–8

A pastor went to visit a church member who had been absent for a few weeks. Showing up at the person's home unannounced, he knocked on the door. The obvious sound of running feet was heard in the house, and the pastor walked over to the garden window in hopes that someone would open the door if he made himself visible. However, nothing happened, so the pastor decided to slip a note under the door. On the back of his business card, he wrote the words of Revelation 3:20: "Behold I stand at the door and knock," hoping this lighthearted approach would bring a response from the absent church member. A couple of days later, the pastor received his business card back in the mail and written underneath his quote were the words "I heard the sound of you walking in the garden, and I was naked and hid myself!"

Isn't it amazing how sin, to this very day, sends us into hiding? When sin is present, guilt creeps in and fellowship slows down. Because we have fallen or stumbled, we feel there is no point in going to church anymore or in praying or reading the Bible. But dear brothers and sisters, this is *never* the will of the Lord! Do you think the Lord was unaware that Adam and Eve had sinned? Do you think their subsequent admission of having eaten from the forbidden tree shocked the Lord? Knowing full well what Adam and Eve had done, the Lord yet walked in the garden and looked for them.

Verse 9 of Genesis 3 tells us the Lord called out, "Where are you, Adam?" That is a very probing question indeed. But the point is, though the fall of man had transpired and the consequences would literally impact every human life ever born, it was the Lord who sought Adam, not Adam who sought the Lord. This is extremely important for us to understand today. The voice that says, "Give up; go back to your old life. God will not forgive you, and He is not interested in you after what you have done" is the voice of the devil.

Adam's sin introduced death into the human race. I would say that is a biggie! Nevertheless, our Lord, in the cool of the day, walked in the garden and looked for him. Yes, Adam was punished for his sin. Yes, he was put out of the garden, but the Lord made a covering for Adam and Eve's nakedness by shedding the blood of another on their behalves. The beauty of this is that right from the beginning, after the first sin ever was committed, the restoration of fellowship with God by the sacrificial blood of another was preached immediately through God's actions.

Dear friend, I am not here to say that you can avoid all consequences for sin; but I am saying, if you have sinned, don't hide from God. He is still longing for and seeking an intimate relationship with you, even as you experience the consequences of your sin. Sin exacts its own consequences, and yes, the Lord does deliver from many of them in this life; but He delivers from all of them in the next by the blood of His own Son slain from the foundation of the world.

If you have failed in your walk, you're in good company. Every other Christian has failed too. But never hide from God. He already knows what you have done and is ready to pardon. He is knocking on the door of your conscience, calling you to come home. The voice that says to run and hide is from the flesh or the devil. Never listen to it. Instead, pray, read the Word, and go to church; and let God walk you through even the consequences of your poor decisions. Remember, He never desires that you face life alone!

November 24

For you are all sons of God through faith in Christ Jesus. For as many of you as were baptized into Christ have put on Christ. There is neither Jew nor Greek, there is neither slave nor free, there is neither male nor female; for you are all one in Christ Jesus. And if you are Christ's, then you are Abraham's seed, and heirs according to the promise.

—Galatians 3:26–29

There are few things as powerful in life as national pride. We see it manifested at events like the Olympics, World Cup, and even during times of war or conflict. National pride runs high at those times. Friends and friendships are often hindered over such things, and two people who have never met or exchanged a word can be enemies just because of their nationalities.

One of the most amazing and undeniable aspects of being a Christian is that we are all one in Christ. No matter our nationalities, genders, or social status, we Christians are family in a way that no one else in the world can understand. I have met Christians whose language I did not speak nor they mine, but we loved each other instantly because we could see Jesus in each other's eyes and smiles. There is nothing quite like it in all the world.

I am not so naïve as to think there are never any schisms in the church based on status or nationality, but those are evidences, not of the work of the Spirit, but of the strength of the flesh. They are wrong 100 percent of the time! We are all sons and daughters of God through faith in Christ Jesus. Our baptism into Christ is the baptism of death to self, pride, and status, and death to the division caused by gender, economics, and nationality. But it is also a baptism into life, new life as an heir according to God's promises, having been made one with others in Christ. There is, therefore, no room for prejudice in the life of a Christian.

Though there is nothing wrong with loving your country, there is something terribly wrong with hating others because of theirs, especially when they are one with you in Christ. We are all sons of God through faith in Christ Jesus. We are family in the truest sense of the word: blood relatives born of the blood of Jesus, a birth more powerful than natural birth. It is a second birth that tears down prejudice and makes all people one.

Do not let the ugliness of prejudice invade the beauty of God's redemptive plan. Your heritage is now heavenly—not national. You have been made one in Him with all others in His family.

November 25

Commit your works to the Lord, and your thoughts will be established.

—Proverbs 16:3

Most of the time, we approach life from the opposite direction of what Proverbs teaches us here. We have all had the experience of following a feeling that seemed to be right only to discover that we were wrong to do so. We allow our thoughts or emotions to lead us, forgetting they are fickle and unfaithful guides much of the time.

This same approach is often used in our spiritual lives as well. We do the things we *feel* like doing or *think* are important, things that are usually pleasing to our flesh. But Proverbs tell us that the works come first; they control or establish (make steadfast) our thoughts. We could well understand this verse, then, as "Do what the Lord says to do, and your thought life will be developed according to His will."

Committing our works to the Lord also includes those things not directly related to the Lord, such as our jobs or schoolwork. Proverbs tells us here to do even these things as unto the Lord; then our thoughts will be established in these areas as well. The interesting part of this proverb is that in an age where mental instability is rampant and multitudes are plagued by depression and oppression, we are given a tool to keep our thought lives from getting away from us. If we commit our works to the Lord, do the Lord's work, and do our work as unto the Lord, we can eliminate any nonmedical, guilt-based causes of depression and discouragement.

When we are born again and have the Spirit of the living God dwelling in us but do not commit our works to the Lord, we grieve the Spirit, and our thoughts become guilt-based discouragements. The prescription to remedy this problem is to serve the Lord, do His work, and do it unto Him. Countless times I have talked to Christians who are merely existing spiritually and cannot understand why their Christian lives seem dull and even depressing. My counsel is always the same: "Do something for God!" Nothing can create joy and a sense of satisfaction like serving God by serving others.

Are you in the doldrums or in a season of dryness and even discouragement? Then tell someone about Jesus today, or help someone out with a meal, a ride, or a listening ear. Do something for God and your thought life will begin to come back in line. Remember, our second birth comes with a new nature that is created in Christ Jesus for good works (Eph. 2:10), and when we are not fulfilling our desires and destinies, we grow very discouraged.

Do something for God today, and do all things unto Him. Then will your thoughts be flooded with the joy of serving the Lord!

November 26

Therefore submit to God. Resist the devil and he will flee from you.

—James 4:7

What a great word of encouragement from James! The word *submit* here simply means "to obey." So, "obey God" is how this great exhortation begins. Next we are told to resist the devil. Too often we see this as some sort of passive resistance similar to just not doing what the devil tempts us to do. But that's not the meaning at all.

The Greek word for *resist* is *anthistēmi* (anth-is'-tay-mee), and it means "to stand against" or "to oppose." It is not passive at all, but rather an active offensive position of opposing the devil. The word for *flee* means "to shun." We can understand the clear meaning, then, if we think of the verse as "Obey God. Actively oppose the devil and he will shun you."

I remind you again that the Christian life is a battleground, not a campground. We are at war with principalities and powers, and the Christian life is not to be spent in a foxhole, but in putting the enemy on the run by obeying the commands of God. Obedience keeps us usable and powerful, and that is why James opened this short exhortation with the great reminder to obey God. Disobedience, on the other hand, weakens us and makes us vulnerable to enemy fire. But when we obey God by the power of the Spirit and actively resist the enemy, he will shun us, or run away from us.

It is also important to remember the enemy does not really run away from us, but from God in us. That is why unregenerate people are simply pawns in the enemy's hands and subject to his will; there is nothing in them to hinder the enemy's advances. As a result, they are powerless against his devices. It is impossible to obey God without first being indwelt by God the Holy Spirit, and when we are indwelt by God, we are then able to resist the devil, to fight back and even cause him to run away from us.

If there is one area I would single out as a major failure in the church today, I believe it would be the impression that we are just here on earth trying to survive this life rather than engaging in active spiritual warfare. It is also important to understand that resisting the devil is far different from rebuking or binding him, as many seek to do today. If the devil could be bound, then this world would be a far better place. He is going to be bound someday, to be sure, but by God. Our call is not to bind, but to resist; our call is not to rebuke, but to oppose. And it all begins with the power that is in us to obey the commands of God and therefore remain battle ready at all times.

Obey God. Actively oppose the devil and he will run away from you!

November 27

All things are lawful for me, but all things are not helpful. All things are lawful for me, but I will not be brought under the power of any. Foods for the stomach and the stomach for foods, but God will destroy both it and them. Now the body is not for sexual immorality but for the Lord, and the Lord for the body.

—1 Corinthians 6:12–13

The church at Corinth had developed some ideas that were evidence of the surrounding culture's influence on it. This led the church to adopt statements like "all things are lawful" and "foods for the stomach and the stomach for foods." The Corinthians had even allowed the casual attitude of the culture around them to infiltrate their mind-set toward sexual immorality. Sex was reduced to an appetite, much like hunger, and was regarded as nothing more than a basic natural desire that was meant to be satisfied. Couple this mentality with the mantra that "all things are lawful" and you end up with a carnal, fleshly, and lust-driven group of people — which is exactly what happened in Corinth.

Paul wrote his letters to the Corinthians in response to questions some were raising about these very things. Paul said that although all things may indeed be lawful, that doesn't necessarily make them helpful. We need to note that Paul is not saying sexual immorality is lawful but not helpful, for that would conflict with other scriptures, including those Paul himself had written. What Paul *is* saying is that the Corinthians had taken not being under the law far beyond its actual meaning. The law that the church was not under was the ceremonial law of Moses; this did not exempt them from obeying the unchanging moral code of God contained in the Ten Commandments. Sexual immorality is never justified by the claim of not being under the law, Paul said.

In an age where we hear terms such as "friends with benefits" and where a casual attitude toward sex as just another physical appetite to be satisfied runs rampant, we need to heed Paul's words now more than ever. The body is not for sexual immorality, but for the Lord. And if the body is not for sexual immorality, then there must be a definition of sexual morality to be followed by God's people. One thing we know for sure: it is not within man's capability to define morality, "for the heart of man is deceitful above all things and desperately wicked" (Jer. 17:9).

God alone can define safe sex, and He has defined it as between one man and one woman who are married; anything outside of that is sin. "All things are lawful" might indeed be the mantra of our day, but it is no more true now than it was in Corinth. The body is not for sexual immorality, but for the

Lord. Any other line of thought regarding sex is nothing less than the mind-set of carnal Corinth—and it is not of the Lord!

November 28

Then all the elders of Israel gathered together and came to Samuel at Ramah, and said to him, "Look, you are old, and your sons do not walk in your ways. Now make us a king to judge us like all the nations." But the thing displeased Samuel when they said, "Give us a king to judge us." So Samuel prayed to the Lord. And the Lord said to Samuel, "Heed the voice of the people in all that they say to you; for they have not rejected you, but they have rejected Me, that I should not reign over them."

—1 Samuel 8:4–7

Every time I read this text, I cannot help but think of the longsuffering of God. The word *longsuffering* means "to withhold wrath." Here in 1 Samuel, the children of Israel, despite their rich heritage of seeing God deliver and provide for them, asked Samuel to appoint them a king like the other nations had. They had seen the hand of God move on their behalves in ways we still marvel at today, yet they protested, "We want to be like other nations." I am amazed at God's withholding of His wrath.

But I also realize every time I read these verses how much I am like the children of Israel. I wish for things that are second best, and I sometimes become upset or discouraged when I don't get them. Yes, that happens to me too, just like it happens to you. But the truth is, God has done so much for me, has granted me so much favor, has provided for me in so many ways, and has gotten me through so many things, why do I even give a second thought to having or not having things that mean nothing? Yet I do, and I'm sure you do too.

Israel wanted what the world had: a king. God warned them through Samuel that the king would plunder their possessions, recruit their sons into his service, and take the best of their vineyards and lands as his own. He warned them that they would cry out to the Lord because of the burdens the king would impose on them (1 Sam. 8:11–18). What was the people's response? To paraphrase 1 Samuel 8:19, "We'll take it; we want what the world has."

There is a reality we need to recognize here, and that is sometimes God lets us have our ways. That, friends, is something to fear. His way is always better than ours, and ours is at best inferior or even, as was Israel's, offensive to God.

So among the myriad of things you have to thank God for, add these two things to your list. First, He does not always give you what you want, but neither does He give you what you deserve. Sometimes His no is the best thing for you. Second, He is longsuffering, even when you desire something other than His best!

November 29

Then David danced before the Lord with all his might; and David was wearing a linen ephod. So David and all the house of Israel brought up the ark of the Lord with shouting and with the sound of the trumpet. Now as the ark of the Lord came into the City of David, Michal, Saul's daughter, looked through a window and saw King David leaping and whirling before the Lord; and she despised him in her heart.

—2 Samuel 6:14–16

Recovering the ark of the covenant and returning it to Jerusalem was a great cause for celebration, and King David rejoiced more than anyone else. Yet the wife he had received as reward from King Saul for the slaying of Goliath, Michal, found his celebration repulsive. David's dancing with all his might before the Lord caused her to despise her husband.

It is quite amazing that many people today despise someone who loves and worships God, but it is true. Many people regard a commitment to the Lord and a belief in the Bible as His word as the actions of weak-minded people. But as David said in Psalm 14:1, "The fool has said in his heart, 'There is no God.'"

The key to all this is what happened after Michal communicated her disgust to David for his worship. In verse 22, David answered her accusations, declaring, "And I will be even more undignified than this, and will be humble in my own sight." David did not allow the bitter disgust of one person to infringe on his worship and praise of God.

Many times Christians find themselves in the presence of one of God's adversaries, and sometimes they alter their normal Christian activities because of the presence of such a person. For example, they may change how they talk, or they don't pray over their meal as usual. These are simple things, to be sure, but nonetheless concessions to someone else's disgust for the things of God.

David gives us the proper response in times such as these. In essence, he says, "If you think I am a fool for loving and serving God, then I will further humiliate myself in your eyes, but I am not going to stop praising and thanking God." Second Samuel also tells us that because of her words, Michal was childless all the days of her life, and the wife of the most famous king in Israel fades into obscurity from the pages of Scripture.

As I write this devotional, Father's Day has recently passed, and I encouraged the men at my church, not just the dads, to act like Christians at all times. I urged them not to let others influence or hinder their walks and certainly not to let anyone silence their worship and praise of God. This is something the enemy loves to do, for his desire for worship was the cause of his fall in the first place. If people won't worship him, he'll settle for hindering them from worshiping God. But don't fall for it. Worship the Lord with all your might—no matter who's watching!

November 30

When the builders laid the foundation of the temple of the Lord, the priests stood in their apparel with trumpets, and the Levites, the sons of Asaph, with cymbals, to praise the Lord, according to the ordinance of David king of Israel. And they sang responsively, praising and giving thanks to the Lord: "For He is good, for His mercy endures forever toward Israel." Then all the people shouted with a great shout, when they praised the Lord, because the foundation of the house of the Lord was laid.

—Ezra 3:10–11

It has been said that new believers are the lifeblood of any church and that the church that does not evangelize will fossilize! This passage bears out that thought.

The laying of the temple foundation was great cause for celebration in Israel. The people had come out of seventy years of Babylonian captivity and returned to a city that had lain in ruin that entire time. There was no temple, there were no walls—the city was a heap of rubble. Yet now, a foundation had been laid.

The temple in Jerusalem contained the inner sanctuary known as the Holy of Holies. Here the ark of the covenant stood as the symbol of God's presence on the earth. But ever since New Testament times, the saints themselves are called the temple of the Holy Spirit, and from Ezra we can well understand that every time a life is delivered from ruin and a foundation laid for the Holy Spirit inside a person's heart, there is great cause for celebration. Someone has been delivered from Babylon (the world) and has become a temple of the Holy Spirit!

The great part about this is that each individual Christian has the opportunity to lay this foundation in someone else by sharing their faith in Jesus Christ. I do believe it is true that the church that does not evangelize will fossilize, but I think we can apply this as an individual truth as well, not just a corporate one. I have spent years watching literally tens of thousands of people get saved, and I can say with all confidence that I never tire of it. It is as exhilarating today as it was the first time I led someone to the Lord or participated in large-scale evangelism.

If you want a Christian life filled with shouts of joy and praise, keep laying the foundation of the church by leading people to Christ. Then your life will be a continual time of praise, even when times are hard.

Tell someone about Jesus today. Their eternal destiny could be changed, and your day could be too!

December 1

Let the elders who rule well be counted worthy of double honor, especially those who labor in the word and doctrine. For the Scripture says, "You shall not muzzle an ox while it treads out the grain," and, "The laborer is worthy of his wages."

—1 Timothy 5:17–18

I have often described ministry as "awfully wonderful." It is the hardest thing a person could ever do and yet the most rewarding thing as well. It is the most discouraging thing at times and the most encouraging thing at other times. It's awfully wonderful, the work of ministry!

Here's an example of what I'm talking about. One of the most discouraging things in ministry is to give people counsel from the Word of God but even as you are talking, you can see on their faces that they have no intention of aligning with the Word. They leave the meeting only to return months or even years later with nothing having changed in their lives. That's awful! The flip side of this, the wonderful aspect, is to watch the lights come on in someone's eyes as God's truth is shared, and by the look on that person's face, you know transformation will take place. This is wonderful!

I say these things for one reason: ministry is hard, so be an encouragement to your pastor, and take care of him. Hebrews 13:17 says, "Obey those who rule over you, and be submissive, for they watch out for your souls, as those who must give account. Let them do so with joy and not with grief, for that would be unprofitable for you." The obvious implication is that we are to obey the Word of God, because when it says, "Obey those who rule," it speaks of the job of the pastor, which is to proclaim the Word of God to God's people.

I have heard many times of families having "roasted pastor" for Sunday brunch, with parents criticizing and dissecting the man, even in front of their children. What a disservice to the kids, and what disrespect for the calling of God this teaches!

If your pastor is growing in his gift but still struggling in it, tell him you love him and are praying for him. Yes, maybe there are better preachers out there, but love your pastor and pray for him.

Ministry is awfully wonderful. Make it your goal to be a part of the wonderful portion in your pastor's life. Remember, those who rule well are watching out for your soul!

December 2

I know how to be abased, and I know how to abound. Everywhere and in all things I have learned both to be full and to be hungry, both to abound and to suffer need. I can do all things through Christ who strengthens me.

— Philippians 4:12–13

Some have stretched verse 13 a little beyond its meaning to imply that some type of superman strength is implied here. Not to diminish the power of Jesus Christ or even to limit what He can do through us, but that is not within the context of what is saying here in Philippians.

If I may be so bold as to paraphrase Paul, I would do it like this: "I don't let circumstances impact my faith and trust in the Lord." Paul was explaining that he trusted God in trials the same way that he trusted Him in triumphs. He offered the same sacrifice of praise (Heb. 13:15) in either poverty or prosperity.

Paul knew how to be abased and how to abound. *Abased* means "humiliated," and *abound* means "superabundance." Both speak to general life experiences, and both can be met without wavering in trust and praise.

Paul also gives us a key in this magnificent verse, and it is found in the little English word *can*. The Greek word used here is *ischuō (is-khoo'-o)*, and it means "to exercise force," "to be of strength," or "to prevail." It very clearly implies a choice: we can do all things, or we can choose not to. We can face trials and triumphs, poverty and prosperity, with an attitude of gratitude, or we can choose not to.

You may know how to do a lot of things you never wanted to know, like suffer need or loss. But you can exercise strength in all things—if you choose to. Each day is a microcosm of opportunity to do all things in Christ's strength—the good, the bad, and the ugly included!

December 3

This is a faithful saying, and these things I want you to affirm constantly, that those who have believed in God should be careful to maintain good works. These things are good and profitable to men.

— Titus 3:8

Paul had entrusted the congregation in Crete to Titus care (Titus 1:5), and now he instructed him about what to teach the congregation. The core of this verse is found in the word *careful*, which means "to exercise thought." In other words, Paul instructed Titus to tell the church that they must always be thinking about what they could do for the Lord.

The word for *careful* can also be translated "anxious." "Be anxious for good works; think about them all the time" is the implication, meaning we are not to let the busyness of life push out the things we should do for God's name and glory. After all, Jesus said in Matthew 5:16, "Let your light so shine before men, that they may see your good works and glorify your Father in heaven." Because our good works bring glory to God, we are to exercise thought about maintaining them.

At this time of year, many people are thinking about what to do for others, what gifts to purchase, how to please someone else. Many give charitable donations and perform acts of service during the holiday season. As wonderful as those things are, the key to what we have read today is to take the Christmas spirit of giving and charity and apply it to our lives year-round.

The holidays are probably the most vivid example of how to employ this truth Paul shared with Titus. We should exercise thought about good works all the time, and, we might add, use the Christmas season as an example of what this looks like. Paul says to affirm this constantly, to bring it up regularly, and not to let this truth ever lie dormant. Those who profess belief in God need to exercise continual thought about good works, for these things are good and profitable to all people, both to those who give and to those who receive the good works.

I am growing in my own awareness of how easily stuff creeps into our lives, how material things can take precedence over the things of God. It is so easy to protest, "I don't have time," "I don't have the resources," "I don't have the opportunity or boldness." Exercise thought about this, dear friends, because life is but a short opportunity to sow into eternity.

As I grow older, the months seem to pass as quickly as days did in the past. Each new day is an opportunity to bring glory to God by doing something good for someone else. But we must consciously think about good works each day and not allow the daily busyness of life to crowd them out.

There is nothing more important than serving God, and we need to think about it all the time. Exercise thought today about good works, look for the opportunity to do good for someone else in the name of the Lord, and then get up and do it again tomorrow!

December 4

Beware, brethren, lest there be in any of you an evil heart of unbelief in departing
from the living God; but exhort one another daily, while it is called "Today,"
lest any of you be hardened through the deceitfulness of sin. For we have become
partakers of Christ if we hold the beginning of our confidence steadfast to the end,
while it is said: "Today, if you will hear His voice,
do not harden your hearts as in the rebellion."

— Hebrews 3:12–14

Though not frequently mentioned, there is a great and chilling reality presented here: continually rejecting God's offer of forgiveness and grace can lead to an irreversible hardness of heart. The example cited is the children of Israel wandering in the wilderness after God had mightily delivered them from the oppression of Egypt. Hebrews tells us that it is the continuing in steadfast confidence in the Lord that indicates a true partaker in Christ.

It is also worth noting that this warning was written to Christian brethren, meaning those who were part of the church. This is significant, because it is the rejection of God's truth, even after hearing it time and again, that leads to a hardened heart. The word *departing* in verse 12 means "to instigate a revolt," and this revolution or rejection begins in the heart. In other words, if we reject portions of the Word of God in our hearts, we will soon become hardened to other portions and eventually to it all.

Again the example is the Jews in the wilderness, who rejoiced when things were good but blamed God when things were tough. Although God had said He would get them to the Promised Land, they departed from His words and accused Him of leading them out of Egypt to die in the wilderness. Their hearts eventually grew so hard that when they finally arrived at the end of their journey, they refused to enter the Promised Land, having been swayed by those who lamented the difficulty of overcoming the giants in the land. This was evidence of an evil heart of unbelief.

Now we all have doubts at times, and we all wonder why God has done this or not done that. That is not what this passage is talking about, frail humans trying to understand an infinite, almighty God. It is referring to rejecting what we do know of God and deciding that it is not true or has become outdated. For example, if we reject God's design for sexual purity, we will soon be hardened against other portions of His Word. If we reject His plan for dying to self, we will soon reject other portions of His Word. Exhort one another daily not to be hardened against the Word of God!

December 5

When the righteous are in authority, the people rejoice; but when a wicked man rules, the people groan.

— Proverbs 29:2

This great proverb is often and rightfully viewed through the lens of the importance of appointing godly and righteous leaders, especially when we have the opportunity to vote them into office. But I want to look at this proverb from another direction, as a sort of a litmus test for those already in leadership.

Being a leader in any capacity is a God-ordained privilege, and we could well say the test of leadership is in the response of the followers. If you are an employer, what do your employees think of you? Are you a pleasure to work for and a cause of rejoicing, or does your name bring a groan from those who work under you? Now I am not so naïve as to fail to recognize that your position in and of itself is going to bring out animosity in some people, no matter what you do. But the real question is, do those who work under your leadership or those who serve under you in ministry consider it a joy or a source of groaning?

It is important to remember that the book of Proverbs is descriptive and not prescriptive; it is Solomon's observations regarding life. And, as he says, when the behavior of bosses or leaders is righteous, the people called to serve under them generally do so with rejoicing. This is because the righteous leader is fair and honest and treats people with respect and dignity. If God has blessed you with the privilege of leadership, to borrow a colloquialism of the day, "How you doin' with that?" Are you a joy to serve with or work for?

Even in ministry, it is so easy to get sucked into the power of position. I often find the cliques that form at pastors' conferences and events very saddening. The "big guys" stick together, and most of the groups are based on church size or pastor popularity. I have to say, it is so refreshing to meet a "big guy" who is just one of the guys. These men stick out from the crowd and stand head and shoulders above anyone else blessed with a large flock. It also makes me believe that those who serve with them do so with rejoicing.

Again I say this as an exhortation to us all, to those called to lead and to those who follow: don't groan without reason as an employee, and don't be a cause of groaning as an employer or ministry head. I have to imagine that serving Jesus was a great joy for eleven of Jesus' twelve disciples (with Judas as the lone groaner in the midst). I have to believe there was much laughter as the Creator of all things interacted with those He had created. The example cannot get any higher than God in human flesh and how He led His flock of twelve.

So take the test, leaders, recognizing you will always have the antiestablishment crowd with you at some level. But also listen to those who work or serve under your leadership; you'll find out more about yourself there than anywhere else, if you are willing. Lead like Jesus is all you need to do!

December 6

O Lord, You are my God. I will exalt You, I will praise Your name, for You have done wonderful things; Your counsels of old are faithfulness and truth.

—Isaiah 25:1

Many of us have heard it said there are some things God cannot do. For example, He cannot lie, and He cannot be wrong. Isaiah adds to this two more things God cannot do: He cannot be unfaithful, and His Word can never be untrue. These are great reasons to praise Him!

We would do well in the midst of difficult times to remember the things God cannot do. It is not even remotely possible that God would fail us. We may fail Him, and we may experience consequences in this life for doing so, but He will never fail us. He will never be unfaithful to His Word, including His promise to never leave or forsake us.

God allows times in our lives when faith is necessary to move forward in our spiritual walks. We may feel nothing, see nothing and spiritually sense nothing; but God is still there, and we must continue to praise Him for all He is and does. We are not nor will we ever be alone. God wants us to walk in the knowledge of His faithfulness. He wants us to trust in the wonderful things He has already done even while we await the sensing of His presence or the recognition of His hand at work. God cannot be unfaithful to us; to do so would deny His very nature.

There was a bumper sticker popular for a while that read, "If you feel far from God, guess who moved?" There is a truth there, to be sure, but there is more to feeling far from God than merely having moved away from Him. Most of us know that when we do something wrong, we will sense it in our spirits, a grieving of the Holy Spirit, if you will. But there are also times when we are doing well in our walks with God, when we are praying, reading, seeking, and serving yet still feel all alone. What do we do then?

When you find yourself in that situation, that is the time to praise the Lord for all the wonderful works He has done. He hasn't moved away from you, and you have not been forsaken. He wants you to remember and trust in the things you know He can and cannot do. His promises cannot fail, and it is impossible for Him not to be faithful.

So I guess the summary of today's devotion is, no matter what you feel, praise the Lord!

December 7

Now when He had taken the scroll, the four living creatures and the twenty-four elders fell down before the Lamb, each having a harp, and golden bowls full of incense, which are the prayers of the saints. And they sang a new song, saying: "You are worthy to take the scroll, and to open its seals; for You were slain, and have redeemed us to God by Your blood out of every tribe and tongue and people and nation, and have made us kings and priests to our God; and we shall reign on the earth."

— Revelation 5:8–10

Most scholars believe that the scroll mentioned here is the title deed to the earth that was sold to Satan because of man's sin. In accordance with Jewish law, the property could be redeemed only by a near kinsman. This is the very reason Jesus came in the "likeness of sinful flesh" (Rom. 8:3), so that He might become that kinsman-redeemer.

A kinsman-redeemer had four qualifications to fulfill in order to redeem a property sold to another. First, he had to be related by blood. Second, he had to have the ability to pay the redemption price. Third, he had to be willing to pay the price of redemption. And fourth, he himself had to be free, meaning not under a bond or debt to another. From this we can better understand the celebration in heaven spoken of in today's passage. There was only one who met the qualifications of kinsman-redeemer for the fallen earth, only one who was worthy, and that one was Jesus.

Jesus became a man so He could become our kinsman. He came as one both able and willing to pay the redemption price to buy back the world. He did not owe sin's debt of death; He was sinless, and therefore death had no right to Him. Thus He was worthy, willing, and able to redeem, and He did so out of every tribe, tongue, people, and nation.

The thing that I love about these verses is that you and I can also sing this new song. We can personalize verse 9 and sing, "You have redeemed me and made me a king and priest to God, and I will reign on the earth with You!" Yes, Jesus did all this for me and for you. As Christians, we can insert our names into the text every time a promise is made to God's church and people. Jesus is going to take back the title deed for the earth, having paid its redemption price with His own blood. You and I are going to be kings and priests on earth when He rules and reigns on this planet after His return!

That's good stuff to remember as you encounter life today: "Jesus died for me. He redeemed me and made me a king and a priest, and I am going to reign with Him someday." Reminding yourself of this truth puts the rest of life in its proper perspective. So as you live out your life in a fallen and darkened world, remind yourself, "I have been redeemed!"

December 8

*As he journeyed he came near Damascus, and suddenly a light shone around him
from heaven. Then he fell to the ground, and heard a voice saying to him, "Saul,
Saul, why are you persecuting Me?" And he said, "Who are You, Lord?" Then the
Lord said, "I am Jesus, whom you are persecuting. It is hard for you to kick against
the goads." So he, trembling and astonished, said, "Lord, what do You want me to
do?" Then the Lord said to him, "Arise and go into the city,
and you will be told what you must do."*

— Acts 9:3–6

Not all of us have a conversion story as dramatic as Paul's, but all of ours are equally fantastic. No matter the story at the point of conversion, the end result was the same. "I once was blind, but now I see" is the testimony of all who have come to faith in Jesus Christ, no matter the specifics. Radically or quietly, the miracle is the same.

There is another element of Paul's conversion that we all share as well, and that is what happens after the moment of conversion. After Paul's encounter, he obviously recognized the divine presence, addressing the voice he heard as "Lord." Then he asked, "What do You want me to do?" and Jesus answered, "Arise and go into the city, and you will be told." In similar fashion, after Jesus becomes our master, we ask Him what He would have us to do. As He answered Paul, Jesus calls us to arise from our past life of sin and failure and begin the journey of a continuing revelation of His will.

This means that "Lord, what do You want me to do?" needs to be a continual part of our Christian lives, even a prayer at the outset of each day. But it is also true that we will need to continually arise as well. As I have said before, salvation could well be defined as a moment of confession followed by a lifetime of conversion. In other words, throughout our Christian lives, Jesus will continue to reveal things we need to arise from.

So begin this day with these things in mind: "Lord, what do You want me to do?" and "What are You calling me to arise from?" Remember, if you ask according to His will, He will hear you (1 John 5:14), so ask today and He will answer. He wants you to know His plan for the day, and He wants you to arise from certain things today. And the great thing is, He'll want the same for you tomorrow.

Before you head out into the day, ask Him, "What would You have me to do, and what do I need to rise above in my life?" Do this today and always, and you will greatly increase the odds of having a magnificent day in Him!

December 9

And do this, knowing the time, that now it is high time to awake out of sleep; for now our salvation is nearer than when we first believed. The night is far spent, the day is at hand. Therefore let us cast off the works of darkness, and let us put on the armor of light. Let us walk properly, as in the day, not in revelry and drunkenness, not in lewdness and lust, not in strife and envy. But put on the Lord Jesus Christ, and make no provision for the flesh, to fulfill its lusts.

— Romans 13:11–14

The "do this" that Paul is talking about is loving your neighbor as yourself, as stated in verses 8–10 of this same chapter. It is noteworthy that this reminder of love is attached to a reminder of the nearness of the Lord's return. The exhortations that follow of walking properly and not in sinful behavior are also acts of love. We might well say that loving our neighbor speaks of our horizontal relationships with others, and walking properly speaks of our vertical relationship with God by putting on the Lord Jesus Christ.

We must also remember that love, as defined in 1 Corinthians 13:4–8, is a series of actions, not emotions. Paul is not telling us to feel good about other people and God since the night is far spent; rather, he is saying to put love into action as the return of the Lord draws near. Christians have always been called to love, and that love is the very factor that informs the world they are Christ's disciples (John 13:35). But in the last days, we are going to need one another more than ever, and love is what will get us through.

As time draws to a close, we are going to need to love one another and love God more visibly. The patient kindness and longsuffering found in love's definition will be critical factors in last-days living. Because of the perilous times of those last days (2 Tim. 3:1), we will need one another's love and support more than ever. We will also need to love God more deeply by living more and more distinctly from the world with each passing day.

I believe we are in the closing seconds of the grand scheme of things and that Christ is coming soon for His bride. I believe He is, even now, at the door. This means someone you will encounter today is going to need an expression of love. Someone is going to need a reminder that God is there for them, that He will get them through and provide strength to meet the day. Someone you meet will need a loving reminder that God will never leave them or forsake them. Someone will need to see your love for God manifested, or made visible, as you walk properly instead of in the ways and lusts of the world.

In these last days, love for one another will get us through, and love will lead others to our Savior as they see us love Him. So do this, knowing the time!

December 10

This is a faithful saying and worthy of all acceptance, that Christ Jesus came into the world to save sinners, of whom I am chief. However, for this reason I obtained mercy, that in me first Jesus Christ might show all longsuffering, as a pattern to those who are going to believe on Him for everlasting life. Now to the King eternal, immortal, invisible, to God who alone is wise, be honor and glory forever and ever. Amen.

—1 Timothy 1:15–17

Paul had a very clear perspective on the magnitude of his own salvation, even as he expressed that it was in part a display of the depth of God's love and forgiveness. In essence, Paul said, "If God can forgive me, He can forgive anyone!" To show His longsuffering was but part of why God saved Paul, however; the heart of why God saved him was simply that He loved him and is unwilling that any should perish.

Paul also indirectly addressed one of the issues I consider a spiritual plague in our day, and that is the lack of fear of the Lord. We often hear this expressed in terms of God being "the big guy" or "the man upstairs." It is also widely expressed in the casualness in which God is approached in prayer and in life.

"Good buddy" God seems to be the mentality of many today, but in my opinion, this does a great disservice to the Lord and the church. Yes, Christ called us His friends, and yes, we are free to cry out "Abba Father," or "Papa." But still we owe Him reverent honor and respect. I find it interesting that people will dress up and be on their best behavior to meet a human dignitary or movie star, but they treat the King eternal, the immortal, invisible God, less respectfully than they do the people He created.

I am not saying we need to diminish the wonderful blood-bought unity we have with the Father through Jesus Christ, but I do think we need to remember that we were saved while we were yet sinners and also keep in mind who it is we are addressing when we come before Him in prayer. That does not mean we need to pray in King James English, and it doesn't mean we cannot speak conversationally with Him. But it does mean we need to be careful about bossing Him around as though He were our servant.

Jesus, in giving the model prayer in Mathew 6, told His disciples to begin in prayer by hallowing the name of the Lord. The word *hallowed* means "to purify" or "to venerate mentally." In other words, when we pray, we are to keep in mind the one to whom we are praying. This example is pictured for us here in the words of Paul. He recognized who he was in light of the one who had saved him, and he knew the one who had saved him was the only one worthy of honor and glory.

Dear friend, come confidently before the throne of grace into the very presence of God through Jesus Christ. There in His presence, remember who is who. You and I are the chief of sinners, and He alone is the King eternal, immortal, invisible—God. You will find this approach leads to a very fulfilling prayer life, which we all need. "Our Father in heaven, hallowed be Your name" will set the tone for any productive time of prayer.

December 11

But concerning the times and the seasons, brethren, you have no need that I should write to you. For you yourselves know perfectly that the day of the Lord so comes as a thief in the night. For when they say, "Peace and safety!" then sudden destruction comes upon them, as labor pains upon a pregnant woman. And they shall not escape. But you, brethren, are not in darkness, so that this Day should overtake you as a thief.

—1 Thessalonians 5:1–4

I am so thankful for the Word of God! It informs us of how things began, and it tells us where things are headed. It assures us that we need not fear an unexpected outcome.

Paul reminded the Thessalonians that they knew "perfectly" about the day of the Lord. The word *perfectly* can also be translated "exactly," so we could understand this as "You know exactly about the day of the Lord and how it will come." Later, in verse 11 of this same chapter, Paul would tell the church to "comfort one another with these words."

We too should find great comfort in knowing both the beginning and the end. We are not unenlightened about either our origin or our future. Many Christians are uncomfortable talking about such things as the world's predicted future, but the truth is, knowing the end of the story takes all the worry out of where things are headed. And that is true even if we know the end is a time of God's wrath.

Paul says that in a time when the world's mantra is "peace and safety," destruction will suddenly come. The phrase *peace and safety* can also be translated "prosperity and security," which indeed is the great concern of our day. It speaks of a godless age, an age when humanity will be lovers of self and pleasure rather than lovers of God (2 Tim. 3:2–4).

The Bible has identified the signs preceding the Lord's return. So when we see a self-absorbed, me-centered society that calls for prosperity and security while denying the God who can give them both, then the day of the Lord is near. If we know this, the day will not overtake us as a thief in the night. As I said, many Christians find the topic uncomfortable, but we would do well to remember Paul's admonition to the church so that this day will not come upon us by surprise.

The most important reason for the generation that will be alive at this time to know this information is motivation. It will stir up an urgency to tell others what we know — to warn them! The church, in many cases, has become ashamed of declaring that God is a just judge and His judgment will not rest forever. Though many have adopted the mind-set that people don't like to hear about hellfire and brimstone, that doesn't make hellfire and brimstone any less of a reality.

We know perfectly what's coming. The perfect thing to do is to tell others what we know because of whom we know! Jesus Christ is coming again, and at His return, He will not come as the Lamb of God, but as the Lion of Judah. Because of the Word of God, we know this perfectly.

Share this truth with someone today. No matter what others may feel about it, feelings do not negate biblical truth!

December 12

*O foolish Galatians! Who has bewitched you that you should not obey the truth,
before whose eyes Jesus Christ was clearly portrayed among you as crucified? This
only I want to learn from you: Did you receive the Spirit by the works of the law, or
by the hearing of faith? Are you so foolish? Having begun in the Spirit, are you now
being made perfect by the flesh? Have you suffered so many things in vain —
if indeed it was in vain?*

—Galatians 3:1–4

Some had taught the Galatian Christians that it was necessary to retain the law of ceremony and sacrifice as part of the Christian life. Paul labeled this action "bewitching." The word *bewitch* means "to fascinate by false representations." This might seem like an obvious thing to avoid, yet it happens quite frequently in our day, just as it did in the Galatians' day. The saving work of grace that births a life lived in the Spirit is often heavy laden with church rituals and traditions that some falsely claim as necessary elements of the Christian faith. Some say you must be baptized in their church to be saved, while others insist you must partake of communion in a certain manner and with certain believers. Still others assert that you must hold to their position on the last days or you're not really saved.

These actions are the same as those of the Judaizers Paul warned the Galatians about. Not that there is anything wrong with traditions and, to a degree, some forms of ritual, but to demand that all true believers do thus and so is to put ritual and tradition on the same level as the indwelling of the Holy Spirit. Having begun in the Spirit, will we now try to be made perfect by ritual and tradition? It is easy to get sucked into this mind-set, if we are not careful.

If there is one thing the church today ought to be known for it is walking in the power of the Holy Spirit. But sadly, the church is better known for its division and manmade rules instead of its spiritual unity and freedom in the Spirit. Some things are indeed nonnegotiable and must be agreed upon by every true church. The deity of Christ, the atoning power of His blood, and salvation by grace through faith are truths that must never be surrendered. But to elevate forms of worship or methods of baptism to equality with such pillars of the faith is bewitching.

We are the people of God, called to walk according to the Spirit and not burdened by traditions and rituals. Nevertheless, we sometimes forget that and get sidetracked by nonessentials. Some insist that contemporary worship is not worship at all; to them, real worship is hymns and a choir. Others zero in on their belief that all true Christians speak in tongues, and they try to force people into doing so. But the fact is, friends, worship is a matter of the heart and a way of life. The gift of tongues is not for everyone, and some even say it is not for today (which I do not agree with). But when we start elevating personal traditions and church rituals to "you must do this or you're not saved," we are seeking to continue the work of the Spirit by walking in the flesh. The question is not how we worship, but whether we worship. It is not whether we speak in tongues, but whether we walk in our gifts.

Walk in the Spirit today, and be led by Him. Let the Spirit be your guide and the Word of God your guard. Remember, the Spirit will never lead you into something that conflicts with His Word.

December 13

Therefore "Come out from among them and be separate," says the Lord. "Do not touch what is unclean, and I will receive you. I will be a Father to you, and you shall be My sons and daughters," says the Lord Almighty.

— 2 Corinthians 6:17–18

How the world today needs to see that we are different — separate, clean, and washed! Paul's quotation here from Isaiah 52:11 and Ezekiel 20:34 reminds us that we have a new identity in Christ. Our lives should look different from when we did not know Christ and glaringly different from the world.

The "therefore" in this verse alerts us that there is something for us to look for that preceded the statement. In this case, it is that He is our God, and we are His people; therefore, we are to be separated unto Him. This does not mean uninvolved with the world, for the world is our mission field, but uninvolved in worldly things because we are of God and not of the world.

There is not one single element of life that knowing Christ does not touch and change. We may have the same color hair and personal tastes in style and food, but the things we derive pleasure from, the things we find important, and the things we consider as goals will change after we come to know Him. Why? Because we are His; He is our God, and we are the temple of His Spirit.

So the question is, what are the unclean things that He does not want us to touch? The answer might seem simplistic and even obvious, but unclean things are things that make us dirty, things that are obviously unrighteous before God.

Most of the time when I counsel people, one thing is consistently true, and that is they already know what to do and not to do. Think about it. Do we really need defined the things that make us dirty? Do we wonder if it is okay to lie, cheat, steal, curse, or have sex outside of marriage? It is pretty obvious that these things are unclean.

But what about the alleged gray areas, things not so clear, such as smoking, dancing, social drinking, and the like? Well, there is a simple test to help you in these areas. Ask yourself two questions when considering a certain action: first, can God be glorified through it, and second, will your witness be harmed by doing it? This gives clear direction on how to define the obvious and not so obvious unclean things you should separate from.

If a Christian is no different from anyone else in the world, there is no reason for anyone to become one. So look for ways to be separate from worldliness as you live out your faith in a world you're in, but not of.

December 14

"And I will bless her and also give you a son by her; then I will bless her, and she shall be a mother of nations; kings of peoples shall be from her." Then Abraham fell on his face and laughed, and said in his heart, "Shall a child be born to a man who is one hundred years old? And shall Sarah, who is ninety years old, bear a child?" And Abraham said to God, "Oh, that Ishmael might live before You!" Then God said: "No, Sarah your wife shall bear you a son, and you shall call his name Isaac; I will establish My covenant with him for an everlasting covenant, and with his descendants after him."

—Genesis 17:16–19

I have always found it interesting that if Sarah was going to be the mother of nations and Abraham the father of a multitude, then wouldn't you expect that they would have had dozens of kids instead of just one, and that one born to them in their old age? But again, God's ways are not our ways. He daily does the impossible, and He does it in a way where only He can receive the glory.

Most of us have done the "Abraham thing" of stepping outside God's perfect will and then asking Him to bless it. Abraham sought to see God's promise fulfilled through Ishmael, the son resulting from his and Sarah's decision to produce offspring through their own methods. Though God had already promised them a son, they simply took matters into their own hands because God's will was taking too long. Then, years later, Abraham did what we have all done: he asked God to bless the actions of his impatience. "I did it my way" might be great lyrics for a song, but they are never appropriate for the life that is lived to please God.

In essence, Abraham said, "Oh, that You would bless what I have done!" But God said, "No, we'll stick to My plan." This is always God's answer when we do that which conflicts with what He has already spoken. "No, what I have said is what will be" is His answer to us when we seek His blessing on our acts of disobedience. Just as God had planned, Isaac was born. He became the father of twin sons, and one of those sons, Jacob, had twelve sons, who became the heads of the twelve tribes of Israel. In God's way and plan, a nation indeed was born, whose descendants are with us yet to this day.

The lesson for us all is not to waste time begging and pleading with God to bless the actions we have taken outside His will. Let's get back to doing His will His way as fast as we can, and His blessings will be upon us once again!

December 15

For to you it has been granted on behalf of Christ, not only to believe in Him,
but also to suffer for His sake.

—Philippians 1:29

The idea of being granted suffering is not something our minds are quick to embrace. When we think of being granted something, our minds instantly go to blessings, favor, or even provision, and the Greek word for *granted* means exactly that: "to show favor or kindness." But in the context of our verse today, we have been *granted* the privilege of suffering for Jesus Christ!

This lofty thought makes my mind spin with questions: If this has been granted to us, are we actually experiencing it? Have we actually suffered for Christ? If not, why not? Have we done things to avoid it? Have we kept silent when we should have spoken up? Have we stood up for right even when we knew we would be the only one doing so? Have we spoken the truth in love even when we knew it wasn't the politically correct thing to do?

The reason Paul made such a bold statement about suffering is simple: living like Jesus will inevitably lead to suffering. It may not come in the form of violence or death, as Jesus suffered, but it could be in the form of betrayal and false accusations, which, too, Jesus suffered. It could be economic, as it was for many of the early Christians, who were ostracized for their faith, had their businesses shunned, and were disowned by their families. It was granted to them to suffer some of the same things that Jesus suffered.

Boldness in the faith will always elicit a reaction from the enemies of the cross. Many people want Christians to be seen and not heard. They have an "I'm glad it works for you, but don't force it on me" type of attitude. But to them, simply living in public dedication to Jesus Christ is objectionable. As long as we keep Christianity in church, they're fine; but the moment we bring it to work or school, they claim we have forced it on others. To be sure, we will suffer persecution and suffering for doing so.

Now I don't believe we should go out of our way to encounter suffering. That is not the intent of this verse at all. However, I do believe we should not abandon the ways of God in order to avoid it. It has been granted to you and me to suffer for Christ's sake, and living our faith in everyday life is going to bring us that very thing. It is not our favorite truth as Christians, but it is true nonetheless.

Have you suffered for being a Christian? Has there been a cost of some sort, not to obtain your salvation, but because of it? If not, maybe some boldness is in order; maybe being a little saltier or shining your light more brightly is the order of the day. You won't have to be anything but bold for Jesus to be granted the favor of suffering for Him. Don't go looking for it, but try not avoiding it today and see what the Lord does in and through you!

December 16

My son let them not depart from your eyes — keep sound wisdom and discretion; so they will be life to your soul and grace to your neck. Then you will walk safely in your way, and your foot will not stumble. When you lie down, you will not be afraid; yes, you will lie down and your sleep will be sweet. Do not be afraid of sudden terror, nor of trouble from the wicked when it comes; for the Lord will be your confidence, and will keep your foot from being caught.

— Proverbs 3:21–26

Here Proverbs identifies the blessings of walking in the wisdom of the Word of God. First, there is life to your soul, or in a word, joy; and grace to your neck, *neck* meaning "throat" and implying the provision of God. Next, safety and a sure footing through life are mentioned, as well as rest and sweet sleep, a scarce commodity for many today. Finally, even when fear threatens and wicked schemes rise against you, you can still remain confident, knowing you are the Lord's and He will keep your foot from getting caught.

God's plan for us is a joy-filled life of victory and safety from self-inflicted wounds, and stability of heart and mind even when everything around us seems crazy. His plan is for us to travel a steadfast and secure journey through life and exercise power over the enemy's schemes and snares. To view the Christian life as anything less is just wrong. The Christian life is not bondage — it's freedom! The Christian life is not a bunch of "thou shalt nots"; the Christian life is a bunch of "you can through Christ."

By walking according to the wisdom of God's Word, you can have peace and enjoy safety from your own wounds of disobedience and need not fear the hidden traps of the enemy. So walk in the confidence of the wisdom of the Word today, knowing the Lord will never lead you into substandard living. The steps He will guide you to take will be the best ones for you and will provide the most joy and safety that can be had in this life.

To live by a negative or bondage-type view of the Christian life is to not understand it at all. Following after God's wisdom is the way to live free. A joyless life void of all pleasure and filled with only boredom and pain is not the way to live and is completely contrary to the truth.

Just do what the Word of God says today and your day will be blessed, safe, and victorious. And the great thing is, you can have another day just like it tomorrow!

December 17

I am the vine, you are the branches. He who abides in Me, and I in him, bears much fruit; for without Me you can do nothing.

—John 15:5

It is not unusual for the Bible, and even Jesus, to approach a point from the negative in order to state a positive truth. It is clearly implied here that without Jesus we can do nothing. However, we are not without Him; therefore, we can do all things!

At the time of this conversation, Jesus was closing in on the cross. John 14 through 16 records His final words of instruction before He prayed the high priestly prayer in John 17. Then, in John 18, we read about Jesus' arrest in the Garden of Gethsemane. Logic tells us, therefore, that Jesus' words in our verse for today must have been vital information, since they were His last words of instruction to the disciples before the cross.

The word *abide* means to "stay in" or, as the illustration implies, "stay attached to" Him. Jesus is the vine, and it is impossible for us, the branches, to bear fruit unless we remain attached to the vine. These words must have created a bit of confusion in the minds of the apostles, since moments earlier Jesus had told them He was going to prepare a place for them. He was leaving them, He had just said, so how could they stay connected to Him?

John 15:26 says, "But when the Helper comes, whom I shall send to you from the Father, the Spirit of truth who proceeds from the Father, He will testify of Me." The Helper is obviously the Holy Spirit, and testifying of Jesus is the fruit we are to bear. We have talked much of the Holy Spirit in our daily devotionals, but it is good to remember that nothing keeps us attached to divine power like testifying of Jesus. This is what Jesus was telling the eleven here (Judas had already left to betray Jesus): "Stay connected to what I came to do. Testify of this, and your life will be fruitful. Cut yourself off from this, and your life will wither away; and in the end, when it is tested by fire (1 Cor. 3:13–15), it will be burned."

As the body of Christ, we must remain attached to His purpose, which is to save sinners. We do this through the power of the Holy Spirit, who provides our attachment to the vine for the purpose of bearing the fruit of lost souls for the glory of His name and the reward of His suffering. So stay connected to sharing your faith. It is the reason you have been given the power of the Holy Spirit.

Tell someone Jesus loves them today!

December 18

For I know your manifold transgressions and your mighty sins: afflicting the just and taking bribes; diverting the poor from justice at the gate. Therefore the prudent keep silent at that time, for it is an evil time. Seek good and not evil, that you may live; so the Lord God of hosts will be with you, as you have spoken. Hate evil, love good; establish justice in the gate. It may be that the Lord God of hosts will be gracious to the remnant of Joseph.

— Amos 5:12–15

Amos was calling upon the people of Israel to repent of their habitual and continual sins and to stop living as though the Lord had not given them commandments and laws to follow. They even spoke that the Lord God of hosts was with them, but the sad truth was, they were not with the Lord God of hosts. Even though they spoke as though they knew Him, their actions showed they did not.

This is a powerful reminder that though God is a just God and His mercies are great and new every morning, His Word is true every day as well. We need to remember that many of the promised blessings of God are conditional. "Seek good and not evil, that you may live" is an example of a conditional promise or exhortation.

But at the same time, I love how Amos mentions the graciousness of God, even to a people steeped in mighty sins. The phrase "it may be" implies a correlation with the conditions that God set, not that God might be gracious to some who repent but not to others.

It is true we often have trouble understanding the depth of God's love and mercy, but it is equally true that we often fail to understand the conditions of His love and mercy. God hates injustice, but He loves repentance. God judges the unjust, but He blesses the repentant who were once the unjust.

However, like Israel, we far too often think if we just say, "The Lord God of hosts is with us," we will automatically receive His graciousness and favor. But we must also take into account His instruction for us to hate evil, love good, and establish justice in the gate, which means to be fair and true in our judgments. The sad truth is, sometimes we have not been fair or just and have held mighty sins in our hearts. At times we have failed to take the necessary steps of repentance, yet still we mouth the words "the Lord God of hosts is with us."

I believe this passage from Amos is warning us not to expect the blessings of repentance without repenting. I am an expert in this area, as I have had much to repent of in my life. But I can also assure you that repentance changes the power and the manner in which you proclaim, "The Lord God of hosts is with me!"

Don't fight the Word of God. Where your life is out of step, repent. It feels great!

December 19

For we have spent enough of our past lifetime in doing the will of the Gentiles —
when we walked in lewdness, lusts, drunkenness, revelries, drinking parties, and
abominable idolatries. In regard to these, they think it strange that you do not run
with them in the same flood of dissipation, speaking evil of you.

—1 Peter 4:3-4

In conjunction with yesterday's devotional, today's devotional provides a rather interesting reality attached to bringing areas of our lives back into line with the will of God. The truth is, when you decide to repent, some people aren't going to like it. Some people will accuse you being a holy roller who thinks he is better than everyone else, just because you took a step of obedience toward God. But Peter reminds us that living in what he calls "the will of the Gentiles" is a waste of time.

Some people will think it strange for you to live a life that is pleasing to God and separate from sin, while others will think it unnecessary. I once spoke with a young person whose parents were so upset about their child's conversion that they forbid their own child from sharing the Word of God with any of their siblings. When the new convert gave the younger brother a Bible, the irate parents confiscated it from him. But this is the Christian life — a life opposed by many for no good reason.

Christians are good and caring people filled with enough of the love of God that they want to tell others about it. They are filled with enough of the Spirit of God that they also want to live in a way that pleases Him, though this decision is becoming increasingly unpopular in our day. But here is the important lesson: Satan knows how hard it is for us to face ostracism by friends and coworkers who make us feel bad for doing good. In school, they call it peer pressure; in later life, it is still peer pressure. But regardless of where it occurs, Satan attempts to pressure us back into his plan by having others think it strange that we now follow God's plan.

Peter would later say in verse 14, "If you are reproached for the name of Christ, blessed are you, for the Spirit of glory and of God rests upon you. On their part He is blasphemed, but on your part He is glorified." I hope you caught that: the Spirit of glory and of God rests upon you when evil is spoken about you because of the good steps you have taken to please and serve God. So ask yourself which you would rather have: the Spirit of glory and of God upon you or the approval of people who blaspheme God by attacking you. I may not be the sharpest knife in the drawer, but the answer seems pretty clear to me!

Remember today, repentance and goodness and living a life to please God may seem strange to others and even cause them to say evil things about you. On your part, God receives glory; on their part, He is blasphemed. Kind of puts their opinion of us in proper perspective, I must say. Live for God, and let them say what they may!

December 20

Let him who stole steal no longer, but rather let him labor, working with his hands what is good, that he may have something to give him who has need.

—Ephesians 4:28

We can usually identify what is important to the faith and vital to living a full life in Christ simply by recognizing what the devil either out and out opposes or seeks to pervert. Giving is one of those things. We see so much abuse in this area today, yet Paul here reminds us that we labor, not just to provide for our own needs, but also to meet the needs of others. The contrast of life realities drawn here is clear. The life of the thief is one of guilt, fear, and shame; the life of the repentant thief is one of labor, reward, and the joy of giving.

We have mentioned frequently the dry times in the life of every Christian and also the things we can do to either shorten their duration or end them altogether. One of those things is giving. Helping other people in even small ways can be such a rewarding experience. It just feels good! But there is another interesting aspect of the pairing of stealing and giving that Paul employs here. Laboring without giving can create the same sense of guilt as stealing, and it can certainly cause dry seasons or create a sense of something missing in a Christian's life.

I often think of the life of John Wesley and what he left behind at his death. He died owning a set of six silver spoons given to him by his mother; six pence, one for each of his six pallbearers; and the worn-out frock he had used for preaching. He also left something else behind: hundreds of thousands of Bibles and the Methodist Church! He literally gave away all he labored to earn. I wonder if in heaven he now has any regrets.

Jesus said, "It is more blessed to give than to receive" (Acts 20:35). Can you imagine if we lived like we believed that? We might not leave much behind at our deaths, at least in the world's estimation, but I am sure there would be untold numbers grateful for our choice, just like the millions that have been blessed by Wesley and the many others who chose to live that way.

Don't forget that your labors are in part to enable you to give to him who has need. Believe me, the words of Jesus can be trusted; you'll be more blessed when you remember to give than when you forsake it and don't!

December 21

The earth also was corrupt before God, and the earth was filled with violence. So God looked upon the earth, and indeed it was corrupt; for all flesh had corrupted their way on the earth. And God said to Noah, "The end of all flesh has come before Me, for the earth is filled with violence through them; and behold, I will destroy them with the earth."

—Genesis 6:11–13

A funny choice of verses to consider right before Christmas, you may think, but they are not really an odd choice at all. The family of Noah and the ark that saved them from judgment are the very picture of what Christmas is all about: God making a way for humanity to avoid eternal judgment. It is important at this time of year to remember such a thing for a couple of reasons. First, Jesus said, "As it was in the days of Noah, so shall it be at My return" (Matt. 24:37, my paraphrase). Second, at Christmastime we often gather with people who need to hear about the Christ child who came to take away the sins of the world.

I was once invited to say a few words at a city-sponsored Christmas event but was asked not to mention Jesus since His name might offend some in attendance. (The community coordinator who made the request was a Jew, by the way). With obvious shock on my face, I incredulously asked, "Are you asking me not to say anything about Jesus at Christmas?" I must say, however, I used my five minutes to tell those in attendance of the love of God who sent His Son to give them eternal life, joy, and peace in a world filled with turmoil and despair. I knew this would be the last invitation I would ever receive from this group, so I had to seize the opportunity!

Like me, you will have that opportunity to speak of Jesus this holiday season. Keep in mind that Jesus was thoughtful enough to give us Noah's day as an example of treating every opportunity as though it might be our last. So speak the truth in love this Christmas season, even as some seek to remove Christ from Christmas.

Christmas is the greatest reminder that Christ is coming again. When the thoughts and intents of man's heart are only evil continually, and violence and corruption fill the earth, we can take comfort in knowing Jesus is coming again to rescue His people from the judgment coming upon the world.

Noah and the ark—a great Christmas reminder of our soon coming King!

December 22

And those who know Your name will put their trust in You; for You, Lord, have not forsaken those who seek You.

— Psalm 9:10

Scripture tells us that this psalm of David was to be set to the music of "Death of the Son," an obviously unknown tune to us. But the heart of the psalm is praising and seeking the Lord at all times, even in times of sorrow and despair.

We often hear at this time of year the quote "Wise men still seek Him," and that is a great reminder for us today. It is wise to seek Him at all times, for the Lord will not forsake those who do. That means seeking the Lord will never be in vain. When God is sought in difficult times, He will be found, and those who know His name will be wise enough to seek Him at all times.

It is no mystery that the holidays are difficult for many people; for some, it is the most difficult time of the year. Some are struggling financially, and it is painful and stressful for them to be unable to do the things they would like to do for those they love. Some will be facing their first Christmas without a loved one, maybe even a son, as the psalm speaks of. For others, the holidays are a reminder of broken relationships or even betrayal. But for those who know the name of the Lord and seek Him, He is there, and He will not forsake anyone who seeks Him.

It is true that the holidays cause some to feel as though they have been forsaken by God, that He wasn't there for them when they needed Him. Consequently, the last thing they want to think about is seeking Him. But this is unwise and the worst thing for hurting and troubled hearts. Life offers no healing for loss; "time heals all wounds" is just a saying. God alone heals broken hearts and restores lost hope.

If the holidays are a hard time for you, seek the Lord and tell Him they are hard. Tell Him you don't understand why certain things have happened and cannot comprehend why He allowed them, but then ask Him to get you through them. He will be there for you, even when life's song is "Death of the Son."

No one who knows the Lord's name will find the effort to seek Him for comfort and strength to be in vain. Listen, even when your heart is not fully in it, He will still be there for you, just because you're His.

Hurting hearts, trust in the Lord. Seek Him, for He has not forsaken you!

December 23

These things I have spoken to you, that My joy may remain in you, and that your joy may be full. This is My commandment, that you love one another as I have loved you. Greater love has no one than this, than to lay down one's life for his friends.

—John 15:11–13

As we mentioned a couple of days ago, the words in chapters 14–16 of John are the last of Jesus' instructions to the disciples before His arrest and crucifixion and are therefore of extreme importance. Because of their place-ment within mere hours of the death of Christ, we often assume that the "lay down" refers to dying for one's friends. This is indeed true, as Jesus was about to demonstrate, and it is also true as proven in the actions of the martyrs throughout the centuries.

But the meaning is broader than that. In the Greek text, the words *lay down* have the additional meaning of "lay aside." This is pictured for us in the very coming of Jesus, as He both laid aside His glory, though never His deity, and laid down His life for His friends. This is His commandment to us: that we love one another like He loves us, and there is no greater love than a love that gives. This is the very heart of our walk of faith and communication of truth to the world.

Back in John 13:35, Jesus said the world would know we are His disciples by our love for one another. Now, here in chapter 15, He says what that love will look like. It's a laying aside and, for some, even a laying down of their lives.

Laying down our lives is self-explanatory, but laying aside our lives requires a little explanation. Though there are many manifestations of how we might lay aside our lives in love for one another, one simple heading could be a banner over them all: servanthood. We are called to lay aside our time, our resources, and our talents for the sake of encouraging and promoting others. This is the life of love we are called to. It's a life contrary to that of the world. It's a life of seeking exaltation through humility; it's a life of not seeking our own but seeking the good and blessings of another.

Not an easy thing, to be sure, and it is also important to remember this is not at the expense of our own families. Rather, it is a practice much like we do within our families. For example, early in our married life, Teri and I some-times willingly went without certain things in order to stretch our resources and provide for our children's needs. There was no begrudging attitude in this; it was natural, loving, wonderful, and even a blessing. This is the mind-set the Lord is urging us to take into the larger family of Christ.

Take what comes naturally and apply it to those who are Christ's friends — the church, other believers. Love doesn't get any greater than this, according to Jesus Himself.

December 24

Blessed be the God and Father of our Lord Jesus Christ, who according to His abundant mercy has begotten us again to a living hope through the resurrection of Jesus Christ from the dead, to an inheritance incorruptible and undefiled and that does not fade away, reserved in heaven for you, who are kept by the power of God through faith for salvation ready to be revealed in the last time.

—1 Peter 1:3–5

Christmas Eve! What a great time to remember why Jesus came: to beget us to a living hope through His death and resurrection and to the incorruptible inheritance reserved for us in heaven. Wow! A reservation has been made for us at the marriage supper of the Lamb. And on the eve of the day when Christ laid aside His glory and came in the likeness of sinful flesh, let us also remember that this great truth became our own because of God's abundant mercy.

This mercy cannot be seen in all its glory except through the lens of God's omnipotence. We cannot fully understand the meaning of Christ's life, death, and resurrection from the dead until we understand that the Father fully knew all that man would do to His Son before He ever gave Him to the world. He knew of the cold reception at the inn and the feeding trough that His Son would rest His tiny back upon. He knew of Herod's evil plot to kill Him while He was still a child. The Father knew the hatred of the Pharisees and the disrespect of the Roman soldiers. The mocking, the scourging, the nails, the spear—the Father and Son knew it all!

Yet the Father still sent Him, and the Son still came. That's abundant mercy! That's the story to remember this Christmas Eve. Before any of it happened, God already knew. He knew what lay ahead even on the eve of the birth of the Christ child. But there was no other way, for man was corruptible and unable to obtain an incorruptible inheritance unless God in His abundant mercy did it for him. And He did, begetting us again to a living hope.

Christmas Eve, the night before a day like no other, a night when God already knew what lay ahead but in His mercy sent His Son to the world anyway. Remember the omnipotence of God this Christmas Eve. It puts the whole story into a much clearer view. God begot us again to a living hope through His Son, because He is abundant in mercy!

December 25

For unto us a Child is born, unto us a Son is given; and the government will be upon His shoulder. And His name will be called Wonderful, Counselor, Mighty God, Everlasting Father, Prince of Peace.

—Isaiah 9:6

Merry Christmas! A Child is born, a Son is given, and all government rests upon Him. His name is Wonderful, Counselor, Mighty God, Everlasting Father, and Prince of Peace! The Hebrew here for *mighty* means "warrior," so we might also say we have been given a warrior God who is yet called Wonderful, Counselor, and Prince of Peace.

Just like many other families, my family has a few traditions that we remember at Christmas, and one of them has a bit of a reputation, both among my family and those who know us. On Christmas morning, I prepare a breakfast that we would never dare eat on a regular basis. Stuffed French toast, several kinds of breakfast meats, cheesy grits, country potatoes, and biscuits abound. It's enough calories to last till next Christmas. But the most treasured part of our Christmas tradition happens before even one gift is opened. As a family, we join hands and gather in front of the beautifully decorated tree to thank God for sending His Son and that His Son is all the things recorded in Isaiah 9.

This Christmas morning, take time to thank God for the matchless gift of His Son, our Savior. There is none like Him, the warrior God and Prince of Peace, the given Son and everlasting Father, the Holy Spirit as the Counselor. Thus we see in Isaiah the Father, Son, and Holy Spirit working in unity as the triune God to save sinners like you and me. And that makes for a merry Christmas indeed!

December 26

Then He who sat on the throne said, "Behold, I make all things new." And He said to me, "Write, for these words are true and faithful." And He said to me, "It is done! I am the Alpha and the Omega, the Beginning and the End. I will give of the fountain of the water of life freely to him who thirsts. He who overcomes shall inherit all things, and I will be his God and he shall be My son. He who overcomes shall inherit all things, and I will be his God and he shall be My son."

— Revelation 21:5-7

Obviously, the fact that the one who overcomes will be God's son or daughter is the major thrust of these great verses. But there is another point of interest. The Lord first says, "It is done!" before stating that the one who overcomes will be His. The logical question is, what must we overcome in order to be His? The answer is found in the following verse: "But the cowardly, unbelieving, abominable, murderers, sexually immoral, sorcerers, idolaters, and all liars shall have their part in the lake which burns with fire and brimstone, which is the second death" (v. 8).

I love this verse in light of the frequent comments you hear about Christians being weak people who need things like God in order to cope with life. The fact is, hell is for cowards, and all of them go there! Notice that the first group listed in the category of "un-overcomers" is the cowardly, those not brave enough to be Christians. To those who overcome cowardice and unbelief, as well as to those who overcome sexual, spiritual, and material sins, the water of life will be freely given. But to those who do not act on the work done by Christ on their behalves, an eternal destiny in hell awaits.

Christianity is not for the weak, but for those made strong in Christ. Those made strong in Him will overcome the habitual practice of the sins He died for. Christ conquered the eternal consequences of death and the temporal power of the things that lead to the second death, such as cowardly unbelief and sexual, spiritual, and material sins. These are the things that are "done" ruling the life of the Christian, and in Christ and through the Spirit, we have power over them.

The point of these verses is really about identification, not qualification. The work of Jesus on the cross is a finished work. Living as an overcomer of cowardly unbelief and sexual, spiritual, and material sins is evidence of being His child. Do not let anyone try to convince you that such things are works in an effort to achieve salvation. Nothing could be further from the truth. Overcoming sin is simply evidence that the finished work of Christ is alive in you!

December 27

Therefore be patient, brethren, until the coming of the Lord. See how the farmer waits for the precious fruit of the earth, waiting patiently for it until it receives the early and latter rain. You also be patient. Establish your hearts, for the coming of the Lord is at hand.

—James 5:7–8

As I have shared before, patience is low on my list of strengths (that's a nice way of saying I don't have much), and I know that many others share this weakness. "Lord, when are you coming for us?" we might well ask. James answers for Him, in a sense, "Soon enough. You just keep producing fruit."

I believe the Bible teaches and history verifies that there are times when the Lord moves in majestic and powerful ways in outpourings of His Spirit. We remember the Great Awakenings in England and America, the Welsh Revival, and Pentecost-like moves of the Holy Spirit. I believe that the early and latter rains mentioned here in James, coupled with the multitude of references to divine activity in the latter days (including the rebirth of the nation of Israel), reveal that in and near the end, God is going to move again in a way that cannot be explained but as a work of the Lord. James urges us to keep bearing fruit as we wait for it and to establish our hearts. The word *establish* here means "to turn resolutely in a specific direction," so we might well conclude we are to be ready for it, even looking for it.

I believe there is yet another reason we should be praying and preparing for a great move of the Holy Spirit. God has set a precedent of showing up preceding the rendering of judgment. The Lord told Noah to build an ark, giving the world a hundred-years notice that judgment was coming. Then God Himself shut the door on the ark (Gen. 7:16). The Lord showed up to talk with Abraham and sent angels to rescue Lot before fire rained down upon Sodom and Gomorrah (Gen. 19:1), and the Lord has promised to send Elijah before the great and terrible day of the Lord (Mal. 4:5).

I believe the Holy Spirit is going to move one last time before the day of the Lord arrives, much like one last thrust of the sickle before winter comes and the harvest is over for that season. The question then is twofold. First, are we currently bearing fruit as we wait for this, and second, are we turned resolutely in that specific direction? In other words, are we ready to be used by the Holy Spirit as the latter rains are poured out one last time in the age of the Gentiles before God moves among the Jews one last time before He comes?

I am excited about that possibility, and even more important, I want to be ready for whatever God is going to do. If it seems like He's taking too long, I'll just keep bearing fruit and try to be patient!

December 28

At the evening sacrifice I arose from my fasting; and having torn my garment and my robe, I fell on my knees and spread out my hands to the Lord my God. And I said: "O my God, I am too ashamed and humiliated to lift up my face to You, my God; for our iniquities have risen higher than our heads, and our guilt has grown up to the heavens. Since the days of our fathers to this day we have been very guilty, and for our iniquities we, our kings, and our priests have been delivered into the hand of the kings of the lands, to the sword, to captivity, to plunder, and to humiliation, as it is this day. And now for a little while grace has been shown from the Lord our God, to leave us a remnant to escape, and to give us a peg in His holy place, that our God may enlighten our eyes and give us a measure of revival in our bondage."

— Ezra 9:5–8

As we wait for the great outpouring of the Holy Spirit in the last-days scenario of yesterday's devotional, we must ask ourselves what else we can do as we bear fruit. What, if anything, can we do to hasten revival? Though I believe God moves in ways and times according to His will and discretion, I also believe we should prepare for His moving by doing what Ezra did, which is to pray.

But Ezra prayed in a particular way, a way we need to emulate. He prayed an honest prayer, an ownership prayer, if you will. This is the type of prayer, I believe, that the American church needs to adopt as its own. Here in Ezra, as well as in Daniel 9 and Nehemiah 9, we can see two key components in the prayers of these three great men for their nations: ownership and repentance. Scripture provides for us the prayer of each of these three great men of whom nothing negative is recorded, and each one was an honest prayer of ownership for the spiritual condition and captivity of the children Israel. Ezra not only acknowledged the long-standing guilt of God's people but also demonstrated a spirit of repentance, saying he was ashamed to even lift up his face to God.

Ownership and repentance ready us for the time when God chooses to move in a more visible and tangible way; therefore, we in the church today must pray for a measure of revival in this age of spiritual bondage. But they must be honest, humble prayers, even as the Lord told Solomon in 2 Chronicles 7:14. Then, should the Lord so choose to move in a radical and significant way, we will be ready for revival.

December 29

Now this I say, brethren, that flesh and blood cannot inherit the kingdom of God; nor does corruption inherit incorruption. Behold, I tell you a mystery: We shall not all sleep, but we shall all be changed – in a moment, in the twinkling of an eye, at the last trumpet. For the trumpet will sound, and the dead will be raised incorruptible, and we shall be changed. For this corruptible must put on incorruption, and this mortal must put on immortality.

—1 Corinthians 15:50–53

Someone who has taken the time to study such things has determined that the twinkling of an eye is the time it takes for light to travel from the iris to the retina. This has been measured as one-sixth of a nanosecond. Now we know how long a second is, but a millisecond is one-thousandth of a second, and a nanosecond is one-millionth of a millisecond. That's fast!

If we add to this equation the words of Jesus from Matthew 24, we have great motivation to remember that today is the day of salvation. Jesus said in Matthew 24:44, "Therefore you also be ready, for the Son of Man is coming at an hour you do not expect." I would say that the twinkling of an eye, or a millionth of a millisecond, is not enough time to get ready; therefore we must *be ready*. In a millionth of a millisecond, God is going to make us into incorruptible immortals. No more struggle with sin, no more troubles with health, no more concerns about death—just incorruptible immortality forever! Who wants to miss that?

But there is another reality that we must face here, and that is millions who think they are ready will find out in a millionth of a millisecond that they are not. We know this from the great mass of people saved during the tribulation from every tribe, nation, tongue, and people (Rev. 6:9–11). The problem with being in this group instead of the group that was ready for the change is that these were all slain for their faith in Jesus Christ; Revelation 20 tells us they were beheaded.

I am a big proponent of being ready now, for if you are not ready when the millionth-of-a-millisecond time comes, you can still eventually put on incorruptible immortality, but it won't be as easy as being changed in the twinkling of an eye. So be ready, and tell others to be ready too!

December 30

Now we exhort you, brethren, warn those who are unruly, comfort the fainthearted, uphold the weak, be patient with all. See that no one renders evil for evil to anyone, but always pursue what is good both for yourselves and for all.

—1 Thessalonians 5:14–15

What a clear mandate for the church's responsibility to all types of people in the body, including the rowdies, the fainthearted, the weak, and the carnal! Pursue what is good for yourself and for all. That means we cannot treat everyone within the body the same. Don't be surprised that there are weak believers and carnal babes in Christ. Don't treat every problem that arises as though the heart of the matter is the spirit of unruliness.

"Don't treat the toe like a thumb or expect the eye's job to be done by an ear" could be one way to understand this exhortation. The body of Christ is made up of different people with different gifts, different personalities, and even different ways of processing problems and difficulties. Don't treat the weak as though they are unruly or the fainthearted as though they are carnal, and vice versa.

There is room for different personality types in the body of Christ, but it requires us to use wisdom, discernment, and—there is that word again—patience. As a pastor, I sometimes find it hard to understand why everyone isn't as committed to the church as I am or others are. It's hard to understand how people can move in and out of ministries with a seemingly casual attitude that someone else will just step in and fill their places. But I have to be patient with such people, as my calling is different from theirs. I cannot have the same expectations for them that I might have of someone called to vocational ministry. Now I am not trying to lessen the importance of serving God, by any stretch, but I am saying we cannot cookie-cutter our expectations of and responses to other people.

There are times when I know the Lord wants me to gently encourage someone in a particular area, while another person with the same struggle may need to be handled differently. Yes, there is one body and one Christ, but all parts of the body play different roles and have different functions.

Be patient with one another. The perfect Christian is not someone who is just like you—or me!

December 31

A man's heart plans his way, but the Lord directs his steps.

—Proverbs 16:9

As another year comes to a close, many of us will be making plans for the next year. Many resolutions, such as daily exercising, will be made, and for the next few weeks, the gyms will be filled with well-intentioned warriors. But after a few weeks, the gyms will empty, and the good intentions will subside.

It's great to make plans and commitments at this time of year, but make sure the Lord's direction is at the heart of all your plans. There are things He wants to do through you this coming year that you will discover only as you seek His direction. There are things He did through you last year that He wants to increase in you this year, and yes, there are things He whittled away in you last year that He wants to decrease even more. So make your plans but submit them to His direction. Ask Him what direction to go in, which steps He wants you to take.

I love New Year's Eve. It's an annual chance to start again and do better. To some, I want to offer a word of exhortation and maybe correction. New Year's Eve is not a time to get in that one last fling or to get drunk or to engage in some other sin. Start the new direction now—not on New Year's Day.

A funny thing happens when you procrastinate on making new commitments: they have a way of never happening. People who want to start the year right often delay their new direction until January 2. After all, they reason, they can't start a new diet or new discipline on a holiday. But it's easy for that day to slip into another day... and then another day... and yet another day without anything changing. So don't wait. Seek His direction now, and begin to follow the path He leads you on now. Don't wait for January 1 or 2, but start today, on December 31.

Plan your steps under and in the Lord's direction. He will take you places you could never have imagined—not next year, but even for the one day left in this year.

Blessed be the name of the Lord, and happy New Year!

CPSIA information can be obtained at www.ICGtesting.com
Printed in the USA
BVOW06s0955100114

341272BV00010B/7/P